Praise for Jeffrey Meyers's *Orwell*:

"The book is admirable for its portrayal of Orwell the man and writer—dark, disturbed, obsessing, contrary—a much more helpful and believable portrait than the many that depict him as St. George. This book is both moving and edifying."　　　　　　　　　—Paul Theroux, author of
The Great Railway Bazaar and *The Mosquito Coast*

"Meyers's admirable *Orwell* . . . illuminates the ruggedly individualistic Orwell without calling attention to the illuminator. . . . [This] fine biography is a reminder of the uniqueness of the man . . . , of just how he lived, and of how morally and intellectually cauterizing was his thought."
　　　　　　　　　—*New York Times*

"Jeffrey Meyers draws an admiring portrait of Orwell, but he doesn't omit the writer's unsaintlike qualities. Orwell was often gentle, but had a violent, even sadistic, streak. He was endearing in his eccentricities, but obliviously selfish in his married life. . . . Orwell's two earlier biographers saw this side of their subject, but Meyers, the first able to avail himself of the materials in Orwell's recently published complete papers, is more specific, and hence his portrait is somewhat darker. . . . [H]is is now the authoritative biography."　　　　　　　　　—*Atlantic Monthly*

"If you think, as I did, that there was nothing further to be written about George Orwell, this book will change your mind. Jeffrey Meyers has uncovered fascinating aspects of Orwell's life that put a new face to one of Britain's most influential authors."　　　　　　　　　—Phillip Knightley,
author of *The First Casualty*

"Jeffrey Meyers traces Orwell's rage through the diverse stages of his life in the absorbing biography *Orwell*. . . . [T]he breadth of his research is impressive."　　　　　　　　　—*New York Times Book Review*

"[Meyers's] book is probably richer in Orwelliana than any of its predecessors, and it is the first study of Orwell to make full use of Peter Davison's superb twenty-volume edition of Orwell's complete works. Meyers presents a story full of new angles and anecdotes, and rich with quotation from a diversity of sources culled from an unusually active and talented literary epoch." —*New York Review of Books*

"Meyers has a lot that is new and interesting to say, and has a different set of emphases than the earlier biographers. . . . The psychological emphasis has resulted in a much darker portrait. Meyers's key claim is that Orwell essentially destroyed himself because he had a fixed, distorted image of himself as a hardy man of action who could invariably take risks and survive them. In Meyers's view, that self-delusion accounted for Orwell's self-punishing behavior." —*Commonweal*

"Meyers [has] widely contributed to the expanding library of Orwell scholarship over the years." —*Newark* (New Jersey) *Star-Ledger*

"Meyers artfully documents Orwell's democratic socialism and talent for satire as he sheds light on a man who reveled in his contradictions: 'Etonian prole, anti-colonial policeman, bourgeois bum, Tory Anarchist, Leftist critic of the Left, puritanical leader, kindly autocrat.' " —*Boston Phoenix*

"In his highly professional and readable new biography, Jeffrey Meyers draws on all the information left by those who knew Orwell in one context or another. It supersedes the other biographies." —*The New Criterion*

"[Meyers] comments incisively on [Orwell's] novels, using passages from them to illuminate the author's private life." —*Philadelphia Inquirer*

"An absorbing account of the correlation between courage and artistry." —*San Francisco Examiner & Chronicle Book Review*

Also by Jeffrey Meyers

BIOGRAPHY

A *Fever at the Core: The Idealist in Politics*
Married to Genius
Katherine Mansfield
The Enemy: A Biography of Wyndham Lewis
Hemingway
Manic Power: Robert Lowell and His Circle
D.H. Lawrence
Joseph Conrad
Edgar Allan Poe: His Life and Legacy
Scott Fitzgerald
Edmund Wilson
Robert Frost
Bogart: A Life in Hollywood
Gary Cooper: American Hero
Privileged Moments: Encounters with Writers

CRITICISM

Fiction and the Colonial Experience
The Wounded Spirit: T.E. Lawrence's Seven Pillars of Wisdom
A *Reader's Guide to George Orwell*
Painting and the Novel
Homosexuality and Literature
D.H. Lawrence and the Experience of Italy
Disease and the Novel
The Spirit of Biography
Hemingway: Life into Art

B IBLIOGRAPHY

T.E. Lawrence: A Bibliography
Catalogue of the Library of the Late Siegfried Sassoon
George Orwell: An Annotated Bibliography of Criticism

E DITED   C OLLECTIONS

George Orwell: The Critical Heritage
Hemingway: The Critical Heritage
Robert Lowell: Interviews and Memoirs

E DITED   C OLLECTIONS   OF   O RIGINAL   E SSAYS

Wyndham Lewis by Roy Campbell
Wyndham Lewis: A Revaluation
D.H. Lawrence and Tradition
The Legacy of D.H. Lawrence
The Craft of Literary Biography
The Biographer's Art
T.E. Lawrence: Soldier, Writer, Legend
Graham Greene: A Revaluation

W. W. NORTON & COMPANY

NEW YORK / LONDON

Orwell

Wintry Conscience of a Generation

Jeffrey Meyers

Copyright © 2000 by Jeffrey Meyers

Printed in the United States of America
First published as a Norton paperback 2001

Lines from the poem "News from Nineteen Eighty-Four"
by Dana Gioia reprinted by permission of the author.
Lines from the poem "George Orwell" by Robert Conquest
reprinted by permission of the author.

For information about permission to reproduce selections from this book, write to Permissions,
W. W. Norton & Company, Inc., 500 Fifth Avenue, New York, NY 10110

The text of this book is set in Electra
with the display set in Horley Old Style
Composition by Julia Druskin
Manufacturing by Quebecor World Book Services, Fairfield
Book design by JAM Design

Library of Congress Cataloging-in-Publication Data

Meyers, Jeffrey.
Orwell : wintry conscience of a generation / by Jeffrey Meyers.
p.   cm.
Includes bibliographical references and index.
ISBN 0-393-04792-X
1. Orwell, George, 1903–1950. 2. Authors, English—20th century—Biography.
3. Literature and society—England—History—20th century. 4. Politics and
literature—England—History—20th century. I. Title.

PR6029.R8 Z736 2000
828'.91209—dc21
[B]   00–038020
ISBN 0-393-32263-7

W. W. Norton & Company, Inc., 500 Fifth Avenue, New York, N.Y. 10110
www.wwnorton.com

W. W. Norton & Company Ltd., Castle House, 75/76 Wells Street, London W1T 3QT

2 3 4 5 6 7 8 9 0

Contents

Illustrations

Maps

Acknowledgments

I WOULD like to acknowledge the help I received while writing this book. Peter Davison, editor of Orwell's *Complete Works*, was a heroic and consistently generous researcher. Several Orwell scholars were also extraordinarily helpful. Stephen Wadhams, Michael Shelden, Peter Stansky and Ian Angus provided addresses and telephone numbers. Gillian Furlong, Orwell Archive, University College, London University, also gave valuable assistance.

I had conversations about Orwell, long before I began work on this book, with several of his old friends, now gone: John Lehmann, Hugh Gordon Porteous, V.S. Pritchett, Stephen Spender, Julian Symons and Tambimuttu. For personal interviews I am grateful to the Hon. David Astor, Anne Popham Bell, Lucy Dakin Bestley, Richard Blair, Henry Dakin, Kay Welton Ekevall, Martin Esslin, Adrian and Stephanie Fierz, Michael Foot, Frank Frankford, Celia Paget Goodman, Waldemar Hansen, Margaret Heppenstall, David Holbrook, Sally Jerome, Robert Kee, Quentin Kopp, Sam Lesser, Michael Meredith, Michael Meyer, Jane Dakin Morgan, Dr. Howard Nicholson, Janetta Woolley Parladé, Sir Steven Runciman, Lady Spender, Geoffrey Stevens, Susan Watson and Dr. James Williamson. It was a great pleasure to meet all these sympathetic and responsive people.

For letters about Orwell from people who knew him I thank Mulk Raj Anand, Guinever Buddicom, Anne Dunn, Fay Fierz Evans, Livia Gollancz, Katie Johnson, Michel Kopp, Pierre Kopp, Catherine O'Shaughnessy

Moncure, Margaret Fletcher Nelson, Lady Violet Powell, Vernon Richards, Dr. Kenneth Sinclair-Loutit and Hugh Trevor-Roper (Lord Dacre).

A number of contemporary writers kindly answered my query about what Orwell meant to them: Margaret Atwood, Alan Bennett, Thom Gunn, Doris Lessing, John le Carré, David Lodge, Alan Sillitoe and Tom Stoppard. I discuss their responses in the Epilogue.

For other letters I am grateful to Victor Alba, William Blair, David Cesarani, Nicholas Comfort, Jerrilynn Eby, Clive Fleay, Albert Gelpi, Sir Martin Gilbert, Christopher Hitchens, James Hopkins, Hans Krabbendam, Michael Macdonald, Philip McClellan, Yasuharu Okuyama and Alan Sheridan; and to the following institutions: Belgian Embassy, Washington, D.C., British Museum, Commonwealth Institute, Edinburgh University Library, Hairmyres Hospital (Sam Miller), A.M. Heath, India Office Library, *Islands* magazine, Jura Hotel, Lilly Library, Indiana University (Sue Presnell), National Museum, Singapore, Netherlands Embassy, Washington, D.C., *Scots Magazine*, Secker & Warburg (Geoff Mulligan), St. Hugh's College, Oxford University, Strand Hotel, Yangon, Swarthmore College Library, Tate Gallery (Caroline Cuthbert), USIS Yangon (Karl Nelson) and University of Texas. The Library of the University of California at Berkeley, a major resource for all my work since the 1960s, has been enormously helpful.

Many friends provided addresses, articles and books, information about Bihar, Burma and Sonia Orwell: Paul Alkon, Elena Balashova, Richard Bascom, Morris Brownell, Keith Crook, Anthony and Sarah Curtis, Gillian Drey (for splendid hospitality in London), Patricia Garside, Michael Howe, Francis King, Ann Kitz, Phillip Knightley, Ian Littlewood, Dr. Robert Michtom, Joan Peters, Roland Schank, William Jay Smith and Paul Theroux. Sandra Dijkstra gave me useful advice.

As always, my wife, Valerie Meyers, helped with the research and interviews, read and improved each chapter, and compiled the index.

Preface

Animal Farm and *Nineteen Eighty-Four* have been translated into more than sixty languages and have sold more than 40 million copies. Why is the man V.S. Pritchett called "the wintry conscience of a generation" so universally appealing? His literary qualities—vigorous style, engaging honesty, sly wit—immediately attract us. And his personal qualities—integrity, idealism and commitment—shine through his writing like pebbles in a clear stream. In his own lifetime Orwell's passionate desire to unite the disparate classes and create a just society in England commanded respect and gave him a special aura. Intensely conscientious, Orwell was hard on himself. His obstinate search for moral values animates his essays and novels, and his lucid prose represents a triumph over the chaos of self-doubt that lies beneath the surface. His legend was partly self-created, and his work has had—still has—extraordinary political and cultural influence. Orwell's books have not dated (though he was born nearly a century ago), and we can now see the complexity of his struggle and the greatness of his achievement.

This is the first biography of Orwell to make use of the rich literary and documentary material in Peter Davison's superb 20-volume, 8,500-page edition of *The Complete Works* (1998). It also includes, through the kindness of his family and friends, a dozen new photographs. My own research and interviews, and the use of unpublished material in the Orwell Archive in London, shed new light on Orwell's strained relations with his weak and passive father, his role in the social and political upheavals of Burma in the 1920s, his career as a teacher in two shoddy schools, his long, loyal connection with his literary agent, Leonard Moore, and his arduous life on the island of Jura. The Soviet police report shows that Orwell was nearly captured and killed in Spain. This biography also describes his close friendships with two shadowy figures, Georges Kopp and Reginald Reynolds, and his literary contacts with Ernest Hemingway, Edmund Wilson and Wyndham Lewis.

Born in the Edwardian era, a child during the Great War, Orwell rejected the stifling English class system and the immutability of the British Empire. His crucial decision to abandon the Burma Police and become a writer enabled him to create a new image and forge a new consciousness. His desire to escape the respectable world—living down-and-out in repulsive slums and working in disgusting restaurants—made him seek out Spartan conditions, and most of his life was harsh and austere. Fighting in the Spanish Civil War, he risked everything, and took personal responsibility for creating a morality based on humanistic Socialism. His constant disregard for his own health, especially on the remote and sodden island of Jura, cut his life short at the age of forty-six.

Orwell also had human failings. He yearned to be rich, handsome and a devil with the ladies. Women were always important to him, from Burmese prostitutes, French "trollops" and Berber girls to Mabel Fierz, his first patron and supporter, his girlfriends Eleanor Jaques and Kay Welton, and his first wife Eileen O'Shaughnessy—the self-sacrificing heroine of this book. He pursued women outside his marriage, including the exotic Russian psychologist Lydia Jackson, and formed close friendships with the writers Inez Holden and Stevie Smith. After Eileen's death, his bizarre marriage proposals to Celia Paget and Anne Popham revealed the hopelessly romantic side of his character. His desperate longing for love—a theme in all his novels—lies at the core of his life and work, and was responsible for his strange deathbed marriage to Sonia Brownell, the model for Julia in *Nineteen Eighty-Four*. The Orwell who emerges from this book is darker than the legendary figure. He had a noble character, but was also violent, capable of cruelty, tormented by guilt, masochistically self-punishing, sometimes suicidal.

In this biography I refer to the subject as Eric Blair until 1933, when he published *Down and Out in Paris and London* and adopted the pseudonym of George Orwell.

I have had a bloody life a good deal of the
time but in some ways an interesting one.
—GEORGE ORWELL

Orwell

1

An Edwardian Childhood,

1903–1914

I

GEORGE ORWELL was burdened from birth by colonial guilt. Motihari, in the state of Bihar in northern India, was an unlikely place for this quintessentially English writer to be born. The town itself, on the broiling dusty plains between the Himalayas and the Ganges River, was a rough colonial outpost, "pleasantly situated on the east bank of a lake," with a jail, a school, public offices crammed with mildewed files and the headquarters of a troop of the Bihar Light Horse. The local people barely survived by making cooking-oil, rugs and string moneybags. The place and circumstances of his birth were crucial factors in Orwell's life. He was brought up to believe in the righteousness of British rule in India and, in his late teens, became a colonial servant himself. But his heritage contained the seeds of its own destruction. He would later abandon this hateful job and condemn the evils of imperialism.

Orwell's family, who originally came from Scotland, had colonial connections that went back to the eighteenth century. His great-great-grandfather, Charles Blair of Winterborne, Dorset, was the absentee owner of tropical plantations and wretched slaves in Jamaica. His great wealth enabled him to ally himself with the aristocracy and marry Lady Mary Fane, daughter of the 8th Earl of Westmorland, a Bristol merchant who'd inherited the title from a second cousin at the age of sixty-two. Orwell inherited her portrait and carried this treasured relic with him on numerous moves to seedy flats and shabby cottages.

His family traditionally served two pillars of Victorian England: the empire and the established church. His grandfather, Thomas Blair, had been an Anglican priest, converting the heathen in India and Australia, and later became Vicar of Milborne St. Andrew, near his ancestral home in Dorset. His father, Richard Walmesley Blair, was born in Milborne on January 7, 1857, the youngest of ten children. Eight of them died before 1908 and his surviving brother emigrated to New Zealand, so Orwell never saw any of the Blairs. Just before leaving to fight for the Loyalists in the Spanish Civil War, Orwell published a bitterly nostalgic poem that recalled his ecclesiastical heritage, and sounded the note of loss and despair that would echo through many of his books:

> A *happy vicar I might have been*
> *Two hundred years ago,*
> *To preach upon eternal doom*
> *And watch my walnuts grow.*
> *But born, alas, in an evil time,*
> *I missed that pleasant haven.*

After breaking with his family traditions, Orwell had to create his own values and way of life in a much more hostile world.

His mother's family also had colonial ties. G. E. Limouzin, his great-grandfather, was born in France and became a prosperous shipbuilder and teak merchant in Moulmein, Burma. His son, Frank Limouzin, who took over the family business, died in 1915. Spiky-haired and beetle-browed, with sharp nose, thin lips and a grim expression, Frank looked exactly like one of Balzac's rapacious misers. The grandparents had nine children, including Orwell's mother, Ida Mabel Limouzin. She was born in Penge, south of London, on May 18, 1875, but had a princely childhood in Burma, in a household tended by thirty barefoot and bowing domestic servants. Ida had a bohemian sister, Nellie, whom Orwell used to see when he lived in Paris in the late 1920s, and a brother, Charles, a lively golfing crony of Richard Blair. Like the numerous Blairs, the other Limouzins, some of them Fabian Socialists and militant suffragettes, seem to have disappeared. Punning on their exotic name, young Orwell called them "Lemonskins" or "Automobiles."

Orwell's father spent his entire working life as a minor, and rather dreary, colonial official. In August 1875, at the age of eighteen, Richard Blair joined the Opium Department of the Indian Government as Assistant Sub-Deputy Opium Agent, 3rd grade. During the course of a long and undistinguished career he slowly crawled up the administrative ladder. In 1891, after working for sixteen years in eight different posts, he was still Assistant Sub-Deputy Opium Agent—though he had now risen to 1st grade. In 1907, after another sixteen years in many far-flung locales, he had snailed his way up from the rank of Sub-Deputy Opium Agent, 5th grade, to 1st grade.

The Opium Department regulated the quality, production, collection and transportation of Indian opium to China. Most of this precious crop was produced in the regions of Benares and Bihar. Richard Blair's job was to supervise the poppy growers in his district and make sure the crop was cultivated in the most efficient way. The government itself "made cash advances to cultivators, purchased their product, carried on the manufacturing process, and made the final sale" of the poppy juice to the factories and exporters in Patna and Calcutta. "The opium revenue, next to that from land and salt, was the largest single increment to the Indian treasury" and generated 16 percent of its total income.

As long as the money came pouring in neither Richard nor the Indian Government was greatly concerned about what happened when the tons of opium—illegal in India—reached the dope fiends in China. In fact, the British quite deliberately used the drug to weaken and undermine the fragile structure of the doomed Chinese Empire, which had fought and lost two opium wars with Britain in the mid-nineteenth century and finally collapsed in 1912.

One authority wrote that "in 1880 nearly thirteen million pounds of opium came into China, mainly from India. . . . In the early part of the twentieth century, $40 million worth of opium came into the port of Shanghai every year. The city had over eighty shops where the crude drug was sold openly, and there were over 1,500 opium houses. . . . At least fifteen million Chinese were confirmed addicts." [1] In China then, as in America now, drugs were a major source of crime. Addicts stole to support their habit, and gangs fought and killed each other to dominate the immensely lucrative trade. By the time Orwell abandoned his own colonial career in the 1920s, he'd developed a keen social conscience and felt intensely guilty about his father's personal involvement in the most vicious and indefensible kind of imperialistic exploitation.

II

IDA LIMOUZIN had grown up in a lavish household in Burma and, when her father lost his fortune, became a humble governess in India. She'd been engaged to a dashing young man but, when jilted, took Richard Blair on the rebound. She had dark eyes and hair, thin features and, according to the poet Ruth Pitter, "an acute mind." She dressed rather picturesquely and was fond of oversize jewelry: jet beads, amber necklaces and dangling earrings. Richard, eighteen years older, had begun his career back in 1875, the year she was born. They married in 1896, in a remote corner of northeast India, far from their large but strangely depleted families. All the Jamaican and Burmese money had disappeared by the time the aristocratic, landowning, clerical Blairs were united with the Anglo-French, commercial, bohemian Limouzins. Their first child, Marjorie, was born near Gaya, Bihar, in 1898. Five years later Eric Arthur Blair was born in a whitewashed brick bungalow in Motihari on June 25, 1903.

Eric became uncommonly tall and gangly, with a shock of dark, stiff hair. But he began life, like most infants, pudgy and almost bald. In a contemporary photograph, the bonny baby, with a quiff of wavy hair, is dressed in a long white gown and lacy collar. Ida holds him toward the camera but, clenching his fist, he shyly looks away. His proud mother, with thick hair parted in the middle and a gap between her front teeth, wears a velvet choker, frilly blouse and long dark skirt. In a companion photograph, with a blurred garden wall in the background, a black Indian *ayah*, a shawl around her head, holds the baby, who tilts his head back and clutches her white sari.[2]

In 1904 Ida had the choice of remaining in India with her husband, as most wives did, or going to England to start Marjorie in school. After eight years of marriage, she seemed keen to leave the remote and rather philistine colonial outpost, and felt she could have a much livelier and more independent life at home. Ida, Marjorie and the year-old Eric settled in Henley-on-Thames, a pleasant Oxfordshire village. The main street descended from the market place and past the square-towered church to the river, lined with boating clubs, where the famous regatta was held in July. Ida and Richard must have corresponded during their long separation—Ida never went back to India and Richard did not retire until 1912—but their letters have not survived.

The Blairs first settled in Ermadale, a house on Vicarage Road they quaintly named for Eric and Marjorie. In 1905 they moved to the slightly larger

Nutshell (a name worthy of Beatrix Potter) on Western Road. In 1912, when Richard finally returned from India, they moved to Rose Lawn on Station Road in Shiplake (two miles south of Henley and also on the Thames), a large, two-story house with an expansive garden for the children to play in. Three years later, after the war began and austerity prevailed, they returned to Henley and rented a smaller, semi-detached house with a tiny front garden at 35 St. Mark's Road. In his novel *Coming Up for Air* Orwell vividly and nostalgically evoked Henley's peaceful rural setting, with the sights and sounds that accompanied the time of day:

> It's always in summer weather that I remember it. Either it's the market-place at dinner-time, with a sort of sleepy dusty hush over everything and the carrier's horse with his nose dug well into his nose-bag, munching away, or it's a hot afternoon in the great green juicy meadows round the town, or it's about dusk in the lane behind the allotments, and there's a smell of pipe-tobacco and night-stocks floating through the hedge.

In 1906 little Eric was photographed wearing short trousers, knee socks, belted tunic and large frilly collar, holding a toy horse and once again turning shyly away from the camera. That year he also stood, moon-faced and chipmunk-cheeked, in front of a painted backdrop of rough ocean waves. Dressed in a sailor's suit, he holds a thick ship's rope as a stage prop and wears a lanyard that coils round his neck and into his front pocket. With feet apart and a stiff posture, he now stares straight out at the seaside photographer— the miniature image of a solid British tar, coddled and content.

Ida could also be very firm with Eric, and her granddaughters, who later visited her in school holidays, found her rather frightening. Tending her nails, doing embroidery and pampering her sleek dachshunds, Ida sat next to a brass cobra lamp. Her Edwardian parlor was crammed with "rainbow silky curtains, masses of embroidered stools, bags, cushions, pin cushions, . . . interesting mahogany or ivory boxes full of sequins, beads, miniature tracts, wooden needle-cases, amber beads, cornelian and ivory, small boxes from India and Burma."

In *Coming Up for Air* Orwell also satirized the stifling oriental decor of the boring Anglo-Indian families who had resettled in England, but still lived in the past: "As soon as you set foot inside the front door you're in India in the 'eighties. You know the kind of atmosphere. The carved teak furniture, the brass trays, the dusty tiger-skulls on the wall, the Trichinopoly cigars, the red-hot pickles, the yellow photographs of chaps in sun-helmets, the Hindustani words that you're expected to know the meaning of, the everlasting anecdotes about tiger-shoots and what Smith said to Jones in Poona in '87."[3] Though Orwell later found all this absurd, in boyhood it stimulated his imagination and inspired him to follow family tradition and serve the Empire.

Orwell disliked frivolity and later characterized his mother as "a pretty silly woman who liked playing bridge." But she seems to have enjoyed life when her dry old stick of a husband was safely occupied in India. Her diary for the summer of 1905 records a modern woman's range of artistic and athletic interests: "went to the theatre and saw Sarah Bernhardt, went swimming, developed photographs. . . . Went to Wimbledon to see the tennis finals. . . . Spent all day on the river" to see the Henley regatta.

But what of Ida's emotional life when she was still in her thirties and separated from her husband? One anecdote suggests that she was tempted, at least, to have love affairs with men who found her attractive. Dr. Dakin, their family physician and father of young Humphrey, who later became the husband of Marjorie Blair, "was unhappily married and had a wandering eye. He and Ida spent time together at the local golf club, and eventually he fell in love with her. There was a brief embarrassing scandal. According to his son, the doctor received no encouragement from Ida."[4] But the lonely woman, though living in a hothouse atmosphere of repression and rigidly defined sex roles, may have yielded to other, more enticing men. Ida's plight influenced Orwell's pursuit of attractive, solitary women. And Richard, sweltering in remote stations with his iced drink and solar-topee, may have taken native mistresses as his son later did.

III

ERIC WAS born in 1903, between the Boer War, which featured guerrilla warfare and concentration camps, and the Russo-Japanese War, in which an oriental country, for the first time, defeated a European power. King Edward VII (after an intolerably long wait) had succeeded Queen Victoria two years earlier and arranged the Entente Cordiale that established friendly relations with France. The Wright Brothers flew the first airplane that year, and the first motor-taxis appeared in London. In Africa, the British conquered Northern Nigeria and Roger Casement investigated the atrocious treatment of rubber workers in the Congo. James McNeill Whistler died and Evelyn Waugh, whom Orwell came to know and admire, was born. Three books by Orwell's favorite authors were published in 1903: Samuel Butler's posthumous satire on Victorian pieties, *The Way of All Flesh*, Bernard Shaw's provocative play *Man and Superman* and George Gissing's autobiographical *The Private Papers of Henry Rycroft*. The modern era had begun and the Great War, which shattered a century of peace in Europe, was looming in the future.

In February 1905, when Eric was eighteen months old, Ida's diary noted the beginning of the lung disease that would plague him for the rest of his life, make him a chronic invalid and kill him at the age of forty-six: "Baby not at all well, so I sent for the doctor who said he had bronchitis." Toward the end of his life Orwell noted that he had defective bronchial tubes and a tubercular "lesion in one lung which was never diagnosed when I was a boy."

Richard Blair, by then a complete stranger to his son, came home on three months' leave in the summer of 1907 and disrupted the placid routine of the suburban household. His younger daughter, Avril, was duly born in April 1908. Richard then went back to India to eke out a tedious existence in a series of minor posts, and didn't turn up again till 1912. During that time Eric and Marjorie attended a day school in Henley that was run by Anglican nuns. Though he became a great reader, Orwell later recalled "the miseries I went through because of the then-prevalent idea that you were half-witted if you couldn't read before you were six." The nuns were the first of many teachers who humiliated Eric during his schooldays and made him feel that he was worthless.

Physically absent most of the time, Richard was emotionally distant even when at home. Eric's relationship with his father was typical of many middle-class boys of the time. W.H. Auden, whose father joined the army in 1914, recalled: " 'I was seven, the age at which a son begins to take serious notice of his father and needs him most . . . and I didn't see him again until I was twelve and a half.' . . . [After the war] the two 'never really came to know each other.' " Later on Auden, like Eric, would remember his father as "henpecked" and "too gentle."[5] Though Eric and his two sisters were essentially brought up by his mother, he was always shy and awkward with women. Nevertheless, he had two wives and a surprising number of mistresses.

Richard had been earning about £650 a year, and after thirty-seven years' service finally retired with an annual pension of £438. He was fifty-five and very set in his ways when he returned to live permanently with his family.

Marjorie was fourteen, Eric was nine, and Avril, the child he had never seen, was four. Chilled by the damp English climate, he kept his room at a tropical temperature. He became the paid secretary of the local golf club and, used to commanding the Indians, threw his weight around. His local tailor, whom he refused for snobbish reasons to recognize on the street, bitterly recalled that "old man Blair was terribly autocratic. If anyone got in his way at the golf course they'd get it in no uncertain terms. . . . He was full of his own importance." Avril, who later opened a tea shop (and was therefore in trade) "was a bit of the same. It was a bit of an honour to be served cakes by her!" The family, income now reduced by one-third, desperately tried to maintain their social status.

Eric's childhood friends found old Mr. Blair a stiff, unsmiling and rather forbidding figure who rarely spoke to them. Tall—with white hair, blue eyes and rosy skin—he strolled around town with a cane, sat in the Conservative Club without joining in the conversation and went faithfully to the cinema, where he always fell asleep. He liked to drink cider and play bridge, but never read a book. Later on, when his grandchildren visited during the holidays, he was completely self-absorbed and took no interest in them.

Though he could be tyrannical in town, at home Richard was bullied by his vivacious and high-spirited wife. His grandson recalled that "he was a most mild bloke, a gentle old boy. I can't remember his making much comment on *anything*, except that the puddings Ida made were never like those his mother made." Ida usually ignored his fatuous comments and ordered him about: "Dick do this, Dick do that!" If she heard him poking the fire to produce a hothouse climate, it was always: "Dick, put that poker down!" Eric felt closer to his uncle Charles Limouzin. Secretary of another golf club near Bournemouth, he was a more worldly and commanding character.

In his autobiographical novel *Keep the Aspidistra Flying*, Orwell described the hero's family as "peculiarly dull, shabby, dead-alive, ineffectual."[6] A reserved and rather self-contained boy, remote and undemonstrative, Eric had always been detached, even impersonal, with his family. A childhood friend, who later wrote a book about him, observed: "I do not think Eric was *fond* of his father, although he respected and obeyed him, but . . . he was genuinely fond of his mother and sisters, especially Avril." Tall and skinny, Avril resembled her father. Short and round-faced, with delicate health, Marjorie looked like her mother. She had a sweeter, more sympathetic and supportive character than the harsher, sharp-tongued Avril.

In "Such, Such Were the Joys," his savage memoir of prep school, Orwell expressed his ambivalence about his parents. His early childhood, he said, had not been altogether happy, but compared to school, home was at least ruled by love rather than by fear. With startling honesty, he confessed: "I do not believe that I ever felt love for any mature person except my mother, and even her I did not trust. . . . I merely disliked my father, whom I had barely seen before I was eight and who appeared to me simply as a gruff-voiced elderly man forever saying 'Don't.' " The young Eric felt that powerful and oppressive adults used their authority to restrict his freedom and could, if he confided in them, be treacherous.

Eric was clearly embarrassed by, even ashamed of, his father's dullness and conservatism, his exploitative yet mediocre career in India and struggle to maintain his precarious position in "the lower-upper-middle class." Richard, who married late and spent most of his life on his own, found it difficult to adjust to family life and problematic children when he retired. As Eric matured and became more critically observant, he found his father distant, henpecked and narrowly focused on the cinema, bridge and golf. Richard and Ida had separate rooms and separate interests, even separate bridge parties, and he was always "rather out of things." Eric was saddened by his parents' lack of harmony and distant, even disdainful relationship. He learned from them how to disguise his feelings and distrust intimacy.

At the end of his life, Orwell noted that the emancipated women in his family were quite hostile to men and that Ida kept Richard at arm's length: "From conversations he overheard as a small boy, between his mother, his aunt [Nellie], his elder sister & their feminist friends . . . he derived a firm impression that women *did not like* men, that they looked upon them as a sort of large, ugly, smelly & ridiculous animal, who maltreated women in every way, above all by forcing their attentions upon them. It was pressed deep into his consciousness, to remain there till he was about 20, that sexual intercourse gives pleasure only to the man, not to the woman." In adult life he developed a keen sense of smell (always prominent in his work), believed he was ugly and felt that women, whose needs he did not fully understand, did not welcome his attentions.

He came to dislike his given names, and when he published his first book he adopted a pseudonym both to slough off the burden of his past and to distance himself from his alienated family. Eric, he felt, not only had "romantic" Norse associations, but was also the name of the intolerably priggish hero of F.W. Farrar's edifying story of Victorian school life—*Eric, or, Little by Little* (1858). At one point a sanctimonious master informs the hero, who seems in danger of losing his moral virginity: "Virtue is strong and beautiful, Eric, and vice downcast in her awful presence. Lose your purity of heart, Eric, and you have lost a jewel which the whole world . . . cannot replace." In Kipling's *Stalkey & Co.* (1899), a popular school story that Eric certainly read and enjoyed, Stalkey's friends make fun of Farrar's book when it arrives as an unwelcome birthday present. Orwell associated his Scottish surname with the snobbish cult of Scotland—kilts, castles and shooting lodges, "all somehow mixed up with the invigorating effects of porridge, Protestantism and a cold climate"[7]—that was encouraged in his loathsome prep school. The name he chose emphasized his English identity.

IV

IN *The Road to Wigan Pier*, his essay on Dickens and *Nineteen Eighty-Four*, Orwell re-created warm, cozy, nostalgic scenes of working-class family life — so unlike his own—which he'd known in childhood before the war. He loved to go bird-nesting and play vaguely erotic games with the plumber's children up the road. "I remember," he wrote, "getting a faint but definitely pleasant thrill from holding a toy trumpet, which was supposed to be a stethoscope, against a little girl's belly." Following natural curiosity, the uninhibited children examined each other's sexual parts. When Ida got wind of this, she forbade Eric to associate with them. The Blairs, who believed the lower classes smelled, had to maintain their social superiority and did their best to turn their son, who found it difficult to make friends, into an odious little snob. He later wrote that "the plumber's daughter, who might be seven, / She showed me all she'd got" and remembered telling her: " 'I mustn't play with you any more, / My mother says you're common.' " Eric's typically Edwardian parents insisted that he have the speech, dress and education that would reflect their social status and prepare him for professional life.

Marjorie's boyfriend, Humphrey Dakin, disliked Eric for hanging about when he wanted to be alone with her. He characterized the weak, miserable child as "a sneak, full of 'nobody loves me' and torrents of tears at the age of five or six." Eric's fortunes improved in 1914 after the Blairs moved to Shiplake and he began to make friends of his own. While standing on his head to attract attention, he met three companionable, exotically named, upper-middle-class children—Jacintha, Prosper and Guinever Buddicom. With Jacintha he established a chaste friendship ("I never had a kiss from him," she said, "and I didn't try to give him one") that provided a strong contrast to his sexual explorations with the plumber's "common" offspring.

In 1915 Mr. Buddicom, an Oxford graduate and lecturer in science, abandoned his family and ran off to Australia. So the children of both families, ignored or neglected by their (long absent) parents, became close to each other and felt much happier on their own. Eric spent most of his time with Prosper, who was a year younger and later went to Harrow. They kept pets, climbed trees, shot rabbits and rats, played tennis and croquet, swam and went fishing—Eric's lifelong passion. Contemporary photographs show Eric—in jacket, tie and long trousers, with hair neatly parted and dangling forelock—standing at ease with croquet mallet, shotgun and fishing rod. He hated rats (which run through all his works until the final horror of the torture scenes in *Nineteen Eighty-Four*) and told Prosper: "I have bought one of those big cage-rat traps. This place is overrun with rats. It is rather good sport to catch a rat & then let it out & shoot it as it runs." [8] He was fond of guns and used them, in war and peace, throughout his life.

As both child and adult, Eric loved explosions. "One of the greatest joys of my own childhood," he wrote with rare enthusiasm about his early life, "were those little brass cannons on wooden gun-carriages . . . [that] went off with a noise like the Day of Judgment. . . . Normal healthy children enjoy explosions." On a more dangerous occasion, ignoring his father's "Don't," Eric and Prosper placed a whisky-still on top of the kitchen stove. When the whole contraption blew up, the cook gave notice and his parents were furious. Jacintha recalled that they also "put chemicals in the fire, thinking they'd have a great explosion, and nothing happened. Then they poked the fire and of course there *was* an explosion. . . . They lost their eyebrows."

There was also a more serious side to Eric. Despite his initial difficulty, he became a serious reader and was keenly interested in ghost stories, detective novels with the gentleman-burglar Raffles, science fiction by H.G. Wells, plays by Shakespeare, and fiction by Poe, Dickens and Kipling. He stole and devoured *Gulliver's Travels*, intended as a present, just before his eighth birthday. Taking a hint from Swift's rational horses, Orwell idealized the horse in *Animal Farm*, and transformed Swift's Floating Island of Laputa into the Floating Fortress in *Nineteen Eighty-Four*.

Eric gave Jacintha a copy of Bram Stoker's *Dracula*, with a hard-to-find clove of garlic, a "proven safeguard against vampires." He thought, even then, of becoming a famous author and chose the appropriate format for his *Collected Works*. Fond of ontological questions, he would cryptically ask: "How can you be sure I'm *me*?"[9] A sophisticated, sharp-witted boy, Eric could also be high-spirited. Carried away in a narrow train compartment, he once "swung from the luggage-rack, scratching himself and declaring he was an orang-outang" until an outraged lady passenger threatened to "call the guard if you don't get down at once, you naughty boy!" A chubby lad, Eric played another prank by answering a fraudulent ad for a weight-reduction course. Pretending to be an obese lady, he deliberately prolonged the cheeky correspondence. " 'Do come before ordering your summer frocks,' the weight-reducer insisted, 'as after taking my course your figure will have altered out of recognition.' . . . This went on for a long time," he recalled, "during which the fee gradually sank from two guineas to half a crown, and then I brought the matter to an end by writing to say that I had been cured of my obesity by a rival agency."

Despite his extreme adult rebellion against his background and class, Eric remained attached to his peculiar family and often relied on their practical help and support. His niece Jane Dakin Morgan pointed out that "when he was ill his mother took him over, when he wanted to write his first book his sister, my mother, offered him accommodation [in Leeds], and later, when his wife Eileen died, it was his sister Avril who [ran] his house" in Jura.[10] After Orwell's death, Avril brought up his adopted son.

Eric's relations with his family in childhood made him defensive and reserved, cynical and aloof. As an adult he always found it difficult to reveal his inner self, express his deepest feelings and get close to other people— even during sexual intimacy. Though he grew up among women, he never felt he understood them. From an early age his acute intelligence made him detached, and critical of his family's conventional values and aspirations. His family inspired his most striking characteristic: a deep sense of guilt that pervaded his personality and his writing. He felt guilty about his colonial heritage, his bourgeois background, his inbred snobbery and his elite education.

2

Misery at St. Cyprian's,
1911–1916

I

THE ENGLISH upper and middle classes are the only people in the world willing to pay schools huge sums of money to cripple their children emotionally. Eric, who must have done well with the Anglican nuns in Henley, was admitted to St. Cyprian's School, on Summerdown Road in Eastbourne, on the Sussex coast, which attracted several other clever little boys. Its distinguished alumni would include the writers Cyril Connolly and Gavin Maxwell (author of *Ring of Bright Water*), the photographer Cecil Beaton, the advertising innovator David Ogilvy and the golfing correspondent Henry Longhurst as well as Major General Bobbie Foote, V.C., and Charles Rivett-Carnac, Commissioner of the Canadian Mounted Police.

Founded in 1898 and named for an obscure martyr in Carthage, St. Cyprian's was one of eighty schools in that prosperous and fashionable retirement town. It was housed in a vast, sprawling, red-brick Victorian building, with a sunken playing field, a cricket pavilion and a rifle range. The ninety boys included a Siamese prince, the sons of South American millionaires and some English aristocrats. Since Eric's family was not wealthy, his fees were reduced from £180 to £90. But this was still a considerable sum, about the average annual wage of a clerk or skilled laborer. His education in snobbery, begun at home, continued at school. Though his academic ability gave him a privileged education, he was never allowed to forget that he was there on sufferance, and had to perform well and win prizes to justify his presence. St. Cyprian's had strong connections to the Empire, drawing children from the Anglo-Indian community and preparing them for future service in India. Its smart uniform was "corduroy trousers and green and pale blue jerseys, and its badge—on a field vert a Maltese cross azure." The extensive staff included "a dozen masters and mistresses, a matron, under-matron, several maids, a school sergeant, a carpenter, two or three gardeners" as well as the proprietors and presiding deities, Mr. and Mrs. Wilkes. They had two sons, who went on to Eton, and two daughters, Rosemary and Marigold, who were sent out of harm's way to a girls' boarding school.

Orwell's masterpiece of polemical autobiography, "Such, Such Were the Joys," one of the best essays in English, memorialized these miserable years. Though he wrote it in about 1948, toward the end of his life, long after the experience he describes, he was still bitter. Since strict English libel laws protected Mrs. Wilkes, who was still alive, it was not published until 1952, but only in America and after Orwell's death. His intensely personal, though brilliant and psychologically astute, adult recollections attack not only the Wilkeses, who mercilessly humiliated and exploited the boys, but also the whole class and educational system that oppressed him. In doing so, he novelizes their characters and dramatizes his own agonizing encounters with them. The essay expresses his pent-up anger and deep sense of shame—the consequence of their moral blackmail.

Other contemporaries, though less bitter, confirmed Orwell's recollections. Behind its ugly but imposing façade, the school offered all the attractions of a penal colony. Cecil Beaton remembered that "the schoolrooms smelt inky and dusty, the swimming pool was stagnant, the lavatories cold and damp. A flat playing-field stretched out to a steep bank with a low brick wall marking the road. It was wartime and things were naturally bleak. In winter the pupils suffered intensely from the cold."[1]

The headmaster, Vaughan Wilkes, was scornfully nicknamed Sambo. He seemed to resemble the character in the popular children's book *Little Black Sambo* (1900) and embodied the Latin source of the name (which appealed to budding scholars) *scambus*, or bowlegged. Gavin Maxwell recalled Sambo's notable ineffectuality: "He spoke little, was inclined to mumble, and was said to spend most of his time playing golf." To Orwell, he was a physical freak, doltish yet infantile: "Sambo was a round-shouldered, curiously oafish-looking man, not large but shambling in gait, with a chubby face which was like that of an overgrown baby." In his official capacity, he cau-

tioned the boys against the horrid vice that bedeviled all schools. He exhort-
ed them to avoid romantic attachments and warned them not to pollute their
bodies by masturbation, and encouraged them to denounce any boys who
attempted to enter their beds or interfere with their persons.

Though generally shy and unaggressive, Sambo, like most masters, had a
sadistic streak and devised ingenious methods to hurt the boys in his care.
"He would tap away at one's skull with his silver pencil," Orwell remembered, "which, in my memory, seems to have been about the size of a banana,
and which certainly was heavy enough to raise a bump; or would pull the
short hairs round one's ears, or, occasionally, reach out under the table and
kick one's shin." Eric kept his hair well greased to avoid the fierce tugs, but
could not evade the other punishments, common enough in most schools.
In Joyce's *Portrait of the Artist as a Young Man*, for example, the terrifying
priest screams at the innocent Stephen: "Lazy little schemer. I see schemer
in your face. . . . Lazy idle little loafer!"; in Orwell's essay, Sambo, echoing
Joyce, exclaims: "Go on, you little slacker! Go on, you idle, worthless little
boy!" [2]

The real power behind the throne was Cicely Wilkes, who was born in
1875, the same year as Ida Blair. She appears in a photograph wearing a flannel shirt and tie, and a military beret pulled firmly down to her eyebrows.
Her prominent cheeks, broad nose and large teeth suggest a masculine
heartiness. Though she liked to be called "Mum," she was a frightening sur-
rogate mother for a group of lonely little boys.

Orwell described her as ape-like or humanoid, "a stocky square-built
woman with hard red cheeks, a flat top to her head, prominent brows and
deepset, suspicious eyes." She would goad the boys shamelessly for disloyal-
ly disappointing their parents, their school and Mrs. Wilkes herself: "I don't
think it's awfully decent of you to behave like this, is it? Do you think it's
quite playing the game by your mother and father to go on idling your time
away, week after week, month after month? Do you *want* to throw all your
chances away?" The boys retaliated with another witty nickname, which cut
her down to size, blunted her power and mocked her gross appearance.
Gavin Maxwell explained that "she was a stout woman in middle age, with
a well-developed bust" that bounced up and down at a passable pulse rate as
she paced briskly through the corridors: " 'Here comes Flip,' someone would
say, '[breasts] flapping nicely, eighty to the minute, everything in clockwork
order.' "

David Ogilvy described how "this satanic woman carried the art of castration to extraordinary perfection . . . [by playing] games of emotional cat-and-mouse against every boy in the school. Each of us was alternately *in favor* or *out of favor*, like the courtiers at Versailles." They all sucked up to the flirtatious queen and vied for her promises of largesse—a rare privilege or excursion, a precious treat or gift. Cyril Connolly, whose memoir "Enemies of Promise" inspired Orwell to write his own account of the school, was more tolerant of her character. But he too emphasized her all-pervasive snobbery, her cruel but effective teaching, and her vainglorious attempts to make the boys fawn and compete for her favor: "Flip, around whom the whole system revolved, was able, ambitious, temperamental and energetic. She wanted her venture to be a success, to have more boys, to attract the sons of peers and to send them all to Eton. She was an able instructress in French and History and we learnt with her as fast as fear could teach us. Sambo seemed a cold, businesslike and dutiful consort." The dominating wife and henpecked husband may well have reminded Eric of his faintly absurd parents. Connolly defined her forceful method with two striking images: "On all the boys who went through this Elizabeth and Essex relationship she had a remarkable effect, hotting them up like little Alfa-Romeos for the Brooklands of life."[3]

Flip claimed Scottish ancestry, favored Scottish pupils and encouraged them to wear their traditional dress. Schoolboys aspiring to "character" were taught to admire the grim and dour aspects of the Scots. Since Flip adored Scotland, Eric hated it. As he cynically told Jacintha Buddicom, "to be a favourite of old Mum you have to be a Duke in a kilt." The real reason for the cult, Eric felt, was that only the very rich could afford the long journey up to Scotland and enjoy luxurious holidays, complete with private trout streams and well-staffed hunting lodges. St. Cyprian's taught him to resent wealth and privilege.

Orwell freely confessed his prejudice against the Highland, Celtic and romantic side of Scottish life, later reinforced by his hatred of the whisky-swilling Scottish merchants in Burma. His early novels contain some characteristically outrageous tirades. In *Burmese Days* he wrote: "The British Empire is simply a device for giving trade monopolies to the English—or rather to gangs of Jews and Scotchmen." In *Keep the Aspidistra Flying* his hero contemptuously derides Scottish names and the dreary legacy of that country: " 'Gordon,' 'Colin,' 'Malcolm,' 'Donald'—these are the gifts of Scotland to the world, along with golf, whisky, porridge and the works of Barrie and Stevenson."[4] This lifelong hostility did not prevent him from spending the last years of his life on the Scottish island of Jura.

The day began at St. Cyprian's with a naked plunge into the school's freezing pool or into the repulsive public baths, where Eric once spotted a floating human turd. The plunge was followed by fifteen minutes of physical exercise, and by a cheerless but mandatory chapel service before breakfast. Though the food was predictably disgusting, the starvelings could never get enough of it. Eric's keen eye spotted the encrusted strips of cold porridge under the rims of the pewter bowls. Poor Henry Longhurst, after getting sick and adding his own vomit to the thick slimy lumps, was forced to stand up and gobble down the nauseous mixture.

David Ogilvy knew the difference between image and reality, and how to run a successful business. He agreed with Orwell that Flip exploited the children, despite frequent protestations of her gracious charity to scholarship boys. Ogilvy remarked that she "made such exorbitant profits out of educating ninety boys that she was able to rent grouse-moors in Scotland during the summer and send her sons to Eton. She achieved wealth by starving the boys. She and her husband never ate our food, but those who were privileged to sit next to Mr. Wilkes at meals pinched food off the plate of that absentminded and henpecked man."

The aim of the school, Orwell wrote, was to produce a boy with "character," who hates intellectuality and worships games, "is insensitive and physically courageous, questions nothing and has no inner life." Such boys were quite different from Maxwell, Beaton and Connolly as well as from Blair himself, who had considerable physical courage, but was also sensitive, introspective and intellectual. A study of St. Cyprian's defined the elements that produced this well-trained, obedient but empty-headed philistine: "a spartan character, enforced with strict discipline; a militaristic atmosphere, with a flourishing cadet corps; an emphasis on school games as a means of fostering physical fitness and inculcating character; an unwritten code of imperial morality; an essentially classical education; a clientele that was to a considerable extent drawn to the Empire; the dissemination of imperial knowledge."[5] No wonder, then, that 155 brave young men from St. Cyprian's eagerly fought in the Great War and that many of them were killed in action.

The school that Eric entered at the age of eight engendered snobbery, philistinism, homosexuality, racism and sadism. Its rigid hierarchy and subordination of younger boys encouraged bullying and flogging. It emphasized athletic ability and physical prowess, disdained art and intellectual pursuits. It stressed loyalty and patriotism, valued money and privilege above everything else, was class-conscious and conformist, despised foreigners and the laboring class. Eric tacitly accepted these values when he joined the Burmese Police in 1922.

I I

LIKE THE hero of *Keep the Aspidistra Flying,* Eric's role as the clever one in the Blair family "was to win scholarships, make a brilliant success in life and retrieve the family fortunes." But, Orwell continued, recalling his mental anguish and deliberately exaggerating, "probably the greatest cruelty one can inflict on a child is to send it to school among children richer than itself." There are far greater cruelties; but both sides kept their devil's pact. The school, seeking prestige, gave Eric excellent academic training; he justified the Wilkes' investment by winning a highly coveted scholarship to Eton.

Orwell achieved devastating effects in "Such, Such Were the Joys" (the ironic title comes from Blake's *Songs of Innocence*) by emphasizing the impact of the school on a rather solitary, sheltered, essentially fatherless eight-year-old. (Richard Blair was still in India when Eric entered St. Cyprian's.) Writing as a boy who'd never been away from home and was ill-prepared for the brutal reality of the place, Orwell begins by abruptly announcing: "Soon after I arrived at St. Cyprian's . . . I began wetting my bed." As Flip (shocked by the outrage) tells a lady visitor, the only cure for this involuntary, humiliating act is a beating. Eric thinks the woman, dressed in full riding kit and armed with a hunting whip, will beat him. Instead, with a certain dream-like consistency, he's beaten by Sambo with the same weapon—a riding whip—instead of with the usual rattan cane. When Eric recklessly boasts that it didn't hurt, Sambo beats him till the whip breaks. He's then left with "a sense of desolate loneliness and helplessness, of being locked up not only in a hostile world but in a world of good and evil where the rules were such that it was actually not possible for me to keep them." The punishment inflicted on the innocent boy provided another profound source of guilt and foreshadowed the world of *Nineteen Eighty-Four*.

The maths master, Mr. Ellis, gruff and peppery with an egg-shaped bald head, was a notorious beater who inspired a parodic headline in the *St. Cyprian's Chronicle*: "Ellis the boy-whipper! Shocking testimony of pupils maimed for life by the monster's kick!"[6] In *Burmese Days* Orwell gives Ellis' name to the fanatical villain who provokes a native riot by beating and blinding a Burmese boy.

The school had disastrous physical and emotional effects, and accentuated Eric's worst characteristics. His defective bronchial tubes and lesion in one lung gave him a chronic cough that made running a torment. Though desperately lonely and keen to fit in, he refused to do so. His cynicism about the school's ethos and arrogance about his own ability made him unpopular with the other boys. So he withdrew (as with his family) into a kind of guarded defensiveness and distrusted all adults. Flip was unaware of his misery and later said that "he was not an affectionate little boy. . . . There was no warmth in him."

Moon-faced, reclusive and often weeping, Eric was bullied by the louts who were jealous of his intelligence and despised his awkwardness—he read books and was no good at games—and were angry at his difference from the herd. One contemporary remembered him as "an unhappy little boy at prep school. Both my brother and he, as intellectuals, were not infrequently 'mobbed' by the school's gang of philistines, and, in great fear, were reduced to tears and then laughed at." As a result of all this, Eric soon became a wretched mass of guilt, self-hatred and self-pity: "I had no money, I was weak, I was ugly, I was unpopular, I had a chronic cough, I was cowardly, I smelt."[7] Adult friendships, a happy marriage and literary success could never completely extinguish these feelings.

Like Kipling at his prep school, Eric felt guilty about his inability to excel or even to belong. Ashamed of his unhappiness, he kept it well hidden from his parents. As he wrote in "Such, Such": "A child which appears reasonably happy may actually be suffering horrors which it cannot or will not reveal." His letters to his mother during his first few months at school (December 1911 to February 1912), though overseen by Flip, *seem* to be written by a happy, well-adjusted child. He sympathizes with his mother's problems, caters to a sick roommate, enjoys explosive toys and responds eagerly to imaginative teaching:

—I am very sorry to hear we had those beastly freaks of smelly white mice back.
—I couldn't get a bit of peace to read for Leslie Cohen kept on worrying and in the end I had to go and read to *him*.
—There's a boy here who's got a kind of cannon that has to have those peas to shoot.
—Mr. Sillar showed us what an eclipse of the moon was, with a football with sugar on the top.

Eric always looked forward to leaving school for summer holidays in Polperro, Cornwall, where the muscular, sunburnt farm hands let him ride on the turnip drill, and would sometimes catch ewes to give him milk.

In June 1912 he appeared at a school dance, dressed as an eighteenth-century footman, with red velvet coat, white flowered waistcoat, red silk trousers, black stockings, lace-frilled collar and powdered wig. In the summer of 1914 he had a rare chance to break out of his misery and adopt other roles. The *St. Cyprian's Chronicle* praised him as cricketer and as actor in dramatic scenes from *The Pickwick Papers*:

> E. Blair. Has improved very much of late, but always starts his innings with a balloon; should with care bat very well. He catches well but must learn to move more quickly. Can bowl a little. . . .
> Eric Blair in the person of Mr. Wardle was exceedingly good in a somewhat difficult part.

During the war, when the guns could be heard thundering across the channel from France, Eric became keenly interested in the school's military events. He admired a guest speaker who delivered excellent lectures on famous battles, like Marlborough's victory at Blenheim and Napoleon's at Austerlitz. The boys practiced drill on the playing field, followed the latest battles on maps in the classrooms and visited the wounded Tommies in army hospitals, where they handed out peppermint creams and Woodbine cigarettes. In chapel they listened reverently as new names of soldiers who'd served and died in the war were added to the Roll of Honour. By contrast, Cyril Connolly emphasized the farcical aspects and told his mother about a mishap that occurred when King George V rode past a military camp near the school: "The wounded soldiers, there were about 1000, all leant on a fence when they saw him, so that it broke and they all fell down a bank into the mud."[8]

While at St. Cyprian's Eric published two utterly conventional poems, in rhyming quatrains, in the local Henley newspaper. The jingoistic "Awake! Young Men of England" appeared one month after the war broke out and urged youths to enlist in the army. It was inspired by the current patriotic fervor, personified in Lord Kitchener's stern, handsome face on the recruiting poster, and by the motto: "Your Country Needs You!" The second poem was an elegy for Kitchener, drowned at sea in 1916 when his ship, en route to the Russian front, struck a mine. Samuel Hynes observed that "all the clichés are there—the evocation of England, the glorification of sacrifice, the image from medieval, romantic battle, the emotive language of courage and cowardice. It is a poem written not so much by a boy as by a tradition, and a tradition that was at its end." When Connolly wrote a poem on the same subject and asked Blair's opinion, he imitated a schoolmaster's pedantic judgment: "*Dashed* good. Slight repetition. Scansion excellent. Meaning a little ambiguous in places. Epithets for the most part well selected. The whole thing is neat, elegant and polished." Delighted by his praise, Connolly responded: "My dear Blair!! I am both surprised and shocked." Their friendship and literary rivalry would continue till Orwell's death.

Eric had surprised Jacintha by asking, "How can you be sure I'm *me?*" and by expressing interest in *Dracula* and vampires. He also impressed Cyril Connolly—a witty, bookish, porcine boy from an Irish military family, his only close friend at school—by casually inquiring: "Would you drink a pint of blood to save your father?" Though Orwell later felt that he was not a real rebel, except when forced to become one, Connolly insisted, in a vivid portrait of his eccentric friend:

> I was a stage rebel, Orwell a true one. Tall, pale, with his flaccid cheeks, large spatulate fingers, and supercilious voice, he was one of those boys who seem born old. . . . Alone among the boys he was an intellectual and not a parrot, for he thought for himself, read Shaw and Samuel Butler and rejected not only [St. Cyprian's], but the war, the Empire, Kipling, Sussex [Kipling's county, and St. Cyprian's] and Character.
> "Of course you realise, Connolly," said Orwell, "that, whoever wins this war, we shall emerge a second-rate nation."

Even in boyhood Orwell could see through hypocrisy and, despite his youthful patriotic poems, predict the decline of England.[9] He longed to be the Wilkes' ideal schoolboy, handsome, athletic, rich—as well as clever. But his subversive intelligence undermined the traditional values of the school.

In "Such, Such Were the Joys" Orwell mocked the hostility to intellect, the rote learning and the hothouse cramming for the sake of exams. In his first year he studied Latin, French, English, History and Maths. But, as with all clever students, his real education came from his own reading. At school, his favorites included not only Shaw and Butler, but Swift, Thackeray, Kipling and P.G. Wodehouse. His great favorite was H.G. Wells' story "The

Country of the Blind." He vividly recalled an idyllic moment—four o'clock
on a summer morning, with the school fast asleep and the sun slanting
through the window—when, impassioned by reading, he crept down the hallway to steal the book from Connolly's bedside table. He later asked Connolly:

> Do you remember one or other of us getting hold of H.G. Wells's "Country
> of the Blind" about 1914, at St. Cyprian's, and being so enthralled with it
> that we were constantly pinching it off each other? It's a very vivid mem-
> ory of mine. . . .
>   And do you remember at about the same time my bringing back to
> school a copy of Compton Mackenzie's *Sinister Street*, which you began
> to read, and then that filthy old sow Mrs. Wilkes found out and there was
> a fearful row.

Sinister Street (1913–14), whose descriptions of bastardy, homosexuality
at Oxford and low life in London were then considered scandalous, cast them
out of Flip's favor. But Wells' story had a deeper appeal. It describes how a
climber falls off a mountain and enters an Andean country in which all the
people are blind. He aspires to be their king, but the people believe that
blindness is superior to sight. When he wants to marry one of their women,
they insist on putting out his eyes, and he finally manages to escape. These
two bright schoolboys, surrounded and oppressed by dull-witted masters and
loutish classmates, were attracted to the idea that the sighted were led by the
blind, that conformist group pressure and mob rule stifled superior individuals. Though Wells' hero escapes from the Andes, the bright boys were
trapped in the school.

Blair and Connolly redeemed themselves, as they'd been trained to do, by
bringing academic glory to the school. St. Cyprian's went so far as to employ
a don from All Souls College, Oxford, to read the boys' examination papers.
He was duly impressed with Blair and Connolly, whom he accurately
described as racehorses running in the Eton sweepstakes: "Of the pupils in
the Scholarship Class, Connolly and Blair invariably topped the bill. At
Greek they both did well, though Blair was far better at grammar; at Latin,
they were neck-and-neck at grammar, but Blair pulled ahead at composition;
Blair triumphed at French translation, Connolly at grammar; Connolly
forged ahead at arithmetic and divinity; at the English essay—the subject of
which was 'What is a national hero?'—Connolly provided 'the best and
fullest contender,' winning 48 out of 50, with Blair lagging behind on 43."

In the spring of 1916, when he was not yet thirteen, Blair (accompanied by Vaughan Wilkes as a kind of academic valet) went up to Eton to take his scholarship exam. This ordeal, the culmination of his years at St. Cyprian's, lasted two-and-a-half days. It included not only Greek verse and a French oral, but an awesome *viva* conducted by the leading dignitaries—Provost, Vice-Provost, Headmaster, Master in College and various Fellows of Eton. Eric passed the exam and was saved from becoming, in Flip's contemptuous words, "a little office boy at forty pounds a year." But there was no place available, and he was not immediately admitted. He left prep school in December 1916, spent the Lent term at Wellington College and entered Eton in May 1917.

The hypersensitive Gavin Maxwell confessed that he finally left St. Cyprian's "in a quaking jelly of misery and self-pity." Eric, considerably tougher, was more like the old boy, quoted by Henry Longhurst, who attributed his ability to emerge "absolutely sane and fit from five years as a prisoner of war" to his previous imprisonment at St. Cyprian's.[10] The school gave Eric basic training for the hardships he eagerly endured (despite weak lungs) in malarial outposts of Burma, as a tramp and kitchen-slave, and on the winter front in northern Spain.

In a perceptive commentary on "Such, Such Were the Joys," Cecil Beaton, comparing his own experiences to Orwell's, said he emphasized the squalid and exaggerated the horror:

> It is uncanny how a boy of that age could have seen through all the layers of snobbery and pretence of the Vaughan Wilkes. It is hilariously funny— but it is exaggerated: God knows I *loathed* the Wilkes and loathed every minute of the school regime, and was just as appalled as he by the stink and squalor of the loos, the swimming-pool, just as appalled by the cold and the filthiness of the food. Even so I never saw a turd floating in the bath. I do not remember the rind of old porridge under the rim of the pewter bowl, and I have the feeling that Orwell made a fetish of the sordid and enjoyed playing up the horror of life among the miners, or the down-and-outs in any city of the world.

On the positive side, St. Cyprian's (using cruel methods) developed his intellectual ability, forced him to fulfill his promise and got him into Eton. It encouraged his enthusiasm for swimming, cricket and boxing, and—after long walks on the smooth downs of Beachy Head—his lifelong interest in natural history. The rifle range and cadet corps awakened his passion for firearms and military exploits. The school toughened him up and taught him to work hard, fired his ambition and made him realize his potential. It also intensified his lifelong guilt and fear of failure, his ingrained defensiveness and reserve, his wariness about revealing his feelings. He always hated the school and in 1939 was delighted to hear that it had burned down.

Orwell confessed that until he was thirty and had published his first book, "I always planned my life on the assumption not only that any major undertaking was bound to fail, but that I could only expect to live a few years longer."[11] It's unlikely that he actually expected to die at Eton or in Burma, and his ability to pass the difficult exams to get to those places did not suggest the prospect of failure. But for him the success was vitiated by the force-feeding and cramming he'd had to endure. He often felt his life was blighted and that nothing he did or could do was any good. He blamed the physical deprivations and emotional blackmail of his prep school for robbing him of his confidence and hope. He cultivated feelings of guilt, self-pity and out-rage, and quite consciously decided to be a failure. Eton, however, would give him what prep school had notably failed to provide: freedom, leisure, stimulating classmates, lively teachers, a civilized environment and a cubicle of his own.

3

Slacking Off at Eton,
1917–1921

I

IN HIS teenage years Eric evolved from a puffy, fat-faced creature, "a bit like a hamster," to "a stork-like figure, prematurely adult, fluttering about the school yard in his black gown." In photographs at Eton he is surrounded by several quite good-looking, even beautifully androgynous boys, and the striking contrast must have made him feel self-conscious about, even ashamed of, his own appearance. A classmate shrewdly noted that "he rather made a point of saying, of course, he was ugly. But I always thought he did it rather almost with enjoyment"—as if there were some positive merit in having the most unappealing countenance and most unhappy childhood, the most foolish parents and most miserable prep school. Malcolm Muggeridge pointed out that since the upper-class boys at Eton were circumcised (like Christopher Isherwood in Don Bachardy's nude drawings), "in the changing-rooms [Eric] was very ashamed at being uncircumcised, and kept himself covered."[1] For Blair, even the appearance of his penis suggested class distinctions.

In January 1917, in a lonely transition from prep school to Eton, the awkward thirteen-year-old Eric was sent to Wellington College, in Berkshire, for the winter term. According to Harold Nicolson, it was (like St. Cyprian's) "designed to provide a large number of standardized young men fitted for the conquest, administration and retention of a vast Oriental Empire." Wellington believed that "intellectual prowess was in some way effeminate," that one could show manliness only by physical force. Eric found the Spartan school oppressively militaristic. His only pleasant memory was of skating on the frozen lake. Asked what he thought of Eton, when he turned up in May, he gave a typically backhanded compliment: "It can't be worse than Wellington. That really was perfectly bloody." But he'd finally arrived and would stay at Eton for four decisive years.

In September of that year the sixty-year-old Richard Blair, who'd seemed comfortably and thoroughly retired, made an astonishing decision. Inspired by patriotism, or perhaps by boredom, he suddenly enlisted in the army. As one of its oldest subalterns, he was posted to an Indian Labour Company and put in charge of a herd of transport mules in a camp near Marseille. Eric may have been impressed at first. His father looked smart posing with his family in military uniform, wearing a clipped mustache, Sam Browne belt and high boots. But he may also have been embarrassed by his father's inglorious, even ludicrous career as commander of coolies and keeper of the King's mules. He never told any of his friends about this strange episode, which would have inspired cruel sniggers when thousands of Old Etonians were fighting and dying at the front. He alludes to his father's military service in *Coming Up for Air*, when the unheroic Tubby Bowling receives "a wire from the War Office telling me to take charge of the stores at Twelve Mile Dump [in Cornwall] and remain there till further notice."

With Richard safely banished to France and her younger children away in boarding school, Ida, relishing her freedom, packed up her dachshunds and embroidery and said farewell to Henley. She and Marjorie found a flat in London, first in Earl's Court, then in Notting Hill Gate, and Ida joined the war effort as a clerk in the Ministry of Pensions. Delicate little Marjorie became a dispatch rider, and looked quite dashing in her uniform, helmet and goggles. Just as Ida had seemed eager to escape her husband and married life in India, so—once in London, free of domestic duties, and perhaps involved with another man—she could not be bothered to see her small children during their longed-for school holidays.

In November 1917 she asked the compliant Mrs. Buddicom, "if you will be so very kind as to have Eric and Avril for their Xmas holidays as paying guests?" The following November, claiming that her children had begged to be with the Buddicoms rather than with their own mother and sister, Ida again asked: "Do you think you could have Eric and Avril for the Xmas holidays, they have implored me to ask you & I promised I would." In December 1918 she said she could not manage to come down to Henley (an hour away

by train) on Christmas day. On January 1, she was sorry to tell the tolerant
Mrs. Buddicom, once again, that "I won't be able to have the children this
week end after all."[2] Ignoring the importance of family holidays to children
who scarcely knew their perennially absent father and spent most of the year
away from home in miserably harsh conditions, Ida enjoyed—as far as
wartime restrictions permitted—her rather self-absorbed life in London.

II

THE MELANCHOLIC poet Thomas Gray, an old Old Etonian, celebrated the
sweet beauty of the school's physical setting in his famous "Ode on a Distant
Prospect of Eton College" (1742):

> Ye distant spires, ye antique towers,
>   That crown the watery glade,
> Where grateful Science still adores
>   Her Henry's holy shade;
> And ye, that from the stately brow
> Of Windsor's heights the expanse below
>   Of grove, of lawn, of mead survey,
> Whose turf, whose shade, whose flowers among
> Wanders the hoary Thames along
>   Her silver-winding way.

In Gray's idealized Eton, the innocent boys exult in the hope and vigor of
youth, blissfully unaware of the bitter disappointments of adult life and the
inevitable decay of "slow-consuming age." The young Blair would be sharply
sceptical about Gray's portrayal of innocent youth.

Cyril Connolly's biographer provides an elegant modern description of
Eton College, only fifteen miles east of Henley, along the winding Thames.
The Tudor king (Gray's holy Henry) who had established the school need-
ed a cadre of bright, well-educated young men to serve the state:

Eton had been founded by Henry VI in 1440: it was, and still is, the grand-
est . . . of the great English public schools, in which middle-class boys [like
Eric] rubbed shoulders with the sons of earls and foreign potentates.
Endowed with a particular blend of stylishness, charm, arrogance and self-

confidence, Etonians went on to rule the Empire, to occupy as if by right the highest positions in the land, and to make an impact out of all proportion to their numbers on every aspect of British life. . . . Eton was still a small country town, just over the river from Windsor, where the huge royal castle frowned greyly down from its heights. It consisted of a main street, with narrow pavements lined with shops and private houses, all apparently built for dwarves. . . . [The boys were] incongruously clad for the most part in grubby black tail-coats, black-and-white striped trousers, scuffed black shoes, black waistcoats, white shirts and white tuck-in ties, and, as if to complete the resemblance to youthful undertakers, black top hats.

Orwell noted that the high stiff Eton collar "sawed your head off," and in *The Road to Wigan Pier* recalled "a couple of savage mass battles" that shattered the uneasy truce between pupils and town boys "in the cold winter of 1916–17."

Eton's ancient buildings, cloistered and cobbled, emanating tradition and privilege, were and still are impressive. The College, built of mellow red brick, consists of two Courts, or quads. The main gate and porter's lodge leads to the larger School Yard, with its imposing statue of the founder in the center. Above the entrance is the Upper School. On the left is the Lower School, the original, late-medieval, lead-windowed classroom. Eric sat on the rough benches and worked at a desk carved by centuries of schoolboys. Opposite is the imposing Chapel, reached by a wide flight of stone steps. A gatehouse leads to the second Court, or Cloisters, and the Dining Room, with its historical portraits and long high table. The College Library, above the Dining Room, is filled with precious rare books. This sheltered cloister is adjacent to the open, vivid green of the playing fields, with the serpentine river in the distance. The 118-yard red-brick Long Wall has an elm tree at one end and a doorway in a right-angled wall at the other. These serve as goals in the arcane Wall Game, a violent version of football peculiar to Eton.

Places at Eton were highly prized. In 1917 there were about 1,100 boys in the school, all admitted after a fierce competitive examination. Eric belonged to an even smaller elite—the seventy "Collegers," or King's Scholars—who had won academic scholarships. Cyril Connolly described their life in the monastic College, which was almost as formal, hierarchical and ritualistic as the Spanish court in the age of Velázquez: "The seventy Eton scholars lived together in a house, part Victorian, part mediaeval where they were governed by the Master in College who had under him the Captain of the School [always a Colleger] and nine other members of Sixth Form, who wore stick-up collars, could cane, and have fags [younger boys who did menial tasks for the older ones]. All boys were divided into elections according to the year in which they won their scholarship; the elections moved slowly up the school *en bloc* and each represented a generation." Living together in the oldest buildings of the school, sitting at rough wooden desks, the Collegers had a distinct identity and were closely connected to the ancient traditions of Eton.

The rest of the boys, about a thousand "Oppidans" (from the Latin, "in the town"), lived in the red-brick Victorian houses that were spread around the village. The Oppidans paid £100 a year for their education. The Collegers paid less than £25 a year for tuition, lodging, board and recreational facilities. Though this was only a quarter of his half-fees at St. Cyprian's, Eric always called it "exorbitant!"

The Collegers, many of whom could not have gone to Eton without a scholarship, were more democratic and intellectual than the snobbish and fanatically athletic Oppidans. Orwell's contemporaries in College included, in addition to Connolly, several boys who went on to brilliant careers: Sir Steven Runciman, the second son of a viscount, a distinguished historian of Byzantium and the Crusades; Sir Roger Mynors, Professor of Latin at Oxford; and Robert Longden, Headmaster of Wellington. The Oppidans included the novelist Anthony Powell (who later became a close friend), the novelist Henry Green, the traveler Robert Byron, the writer and aesthete Harold Acton. John Lehmann wrote that the Collegers "were proud of our separateness from the thousand-odd other boys in their Houses, and gloried in being thought bookworms . . . in having our own privileges and honours, our special places in Chapel, our own inscrutably ancient game in the Wall Game . . . in having a kind of brotherhood of intellectual apartness." It was a great intellectual advantage for Orwell to be educated in that "nest of clever boys," that "hothouse of bright young things."[3]

III

CHRISTOPHER HOLLIS, an Eton contemporary, went to Oxford, met Orwell in Burma, and later became a publisher and Conservative M.P. He reported that initiation at Eton was considerably milder than the brutal rites at St.

Cyprian's: "all new boys in College had one by one to stand upon a table in their dormitory which was known as Chamber and each to sing a song" in front of the rest of the College, who were asssembled around a big fire. "Orwell sang—not very well—'Riding Down from Bangor,'" later on, the subject of one of his *Tribune* essays. That nineteenth-century American song, which Eric found in the *Scottish Students' Song Book*, begins:

> *Riding down from Bangor*
> *On an Eastern train,*
> *Bronzed with weeks of hunting*
> *In the woods of Maine—*
> *Quite extensive whiskers,*
> *Beard, moustache as well—*
> *Sat a student fellow,*
> *Tall and slim and swell.*

The song describes the intimate encounter of the backwoods huntsman with a delicate lady, who removes a cinder from the hero's eye and finds her earring entangled in his beard. Eric's song appealed to the boys and was a great success, and he avoided the opprobrium of being pelted with books and apples.

Eric also gave a dramatic reading of Robert Louis Stevenson's short story "The Suicide Club." The *Eton College Chronicle* reported that "Blair's speech was skilfully chosen. . . . The even and unmoved coolness with which Blair let the story make its own effect was certainly very successful." In the tale a group of young gentlemen gather to play cards and drink champagne while deciding which of them will offer the ultimate response to ennui. One character sets the sophisticated, world-weary tone—which would also have appealed to the boys—when he thinks: " 'It does not seem to me a matter for so much disturbance. If a man has made up his mind to kill himself, let him do it, in God's name, like a gentleman. This flutter and big talk is out of place.' "

Eric's interest in natural history, in vampires and the supernatural, took more extreme—even bizarre—forms at Eton. He and Roger Mynors dissected animal organs acquired from the local butcher. They also killed a jackdaw with a catapult, spirited it away to the biology lab and slit its gall bladder, which squirted out its disgusting contents and made a foul mess. According to Christopher Hollis, Blair also dabbled in dark arts and had once "made out of soap an image of his hated enemy. He had extracted all the pins out of his returned washing and stuck them at odd angles into this soapen image."[4] This bit of voodoo proved remarkably effective. The victim suffered a series of evil accidents and beatings until Eric finally relented and lifted the curse.

Abandoning these childish pranks, Eric took on the role of learned cynic. Assuming disdainful superiority, he mocked everything that was sacred to the conventional mind: compulsory games, the Officers Training Corps, the Christian religion and the Royal Family. Just as he'd rejected "war, the Empire, Kipling, Sussex and Character" at St. Cyprian's, so at Eton, wrote Connolly, he "perpetually sneered at 'They'—a Marxist-Shavian concept which included Masters, Old Collegers, the Church and Senior reactionaries." His cynicism, however, did not affect his loyalty. Connolly remembered that Eric came to his aid and knocked down a bully "when he found him tormenting me."

Blair had a sophisticated sense of humor and relished the absurd. One of his star turns was to go around inquiring about the religions of new boys and naming a series of extinct creeds. "Are you Cyrenaic, Sceptic, Epicurean, Cynic, Neoplatonist, Confucian or Zoroastrian?" he would ask a bewildered youngster. "I'm a Christian." "'Oh,' said [Eric] 'we haven't had that before.'" Sceptical about religion, he sneered at the ordained masters and told another Eton friend: "There are at least six masters on the staff who make a very good living out of the Crucifixion. It's worth over £2,000 a year between them. . . . I reckon that must have been the most profitably-exploited event in history—and they all have to talk as if they wish it hadn't happened."

When provoked he engaged in some memorable repartee. "Well, Blair," said one master, risking a cheeky retort, "things can't go on like this. Either you or I will have to go." "I'm afraid," Blair inevitably replied, "it will have to be you, sir." Reading Butler and Shaw encouraged his hostility to traditional religion and the conventions of family life, and he shocked his contemporaries by running down his parents in public. He'd once described his mother as "a pretty silly woman." Now, he dismissed her as a "frivolous person who wasn't interested in any of the things he thought people should be interested in and said his father wasn't apparently interested in anything."[5] In all these remarks Eric was parading his learning, speaking for effect, impressing his friends as cynical, witty, rebellious—even outrageous. But he was also genuinely different from the other boys.

At Eton Eric seemed to his friends to be unusually grown up, literate and satirical. Steven Runciman, who retained a vivid impression, agreed with Connolly that Eric had "much the most interesting personality. I enjoyed his company. His mind worked in rather different ways, his reactions were different from the ordinary schoolboys. . . . He loved airing his knowledge, particularly to the masters who were slightly shocked to find someone so well read."

Runciman, like most of his classmates, felt uncertain about Eric's friendship, and worried about whether he himself was an interesting and stimulating companion. Unable to pierce his curious aloofness, he thought Eric seemed interested in humanity but not in what individual human beings actually thought or felt. He "believes in free love," as another classmate put it, "but never seems to love anybody." Runciman believed his later novels reflected that inhuman detachment, and said that Eric "was a curious boy. He didn't really *like* other people. He liked their intellectual side, someone to talk to, but friends didn't really mean anything to him." But Eric, who needed friends as much as anyone else, deliberately tried to do without them. His disappointment with his mother and disgust with Mrs. Wilkes convinced him that no one really cared for him and that he didn't deserve to be loved. He protected his innermost feelings with studied aloofness and cynical disdain.

Runciman invited Eric home for the holidays—when Ida couldn't, or wouldn't, have him—but he always perversely refused the invitations. Runciman believed he would never attempt to make a good impression, to desert his own individualistic standards, to conform to a different, more socially acceptable mode of behavior. Eric always claimed to be much poorer than everyone else at Eton. "I frankly don't believe he was as poor as that," Runciman noted. "It was all rather part of the legend [of hardship] about himself that he began to create, and which I think dates from when Burma went wrong."[6]

I V

ERIC'S CHRONIC cough continued, and while at Eton he twice became ill with pneumonia. At St. Cyprian's Sambo noticed that he "wheezed like a concertina" and, despite the lean rations, claimed his illness was caused by overeating. The food at Eton was marginally better, and only slightly more abundant. The boys had no solid meal after midday dinner. For afternoon tea they ate only bread and butter; and at eight o'clock gulped down a miserable supper of soup or fried fish—more often bread and cheese—with only water to drink. Public school boys usually received food packages from home, and supplemented their meager rations with toasted muffins and sausages cooked on the fire, but Blair never mentioned these special treats.

Despite the torments of poor health, Eric energetically threw himself into sporting activities. Keenly interested in rowing, swimming and fishing, as well as floating down the Thames or lazily lying on the banks, he was known in Eton parlance as a "wet bob" (as opposed to a "dry" one). In his poem "Wall Game" (1919), an obvious parody of Kipling's "If," Eric wrote:

> *If you can keep your face, when all about you*
> *Are doing their level best to push it in. . . .*
> *Yours is the game and everything's that in it,*
> *And you may wear your College Wall, my son.*

Christopher Hollis recorded that "the College Wall book commends [Eric's] cool and skilful kicking, both on St. Andrew's Day and throughout the season. 'Blair made some neat kicks.' 'Blair kept his head and stopped the rush.'" He also noted that "the throw is inordinately difficult and for years on end no one ever scores a goal." But in a match on October 6, 1920, Eric (later remembered for playing football in Burma) reached the peak of his athletic career and Eton glory by scoring one of these rare goals.

Eric's school offered extensive military training, which he put to good use in Burma, Spain and the Home Guard. As he wrote at the beginning of World War II: "At seven years old I was a member of the Navy League and wore a sailor suit with H.M.S. 'Invincible' on my cap. Even before my public-school O.T.C. I had been in a private-school cadet corps. On and off, I have been toting a rifle ever since I was ten." At Eton, he said, "to be as slack as you dared on O.T.C. parades, and to take no interest in the war, was considered a mark of enlightenment."[7] On Field Day in 1919 he encouraged the cadets to take off their hot uniforms and amused them by reading from the much-loathed *Eric, or, Little by Little*, which he'd brought with him specially for the occasion. But he greatly enjoyed the compass work and map reading, rifle and bayonet practice, and later regretted that he had not been old enough to test his manhood and fight in the Great War.

He cynically recalled that during the war "a huge map of the western front was pinned on an easel, with a red silk thread running across on a zig-zag of drawing pins. Occasionally the thread moved half an inch this way or that, each movement meaning a pyramid of corpses." Though he followed the bloodthirsty battles and remembered the war map all his life, Eric was mainly concerned with the deterioration of food at school and the substitution of margarine for butter.

On Armistice Day in 1918 the school was given a patriotic holiday and marched down the High Street waving flags and cheering until they were hoarse. Eric believed that in the midst of this euphoria the boys were wiser and more humane than their teachers. As he wrote in *The Road to Wigan Pier*: "Our elders had decided for us that we should celebrate peace in the traditional manner by whooping over the fallen foe. We were to march into the school-yard carrying torches, and sing jingo songs of the type of 'Rule Britannia.' The boys—to their honour, I think—guyed the whole proceeding and sang blasphemous and seditious words to the tunes provided." The young men, as opposed to the old gang, realized there was little to celebrate when nearly half of the 5,700 Old Etonians who fought in the war had been killed or wounded while leading their men into combat.

Eric made use of his camping skills when, en route to a family holiday in Polperro in August 1920, he had his first experience as a tramp. After missing the connecting train, he was stranded in a village without a telephone and left with only sixpence in his pocket. Faced with the choice of either food or room, he bought twelve buns and slept out in a farmer's field. "I am very proud of this adventure," he told Runciman, "but I would not repeat it."[8] Roughing it did not come naturally, and he later had to force himself to become a tramp.

Eric appears relaxed and self-possessed in a number of photographs taken at Eton between 1919 and 1921. Legs crossed and hand on hip, with wet hair and a striped bathing costume, he joins a group of youthful swimmers. In cap and open shirt with rolled-up sleeves, he swaggers with eleven other youths before the Wall Game, or, shaggy-haired and leather-gloved, smiles outside the Fives Court. In uniform and on maneuvers during Field Day, he half smiles and clasps a rifle that rests between his puttee-wrapped legs. He posed more formally with a group of King's Scholars, all in stiff white shirts, high collars and bow ties. With hair sleekly parted, he leans against a stone wall and casually drapes one of his large hands over his leg. In his most relaxed pose, under a large floppy sunhat, with rolled towel and dangling cigarette, he stands on the river bank after a swim. After leaving Eton in 1921 he sat for a studio photograph. In a three-quarter view, head-and-shoulders portrait, with his thick hair neatly combed and parted, he's dressed in a three-piece flannel suit, with spotted necktie fastened to his shirt with a gold pin.

Toward the end of his time at Eton, the normally aloof and austere Eric, succumbing to a common emotional hazard of public school life, developed a crush on a younger boy. To make matters worse, his rival for the boy's affections was Cyril Connolly. Eric was self-conscious about his looks; and though Cyril was physically unattractive, he had great charm and wit. He knew he'd easily win this romantic contest and relished his victory over Blair. In a letter to another friend, he quoted a rather pathetic letter from Eric, begging Cyril not to spoil his chances; then (in parenthesis) mocked him and twisted the knife with his own malicious comments:

> I got this curious communication from Blair this hols. I will only quote part of it.
>
> "I am afraid I am gone on Eastwood (naughty Eric). This may surprise you but it is not imagination I assure you (not with shame & remorse). The point is that I think you are too (to the pure all things are pure) at any rate you were at the end of last half. I am not jealous of you (noble Eric). But you, though you aren't jealous, are apt to be what one might call 'proprietary.' . . . Having a lot of influence over Eastwood you would probably have put him against me somehow, perhaps even warned him off me. Please don't do this I implore you. Of course I don't ask you to resign your share in him only don't say spiteful things." . . .
>
> Of course I like him very much and shall steal him from Blair who deserves no commiseration. When gone on someone you do not ask for a half share from the person who owns the mine. . . . Anyhow Eastwood has noticed it and is full of suspicion as he hates Blair.

Eric probably felt guilty about this homosexual crush, and later condemned Auden and Spender as "Nancy boy" poets to distance himself from these feelings.

Another incident, in which Eric was again a passive victim, was even more out of character. He had always opposed corporal punishment and considered it "completely disgusting and barbarous." His fag remembered him as "kind and nice, very withdrawn, a very pleasant, kind and decent fagmaster." But Eric was also tough and could defend himself. At St. Cyprian's he'd taken swift revenge on an older boy who'd cruelly twisted his arm: "[I] walked up to Burton with the most harmless air I could assume, and then, getting the weight of my body behind it, smashed my fist into his face." At Eton he'd beaten a bully who'd picked on Connolly. And in *The Road to Wigan Pier*, when comparing a tough lower-class lad who goes down the mines with a middle-class boy who remains in school, he concluded: "Just fancy a working-class boy of eighteen allowing himself to be caned!"

Yet in 1921, when Eric was eighteen, *he* allowed himself to be whipped — not by a master, but by fellow students. Connolly reported that the "super-senior election were in power and beatings were frequent. To our indignation they beat Orwell for being late for prayers. . . . Orwell and Whittome were boys of eighteen; they were just outside Sixth Form, and were beaten by boys of the same age in their own senior election, as if they were fags. . . . [They beat him] on trumped-up charges for political reasons."[9] This humiliating punishment by his peers was very different from being beaten for a crime he had actually committed.

It is not clear why Eric submitted. He may have been intimidated, or forced to yield, by the powerful senior clique. After four years at Eton, he may even have accepted this brutal system and, not wanting to seem cowardly, felt he had to submit. He may also have been threatened with expulsion had he refused. In any case, "the trumped-up charges for political reasons" reinforced an idea, already forming in his mind, that boarding school had many features of a totalitarian society.

V

IN "Such, Such Were the Joys" Orwell wrote that at Eton, compared to St. Cyprian's, he was "relatively happy." For him, this was a great concession. "I knew that at a public school there would be more privacy, more neglect, more chance to be idle and self-indulgent and degenerate." He had resolved, after winning his scholarship, to " 'slack off' and cram no longer." And he declared that, "between the ages of thirteen and twenty-two or three I hardly ever did a stroke of avoidable work." The key word is "avoidable," and once again (as with his "ugliness") he indulges his taste for exaggeration. The opportunities for degeneracy — cigarette smoking and homosexual flirtations — were limited. Too individualistic to be a good scholar, he was academically undistinguished during his five years at Eton, and in 1920 was a sluggish 117th in a class of 140. But he worked quite adequately and the vigilant masters made sure that he kept up with his studies. In his early twenties, after he'd left Eton, he had to work very hard, first in preparation, entrance exams and training for the Burmese Police, and then in carrying out his arduous duties as an officer.

Eton had a strict academic schedule that did not allow much leeway for slacking off. "There was 'Early School' at half-past seven, a class before breakfast, then three hours of lessons and an hour with, or doing work set by, their tutor. Three afternoons a week began with organised games followed by two more hours of classes and preparations." In 1918, his second year, he took classes in Greek, Latin, English, French, Divinity, Maths and Science. The following year he continued Latin, French and Divinity, and also studied Ancient History, Geography and Shakespeare. He had started Latin at the age of eight, Greek at ten, and was thoroughly sick of both of them. When in boyhood he read about the great fire in Alexandria, which destroyed the texts of many ancient Greek tragedies, the little philistine was "filled with enthusiastic approval. It was so many less words to look up" in the Liddell and Scott dictionary.[10]

Compared to the writing of more sophisticated contemporaries like Harold Acton and Brian Howard, who dominated the Eton magazines and also managed to publish their work in London, the stories and poems Eric brought out in the *Election Times* and *College Days* were conventional and rather dull. But in the summer of 1920 he and his friend Denys King-Farlow printed two issues of *College Days*, and filled them with advertisements and contributions from well-known authors. They sold them at the Eton-Harrow cricket match at Lord's and made a handsome profit of about £200—eight times more than the annual fees for a Colleger. John Lehmann, who later took over the magazine, explained that "if one displayed enough energy and a moderate amount of canny business sense, one made money, more money than we had ever dreamt of."

Despite his intellectual swagger, Eric respected some of the masters. He admired M.R. James, the Provost and author of well-known ghost stories, who gave the impression that rules and exams were rather ridiculous. He was fascinated by the highly eccentric and rather miserable figure of Aldous Huxley, who'd replaced a French master serving at the front and vainly tried to teach English and French. An Old Etonian, Huxley had by 1917 published two volumes of poetry, which appeared in the window of Spottiswoode's bookshop on the High Street. Half-blind, inexperienced and insecure, unable to keep order, Huxley absolutely hated every moment he had to spend in the classroom. He especially resented "the unceasing pretence of knowing better, of being respectable and a good example."

Edward Sackville-West wrote that the boys treated Huxley with appalling incivility: "Poor Aldous! He must have been one of the most incompetent schoolmasters who ever faced a class. . . . From time to time, Aldous would pause, look up, and say, in an imploring tone, 'Oh! Do be quiet!' No one took the slightest notice." In the first chapter of his novel *Antic Hay* (1923) Huxley expressed his own deep despair as his hero reflects on an agonizing day in class and an evening spent on a heap of dreadful papers: "Definitely, it couldn't go on, it could not go on. There were thirteen weeks in the summer term, there would be thirteen in the autumn and eleven or twelve in the spring; and then another summer of thirteen, and so it would go on forever. For ever. It wouldn't do. He would go away." No wonder that Aldous' brother, Julian, once warned Steven Runciman: "You must never, never mention Eton to him!"[11]

Runciman felt that Huxley didn't know how to reach the boys and taught them very little. But he appreciated the quality of Huxley's unusual mind, and gave a more sympathetic account than Sackville-West's:

[He had] that long, thin body, with a face that was far younger than most of our masters' and yet seemed somehow ageless, and, usually hidden by an infinite variety of spectacles, eyes that were almost sightless and yet almost uncomfortably observant. He stood there, looking something of a martyr but at the same time extraordinarily distinguished. . . .

I cannot now remember a single thing that he taught us. But he was an educator in a wider sense. He showed us a glimpse of the fascination to be found in an unhampered intellectual approach to things.

Eric also saw beyond Huxley's physical disability and pathetic attempts to maintain order, and disliked the cruel jeers of his fellow students. He, too, enjoyed Huxley's "use of *words*, the phrases he used, and that was a thing that Eric Blair very much did appreciate." Always defending the underdog, "he rather stood up for Huxley because he found him interesting."[12]

The indolent, cocky and rather bolshy Eric inevitably clashed with the more overbearing and uncongenial masters. The most significant figure in Eric's academic life was his tutor Andrew Gow, who supervised his studies and taught him classics. Gow (1886–1978), the son of the headmaster at Westminster School, epitomized the stuffy classics tutor. Educated at Rugby and at Trinity College, Cambridge, he taught at Eton from 1914 to 1925 and then became a Fellow at Trinity. He edited many scholarly volumes on Greek literature and in 1936 published a memoir of his friend A.E. Housman. Eric had memorized many poems in A *Shropshire Lad* and might well have discussed them with Gow.

Eric found "Granny" Gow—or "Wog" (his name derisively spelled backwards)—fussy and old-maidish. Unresponsive to Gow's precise and probing teaching, he was bored by the long hours spent on Latin and Greek translation and composition. In a crude but heartfelt poetic squib, he satirized Gow's adoration of Homer as sentimental and his aesthete's appreciation of Italian pictures as "escapist posing." He also took a crack at another master, the bald, bespectacled John Crace, who tended to be "overfond" of pretty boys:

> *Then up waddled Wog and he squeaked in Greek:*
> *"I've grown another hair on my cheek."*
> *Crace replied in Latin with his toadlike smile:*
> *"And I hope you've grown a lovely new pile.*
> *With a loud deep fart from the bottom of my heart!*
> *How d'you like Venetian art?"*

Gow may also have inspired Orwell's ambivalent portrait, in *Coming Up for Air*, of the scholarly schoolmaster Porteous. He's one of those "cultivated Oxford blokes [who] stroll up and down studies full of books, quoting Latin tags and smoking good tobacco out of jars with coats of arms on them"—and are completely out of touch with the real world.

Gow, who disliked Eric and resented his laziness, could never get him to use his brains and fulfill his promise. He remembered Eric as "always a bit of a slacker and a dodger," as a cheeky boy who "made himself as big a nuisance as he could" and "was very unattractive." But Runciman (later on, his colleague at Trinity) found "Granny" Gow aloof and arrogant. Gow was, he felt, a good but not remarkable scholar, a competent but not stimulating teacher, who prodded Eric out of his comfortable indolence and made him work hard. "He disliked little boys," Runciman said. "He didn't understand them at all. I disliked Gow very much at that time. . . . Eric was everything Gow couldn't understand. My sympathy is entirely for Eric"[13]—who was desperate to break out of the restrictive school routine and start doing something exciting and significant.

V I

IN THE years between 1927 and 1933, shortly after Eric left Eton, "57% [of the students] went on to Oxford and Cambridge, 20% to the army, 16% straight into business." Of the fourteen boys in his election who left Eton in 1921, eleven went on to Oxford and Cambridge, two entered family businesses. Eric joined the Burma Police. What made him veer so wildly off the traditional track?

I asked Andrew Gow this question, and on January 1, 1969, he replied:

> Some time before G.O. left Eton his father came to see me to talk about his future. He said that O. could not go to a University unless he got a scholarship, and I said, as was obviously true, that there was not the faintest hope of his getting one and that it would be a waste of time to try. I do not remember whether I added, though I certainly thought, that he had shown so little taste or aptitude for academic subjects that I doubted whether in any case a University would be worth while for him. . . .
>
> Mr. Blair spoke of the Burmese Police and said that he had made, or would make, enquiries into the service. . . . It is highly unlikely that Mr. Blair consulted anybody else at Eton on this subject.[14]

In 1975 I published this apparently authoritative letter, which has often been quoted. In retrospect, considering Gow's character and relations with Eric, his letter now seems dubious and self-serving. Eric *could* have gone to university without a scholarship; and it was not "obviously true," except to Gow, that there was no hope of getting one. Eric was good at exams. His taste and aptitude for academic subjects had got him into Eton College, a far more selective process than entry to Oxbridge, and would later get him into the Burmese Police. In any case, the worth of a university education could not be measured by academic studies alone.

Eric's contemporaries had a very different view of his academic prospects. Connolly asserted that it was very easy for Eton scholars to gain admission to Cambridge: "most Collegers went on to King's, where there were safe scholarships for them and a reprieve for several more years from expulsion from the womb." His statement was confirmed by Michael Meredith, currently a master and librarian at Eton, who said: "Eric could have walked into Oxbridge from Eton. All the boys got in." Though it would not have been a waste of time for *Eric* to try for a scholarship, Gow did not want to waste his *own* time on a pupil he considered lazy and unambitious. Runciman thought Gow preferred solid scholars, whom he could teach and nourish. The universities, by contrast, looked out for promising, unusual characters, and made enlightened choices. Eric, with all his eccentricities, would have been their man.

Christopher Hollis, contradicting Gow, emphasized that Eric could have gone to university with or without a grant: "He could easily have won a scholarship, and if the emoluments of a scholarship were not sufficient, Eton, as I had the happy occasion to learn, was generous in making up scholarships to a figure which would make it possible for a poor boy to go to the university. . . . The question of family poverty, however freely it may have been brought in, had really nothing to do with it. . . . There is no doubt that Orwell could have gone to Oxford or Cambridge without costing his father a penny."[15]

Eric himself rebelled at the thought of university. He had been forced into St. Cyprian's and then into Eton. When able at last to make his own decision, he didn't wish to prolong his schooldays in the womb of a university. If he wanted to enter the illustrious Indian Civil Service, he'd have to spend three more years reading for a degree at Cambridge and another year studying for the competitive entrance exam. His father might have been willing to pay for university (if absolutely necessary) in order to get him into the ICS. But the son (as Orwell later wrote in *Keep the Aspidistra Flying*) didn't want to follow a smooth path and be one of "those moneyed young beasts who glide so gracefully from Eton to Cambridge and from Cambridge to the literary reviews." He would eventually make his way into the literary reviews but, struggling, not gliding, would get there by his own tortuous route.

"Where to?" then, was the question. Eric's childhood friend Jacintha Buddicom claimed that Richard and Ida Blair quarreled about Eric's future, and that Richard (for once) prevailed. Ida deplored "old Mr. Blair's obstinate attitude regarding Eric's future," his insistence that service in India "was the only career he would tolerate for his son." Mrs. Blair made "a desperate last-minute stand for a final last-minute chance of Oxford."

The Burma Police was a compromise that allowed Eric to follow his father's footsteps and serve in the East, though in a far less prestigious position than the ICS. Weary of school, but still influenced by the imperialist ethos, he admired the British Empire. He was drawn to India by his birth in Motihari and to Burma by his mother's memories of her exotic, even regal girlhood. His grandmother, who'd adopted native dress but after forty years could not speak a word of the language, still lived in Moulmein.

Eric was strongly attracted to the uniform, the money, the adventure, the danger, the authority and the power of the quasi-military police force, which would put him in charge of a small bit of Empire. Though the job might seem completely unsuitable for the writer we know as Orwell, the young Eric Blair seemed eager to go. Steven Runciman explained his character and motives: "the Burma Police was in those days quite a good job, quite a well-paid job. You started with . . . a certain amount of independence and responsibility. You were on your own quite a lot. And I think that was what attracted him. I always knew that he had no intention of going to the university. He had no wish to. And again, all this talk of him being too poor to go to university . . . that was all nonsense. He wanted to go to the East."[16]

VII

IT WAS customary for Eton students to present a book to the College Reading Room. Eric expressed his ambivalence about the school by presenting a copy of Bernard Shaw's play *Misalliance* (1910).[17] Orwell's later comments on Eton, especially during World War II when privilege was anathema to him, were quite negative. Looking back, he tended to underestimate its intellectual value and its influence on his life. He described a public school education as "five years in a lukewarm bath of snobbery" and insisted the whole value of Eton and Harrow, "from the point of view of the people who go there, is their exclusiveness." He regretfully told a woman friend: "If only I'd been sent to another school, a freer co-educational school, I should have been much happier than at Eton." In a biographical sketch of April 1940, he flatly but misleadingly asserted: "I did no work there and learned very little, and I don't feel that Eton has been much of a formative influence in my life."[18]

On other occasions he recognized the positive side of the experience. David Astor—an Old Etonian himself, editor of the *Observer*, his friend and patron—emphasized that Orwell enjoyed great freedom at school and was allowed to read whatever he wanted. Eton was, in fact, his university. Orwell felt he'd had a good education, and said he'd send his own son there if they'd change the stiffly formal clothes. Reviewing a book on Eton for the *Observer* in August 1948, Orwell praised the traditions that went back to the medieval period and the humane milieu that enabled, even encouraged the boys to develop an independent character:

It has one great virtue . . . and that is a tolerant and civilised atmosphere which gives each boy a fair chance of developing his own individuality. The reason is perhaps that, being a very rich school, it can afford a large staff, which means that the masters are not overworked; and also that Eton partly escaped the reform of public schools set on foot by Dr. Arnold and retained certain characteristics belonging to the eighteenth century and even to the Middle Ages. At any rate, whatever its future history, some of its traditions deserve to be remembered.

It's typical of Orwell to praise Eton for escaping the Victorian reforms of the pious and fanatical Dr. Arnold, who had turned lively schoolboys into earnest prigs.

Apart from some inconsequential writings, a few cynical remarks and a rare goal in the Wall Game, Eric left no great impression at Eton. Except for Connolly, he had no close friends at all until he met Sir Richard Rees in 1930. There was nothing extraordinary about Eric as a young man, no great promise of genius, very little to suggest that he'd become a brilliant stylist and the most influential English author of the century.

Eton, however, left its lasting mark on him. Years later, when Rees, a former Oppidan and the editor of the *Adelphi*, alluded to the academic gowns (or "togas") they wore and casually used a derisive nickname for the Collegers, Orwell revealed his still-keen sensitivity about having been a scholarship boy: "One day in 1948, when I had known him for eighteen years, I incautiously used the word 'Tug' and although he was too polite to say anything he winced as if I had trodden on his tenderest corn." He maintained close and crucial friendships with many Old Etonians, based on their common bond, throughout his life: with contemporaries like Cyril Connolly, Anthony Powell and Christopher Hollis, as well as with David Astor and Richard Rees. The writer John Strachey and novelist L.H. Myers, the publishers Roger Senhouse and John Lehmann, the philosopher A.J. Ayer and the laird in Jura, Robin Fletcher, also played significant roles in his life.

Orwell retained the languid, weary manner of an Old Etonian, yet also had a commanding presence (intensified by his ascetic gauntness) that enabled him to assume authority in dangerous situations. W.H.J. Christie, an Old Boy at St. Cyprian's, quoted a woman who'd known Eric in Burma to show that his liberal beliefs and conscientious character, the idealistic values and inner resources he drew on in difficult circumstances, were strongly influenced by his public school. "I once remarked to him," she said, "on the minute care with which he sifted each case, his passion for justice, his dislike of prejudiced remarks about anyone, however lowly, and his sense of utter fairness in his minutest dealings. He replied: 'This was the most important part of the education I received at Eton—this and the capacity to think for myself.' "[19]

4
—

Policing Burma,
1922–1927

I

ERIC BLAIR thought his career in Burma would be a great adventure, yet his five years there intensified his loneliness and ended in bitter disillusionment. In the Police he learned to live with inner conflict, to see himself as an individual and, at the same time, as a cog in the wheel of Empire. Burma made him think seriously about his own beliefs, and he spent the next twenty years working out these conflicts in his books and essays.

In the spring of 1919 Richard Blair finally left the army, once again emerged from foreign parts and came home to his unfamiliar family. The Blairs returned to their old house, which they had leased during the war, on St. Mark's Road in Henley. In July 1920 Marjorie married her childhood sweetheart Humphrey Dakin. In December 1921, when Eric left Eton, the Blairs moved to 20 South Green, Southwold, Suffolk. After the Christmas holidays Eric entered Mr. P. Hope's tutorial establishment in Southwold to prepare for his competitive examinations. His father agreed to provide his uniform; Hope and John Crace, the Eton master, supplied testimonials of his good character.

After cramming for six months, in June–July 1922 Eric took eight days of examinations in Greek, Latin, English, French, History, Geography, Maths and Drawing. He earned his highest grades in Latin, his lowest in History and Geography. He finished creditably but not brilliantly in the top quarter—7th in a class of 29—and was academically the best of the three men sent to Burma. He chose Burma because he "had relations there." His second choice was the United Provinces in northeast India, where his father had served for some years. At the bottom of his list was Bengal, with its capital, Calcutta, the increasingly active seat of Indian nationalism.

On September 1, Blair was certified physically fit; three weeks later he passed his riding test by a narrow margin. The following month he was appointed Probationer in the Burma Police and was advanced £30 against an annual salary of £444 plus bonuses (which was more than his father's annual pension). This was most encouraging to his parents. All their sacrifices, as well as the extra expense of crammer's fees, clothing and uniforms, were finally beginning to pay off. Marjorie was married, Eric was launched on his career and only Avril still remained at home.

On October 27, aged nineteen, Blair traveled first-class on the thirty-day journey from Birkenhead to Rangoon on the S.S. *Herefordshire*. The voyage out provided important lessons about the status of working men and the petty despotism of colonialism. One day after lunch he was astonished to see the European quartermaster, whose job it was to steer the ship, scurrying along the deck trying to conceal a stolen custard pudding. The young man, about to begin his own first job, suddenly recognized the disparity "between function and reward": "the revelation that a highly-skilled craftsman, who might literally hold all our lives in his hands, was glad to steal scraps of food from our table, taught me more than I could have learned from half a dozen Socialist pamphlets."

When the ship reached Ceylon, he watched the brutal treatment of a native porter and felt sympathy for the underdog. This gave him a bitter foretaste of what *his* police job would be like, and made him realize how imperialism corrupted both English officials and civilians:

The liner I was travelling in was docking at Colombo, and the usual swarm of coolies had come aboard to deal with the luggage. Some policemen, including a white sergeant, were superintending them. One of the coolies had got hold of a long tin uniform-case and was carrying it so clumsily as to endanger people's heads. Someone cursed at him for his carelessness. The police sergeant looked round, saw what the man was doing, and caught him a terrific kick on the bottom that sent him staggering across the deck. Several passengers, including women, murmured their approval.

The British had gradually conquered Burma in three Anglo-Burmese Wars, which began in 1824 and ended sixty years later. In 1885, when the king was finally driven into exile and the monarchy abolished, the entire country was brought under British rule and became part of the Indian Empire. Blair soon realized that Burma's timber, rice and oil were extremely profitable and that the country was relatively easy to control. In one of his earliest professional articles, published in May 1929 in the radical French journal *Progrès civique*, he wrote that Burma "is three times the size of England and Wales, with a population of about fourteen million, of whom roughly nine million are Burmese. The rest is made up of countless Mongol [hill] tribes who have emigrated at various periods from the steppes of Central Asia, and Indians who have arrived since the British occupation."[1] Twelve thousand armed Indians, commanded by British officers, were enough to subdue the entire population. Rangoon, the capital of Burma, had in Blair's time a population of 340,000: about one-third Burmese, one-third Hindu, and the rest Moslems, Chinese and Christians. The lush, tropical country had three seasons—cool, hot and wet—and for a depressing third of the year the rain "pours down with an unceasing rattle that grows into a nervous obsession and seems to fill your mind with the mildew that rots your clothes."

Sir Herbert White, a colonial civil servant, writing a few years before Blair arrived, claimed that British civilization was superior and expressed the prevailing authoritarian beliefs. Our job, White insisted, is to bring "law and order to parts of barbary and to maintain them there." Another official, writing in 1921, expressed the racism and paternalism that justified the policy of strict law and order: "[The Burman] has great pride of race and self-reliance, and these, when he is clad with a little brief authority, too often develop into arrogance. . . . [He is] lamentably wanting in self-control, sometimes passing into wild outbursts of brutality."

Joseph Conrad's friend Richard Curle, who worked as a journalist and traveled in the East in the early 1920s, gave a perceptive account of the kind of social life Blair found in Rangoon. Curle emphasized the limitations of white society, the profound ennui and isolation of the officials, which Blair would portray in the club scenes of *Burmese Days*: "People thoroughly on each other's nerves meet night after night in a desperate effort to forget the boredom of their own existence. . . . The Club is not alone a place of enjoyment, it is a symbol of racial solidarity." Curle described the principal club, which the unsociable Blair (it's difficult to imagine him dancing in a ballroom) sometimes frequented when he visited Rangoon: "The largest and

Burma
c. 1920

most generally popular is the Gymkhana Club, known all over Burma as the Gym, which, founded as a sporting club, is now equally notable for its dances and its bar. Its large buildings and playing-grounds, situated on the borders of the town, wake into life each evening about dusk and are shrouded again by half-past nine. But during these few hours Rangoon society, especially on the three nights a week when the Club's own band plays in the Club's own ballroom, is to be found there in force."

Somerset Maugham, a wealthy celebrity in great demand, took a less jaundiced view of colonials at play when he passed through Rangoon in 1930. A keen observer on a short stay, Maugham enjoyed a pleasurable round of social events in a comfortable but constricted setting. He found it "an agreeable life, luncheon at this club or that, drives along trim, wide roads, bridge after dark at that club or this, gin *pahits* [gin and bitters], a great many men in white drill or pongee silk, laughter, pleasant conversation; and then back through the night to dress for dinner and out again to dine with this hospitable host or the other, cocktails, a substantial meal, dancing to the gramophone, or a game of billiards, and then back once more to the large, cool, silent house."[2]

I I

TWO DAYS after arriving in Rangoon, Blair, keen to begin work, took the comfortable sixteen-hour train ride north to Mandalay. He was drawn to the land of tigers, elephants and pagodas by Kipling's evocative "Mandalay," which (according to Malcolm Muggeridge) he considered "the most beautiful poem in the English language":

> Come you back to Mandalay,
> Where the old flotilla lay;
> Can't you 'ear their paddles chunkin' from Rangoon
>   to Mandalay?
> On the road to Mandalay,
> Where the flyin'-fishes play,
> An' the dawn comes up like thunder outer China
>   'crost the Bay!

Fresh to the country, the young Blair may still have believed that life in Burma would follow the ancient Asiatic pattern—one long round, beneath friendly skies, "of singing, dancing, concubinage . . . hunting and religious observances." In their memoirs the old-timers, following Kipling, conjured up the romance of the East (see Appendix I). The authoritarian Sir Herbert White nostalgically wrote, in mandarin prose and from his comfortable retirement in England: "Never to be forgotten are the battlements of the walls, the purple shadows on the eastern hills, the glowing sunsets on the moat, the splendour of moonlight in the Palace corridors." And V.C. Scott O'Connor, a few years earlier, summoned up another idyllic remembrance of things past: "Evening after evening the women come here, a little pale, as English women are in the East; evening after evening the men gather here from the polo-ground and the tennis court; the band plays, the markers call the scores at the billiard tables. . . . Long men lie in the easy-chairs under swinging fans or sit . . . playing at whist and poker. The swish of soda-water bottles, the crack of ice, the click of billiard balls;—of such is the western end of the palace" in Mandalay.[3]

But Blair, uninterested in bridge and billiards, was soon disillusioned. He came to accept the more realistic, even embittered views of his contemporary Maurice Collis, an experienced civil servant and judge, and the caustic observations of Richard Curle. Emphasizing the exhausting, choking horrors of the hot season, Collis wrote that Mandalay "had an hallucinatory aspect, as it lay tranced under an overpowering sun, extremely dry, buffeted by a tearing wind, enveloped in dust clouds, the temperature at 100 degrees." Curle stressed the oppressive decay of the once-glorious town: "Mandalay, with its palaces and its temples, is a city of yesterday crumbling visibly before the stress of the modern world. It is old Burma dying by inches, and vilely set upon by the fungus of European civilisation. The great distances of the town, the moated walls of the Fort, the thousand pagodas, yes, even the number of forlorn dogs, all are symbolic of faded glories in their present heavy sense of exhaustion." In *Burmese Days* Orwell called Mandalay "rather a disagreeable town—it is dusty and intolerably hot, and it is said to have five main products all beginning with P, namely, pagodas, pariahs, pigs, priests and prostitutes."

The Police Training School—where Blair and the twelve other Probationers ate, slept and took classes—was inside the Mandalay Fort. "It is a vast square," Curle noted, "one and a quarter miles in each direction, and it is surrounded by a crenellated red-brick wall. . . . Within the wall, a moat of clearest water . . . invests the citadel, and gives to that parched scene an air of sumptuous serenity." A later trainee described the barracks-like mess,

built to retain the cool breezes and tended by a small army of personal servants: "The ground floor consisted of a large dining room, an equally large
ante-room and a billiard room. . . . The upstairs had a dozen bedrooms also
in line, each with its own primitive bathroom, with a wide covered verandah
and deep overhanging eaves that provided good shade throughout the day.
A narrow balcony ran continuously along the back of the bedrooms, with a
set of steps at each end allowing access for the servants."[4]

Most of his fellow officers were several years older than Blair and had
fought in the Great War. Orwell later recalled that "they talked about it
unceasingly, with horror, of course, but also with a steadily-growing nostal-
gia." He felt "less than a man" for missing the war, but all the more eager to
make his mark in the Police. In a photograph taken in Mandalay in 1923,
Blair, rather pale and wearing a uniform, stands beneath a brick archway
holding his solar topee. In his late teens he'd suddenly shot up and grown
up, and towers above the others. His face is longer and thinner, his jaw firmer.
He rather surprisingly gave the actual name of the only Burmese officer, U
Po Kyin (standing on the far left), to the villainous magistrate in his novel.

During his fourteen months in Mandalay (November 1922 to January
1924) Blair prepared for the exams he would have to pass, within his two-
year probation period, in Criminal Law and Procedure, Police Regulations
and Rules of the Province, and two oriental languages—one of them to the
higher standard of reading and writing as well as speaking. Roger Beadon,
the only contemporary in Burma who left a record of his time with Blair, was
impressed by his mastery of two difficult alphabets and languages. He recalled
that "we attended instructions in law, Burmese and Hindustani, and we used
to do an hour's Burmese and then have to switch straight over to Hindustani
. . . which didn't seem to worry him at all."

Studying Greek, Latin and French since boyhood, and coming directly
from a public school to the Police School, instead of fighting in the war,
made studying oriental languages relatively easy for him. Maung Htin Aung,
future Vice-Chancellor of the University of Rangoon and the only Burmese
to write about Blair's career, was also impressed by his linguistic ability and
academic success. "He passed his examination in Hindustani in no time, and
he passed without real effort all the compulsory examinations in Burmese
and the highest 'proficiency' test. He also passed an examination in Shaw-
Karen, which was optional and a rare language qualification"—and earned
a thousand-rupee bonus for each exam that he passed. (In 1937, while fighting in the Spanish Civil War, Orwell learned some Spanish and some

Catalan. This brought his knowledge of foreign languages—two classical, three oriental and three European—up to the extraordinary total of eight.) Their training, however, was purely academic and theoretical, and in fourteen months they never set foot in a police station.

Beadon found Blair a rather lugubrious fellow who kept very much to himself. The gregarious Beadon was fond of going to the club and playing snooker and dancing; but this sort of thing didn't appeal to Blair, who spent a great deal of time reading in his room. Beadon always had an eye out for the girls, but in Mandalay he never saw Blair with "female company." He remembered with some amusement that Blair—who liked to work with his hands and thought of himself as a practical chap—actually had very little mechanical ability. He owned a small American motorbike which he rode around the huge Fort. In a slapstick scene he once roared up to one of the gates, not realizing until it was too late that it was shut. Using his unusual height to avert disaster, "[he] just stood up and the bike went straight on between his legs and sort of hit the gate and came down."[5]

III

FROM THE 1880s to the end of World War I relations between the English and Burmese had been quite friendly. But the political situation had deteriorated dramatically between the end of the war and Blair's arrival in 1922. One Burmese historian stated that "before 1919, the English and the Burmese were friends, and after 1930 they were merely political opponents; but during that dark period between 1919 and 1930 they were bitter enemies, each despising the other." In the 1920s nationalist passions ran high.

In 1915 Mohandas Gandhi returned to India from South Africa and organized civil disobedience campaigns to achieve Home Rule. In 1919, partly as a result of Gandhi's movement, the recommendations of the Montagu-Chelmsford Report, advocating constitutional reforms that would lead toward "responsible self-government" in India, were enacted by Parliament. The Government of India Act—granting diarchy, which allowed Indians to help rule the country—took effect in 1921.

The British reforms excluded Burma, which was part of the Indian Empire. This inevitably angered and embittered the Burmese, whose monasteries became centers of activism and dissent. In 1920 "there was a storm of protests, resulting in the boycott of all English goods. Young Buddhist monks, for the first time in the history of Burma, entered the political arena, going about armed with small canes, with which they beat anyone found using English goods." These young men were not monks in the Western sense, but students who entered a monastery, for a few weeks or years, to prepare for adult life. Blair hated these intensely politicized students, who jeered at him and tripped him up on the football field. During these endless torments and provocations, which clashed with their traditionally placid image, he "thought the greatest joy in the world would be to drive a bayonet into a Buddhist priest's guts."

The boycott led to the founding of national schools that were free from British support and control, and of a national university, which inevitably fired up the movement for constitutional reform. In 1923 the British government, realizing it had made a mistake, extended India's limited form of parliamentary government to Burma and allowed Burmese to be elected to the legislative council. So the 1920s, when Blair served in the Police, became "a period of transition for Burma. The associations which had begun as institiutions for the preservation of Buddhism and Burmese culture had taken on a political aspect. The newspapers had matured as organs for expressing popular sentiment, in particular the nascent mood of nationalism."[6]

On January 1, 1923, when Blair was still being trained in Mandalay, the new constitution took effect. Sir Harcourt Butler—who had been to Harrow and Balliol College, Oxford, and spent his career in India and Burma—became governor of Burma and held the post until 1927. His relations with the legislative council were marked by tact and skill, but the 1920s were (according to one historian) "a period of meager positive achievement. The welter of political unrest which attended these governmental changes was aggravated by tangible economic grievances and by a rising tide of communal opposition to the presence and activities of Indian residents." Burmese nationalism aroused violent hostility to Indian shopkeepers and traders, who controlled commerce and were condemned as exploiters. As the revolutionary movement developed toward the end of 1924, there was great tension between Burmese, Indians and English, between civilians and police.

Orwell later expressed his ambivalent attitude to Burmese politics. He wittily condemned the colonial bureaucrats in Whitehall, dressed in clothes he'd never wear, as "well-meaning, over-civilized men, in dark suits and black felt hats, with neatly-rolled umbrellas crooked over the left forearm, imposing their constipated view of life on Malaya and Nigeria, Mombasa and Mandalay." But in 1943, only a few years before Burma became independent, he thought the idea was absurd: "Burma is a small, backward agricultural country, and to talk about making it independent is nonsense in the sense that it will never be independent. There is no reason for turning Asia into a patchwork of comic opera states." [7] He despised the British bureaucrats who formulated policy without understanding the practical difficulties; but he also felt that Burma was too poor to be self-supporting, and that its leaders were incapable of running the country. In principle, he believed in independence; in practice, he thought Burma was better off under British rule.

Nationalist agitation inevitably intensified criminal activity and made Blair's job more difficult and dangerous. As one of his friends, who'd also served in the East, put it: "The Burmese were perfectly harmless people but riots used to be stirred up and they had to put them down. And chaps would get beaten over the head." In a few years violent crime more than doubled, from 1,456 offenses in 1918 to 3,257 offenses in 1925. A historian noted that "by the mid-twenties Burma's jails were filled to overflowing, so that tickets of leave [paroles] had to be granted before old sentences expired in order to make room for the newly convicted. Nearly all of those consigned to prison were men."

As crime rose, the police also came under attack in the legislative council. They were criticized for gross inequities in salary, for bribery and corruption, and for crushing patriotic activity instead of investigating crimes: "the Nationalist members seized the occasion of the budget debates to attack the police system. They insisted that the entire policing operation was too costly. The pay of the higher-bracket salaries was too high in comparison to that of the inadequately paid constables . . . who allegedly made good their income deficiencies by corrupt practices. . . . The Criminal Investigation Department in particular was criticized for devoting too much attention to the suppression of political agitation while neglecting the basic work of crime detection. One Nationalist Party spokesman referred to the exciting and exhilarating popular sport of police baiting."[8]

I V

THE BRITISH officer, one of ninety in the Burma Police, had considerable independence and responsibility. He had to tour the villages in his area, by day and night, throughout the year. He had to recruit, train and discipline his native policemen in weapons, drill, field maneuvers and regulations, to "build up their physical strength, their self-confidence and their integrity." He ran the office, supervised the payroll, managed supplies and equipment. He led the thirty to fifty men under his command at headquarters, both on patrol duty or when escorting prisoners to trial or jail. He prepared cases for prosecution and compiled crime reports. "Whenever a major crime was reported, he was called to the scene to supervise the investigation. Whenever a dangerous criminal was at large, he directed the effort to capture the man. He settled quarrels between village leaders, disciplined errant constables, observed interrogations of prisoners, and testified at important trials and inquests." In Blair's time superintendents took charge of each of the thirty-six districts of Burma and fifty-nine assistant superintendents controlled the more important subdivisions. In the 1930s an officer on his first post, Pegu, north of Rangoon, had a large subdivision of about 2,000 square miles and commanded 400 policemen, which was as great as the total force of some districts.

Blair, like his father, did "the dirty work of Empire." But unlike his father, who never saw the disastrous effect of the thousands of tons of opium he helped ship to China, he saw at close quarters the sentencing, whipping, jailing and hanging of prisoners. He would never have become a policeman in England, where the work had far less glamour, prestige and moral authority, and didn't get much satisfaction from maintaining law and order. After the cramming course and voyage out, the training and examinations, he was surprised to find that he actually hated the job. If he'd chosen a different kind of service and been trained as a missionary, teacher, doctor, architect or engineer, instead of an oppressor who handed out harsh punishments every day, he would have done more constructive work—had converts, pupils, patients, houses and bridges instead of convicted criminals—and felt less guilt.

When a "cock-virgin" American missionary condescendingly told him, "I wouldn't care to have your job," he felt ashamed of his own inhumane behavior to "the wretched prisoners squatting in the reeking cages of the lock-ups, the grey cowed faces of the long-term convicts, the scarred buttocks of the men who had been flogged with bamboos, the women and children howling when their menfolk were led away under arrest." In *The Road to Wigan Pier* he also confessed that "things like these are beyond bearing when you are in any way directly responsible for them."[9] Once he'd left Burma, and secretly while still there, he abandoned the belief that the forces of law and order were always right and sided with the oppressed against their natural enemy, the police.

Though he had learned Shaw-Karen, one of the three main languages of the Karen people, he was never sent to their district. He never had a chance to get to know, help and protect the colorful and exotic tribes who lived in the remote mountains along the borders with India and China. In January 1924, when Blair finished his police training course, his schooldays were finally over. In the next four years he served from four to nine months at a time in six more prosaic and often unpleasant places. His first post, Myaungmya—in the brown, alluvial Irrawaddy Delta, southwest of Rangoon—was one of the worst districts in Burma. There were no through roads and waterways were the sole means of travel. Blair traveled eighty miles from the capital on a river steamer of the Irrawaddy Flotilla Company, which covered 900 miles of the 1,200-mile-long river. His superintendent here (and in two other places) was Burmese, and he had four inspectors serving under him. According to the *Imperial Gazetteer*, the huge jail at Myaungmya had an enclosure capable of providing for 1,000 prisoners, "who manufacture jail clothing and do gardening."

The district lay among the tidal creeks of the delta, which formed a fertile rice plain but was flat, monotonous and malarial. Blair, who may have lived on the boat he used to patrol the district, later recalled the torments of trying to read by oil lamp and sleep with the windows shut tight in that stifling hothouse: "in an eastern country, you keep thinking you have killed the last mosquito inside your net, and every time, as soon as you have turned the lights out, another starts droning." One colleague described the delta as "the most dismal and pestiferous tract in Burma . . . a vast featureless plain of alluvium extending for hundreds of square miles [and filled with mangrove swamps]. . . . Mosquitoes both by night and day exist in their millions. In the rain, the greenfly from the paddy fields invades the houses and makes it difficult to eat meals or drink without swallowing quantities of the insect."[10]

After five grueling months in Myaungmya Blair was transferred to Twante. Situated on the edge of the low-lying, thickly populated delta, it was connected to Rangoon, about ten miles northeast, by a sluggish creek that ran through the center of town. Seven months later he was transferred to Syriam, half an hour's ferry ride across the river to Rangoon. It had a population of 15,000 and a huge Burmah Oil Company refinery, whose tall chimneys polluted the air with the noxious smell of sulphur dioxide, killed off the vegetation and turned the surrounding area into a wasteland. The miasmic humidity of Myaungmya and the toxic fumes of Syriam had a devastating effect on his delicate lungs. He commanded almost 200 men and had the routine job of guarding the strategic yet vulnerable refinery, which supplied most of the oil to India, as well as maintaining law and order in the town. Later on, in a letter to a novelist who also wrote about Burma, Orwell bitterly recalled "the economic milching of the country via such concerns as the Burma Oil Company . . . [and] the disgusting social behaviour of the British."

In September 1925 he again packed his bags and moved on to Insein, just north of Rangoon. The Burma Railways Company, with its principal workshops, dominated this important terminus just as Burmah Oil had dominated Syriam. The town boasted, among its attractions, a reform school and the largest jail in the province, but was becoming a popular residential suburb of the capital. Richard Curle gave a vivid portrait of the nightmarish atmosphere. Insein, he wrote, "is a dismal hole at best. . . . There was a waste field there on the edge of a sort of swamp which represented, if I may say so, the quintessence of a charnel-house in its mixture of bones, smells, dreariness, furtive pi-dogs, and waiting vultures, who would flop down upon the thrown-out refuse with a tearing hiss."

After seven months in Insein and four unhealthy jobs within eighty miles of Rangoon, Blair may well have protested and was finally given a decent posting. From April to December 1926 he worked in Moulmein, ancestral home of Ida Blair, the Limouzin grandees and that old Burma hand, his Grandmother Theresa. Moulmein, like Twante, was a subdivision on its own and Blair was in sole charge there. More substantial than his previous posts, it had an old cantonment, jail, hospital, schools, churches, newspapers, Commissioner's house and a branch of the Bank of Bengal. The low hills along the banks of the Salween River were filled with glistening pagodas.

Murray's Handbook called Moulmein—across the Gulf of Martaban to the east of Rangoon, but a long way round the coast by road—"the most beautiful town in Burma." The *Imperial Gazetteer* also praised its gorgeous setting and scenic beauty: "The river banks are crowned with the most varied of ever-green foliage, a marked contrast to the low-lying muddy flats at the mouth of the Irrawaddy. . . . To the north and west lie the meeting place of the rivers, the shipping in the stream, the wooded islands in the channel, Martaban with its glistening pagoda overhanging the water, and the dark hills of Bilugyun." Maurice Collis, experiencing the sense of relief that Blair also felt when transferred there, wrote that "from a social point of view Moulmein was one of the best stations in Burma, with its large club, numbers of English people, golf and tennis, dinners, and so on. Coming from the grim loneliness of Myanaung, I found this very agreeable."

A small incident revealed Blair's kindness to a young Irish officer. Neil McCue had just married a Burmese woman and been posted to Moulmein. Dressed in khaki shorts and shirt, and holding a police helmet, Blair called on his new colleague, who confessed he didn't know Burmese well enough to take on his new job. His wife recalled that "he was still worried when Mr. Blair called again a few days later and discussed his position with him. He was sympathetic and advised Neil to stick it out for a month or so and then apply for a transfer to the River Police, where he would gain considerable experience."[11]

Blair's last post was Katha (December 1926–January 1927), the setting of *Burmese Days*, at the edge of the hills and on the east bank of the Irrawaddy, almost 200 miles north of Mandalay. Tigers, leopards, elephants and bison roamed the jungle, and bears were common in the uplands. Rice was the principal crop in the plains; tea, cotton and sesame in the hills. Teak was logged in the forests, and precious minerals extracted from the ground. In 1921 the population, made up of Burmese, Shans and Kadus, was 255,000.

The rather bare, shabby settlement, laid out along five roads running north-south and parallel to the river, contained a bazaar and the main public buildings. In addition to Blair's Burmese superior and an inspector below him, there were 300 head-constables, sergeants and constables. The prisoners were kept busy in jail, grinding wheat for the military police and doing carpentry and cane-work for the government offices.

V

WHILE IN the East Blair grew a straight, narrow mustache, which left a bare strip under his nose. It must have taken some trouble to maintain, but distinguished him from the clean-shaven Burmese and made him look more military and authoritative. Anthony Powell was fascinated by this idiosyncratic mustache, which always remained "a bit of a mystery. . . . It was perhaps Orwell's only remaining concession to a dandyism that undoubtedly lurked beneath the surface of his self-imposed austerity. . . . Perhaps it had something to do with the French blood inherited through his mother." His mustache seemed to go with the masculine thrill of wearing trouser straps under his boots, which, he told Powell, "give you a feeling like nothing else in life." When discussing riding breeches with his Southwold tailor, he remarked: "We *always* put buckskin strappings on."

Shifting frequently from post to post, remaining aloof, Blair had no close friends and made no greater impression in Burma than he had at Eton. Accounts of him are rare and unreliable. An engineer on the Burma Railways in Katha left a rose-tinted misconception of a happy-go-lucky Blair that contradicts most of what's known about him. But it's worth quoting to show the mask he had to wear to conceal his true feelings: "Orwell was easy-going and keen about his job; he was the life and soul of parties, and very fond of animals, rescuing waifs and strays. He spoke slowly and softly, was not anti-establishment, was very popular and an excellent linguist. . . . Even at that time, he had a weak chest and failed to look after himself, so he suffered badly now and then. Orwell was sent to Katha as punishment for shooting an elephant."

Blair certainly liked animals, was good at languages and had poor health. But his writings about Burma reveal that he was also lonely and unhappy. Very much the odd man out, he developed a covert anti-colonial point of view and came to loathe his job. There is no evidence that he was reprimanded or penalized for shooting the elephant. In any case, in contrast to the delta, Katha was an attractive post. An Englishwoman who knew him in Burma characterized him, more accurately, as "a delicate and shy man, brusque and unsociable, with no small talk."[12]

The waifs and strays made their presence felt. The shipshape Beadon "was surprised to find Blair's Insein house in a mess, with 'goats, geese, ducks, and all sorts of things floating about.' " When he was stationed in Moulmein his mobile Animal Farm seemed to menace public order. Another Englishman was shocked to see him "in Martaban station loading . . . a lot of farmyard creatures like hens, ducks and so forth, which happened to escape on the platform and caused quite a commotion."

Blair dropped his clothes and cigarette butts on the floor for his servants to pick up, and allowed himself to be dressed and undressed by his Burmese "boy." (Kipling even trained his servant to shave him while he was still asleep.) He later noted with disapproval that "Tolstoy himself did not give up beating his servants till he was well on into adult life." In *The Road to Wigan Pier* he expressed contrition about the "servants and coolies I had hit with my fist in moments of rage," yet also explained that "orientals can be very provoking."[13] After only a few years in Burma, he'd become corrupted, like the police sergeant who kicked the coolie on the ship in Colombo. He resented the job above all because it had turned him into a brute.

In his memoirs Maurice Collis described his circle of cultured and artistic Englishmen in Burma, some of whom had published their work in London. But Blair, a natural solitary, never met any of them. Though his first four posts were close to Rangoon, where he frequented Smart and Mookerdum's bookshop, he felt isolated in Burma—"up against petty minds and starved for intellectual debate." His prejudice against the Scots was reinforced by "the whiskey-swilling planters in Burma," and in *Burmese Days* the fatuous District Commissioner is called Macgregor.

Though his duties were arduous and the climate enervating, Blair had plenty of leisure time to write. He'd published a considerable amount of juvenilia while still at school, but apart from twenty pages of inconsequential stories, plays, poems (one of them about a visit to a whorehouse) and sketches for *Burmese Days*, written on official stationery, the would-be writer published nothing between 1920 and 1928. If he ever wrote for the *Rangoon Gazette* or other local papers, police regulations would have forced him to use a pseudonym, and nothing by him has ever been traced. His main intellectual pursuit was reading a little magazine, the *Adelphi*, sent out from London. When he disapproved of a particular article, he'd prop the magazine against a tree and "fire his rifle at it till the copy was a ruin."[14]

Blair was almost certainly a virgin before he went to Burma. Once there, he tried to assuage his loneliness (as he once confessed, in an unusual burst of candor) in the waterfront brothels of Rangoon. He may also have had an emotionally troubling and extortionate liaison with a native girl, like John Flory's with Ma Hla May in *Burmese Days*. Harold Acton, an Old Etonian who met him in Paris in 1945, reported that "his sad earnest eyes lit up with pleasure when he spoke of the sweetness of Burmese women" (whom Kipling thought were the most beautiful in Asia). "But for his nagging 'social conscience' I suspected he might have found happiness there." Anthony Powell, a close friend, recorded Orwell's impersonal account of the adolescent bonds that formed between policemen whose sexual life had been retarded by the war: "George spoke of the Burmese police officers having native mistresses, but said their emotional life really centred on each other, not in a directly homosexual way, but commenting about who played tennis with whom . . . like a lot of schoolgirls."

Maung Htin Aung, who tried to follow Blair's faint trail in 1935 (eight years after he'd left the country), reported that the handful of people who could recollect anything about him "remembered him merely as a sporting and skilful centre-forward who scored many goals for the Moulmein police team." Though Blair was sporting, his Burmese opponents were not. In a prophetic essay on nationalistic violence in sporting events, he later wrote that football was pretty rough in Burma: "I have seen the supporters of one side break through the police and disable the goalkeeper of the opposing side at a critical moment." Explaining his own state of mind in the opening paragraph of "Shooting an Elephant" and using volatile words like "hideous," "sneering" and "hooted," he described how he was publicly victimized and humiliated: "When a nimble Burman tripped me up on the football field and the referee (another Burman) looked the other way, the crowd yelled with hideous laughter. This happened more than once. In the end the sneering yellow faces of young men that met me everywhere, the insults hooted after me when I was at a safe distance, got badly on my nerves. The young Buddhist priests were the worst of all."[15] The scarcity of European women and the comparative geniality of the Burmese had made social relations friendlier in Burma than in India. But the considerable hostility between the two races in the 1920s made Blair an obvious target.

It was only a short step, apparently, from tripping him up on the football field to knocking him over in the train station. In November 1924, wrote Maung Htin Aung, he was a university student and Blair was serving in Twante,

> a small town across the river from Rangoon. One afternoon, at about 4 p.m., the suburban railway station of Pagoda Road was crowded with schoolboys and undergraduates, and Blair came down the stairs to take the train to the Mission Road station, where the exclusive Gymkhana Club was situated. One of the boys, fooling about with his friends, accidentally bumped against the tall and gaunt Englishman, who fell heavily down the stairs. Blair was furious and raised the heavy cane which he was carrying, to hit the boy on the head, but checked himself, and struck him on the back instead. The boys protested, and some of the undergraduates, including myself, surrounded the angry Englishman. The train drew in and Blair boarded a first-class carriage. But . . . some of us had first-class season tickets. The argument between Blair and the undergraduates continued. Fortunately, the train reached Mission Road station without further incident, and Blair left the train.

Though this oft-quoted incident seems to be a reliable firsthand account, it's doubtful that a Burmese boy could or would knock Blair down the stairs. The description of him raising his stick to beat the boy recalls the scene in

Burmese Days when Ellis strikes and blinds the jeering student. In the novel the Englishman's response is excessive; in Aung's story Blair's reaction seems far too weak. His official position and personal dignity, let alone his quick temper and propensity to violence, would not have allowed the boy to get away with it. Blair's engaging in argument in the train carriage is even more improbable. The whole story seems more like nationalist propaganda than an actual event. The narrator is pleased to report that Burmese students humiliated an English policeman (later on, a famous author), who was on the way to the club from which they were excluded.

Blair discussed his alienation from the English and hostility to the Burmese over two dinners with Christopher Hollis in Rangoon in the summer of 1925. Since leaving Eton, Hollis had been at Oxford, where he became president of the Union, a friend of Evelyn Waugh and a Catholic convert. He thought Blair's "loneliness certainly was sharpened and embittered by a life in Burma, in which none of his fellow Europeans were people at all sympathetic to him." His liberal opinions at Eton had been transformed by the harsh reality of his work and "he was at pains to be the imperial policeman, explaining that these theories of no punishment and no beating were all very well at public schools but that they did not work with the Burmese."

Blair had by now been in Burma for two years, had worked as a fully trained policeman for about a year and was still pro-imperialist. His job demanded that he maintain law and order. He soon realized that his liberal ideas were naive, ill-informed and largely inconsistent with the daily realities of occupying and controlling a foreign country. Trying hard to fit in, do a conscientious job and believe in his work, he told Hollis, who was briefly in Burma on a jaunt through the East: "You don't know what it's like—and I do." As time wore on, however, he began to see the hypocrisy of his own position and regretted his corrupt imperialistic role. After leaving Burma, his past justification of police brutality turned into guilt that haunted him forever.

His conflicts later helped him to understand the psychological pressures of living in a police-state. In *The Road to Wigan Pier* he described a conspiratorial but therapeutic conversation—which foreshadows the forbidden talks between Winston and Julia in *Nineteen Eighty-Four* and provides a strong contrast to his pukka-sahib talk with Hollis—with a teacher in Burma who didn't have to do "the dirty work of Empire," but shared his new hostility to imperialism: "I remember a night I spent on the train with a man in the Educational Service. . . . It was too hot to sleep and we spent the night in talking. Half an hour's cautious questioning decided each of us that the other was 'safe'; and then for hours, while the train jolted slowly through the pitch-black night, sitting up in our bunks with bottles of beer handy, we damned the British Empire—damned it from the inside, intelligently and intimately."[16]

VI

BLAIR WAS good at his job, but his uneasy relations with his English superiors sharpened these conflicts. A policeman on the scene at the time noted that Blair obviously suffered at the hands of several Superintendents of Police "whose ideas of training a young probationer was to throw him in at the deep end and tell him to get on with it." Maung Htin Aung also emphasized that he "was posted to the mosquito-ridden and oil-lanterned purgatory of the Irrawaddy Delta, had to cope with burdens of office beyond his tender years and experience and, above all, had to serve under unsympathetic superiors, one of whom was a bully, another a neurotic, and the third an Etonian-basher." He had to tread carefully with these superiors, whose official reports on his job performance (destroyed during the Japanese occupation of Burma) would determine his future career. But his clash with such people was inevitable. They resented his elite education, comparative youth, lack of war experience, intellectual interests, general unsociability, eccentric behavior, untidy uniform, messy house and solitary reading habits. To Blair, they stood for the decaying ideals of British imperialism, and he could scarcely disguise his growing distaste for their beliefs and their conduct.

His superior at Myaungmya was "a bit difficult." Henry Lanktree, at Twante, was (according to one contemporary) "a bad fellow, not one of us, if you know what I mean. He was ex-Army, but he was not a good officer. He didn't know how to handle men, and I gathered that Blair did not like him." Another superior, Colonel Welbourne, the police chief in Moulmein, disliked the way Blair mocked the bores at the club and failed to show enthusiasm for the Empire. "Welbourne deliberately set out to denigrate him, describing him as a disgrace to Eton. According to George Stuart, 'Everyone was disgusted with the way he ran Blair down.' "[17] Roger Beadon believed bad treatment by his superiors was the main reason why "he chucked it" and left the Police.

The sink-or-swim method of treating young probationers, while subjecting them to extreme loneliness and a foul climate, drove several contemporaries to suicide. H.H. Munro—who served in Burma, was invalided out with
severe malaria and later wrote short stories under the name of Saki—gave a
grim, Graham Greeneish view of an officer's life:

> He would be in some unheard-of sun-blistered wilderness, where natives
> and pariah dogs and raucous-throated crows fringed round mockingly on
> one's loneliness, where one rode for sweltering miles for the chance of
> meeting a collector or a police officer, with whom most likely on closer
> acquaintance one had hardly two ideas in common, where female society
> was represented at long intervals by some climate-withered woman mis-
> sionary or official's wife, where food and sickness and veterinary lore
> became at last the three outstanding subjects on which the mind settled,
> or rather sank.

Blair himself was morbidly fascinated by the career of a soldier he'd met
in Mandalay. Captain H.R. Robinson lost his commission, went native,
became addicted to opium, ruined his life and botched his suicide attempt.
He described his self-destruction in A Modern de Quincey, which Orwell
reviewed in September 1942:

> An officer of the Indian Army, seconded to the Burma Military Police, he
> was axed in 1923 and settled down for a couple of years in Mandalay, where
> he devoted himself almost exclusively to smoking opium, though he did
> have a brief interlude as a Buddhist monk. . . . On being arrested for debt
> [he] attempted suicide—a ghastly failure, for instead of blowing out his
> brains as he had intended he merely blew out both eyeballs, blinding him-
> self for life. . . . Those who knew the author in Mandalay in 1923 were
> completely unable to understand why a young, healthy and apparently
> happy man should give himself up to such a debilitating and—in a
> European—unusual vice.

In Burmese Days Orwell's hero condemns colonialism, the English hostility to the Burmese and the fatuous ethos of the Club. But he also shows
great fondness for his servants and the Indian doctor as well as for the local
customs and culture. Blair himself was fond of visiting temples and con-
versing in high-flown Burmese with contemplative priests. He liked the coun-

try, but the fierce tropical conditions had a terrible effect on his health; he didn't look after himself and suffered a severe bout of dengue fever. Orwell later wrote: "I gave it up partly because the climate had ruined my health, partly because I already had vague ideas of writing books, but mainly because I could not go on any longer serving an imperialism which I had come to regard as very largely a racket."[18]

Blair had served for five years—the peak of his youth—and now realized that he was temperamentally and morally unsuited to be a colonial police-man. Though he'd saved quite a bit of money, and had accumulated eight months medical and home leave, he didn't spend any of it traveling in the Orient on the way back to England. Eager to be home, he sailed on the M.V. *Shropshire* in July 1927 and went straight back to dull, quiet, respectable Southwold. He disembarked in Marseille, planning to travel across France by rail, and while there witnessed a massive political protest. A vast crowd had turned out to support Sacco and Vanzetti, Italian immigrants in America, who had been convicted of murder in a highly controversial case. "All these people," Orwell wrote, "—tens of thousands of them—were genuinely indig-nant over a piece of injustice, and thought it quite natural to lose a day's wages in order to say so. It was instructive to hear the [English bank clerks in Marseille] saying 'Oh well, you've got to hang these blasted anarchists.' " He used this comment in *Burmese Days* when Westfield, the police officer, says of the men who've killed Maxwell, the forest officer: "They won't go free, don't you fear. We'll get 'em. Get *somebody*, anyhow. Much better hang the wrong fellow than no fellow."

Burma had lasting effects; some were practical, others shaped Orwell's personality. His streak of violence, expressed in beating his servants and using his fists, occasionally erupted in later life. His police training and experience enabled him to assume authority and to become a good soldier in the Spanish Civil War and in the Home Guard during World War II. There is no record of him speaking Burmese after he returned to England, but he made good use of Hindi when broadcasting wartime propaganda to India during his two years at the BBC. He reviewed many books on Burma and India; and he per-suaded David Astor, editor of the *Observer*, to advocate independence for India after the war. His police duties also disciplined him and gave him the capacity for hard work; and he was a capable administrator both as Talks Producer at the BBC and literary editor of the *Tribune*.

In a review of 1936 he described his longing for England while in the East and, paradoxically, for the Orient while he was in Europe: "Live among palm

trees and mosquitoes in savage sunshine, in the smell of garlic and the creaking of bullock-cart wheels, and you pine for Europe until the time comes
when you would exchange the whole of the so-called beauties of the East for
the sight of a single snowdrop, or a frozen pond, or a red pillar-box. Come
back to Europe, and all you can remember is the blood-red flowers of the
hibiscus and the flying foxes streaming overhead."[19]

VII

ORWELL WROTE two major essays about police work in Burma, "A Hanging"
(1931) and "Shooting an Elephant" (1936). They justify, years after the event,
his decision to resign. These autobiographical, confessional pieces, the result
of intense psychological self-searching, show Orwell mastering the experience and conquering his sense of failure, shame and guilt. He had learned
to do what he could not do while still in Burma: dissociate himself from the
colonial system and atone for what he thought were his sins.

Maung Htin Aung wrote: "It is not certain whether 'A Hanging' took place
in Insein or Moulmein. It is true that condemned prisoners were sent to the
Insein jail for execution, but hangings also occasionally took place at other
jails." Wherever it took place, there is no question that the essay was based
on his close observation of an actual event. In an "As I Please" column in
November 1944, Orwell noted: "I watched a man hanged once. There was
no question that everybody concerned knew this to be a dreadful, unnatural
action. I believe it is always the same—the whole jail, warders and prisoners
alike, is upset when there is an execution." He does not mention, however,
that there were hundreds of hangings every year in Burma, that the warders
and hangmen, and perhaps even the prisoners, eventually became hardened
to them. In this column, as in his essay, Orwell (who saw only one hanging
and was horrified by it) projected his own feelings onto everyone else. In his
notebook he went even further by stating the implicit theme of the piece:
"When a murderer is hanged, there is only one person at the ceremony who
is not guilty of murder."

"A Hanging" is Orwell's first distinctive work. It gives an apparently objective account of a ritualistic execution—from fixed bayonets to a bag over the
head of the condemned—in which the narrator officially and actively partic-
ipates. It begins with the sodden prison in the rainy season, the prisoner and
guards who handle him "in a careful, caressing grip, as though all the while

feeling him to make sure he was there" and with the doctor-superintendent. The procession to the gallows is interrupted by a stray dog that leaps about and disturbs the solemnity of the occasion. In a strikingly human detail, the prisoner, who'd pissed on the floor when he heard his appeal had been dismissed, steps aside to avoid a puddle on the path—as if he feared he might catch cold on the way to his execution. This act of conscious will confirms his human existence. At this halfway point Orwell states his theme: "till that moment I had never realised what it means to destroy a healthy, conscious man. When I saw the prisoner step aside to avoid the puddle, I saw the mystery, the unspeakable wrongness, of cutting a life short when it is in full tide." Instead of invoking religion, he asserts a quasi-religious sense of life's sacredness—the first expression of the instinctive humanism that characterizes all his work.

The walk to the gallows continues, the convict-hangman appears, the prisoner cries out his last prayer to the Hindu god and then vanishes in the drop as the rope twists on itself. The dog stops barking and retreats to the corner of the yard. The superintendent, poking the dead man (now a thing) with his stick, exclaims: "*He's* all right," which is at once ironic and, in an awful sense, true. Breakfast is handed out to the other prisoners and the Eurasian warder mentions some disagreeable details in previous executions. The superintendent offers the narrator a shot of whisky, and they all break into uneasy laughter to relieve the tension. "The dead man," Orwell concludes, "was a hundred yards away."[20] There is a striking contrast throughout the essay between the condemned man who passively accepts his fate and the executioners who feel uneasy about killing him. Orwell, of course, never mentions the crime that justifies the execution: that would make the doomed convict less of a victim and weaken his rather one-sided argument. After the war, he joined forces with his friend Arthur Koestler to oppose capital punishment.

His second Burmese essay also concerns an unjustified killing, but this time the victim is an elephant and Orwell himself delivers the death blow. In timber towns like Moulmein, elephants in heat sometimes ran amok through the streets and bazaars, and had to be shot by the local police officer. George Stuart, on the scene at the time, recalled: "When a message was brought to the club in Moulmein one Sunday morning, Orwell 'went off in his old Ford to pick up a rifle and went in search of the elephant which was causing great damage on a semi main road and causing danger to life and limb and shot this elephant.' He was very nonchalant about the whole affair

. . . but got into serious trouble because the elephant was valuable and because of 'the influence these big [timber] firms had over the government.' "

The simple, straightforward job described by Stuart differs in many details from Orwell's "Shooting an Elephant." Blair mounts a pony and grabs a useless old Winchester rifle, mainly for show. He has no intention of killing the elephant, and it's by no means clear that he will. The essay, however, becomes far more interesting than a dramatic description of an exciting event. Its significance lies in the interplay between the young man's view of the situation and the older, wiser, more reflective voice of the narrator.

Orwell dramatizes the panicky feelings of a young policeman who's out of his depth. He's "hated by large numbers of people," which clearly bothers him, perhaps more than it should. He's suffering from an intolerable sense of guilt and feels too young and ill-educated for the role he's forced to play. He hates both the Empire he serves and the Burmese he's policing: "I did not even know that the British Empire is dying, still less did I know that it is a great deal better than the younger empires that are going to supplant it. All I knew was that I was stuck between my hatred of the empire I served and my rage against the evil-spirited little beasts who tried to make my job impossible. With one part of my mind I thought of the British Raj as an unbreakable tyranny . . . upon the will of prostrate peoples; with another part I thought that the greatest joy in the world would be to drive a bayonet into a Buddhist priest's guts." In a deceptively casual, conversational style, the essay focuses on an incident which exposes his conflict and seeks to resolve it.

At the beginning of the rainy season (June 1926) the officer hears that an elephant (in "must" or heat) has broken loose from its chains and trainer. He rides to the poverty-stricken shantytown where the elephant has ground into the earth a black Dravidian coolie, whose face is twisted in agony. He hastily sends for an elephant gun. An immense crowd of 2,000 people gather round him and think he's going to shoot it. Though reluctant to destroy the huge and costly four-ton elephant, who by now is quietly eating grass with a grandmotherly air, he decides he'll have to kill it. The ground is too soft for him to approach and test the elephant's willingness to attack: if he tries to get close he'll be flattened like a toad under a steamroller. More importantly, he must now meet the expectations of the crowd, who want some entertainment and free meat. It takes considerable skill, especially for a novice, to kill an elephant. He hits it with his first shot, then keeps shooting until he has no more bullets. At this point Orwell signals the theme of the essay: "I perceived in this moment that when the white man turns tyrant it is his own

freedom that he destroys. . . . I had done it solely to avoid looking a fool."
The elephant, "dying, very slowly and in great agony" symbolizes the death
throes of the British Empire.

The logic of the essay is not entirely persuasive. A well-trained elephant,
who penetrated the forest and transported huge logs of teakwood, was worth
much more than £100. The crowd of Buddhists—unwilling to take life and
often going out of their way to avoid stepping on an insect—did not neces-
sarily expect him to shoot it. He has a genuine dilemma: on the one hand
the elephant is highly trained and presently peaceful, and could have been
recaptured by its trainer and chained down. On the other, his "must" has lasted for a month and made him potentially dangerous during that time, and
he's already killed one man. The crowd came to see what would happen, but
they do not force the policeman to act, nor does he shoot to avoid looking
foolish. Brutalized by the system and out for blood and glory, he actually
wanted to shoot the elephant. His official position allowed him not only to
kill the huge animal, but also to get away with it. The policeman had a valid
excuse, and since the owner was only an Indian, not a powerful timber company, he couldn't do anything about it.

Blair had been brought up to believe that imperialism was justified
because British civilization was superior to that of the barbaric people they
ruled, but experience taught him otherwise. In Burma his Etonian detachment, scepticism and anti-establishment spirit came to the fore, and the
longer he stayed, the more tainted he felt. Captain Robinson's mental breakdown and Flory's suicide in Burmese Days suggest what he feared might be
his own fate. As he wrote in a review of 1936: "When a subject population
rises in revolt you have got to suppress it, and you can only do so by methods which make nonsense of any claim for the superiority of Western civilization. In order to rule over barbarians, you have got to become a barbarian
yourself."[21] He turned to writing to begin the long process of healing, of erad-
icating the barbarian in himself.

5

The Joy of Destitution,
1927–1932

I

In September 1927 Blair, aged twenty-two, came home to Southwold, on the North Sea coast in Suffolk. Once a fashionable Edwardian bathing resort, it was now a fishing port and a genteel, old-fashioned retirement town for many Anglo-Indian families. Prosperous trade with the Low Countries had influenced its architecture, and in the old streets tidy English cottages mingled with houses in the Dutch style. The family found their boy transformed into a tough and experienced young man. A rather seedy sahib, still suffering from fever, he had reached his full height of six feet, two-and-a-half inches. In an uncharacteristic photograph, taken about this time, he seems fattened up on hearty English food. Round-faced, even fleshy, he sports a dandified patterned cravat. As the family welcomed him and proudly showed him off to their friends, he waited for the right moment to break the bad news. He was now making £696 a year (plus bonuses), but before leaving Burma he had definitely decided to quit.

Though officially on leave until March 12, 1928, Blair resigned as Assistant Superintendent of Police as of January 1. By doing this he sacrificed about £140 in salary, but he wanted to show his family that he would not change his mind. He knew he'd need money to live on, but once his decision was made he felt conscience-bound not to accept any more of his salary. He gave no reason for his resignation. His superiors were annoyed that he'd wasted fourteen months of training (one-quarter of his time in Burma), but they grudgingly approved his request.

His family and their friends, appalled by his decision, rolled out all the commonsensical arguments. His father, "forever saying 'Don't' " in Blair's childhood, now said "Don't" once more, and urged his son to consider his career, his future—and his pension! His mother, worried about his loss of security and no doubt reduced to tears, accused him of being ungrateful and ignoring the great sacrifices the family had made to give him an expensive education. Ida's friend Ruth Pitter exclaimed: "having chucked his Burma job filled us all with holy horror. It was like turning down a cheque for 5,000 or 10,000 pounds. His mother had thrown everything, all she had, into getting him up to be somebody in the British Raj." The Blairs' careful plan to realize their investment in Eric had failed, and from a financial point of view they were perfectly right. For the next fifteen years, as he made his way as a writer, he lived hand-to-mouth. He did not equal his starting salary in Burma until he became a BBC Talks Producer in 1942. For someone so concerned, even obsessed about money, Eric's choice seemed to them inexplicably self-destructive.

Relatives badgered him day and night for failing to get on in the world. As he wrote in *Keep the Aspidistra Flying*, in which Gordon Comstock's chucking the advertising job in London is the fictional equivalent of Blair's abandoning the police job in Burma: "There were fearful rows, of course. They could not understand him. It seemed to them a kind of blasphemy to refuse such a 'good' job when you got the chance of it. He kept reiterating that he didn't want *that kind* of job. . . . He wanted to 'write,' he told them sullenly. But how could he possibly make a living by 'writing'?"

Richard Blair had encouraged, urged and (according to Jacintha) even forced his son into the Police, and now had to suffer the consequences. Eric could not convince his parents that the job was abhorrent to him. Mabel Fierz, his friend and patron in London, recalled that "when he left the Burma post, his father was very disappointed. And looked upon him as a sort of failure. He felt that deeply. . . . The son who couldn't make money in old Mr. Blair's concept was not the right sort of son." Yet Eric still wanted to please his father and earn his respect. As Mabel observed: "His one idea was to convince his father of his own worth, because he loved his father and he wanted his father to love him."[1] And, she might have added, he didn't want to have the same mediocre career as his father.

Though fond of her brother, even Avril expressed disapproval. Living at home and running a tea shop, the Copper Kettle, she was well on her way to becoming a sour spinster. "A bitter pill . . . wickedly amusing at the expense of other people," she criticized Eric's sloppiness, selfishness and indolence: "I suppose being used to a lot of servants in India [i.e., Burma] he'd become terribly—to our minds—untidy. Whenever he smoked a cigarette he threw the end down on the floor—and the match—and expected other people to sweep them up." While he apparently loafed about, living on his Burmese savings, as she worked hard for small profits and endured an emotionally empty life, she became increasingly stern and reproachful.

Though he'd told his family he was determined to write, he'd written almost nothing during the past five years and didn't *seem* to be writing much at present. He certainly had no history of literary success, had won no school prizes, had published no adult work. Referring to his father and to other well-intentioned advisers, he later remarked: "I had to struggle desperately at the beginning, and if I had listened to what people said to me I would never have been a writer."[2]

Blair also sought advice from another father figure who'd been instrumental in propelling him to Burma. As he told his classmate Denys King-Farlow: "I went & stayed at Cambridge with Gow when I came back from Burma at the end of '27, but though he was very kind it seemed to me I had moved out of his orbit & he out of mine." As an adult with years of practical experience in the world, he felt more remote than ever from Gow, who may well have felt embarrassed to discover his advice had backfired. He sat Blair next to his old idol A.E. Housman at High Table in Trinity, but Housman was always rather withdrawn and it's unlikely that they had much, if any, conversation. Though he received little understanding from father or teacher, Blair wanted to please them. As late as April 1946, after *Animal Farm* had become his first great literary success, Orwell modestly wrote Gow: "I'd be happy to send you a copy. It is very short and might amuse you."[3]

I I

AFTER BLAIR'S return from Burma, his family thought he was spoiled, selfish, vain and egotistical. He acknowledged their viewpoint in his satirical self-portrait of Gordon Comstock, the would-be writer who throws up his job in *Keep the Aspidistra Flying,* when Gordon expresses Blair's self-consciously perverse attitude: "There are two ways to live, he decided. You can be rich, or you can deliberately refuse to be rich. You can possess money, or you can despise money. . . . He would refuse the whole business of 'succeeding'; he would make it his especial purpose *not* to 'succeed.' " Though he did not want conventional prosperity and never expected to be rich, he desperately wanted to be a successful author. In a curious way, unique in English letters, he found it necessary to live in destitution in order to get himself started as a writer. It seemed he could assert his right to be an author only by subjecting his ego and pride to the severe test of living in poverty.

In the winter of 1927, eager to escape from the nagging at home and to begin his new life, he got some help and support from two women: his mother's friend, the poet Ruth Pitter, and his sister Marjorie Dakin. Six years his senior, Ruth Pitter was born in Essex, the daughter of artisans and schoolteachers in the working-class East End of London. She first published in A.R. Orage's *New Age* magazine, worked as a clerk in the War Office during World War I and brought out her *First Poems* in 1920. After the war, she earned her living as a painter and decorator of tea trays and pots. With her companion Kate O'Hara she set up a gift shop in Notting Hill Gate, where she'd first met Ida Blair.

In the fall of 1927 Ruth helped Blair find a room on Portobello Road. In a kind of reverse culture-shock, he had to adjust to England all over again. With no servants to cook or clean for him, eking out his savings as long as he could, he lived the *vie bohème* in a freezing room and warmed his hands with a candle during the London winter. Ruth gave practical support, but shared his parents' view of his literary ambitions. Mocking his lack of imagination, his earnest if amateurish efforts, she emphasized the egoistic aspects of being a writer. Though she was a poet herself, she dismissed him out of hand: "he was a wrong-headed young man who had thrown away a good career, and was vain enough to think he could be an author. . . . We lent him an old oil-stove and he wrote a story about two young girls who lent an old man an oil-stove. . . . One story that never saw the light of day began 'Inside the park, the crocuses were out.' Oh dear, I'm afraid we did laugh." Ruth also criticized his beliefs, his character and his behavior. She said "he had a deep-seated grudge against life," and maintained that his "cruel streak" came from Ida: "He could be spiteful. He could be very spiteful. He might give one a cruel pinch and he could say very cutting things too at times. Very true. His mother, you see, was waspish."

While living on the distinctly unfashionable Portobello Road, Blair witnessed a classic example of English snobbery. He and his landlady (once a lady's maid to a titled woman) had both locked themselves out of the house. When he suggested borrowing a ladder from the people next door, she refused: "We've been here fourteen years and we've always taken care not to know the people on either side of us. It *wouldn't do*, not in a neighbourhood like this. If you once begin talking to them they get familiar."[4] So Blair and her husband had to borrow a ladder from a relative, and carry it for a mile with great discomfort.

Blair's elder sister, Marjorie, the pink-cheeked motorcycle rider, had moved with her husband, Humphrey Dakin, to Leeds, in Yorkshire. More tolerant than Avril, she was a sympathetic listener who invited confidences. In between tramping expeditions in the north or retreating from the rigors of his London room, Blair stayed with the Dakins in their comfortable middle-class house, and sometimes strained their patience. The son of a Southwold doctor, Dakin had been educated at Cheltenham College, worked as an office boy on Wall Street in New York and (like his father) fought in World War I. He'd spent two years on the Western front, lost an eye and wore a glass replacement. After the war he became a factory inspector for the Board of Trade.

A rather irascible man, Dakin had little in common with Blair. He felt Eric had been a nuisance as a child and was troublesome once again. The jowly, florid, jovial Dakin was a great raconteur in pubs, while Blair, his temperamental opposite, withdrew from the conversation and quietly watched the scene. Describing, perhaps imitating, an idealized working-class scene that Orwell himself later portrayed in several works, Dakin said that his favorite Leeds pub "was always bright, cosy, and warm, with a big fire going and quite a merry crowd in the evenings. . . . [Blair] used to sit in a corner by himself, looking like death, until it was with some relief that we'd hear him say: 'I must go home.' " Dakin thought Blair's reserve was standoffish and superior, and he didn't realize that the would-be writer had been carefully listening and observing.

Dakin later criticized Blair, who'd suffered chronic ill-health since childhood, for wearing threadbare clothes and a huge muffler, "like an aristocrat who'd seen better days," but no overcoat, even in winter. He thought his brother-in-law was partly angry about, partly ashamed of, his poverty, that he had sought out squalor and had found it. Dakin disliked *The Road to Wigan Pier* and (ignoring its polemical purpose) complained that it didn't show the positive side—the pubs and football matches—of working-class life. As sceptical as Ruth Pitter about Blair's potential as a writer, he thought he should get a proper job instead of cadging off his family. But, encouraged by Marjorie, Eric wrote in their house for several weeks at a time.

The Dakins' elder daughter, Jane, had a vivid childhood memory of the whole family setting out for the Christmas holidays in their small canvas-topped Rover, while Uncle Eric, isolated from the chaos, buried himself in a book: "In the front of the car sat my mother with [my sister] Lucy on her knee, in the back sat my brother, aged about four, myself aged about seven or eight, our pug dog, our cat, two or three guinea pigs and a kid goat called Blanche in a straw fish basket with her head sticking out. Rugs and food and baskets and the usual clamor. And behind the driver, on the back seat, sat Eric, quite unruffled and amiable although dissociated from any responsibility, with his knees up near his ears, reading French poetry."[5]

III

AROUND THIS time Blair began his expeditions as a tramp and continued, on and off for the next four years, the self-punishing experiments that mystified his family and friends. To go from policeman to tramp was a radical venture: part expiation, part social exploration, part self-scrutiny. Tramping won him time to examine his life, to find his purpose, to focus his aspirations. It gave him original material to write about, made him more worldly and less self-absorbed. But like so many other aspects of his life, guilt provided the initial impetus—an irrational yet deep-rooted guilt that fed on past guilt and formed a kind of disfiguring hump that he always carried around with him.

He felt guilty about his family's colonial background—slaveowners in Jamaica, exploiters in Burma, opium dealers in India—as well as his own too comfortable bourgeois family, his snobbish upbringing, which had taught him to despise the working class, and his education at Eton. Tormented by a social conscience, he felt uneasy (even when relatively poor) about having more money than anyone else. His colleagues in Burma made him feel guilty about being too young to serve in World War I, and this guilt was revived when he proved medically unfit to serve in World War II. He felt guilty about enjoying the oppressive power of his job as policeman. Finally, his family made him feel guilty about giving up a promising career, for disappointing them and cadging off them instead of getting a proper job.

But in a sense Blair also *liked* having a sense of guilt and needed to prolong it. This inner conviction of his own guilt—of being obscurely to blame—

gave him a purpose and inspired his early work. In a famous autobiographical passage in *The Road to Wigan Pier*, he explained that after his experience in Burma he became violently opposed to a settled, normal, prosperous, comfortable middle-class way of life, and saw tramping as a kind of expiation. Though he knew he couldn't really belong to this harsh world, he desperately wanted to be accepted by the tramps and to shed his guilt:

> I was conscious of an immense weight of guilt that I had got to expiate.
> . . . I felt that I had got to escape not merely from imperialism but from
> every form of man's dominion over man. . . . At that time failure seemed
> to me to be the only virtue. Every suspicion of self-advancement, even to
> "succeed" in life to the extent of making a few hundreds a year, seemed to
> me spiritually ugly, a species of bullying. . . . My mind turned immediately towards the extreme cases, the social outcasts: tramps, beggars, criminals, prostitutes. These were "the lowest of the low," and these were the
> people with whom I wanted to get in contact. What I profoundly wanted,
> at that time, was to find some way of getting out of the respectable world
> altogether.

Living rough and becoming a writer were part of the same route out of the respectable world.

Blair's tramping was certainly penitential. His first tentative step from comfort to squalor was extremely difficult and took considerable courage. He had (according to Avril) a "mania about personal cleanliness," and was very squeamish and sensitive to smell. The revolting experiences to which he subjected himself had a powerful impact on the man who emphasized the repulsive hygiene at St. Cyprian's—the crust of porridge in the bowl and the floating turd in the bath. In *A Clergyman's Daughter* Dorothy cringes when she has to drink from a communion cup after old Miss Mayfill has drooled into it. When starving in *Down and Out in Paris and London* Orwell throws his precious hot milk away when a bug falls into it. His deliberate immersion in the filth and indignity of the homeless tested his endurance to the limit— and beyond.

He had to have something to write *about*, but had not yet objectified, absorbed and understood his experience in Burma. He was drawn to the marginal, the destitute and the dispossessed, and saw a parallel between the British domination of the Burmese and the English treatment of the poor. Characteristically, he did not simply live like a poor working man in

England—though he later did so in Paris—but moved from being an oppressor to becoming one of the oppressed. He went to the very bottom of the social scale by becoming one of the thousands of unemployed, homeless men. The Vagrancy Act forced them to tramp from town to town, village to village, all across England, and they could stay in charitable hostels for only one night at a time. He dressed the part by buying some ragged old clothes in a secondhand shop and tried, less successfully, to disguise his posh accent.

He could, and did, abandon the road and return to a comfortable life with family and friends at Southwold, Golders Green or Leeds whenever he wanted a bath, a rest, decent food and time to write. Yet his down-and-out phase—his tramping, hop-picking and arrest, his physical collapse, destitution and dishwashing—lasted for four long years. During that time—more than sufficient to gather the material he needed—he recklessly gambled with his health, his reputation and his future. His fascination with tramping revealed two important aspects of his character: the wanderer and the outsider. He could never remain in one place for long and he only felt right with the world when he stood at a slight angle to society.

"Down there in the squalid and, as a matter of fact, horribly boring subworld of the tramp," wrote Orwell, the sahib who "went native" in his own country, he had "a feeling of release, of adventure," which he'd also experienced in Burma. He must have enjoyed thinking of how shocked Flip and Granny Gow would be to see their Eton scholarship boy plunged into the lower depths. He got an occasional thrill by passing through familiar places in disguise. A Southwold friend, Dennis Collings, recalled that Blair put up at the Spike (a lodging house run by the local council) at Blythburgh and planned to move on to the next workhouse in Southwold. Then he thought better of it and said, with a mixture of pathos and black humor: "no, I couldn't possibly do it, if my father were to see me it would really kill him."[6]

Expiation and release were psychologically valuable, but another important motive emerged as he began to look outside himself and collect firsthand information. In all his documentary works, he had to be an eyewitness of the conditions he wrote about in Burma, London and Paris, Wigan, Spain, Marrakech and postwar Germany. Only in this way could he give his readers the sense of actual experience and humanize the social outcasts with whom he chose to live. When down-and-out, he was exploring his subject and discovering his method. He was also trying to create a living bridge between Left-wing intellectuals and the most oppressed people in English society, to compensate, as he once wrote, for "the tragic failure of theoreti-cal Socialism to make any contact with the normal [or abnormal] working class."

In this respect, his model was Jack London, who'd explored the East End of London, written about his brief firsthand experience in *The People of the Abyss* (1903) and tried to improve the grim lives of the urban poor. In the Preface to that book London wrote:

> The experiences in this volume fell to me in the summer of 1902. I went down into the under-world of London with an attitude of mind which I may best liken to that of the explorer. I was open to be convinced by the evidence of my eyes, rather than by the teachings of those who had not seen, or by the words of those who had seen and gone before. Further, I took with me certain simple criteria with which to measure the life of the under-world. That which made for more life, for physical and spiritual health, was good; that which made for less life, which hurt, and dwarfed, and distorted life, was bad.

Like Jack London, Blair learned how to get on with ordinary, even dispos-sessed people, and actually enjoyed their company. He neither patronized nor scorned them, but showed real sympathy and interest in their lives—a considerable imaginative leap for an Old Etonian and ex-policeman.

In 1931 Blair published two articles in the *Adelphi*, "The Spike" and "Hop-Picking," the raw material of scenes in his early books, *Down and Out in Paris and London* (1933) and *A Clergyman's Daughter* (1935). The first essay describes the prison-like setting of the typical casual ward, condemns the system that humiliates the tramps and arouses compassion for their plight. The second portrays the working-class Londoners who escape from the city and spend their summer holidays doing this disagreeable and low-paying job in the fields of Kent. In a letter to Dennis Collings he described, with a cer-tain bravado, the harsh conditions on the way to Kent and his carefree atti-tude to the work that left his back aching and fingers bloody: "We got most of our food on the way by begging, & did not go short of anything except tobacco, but the cold & discomfort of sleeping out of doors are worse than you would believe. . . . Still, it is rather fun for a short while, & I shall at any rate be able to make a saleable newspaper article out of it."[7]

IV

IN THE spring of 1928 Blair went to Paris, and lived there for nearly two years. For a year and a half he survived on his savings, supplemented by teaching English, until the last of his money was stolen. First he pawned most of his belongings, then he got work as a dishwasher. "When you are in a foreign country," he observed, "unless you are there because you are obliged to work there, you do not live fully and you do not usually mix with ordinary people. You tend to spend your life in cafés or brothels or picture galleries rather than in ordinary homes, and if you are also short of money your experiences will be more sordid than they would be in your own country." He contrasted his own experience in Paris with that of the thousands of American expatriates who flocked there in the 1920s, when everything was cheap. As he wrote in "Inside the Whale," his essay on Henry Miller: "During the boom years, when dollars were plentiful and the exchange-value of the franc was low, Paris was invaded by such a swarm of artists, writers, students, dilettanti, sight-seers, debauchées and plain idlers as the world has never seen."

Blair's Paris was altogether different from Hemingway's or Joyce's, though in 1928 he thought he saw James Joyce in one of his favorite hangouts, the café Deux Magots. The following year he did see Philippe Pétain, the defender of Verdun, at the state funeral of Marshal Ferdinand Foch, the supreme commander of the victorious French armies in World War I. Blair lived in the squalid rue du Pot de Fer (called rue du Coq d'Or in *Down and Out*) in the Latin Quarter. Hemingway had lived in the district with his first wife in the early 1920s, but by the time Blair arrived he'd moved on to a richer wife and better address. In his nostalgic *A Moveable Feast*, Hemingway described the simple flat where they lived on his meager earnings and his wife's small trust fund. He remembered a beautiful city and seemed to enjoy their cozy, even glamorous poverty: "When we came back to Paris it was clear and cold and lovely. The city had accommodated itself to winter, there was good wood for sale at the wood and coal place across our street, and there were braziers outside of many of the good cafés so that you could keep warm on the terraces. Our own apartment was warm and cheerful."

Blair did not frequent the same restaurants and cafés. For two years he lived a more or less solitary existence, finding his own kind of dissipation in low life. He naturally sought out the most uncomfortable place he could find and reveled in his ability to live on a few francs a day. His book emphasized "the sour reek of the refuse-carts," the extreme decay of the place and the consolation of real poverty: "I believe everyone who has been hard up has experienced it. It is a feeling of relief, almost of pleasure, at knowing yourself at last genuinely down and out. You have talked so often of going to the dogs—and well, here are the dogs, and you have reached them, and you can stand it. It takes off a lot of anxiety."[8] Like other expatriates, Blair tried to write in Paris, and actually wrote two novels that he later destroyed. But his real purpose was far more complicated: not only to observe life and test his capacity for survival, but also to find a method of writing about his new way of life.

His aunt Nellie Limouzin, Ida's sister, was then living in Paris and, though he rarely sought her help, could always be counted on for a handout. A real bohemian, she'd acted in vaudeville and was married to a Frenchman, Eugène Adam, who'd been involved in the October 1917 Revolution in Petrograd. A fanatical teacher of Esperanto, he refused to speak any other language. "The marriage was not happy," according to one of their friends. "She had no character. She was soft, without backbone, without willpower." Adam later abandoned Nellie, went on a world tour, wound up in Mexico and killed himself in 1947. Blair may have met his first Socialist cranks, whom he satirized in a notorious passage of The Road to Wigan Pier, in Nellie's household.

Ruth Pitter had observed Blair's strong masochistic streak in Notting Hill. "I felt quite sure he was in what is called the pre-tubercular condition," Pitter recalled. "And here he was, exposing himself in such weather in totally inadequate clothing. It wasn't just poverty. It was suicidal perversity." This stubborn self-testing endangered his always precarious health, and in Paris he suffered a serious bout of influenza. In March 1929 he spent two weeks in the grim public wards of the Hôpital Cochin, which he described in his moving essay "How the Poor Die" (1946).

After filling out a lot of forms in the hospital and learning he had a temperature of 103°, he was forced to take a cold bath and, wearing a thin nightgown, had to walk 200 yards across the open grounds to reach the charity ward. Not surprisingly, he emphasized its "foul smell, faecal and yet sweetish." He then suffered agonies as the inhuman staff first cupped him with hot glasses and then applied an excruciating mustard poultice to his chest. During all this time there he was nothing more than a mute specimen for medical students, who didn't seem to realize that he and the other patients were actually human beings. In his essay the poor die slow, smelly and painful "natural" deaths.[9]

After he left the hospital, his marginal existence suddenly became desperate when his room was robbed and his money stolen. In *Down and Out* the thief is an Italian compositor and fellow-lodger who duplicates the keys and robs a dozen rooms. But Blair gave a friend a more convincing account of what happened. He was deceived, in fact, by a girl whose haircut and slim figure reminded him of the boys at Eton: "he once said that of all the girls he'd known before he met his wife, the one he loved best was a little trollop he picked up in a café in Paris. She was beautiful, and had a figure like a boy, an Eton crop and was in every way desirable. Apparently he came back to his room, and this paragon had decamped with everything he possessed. All his luggage and his money and everything." Reduced to destitution, Blair tried unsuccessfully to catch dace in the Seine (Hemingway claimed to have caught pigeons for dinner in the Luxembourg Gardens). With no rent money, he was forced to sleep outdoors: "I passed the night on a bench on the boulevard. It was very uncomfortable—the arm of the seat cuts into your back—and much colder than I had expected."

Finally, through Boris—a Russian émigré and former soldier whom he had met in the hospital—he worked thirteen hours a day for ten weeks, first as a dishwasher in a luxurious hotel, then in a Russian restaurant. His experiences as a *plongeur* occupy most of the Paris section of *Down and Out*. The lowest of the low in the hotel hierarchy, he had to shave off his cherished mustache, which was considered insubordinate by the management. Abused by the waiters, he had to use his fists to get common civility. Some of the more ambitious waiters went to English classes in the afternoon, yet he never tried to escape from dishwashing by teaching them. He had no presentable clothes and was too exhausted to try to earn more money.

In her memoirs the Duchess of Westminster, who often stayed in the hotel where Blair worked, told a story of how a déclassé employee was forced to satisfy the late-night cravings of her husband, an Old Etonian:

> At a party, I met a frail-looking man who said, "You won't remember me, but I have a very vivid recollection of you and your husband." He then told me that he had once worked at the Hotel Lotti. Late one night Benny had rung the bell for the floor waiter and asked for a peach. It turned out that there was not a peach in the hotel so my friend, who was an apprentice waiter, was sent out into the streets and, under threat of instant dismissal, told not to return without at least one peach. Of course all the shops were shut, so he wandered forlornly about (I tell the story as he told it to me)

until he saw a small green-grocer's with a basket of peaches in the window. Desperately he rattled the door, pounded on it, but all in vain. He dared not go back empty handed so, as the street was quite deserted, he picked up a cobble stone from a heap where the road was being mended, smashed the window, seized a peach and dashed back to the Lotti, happy to think that he had kept his job. However, soon after that he gave up trying to be a waiter and became a writer. His name? George Orwell.[10]

The duchess' tale, however, is derived from an anecdote in *Down and Out*. In Orwell's version an English lord came to the hotel and asked for peaches, and a German dishwasher stole some from a neighboring restaurant. Since Blair was a dishwasher, not an exalted waiter, and probably never met the duchess at a party (he didn't move in such circles), her story reveals how biographical material is frequently recycled and distorted.

V

ON THE promise of a job that did not materialize, Blair returned to England toward the end of 1929, and for the next two years continued his almost pathological commitment to tramping. In "Clink" (1932) he described his last adventure: a futile attempt to spend some considerable time in prison. In mid-December 1931 he got extremely drunk on beer and whisky. He approached a policeman, who seized his bottle, gently took him to the station and put him in a cell, where he became horribly hungover and sick. He was then confined to another huge cell at the police court, and released, in lieu of a fine, after only one day in custody. During the next few days he made several more attempts to get arrested by begging in front of policemen, but he led a charmed life and they paid no attention to him.

The anthropologist Geoffrey Gorer, who wrote him a fan letter and became a friend in the 1930s, noted Orwell's physical and social awkwardness. A typical public schoolboy, until 1927 he'd spent his entire life in all-male institutions, and had little experience of women apart from Burmese prostitutes and French "trollops." He himself spoke of "the star-like isolation in which human beings live." Shy, inhibited and self-conscious, he thought English women were distant and unattainable, and his impoverished way of life made things even more difficult. Despite these limitations and his late start, the reserved, austere Orwell went on to have many liaisons. Several women in Southwold were important to him in these years of struggle, and he kept in contact with them in between his tramping expeditions.

Blair met Brenda Salkeld in 1928, when they were both twenty-five. A clergyman's daughter and gym-mistress in a girls' school in Southwold, she was bookish, proper and demure, but liked social life. She couldn't understand why he preferred to keep typing in his room instead of joining her in a game of bridge. Brenda refused to sleep with him, which intensified his attraction, but they managed to remain good friends. She disagreed with his dogmatic opinions, which he referred to in a letter of September 1932: "It was ever so nice seeing you again & finding that you were pleased to see me, in spite of my hideous prejudice against your sex, my obsession about R.C.s, etc."[11] Brenda described his face as "pale with smallish, rather bright blue eyes," and thought him "good company when he wasn't gloomy and complaining." "He didn't really understand people," she said, "women in particular, he couldn't give himself. . . . He liked to shock. Writing was the one great thing in his life. Nothing—not even people—got in the way of that."[12]

Eleanor Jaques, whom Blair met at about the same time, was three years younger than Brenda and a very different kind of woman. Her parents, of Huguenot background, had moved from Canada to Southwold in 1921, when she was fifteen, and lived next door to the Blairs. Much livelier and sexier than Brenda, the attractive, dark-haired Eleanor was willing to sleep with Blair while being courted by his friend and her future husband, Dennis Collings. Though Blair was more practical than romantic, more polite than passionate, more likely to win their bodies than their hearts, women felt they could trust him. Brenda was the model for the prim Dorothy Hare in *A Clergyman's Daughter*, Eleanor for the responsive Rosemary in *Keep the Aspidistra Flying*.

The seduction scene in the latter novel conveys the flavor of Blair's approach to women:

> "You do like me, don't you?"
> "Adore you, silly."
> "And you're going to be nice to me, aren't you?"
> "Nice to you?"
> "Let me do what I want with you?"
> "Yes, I expect so."
> "Anything?"
> "Yes, all right. Anything." . . .

"Take your clothes off, there's a dear. . . . May I—now?"
"Yes, all right."
"You're not frightened?"
"No."

The most intensely erotic moment in Blair's life took place in June 1932, after several years of courtship, when Eleanor surrendered to him in an idyllic setting, the banks of the Blyth River near Southwold. "I cannot remember when I have ever enjoyed any expeditions so much as I did those with you," he nostalgically wrote to her in September, when their affair had peaked. "Especially that day in the wood along past Blythburgh Lodge—you remember, where the deep beds of moss were. I shall always remember that, & your nice white body in the dark green moss."

This natural, primal scene recurs in four of his novels. In each work a shy, passive, virginal, smiling and willing woman, deep in the wood and naked in the grass, surrenders to a powerful but hesitant man:

—She lay and let him do as he wished with her, quite passive yet pleased and faintly smiling.   (*Burmese Days*)

—Naked, she lay back, her hands behind her head, eyes shut, smiling slightly. . . . "I'll be as gentle as I can with you." "It doesn't matter."
                                        (*Keep the Aspidistra Flying*)

[I] stood over her for a moment. She was lying on the grass with her arm over her face. . . . You could do what you liked with [her]. She was mine and I could have her, this minute if I wanted to.   (*Coming Up for Air*)

—He had pulled her down onto the ground, she was utterly unresisting, he could do what he liked with her.   (*Nineteen Eighty-Four*)[13]

Blair's letters to Eleanor that summer and fall were naturally more intimate than the ones he wrote to Brenda. In June (while teaching near London) he referred to temptations of the World, the Flesh and the Devil, and playfully alluded to their affair. He said: "you can decide which of these categories you belong to," then added, with characteristic reticence: "if you are ever to be in London please let me know, as we might meet, that is, if you would like to." Three weeks later, when their plans went wrong, he sought reassurance and apologized for the misunderstanding: "tell me you were not hurt at my not after all coming to meet you that Sunday—you did not write & I thought it might be that. I should be sorry if you became angry with me. I would gladly have come if I could."

In mid-October, the affair apparently over, he was glad, at least, to be fondly remembered. Though he hoped for more "kindness," he was grateful for what he had received. Like most men of that era, Blair had been taught to consider sex a favor that women bestowed on men. "It was so nice of you to say that you looked back to your days with me with pleasure," he wrote to Eleanor. "I hope you will let me make love to you again some time, but if you don't it doesn't matter, I shall always be grateful to you for your kindness to me." In late November, still trying to revive the affair, he asked her if she would "go out some Sunday into the country, where we could go for a long walk & then have lunch at a pub? London is depressing when one has no money." He then adopted a passive, even boyish role (sex as treat), referred to her inconvenient involvement with Collings and anticipated her refusal: "When we were together you didn't say whether you were going to let me be your lover again. Of course you can't if Dennis is in S'wold, but otherwise? You mustn't if you don't want to, but I hope you will."[14] Blair's gentleness and unfailing good manners enabled him to remain on good terms with women at the end of an affair. As a sly joke, he gave Eleanor's surname to the melancholy Irish tramp, Paddy, in *Down and Out in Paris and London.*

V I

MABEL ROBINSON Fierz was the most important of Blair's three women in Southwold. Mabel was born in 1890 of English parents in Rio Grande do Sul, Brazil, near the southern border with Uruguay. She knew Portuguese and spoke English with a slight accent, was tutored a bit at home and came to England in 1908, when she was seventeen. Though she had no formal education, she loved swimming and qualified (like Brenda Salkeld) as a gymmistress. According to her son, she had only a smattering of learning and no great powers of discrimination; she would often open a book, read a few pages and impatiently toss it aside. But she had a genuine curiosity and thirst for knowledge. She was a great joiner, followed the latest intellectual fads, like mysticism and Social Credit, and attended Socialist summer schools. She loved the *New Statesman* and reviewed for the *Adelphi.* Her husband,

Francis, was an engineer in London, and the family, including an adolescent boy and girl, spent their summer holidays in Southwold.

The writer Rayner Heppenstall, a keen observer who lived with Orwell in the early 1930s, wrote that "Mabel inspired rather a fond complicity than any steady warmth of feeling. She was a woman of great energy, activated by transient enthusiasms. These, at various times, included Nature Cure, Adlerian psychology, Yoga, Roman Catholicism (she had been brought up a Catholic in Brazil) . . . [and] Anglo-Catholicism." Though lively and responsive, Mabel could also be irritating, affected and pretentious (the very opposite of Eric Blair) as well as pushy, meddlesome, opinionated, willful and dogmatic — even when completely ignorant of the subject. She would, for example, baldly but ignorantly contradict her daughter-in-law, a trained chemist, when discussing scientific matters. Mabel's daughter described her as "emotional, extrovert, lively, gregarious and full of enthusiasm for all sorts of issues: an ardent campaigner for socialism, pacifism, animal welfare and naturopathy. She was a very determined character and wouldn't take no for an answer." Her son added, more critically, that "Mother was a strong left wing supporter but she was not above some petty snobbery and had little grasp of the fundamental economic issues. Her attitude to the poor would today be called paternalistic."[15]

Alienated from his family, with no job and only vague plans about writing, Blair was still drifting about in the summer of 1930. Painting watercolors on the beach at Southwold one day, he met Mabel. She was at once sympathetic, attentive, supportive, maternal and flirtatious. She soon took him under her wing, and he often stayed at her house on Oakwood Road in Golders Green, north London, between tramping expeditions. "He felt with us entirely at ease," Mabel said, "and would tell us anything. He knew that we liked him and were tolerant, and he was completely at home in our house. He and my husband used to talk endlessly about Dickens."

Blair took an interest in her son Adrian, who was thrilled to spend time with the adventurous policeman from Burma. He introduced Adrian to some of his favorite books: *Gulliver's Travels*, the stories of Conan Doyle and P.G. Wodehouse. He took him to see *Hamlet*, with Maurice Evans, and to the British Museum, where he explained the exhibitions in the galleries. He remained fond of Adrian and attended his wedding in 1941.

Though Mabel was extremely bossy with her family, she habitually deferred to Blair. She was thirteen years older, but he dominated, even dazzled her intellectually. She took him so seriously that she often failed to recognize his dry humor. "In an amusing way," Adrian remarked, "my mother always quoted Eric's sayings as gospel, even when, I suspect, they were said tongue-in-cheek. Examples are 'all scoutmasters are homosexuals' or 'all tobacconists are fascists.' The preamble 'Eric says . . .' was always the prelude to what she assumed was an incontrovertible truth." As he grew up Adrian was struck by the paradoxical aspects of Blair's Socialist beliefs: "[His taste in] books and food and wine and all these things and then his voice were very much of the upper classes. . . . He was not very much interested in complex economic theory, about bank rates and interest rates and investment and all these things. And I don't think he even was much interested in the writings of Karl Marx even when he was a socialist." Blair's Socialism was not based on political and economic principles, but on liberal and humane beliefs.

When the Fierzes discussed Blair's tramping and Francis asked "why does Eric make himself suffer?" Mabel justified his self-punishing quest for experience by explaining that "he always wanted to make out that he was tougher than he actually was." When Blair was depressed by his sense of failure, discouraged by his family and by Ruth Pitter, Mabel recognized his potential and encouraged his literary ambitions. She believed, early on, that he was "a very interesting young man, a man with a terrific vision of life as a whole; and an enormous curiosity, awfully keen on learning."[16] Mabel, in fact, gave Blair precisely what he lacked at home: affection, approval and intellectual stimulation. He was loyal to his family, she said, but had "absolutely no warmth of contact. They hadn't the vaguest idea what he wanted to do, or what he felt. He used to say, my mother would forgive me whatever I did," but his tramping and writing were "something beyond their concept."

A local woman made the surprising assertion that Blair had had several adulterous affairs: "Married women around Southwold [were ready to] bed with him. He had quite a few little *affaires* that didn't count for anything. One or two that did. But all this talk of the ascetic Orwell? Not Eric!" It seems unlikely that he could have managed to sleep with various women and avoid scandal while living at home in that small, respectable, gossipy town. But a letter from Mabel to Eric, written in the summer of 1932 when he was teaching school and living near London, reveals that she was one of his married lovers and that they met in London or in the country. Mabel gave him love as well as sex. Arranging to meet him for a day's outing, she wrote:

Darling, how splendid! 2.30 then at Hayes Station on *Monday*. Take me then by the quickest route to a point on the river. I adore a warm sunny day in a punt. I will punt you carefully along the *prettiest* ways and not upset your male dignity into the Thames! Take your costume in case we find a suitable place. I hate the usual swimming bath. Will also take tea. It *will* be nice. Not as you say a *decent walk*. I prefer the opposite! If it rains, well, we will visit the pubs in turn. The great thing is to waste as little time as possible, so try and find out the route. I have often passed through Hayes going to Maidenhead.—So amusing, hey! You will know better where to go. Thanks so much cheri for the recipe.

My friends go Leningrad tomorrow from Days Wharf. I am going home, they [are] all off, cruelty to animals, I call it! The Greek history progress-es. Why, alas, why can't some one write a colorful and yet exact account of those times, beginning at Simonides and Pindar? I have tried many, all so dull and heavy and stamped with academic labour! I am working at a poem, but it simply *won't* come right.

Most precious and adored one,

au revoir,

Mabel

This characteristically emotional, even gushing love letter, full of excla-mation points, shows many sides of Mabel's personality: her eagerness to meet, enjoyment of swimming and the outdoors, her zest for life, good humor and affectionate nature as well as her pretentiousness, her passion for poetry and self-improvement. She felt free to make sexual allusions and, unlike Brenda and Eleanor, openly expressed her feelings for him. Adrian "once asked mother what father thought about her relationship with Eric, as we called him. She said 'father didn't want to know.' " When Adrian questioned her late in her life (she lived to be a hundred years old) about her affair with Eric, she confessed: "Yes, you could say so. He was my lover."[17]

VII

IN THESE years Blair was developing into the figure we know as "George Orwell." Like his contemporary and colleague Graham Greene, he was unusually tall and thin, but while Greene dressed conservatively in striped suits and looked like a man of the upper-middle class, Blair adopted his "*New Statesman*-dress"—battered tweed jacket, dark trousers, rough blue shirt and tie—to show his distaste for convention and blend into the working class. He could not change his cultivated tastes or educated accent, but he could make a political statement with his clothes. He had a workingman's cropped haircut above his invalid's long furrowed face, his Frenchman's odd pencil-thin mustache. His thick hair, parted in the middle, billowed up like a wave about to break. Toward the end of his life, he told Richard Rees: "Mat Kavanagh . . . an old Irish I.R.A. Anarchist hairdresser . . . used to cut my hair in Fleet Street. He now tells me . . . that when a person with my sort of hair comes into the shop there is a sort of competition not to deal with him." Even his barber had a political identity. Rayner Heppenstall echoed Steven Runciman's view that he deliberately cultivated a proletarian style and eccentric manner that helped promote the "Orwell legend." In the 1960s Heppenstall complained of "a whole Orwell mythology which seemed to bear little relation to the man I had known."[18]

Photographs in the 1930s show Blair recovering from tramping expeditions in Mabel's garden, wearing heavy brogues, baggy trousers, jacket and tie, with a handkerchief (used often when he coughed) dangling from his front pocket. In a companion piece, he sits in a deck chair, forcing a rather wan smile as he tenderly holds Hubert, the Fierzes' pet rabbit. On the stony beach at Southwold, he leans over to stroke Ida's dachshund as the gusty wind blows his tie across his shoulder. A few years later he looks relatively smart in a wool jacket with peaked lapels, vee-necked sweater, tie and shirt, though the points of his collar are curling up and his hair is cut too closely above his ears. Though he's still in his early thirties, deep grooves are beginning to form in his face, but his eyes are clear and he now seems more sure of himself. In the down-and-out years he gained confidence and a sense of direction.

When he returned to England from Paris he tried to advance his literary career by offering to translate Jacques Roberti's À la belle de la nuit, the story of a prostitute. In March 1930 his luck turned. While working on the early version of Down and Out he began to contribute the first of fifty reviews, poems and essays, like "The Spike" and "A Hanging," to the Adelphi, the magazine he'd occasionally riddled with bullets in Burma.

Like most professional authors, he knew it was easier to write a piece than to place it, and when he became connected with a paper, he stayed with it as long as possible. Everyone emphasized how hard he worked and how he constantly pounded away at the typewriter, and this too became part of his legend. But no one ever mentioned him sitting quietly (if not comfortably) in a chair and actually reading the books he was writing about. He always relied on reviewing for a substantial part of his meager income. As he put it in his witty, exasperated "Confessions of a Book Reviewer," "the indiscriminate reviewing of books is a quite exceptionally thankless, irritating and exhausting job." The chief bore was having to read at least fifty pages of each one to avoid making a howler, but he eventually learned to skip expertly through these worthless books.

Getting into this Left-wing review opened a stimulating new social and intellectual world for him. The *Adelphi* had been started by John Middleton Murry as an outlet for the work of his late wife, Katherine Mansfield, and his sometime friend D.H. Lawrence. It never had a large circulation, but encouraged young authors and allowed them to say what they wished. When Blair began to contribute the co-editors were Max Plowman and Sir Richard Rees, both of whom became his lifelong friends. He later wrote that Plowman, author of the Great War classic *A Subaltern on the Somme* (1928), "was by nature a rather pugnacious man, of strong physique and simple tastes, a lover of cricket and gardening, and in a sense not an intellectual." Rees was the first man in his life whom Blair could fully trust and respect, and he later made Rees his literary executor. If Mabel gave him the emotional support and encouragement he needed to keeping writing, Rees and the *Adelphi* provided regular reviewing and an outlet for his original essays. Together, they helped launch his literary career.

Rayner Heppenstall, also in the *Adelphi* circle, gave an incisive account of Rees' background and character: "Rees was of noble birth on his mother's side. She, a sister of the fourteenth Lord Dorner, had married a South Wales coal-owner, awarded his baronetcy for political services to Lloyd George. His son hated him and viewed his mother with the kind of devotion which commonly produces homosexuals, among whom Rees belonged to the non-practicing variety, or so I was to be told by George Orwell."

Rees's father, the first baronet, worked in the Indian Civil Service. wrote many books on India and did refugee work in World War I. Born in 1900, Rees was educated at Eton and Trinity College, Cambridge, served in the diplomatic service, worked for Cambridge University Press and taught for the Workers' Educational Association. He drove an ambulance during the Spanish Civil War and won the Croix de Guerre in World War II. He also exhibited his paintings, and wrote books about Orwell and Simone Weil.

Thin, deep-voiced and bald, the modest and generous Rees was always helping other people. John Middleton Murry's daughter characterized him as "kind, good-humoured, gentle, well-bred, with that natural breeding beyond caste."[19] Mark Benny, a former jailbird and *Adelphi* writer, noted

Rees' proletarian clothing which—like Blair's—clashed with his upper-class demeanor: "He must have gone to some pains . . . to find the kinds of villainous hand-me-downs in which he was wont to clothe himself; yet inevitably his voice and bearing, still carrying all the unconscious patrician assurance he had acquired at Eton, Trinity and the Berlin Embassy, gave them a kind of distinction."

Orwell portrayed Rees as Gordon's patron and editor, Ravelston, in *Keep the Aspidistra Flying*. He was "a tall distinguished figure, aristocratically shabby, his eye rather moody. . . . Ravelston had not merely a charm of manner, but also a kind of fundamental decency, a graceful attitude to life." In his book *For Love or Money*, Rees described Orwell as "haggard with social guilt . . . he possessed, or was possessed by, a moral force which drove him to violent extremes of expiation."[20]

The two men shared similarities of background as well as temperament. Both had fathers who'd worked in India; both were Old Etonians and would serve in the Spanish War. Both wore threadbare clothes, which failed to disguise their true social class. As the Tramp Major says to Blair in "The Spike," after staring hard at him: "You are a gentleman?" "I suppose so." . . . "Well, that's bloody bad luck, guv'nor." And both, as Rees said, were "haggard with social guilt." Rees' habitual generosity relieved his guilt about having a large unearned income.

The Paris-born poet and translator Edouard Roditi, who met Blair through the *Adelphi* in 1931, described how this gnawing social conscience prevented them from enjoying a decent meal or a walk through town. When Blair adopted his Jeremiah persona, he became a comically lugubrious companion. As they dined together, Roditi recalled, Blair described, "as if to discourage me from eating, the filthy conditions that he had observed in the kitchens and pantries of so many of the restaurants where he had worked." After lunch they assiduously avoided the parks and wandered for several hours "in some of the most depressing areas of London."[21]

6

Among School Children,

1932–1934

I

AFTER MONTHS of strenuous kitchen work in Paris, Blair turned to teaching, a more suitable job for an educated man. In *Down and Out* he wrote that toward the end of 1929 an English friend got him a job looking after a "congenital imbecile" and sent him £5 to return home. When he arrived he found the parents had taken the boy abroad, and he lived for a month as a tramp till they returned. In 1940 he told Sacheverell Sitwell that the boy "was not only very backward but was a cripple and so clumsy with his hands as to have been quite incapable." Dennis Collings, who lived near the boy in Southwold, and probably got him the job, said that Blair did his best and was saddened by his failure: "he had that rather unpleasant time when he looked after a batty boy in Walberswick, who really was, poor child, incapable, there was something wrong with his brain. He had to try and teach him something. . . . And that affected him very much. The sight of this poor child, incapable of improvement in any way."[1] Sophisticated and literary, but not trained to teach the handicapped, he soon gave up.

With bright or normal children, he was an excellent teacher, who knew how to appeal to boys and inspire their admiration. During the school holidays in Southwold in 1930–31, he tutored three sons of an officer in the Indian Imperial Police. The oldest boy, Richard Peters, became a professor at London University and wrote an essay about his unusual teacher. Peters described him as "a tall spindly young man with a great mop of hair waving on top of a huge head, swinging along with loose, effortless strides and a knobbly stick made of some queer Scandinavian wood." Like Adrian Fierz, Peters found him "a thoroughly lovable and exciting companion." "A mine of information on birds, animals and the heroes of boys' magazines," as well as on H.G. Wells, ghosts, archeology, military maneuvers and how to kill eels with a shotgun, "he was really at home only with animals and children." In *Coming Up for Air*, George Bowling remembers that in childhood "we used to catch toads, ram the nozzle of a bicycle pump up their backsides and blow them up till they burst." Regretting this cruelty, which he may have once practiced himself, he told Peters "how he thrashed a boy whom he caught blowing up a frog with a bicycle pump."

Remembering the explosive brass cannons that had given him great pleasure as a child and the disastrous experiments with nitroglycerin that had once singed his eyebrows, he encouraged the boys to make bombs: "[He] taught us a very special way of making gun-powder and he had a patent firing mechanism which involved tipping a test-tube of sulfuric acid from a distance."[2] He also impressed the boys by nonchalantly striding across a narrow girder high above the Blyth River.

Like many modern writers—Wells, Joyce, Lawrence, Eliot, Huxley, Waugh and Auden—Blair spent several stopgap years as a schoolmaster. He was influenced by Wells, admired Joyce, was taught by Huxley, befriended Eliot and Waugh, and satirized Auden. But the writer he most resembled was D.H. Lawrence, who died in 1930, just as Blair was beginning his literary career. Two years after Lawrence's death, Blair, who lacked his passion and his taste for personal revelations, told Eleanor Jaques: "everywhere in his work one comes on passages of an extraordinary freshness, vividness, so that tho' I would never, even given the power, have done it quite like that myself, I feel that he has seized on an aspect of things that no one else would have noticed." Both writers lived in restless poverty for most of their lives, were fiercely independent and had a crusading spirit. They were good at household tasks: cooking and mending clothes. They idealized working-class life, believed that workers were warmhearted and in touch with their emotions. They disliked cities, machine civilization and the worship of money, loved the countryside and had a deep knowledge of nature. They hated the class system, attacked bourgeois values and had their defiant books suppressed. In private life they had a puritanical streak, refused to use contraceptives and feared or believed they were sterile. They were given to ferocious exaggerations, violent fantasies, outbursts of rage and prophetic doom. They suffered poor health all their lives, were treated by the same doctor and died of tuberculosis in their mid-forties. Above all, they were courageous writers, faced with formidable adversaries, who spoke the truth. As Connolly wrote of Orwell: "He was a man, like Lawrence, whose personality shines out in everything he said or wrote."

From April 1932 until July 1933 Blair taught and lived in The Hawthorns School for Boys on Church Road in Hayes, west of London, near what is now Heathrow Airport. The school, housed in a former vicarage, had only two masters and about fifteen boys (seven in a class) between the ages of ten and sixteen. They were mostly the sons of shopkeepers, office employees, small business and professional men. Geoffrey Stevens, whose father owned a joinery firm, was one of his thirteen-year-old pupils. He remembers how Blair, never smartly dressed, disguised his height by slouching. He fascinated the boys by showing them the scar on his wrist from a hornet's bite in Burma. Stevens thought he was very much an introvert and that his mind was elsewhere: "He would sit at his desk and start smiling and no one knew what he was laughing at. He was aware that this was strange, so if it happened at mealtimes, he would turn round and feed the proprietor's parrot to hide his face."

Blair taught every subject: English, French, History, Geography and Maths (there was no science). He seemed to enjoy teaching and was the best teacher of the school—not a great compliment since there were only two. There were no textbooks and he had to make up his own lessons. He didn't read to the class nor recommend his favorite authors, but was keen on essay writing, and had the boys memorize and recite forty lines of Shakespeare from *The Merchant of Venice* and *The Tempest*.

Blair never raised his voice, but was a strict disciplinarian. He kept a thick cane near his desk, used it frequently and "would cane you unmercifully at the slightest provocation." When the boys brought their work up to his desk, he would prod them in the stomach with a ruler. On one occasion Stevens returned to his seat and playfully imitated his teacher by prodding the boy next to him. Blair caught sight of him and gave him six of the best. Though Stevens thought the punishment excessive and unjust, he felt no resentment and didn't tell his parents about it. He looked up to his teacher and invited him to tea. When he came to the house and had a long talk with his father, Geoffrey's homework doubled. After that visit, he stopped inviting him.

Though severe in class, Blair could be quite genial outside the schoolroom with boys who shared his interests. He gave Stevens sixpence, which seemed a lot of money at the time, for spotting a spelling mistake on a sign. On natural history outings to the marshes, he taught the boys to stir up methane with a stick and hold a bottle upside down to catch the gas. They lit it, and it burned like a candle. Twin boys and their two brothers in the school suggested dramatic possibilities and inspired Blair's short play, "King Charles II," which divided the boys into Cavaliers and Roundheads. The play, put on just before Christmas in 1932, lasted half an hour and had only two performances. But he took enormous trouble during the fall term with the costumes, props and sets, and seemed to enjoy the elaborate preparations.[3]

Writing to Eleanor Jaques in 1932, Blair called Hayes "one of the most godforsaken places I have ever struck" and said the work was extremely demanding: "I am living in a sort of nightmare—schoolwork, rehearsing boys for their parts in the play, making costumes, & playing football. . . . I don't find the work uninteresting, but it is very exhausting. . . . My sole friend is the curate—High Anglican but not a creeping Jesus & a very good fellow." The vicar kept a "Holy Goat," which he taught Blair to milk, and goats would recur in his life and work. Though generally hostile to religion, Blair cherished his friend, and gilded a cigar box and an oil painting for the church, St. Mary the Virgin.

Geoffrey Stevens thought the school (and school play) in A Clergyman's Daughter was exactly like The Hawthorns. In that novel the repellent suburb is filled with "labyrinths of meanly decent streets, all so indistinguishably alike," and the school is in "a dark-looking, semi-detached house of yellow brick, three storeys high." Like Blair, the heroine, Dorothy Hare, "had no privacy and very little time that she could call her own." But she's determined to work hard for the school and "be proud of it, and make every effort to turn it from a place of bondage into a place human and decent."

Most teachers in Blair's position, poorly paid and overworked, would use a published play instead of writing a new one. Though he desperately wanted time to work on Burmese Days (the owner's wife played hymns on the piano and interfered with his writing), he was extremely conscientious and tried very hard to give a few boys, in a terrible school run entirely for profit, a decent education. In May 1940, reviewing a prep-school novel by Stephen Spender, he wrote that "these schools, with their money-grubbing proprietors and their staffs of underpaid hacks, are responsible for a lot of the harm that it is usual to blame on the public schools."[4]

From August to December 1933, without taking a real summer holiday, Blair taught and lived at a much better school. The coeducational Frays

College was located on Harefield Road in Uxbridge, a few miles northwest of Hayes. It had about 200 students, thirty of them boarders, between the ages of five and fifteen. The staff of sixteen prepared them for the professions, the universities and the Civil Service. Blair taught French and English, and supervised hockey and cricket after school. In the little time he had to spare, he went fishing, rode his new motorbike (as he done in Mandalay) and worked late into the night on his novel. Colleagues remembered that he had a rather austere temperament, was always friendly and courteous, but distant and cool.

Blair described this depressing area, which had an ugly urban sprawl and was polluted by the neighboring factories (reminding him of the blighted landscape of Syriam), in his rather labored poem "On a Ruined Farm near the His Master's Voice Gramophone Factory":

> *The acid smoke has soured the fields,*
> *And browned the few and windworn flowers;*
> *But there where steel and concrete soar*
> *In dizzy, geometric towers . . .*
> *There is my world, my home; yet why*
> *So alien still?*

Blair looked after himself no better here than he did in Paris, and was often quite reckless about his delicate health. In December 1933, while riding his motorbike without an overcoat, he got completely soaked in a freezing rainstorm. He caught a severe chill that developed into pneumonia and landed him in Uxbridge Cottage Hospital for two weeks. His mother and sister rushed down to look after him, and Avril recalled:

He was very ill indeed, but the crisis had passed then, and he was recovering. He was very worried about money, so the nurse told us. He'd been delirious, and he'd been talking the whole time about money. We reassured him that everything was all right, and he needn't worry about money. It turned out that it wasn't actually his situation in life as regards money that he was worrying about, but it was actual cash: he felt that he wanted cash sort of under his pillow.[5]

The delirium brought out his fears about poverty, which could only be assuaged with a stack of sovereigns. In any case, he was too weak to continue teaching and, like D.H. Lawrence, was permanently released from that dead-end job by illness. His first book was published in 1933, and from then on George Orwell (as I shall now call him) lived as a professional writer.

I I

IN 1940 Orwell wrote that the authors he cared most about and never grew tired of were mainly classic realistic novelists, innovative modernists and, somewhat surprisingly in this group, a traditional author who often wrote about the East: "Shakespeare, Swift, Fielding, Dickens, Charles Reade, Samuel Butler, Zola, Flaubert and, among modern writers, James Joyce, T.S. Eliot and D.H. Lawrence. But I believe the modern writer who has influenced me most is Somerset Maugham, whom I admire immensely for his power of telling a story straightforwardly and without frills." Maugham's utterly plain style and his precept "write about what you know" clearly left their mark on Orwell. Both were "odd men out as writers, and as individuals, honest journeymen, telling plain unvarnished tales, about unfashionable people." Orwell's prose style matched his blunt, forceful mode of argument and his direct portrayal of actual experience. As Wyndham Lewis wrote in *One-Way Song* (1933):

> *These times require a tongue that naked goes,*
> *Without more fuss than Dryden's or Defoe's.*[6]

Orwell, who wrote most effectively about things he had actually observed, deliberately sought out experiences he could use in his work. The nastier the experience, the more he suffered in prep school, tramping, Wigan, Spain and the London Blitz, the better equipped he was to describe it. Hardship and injustice, violence and oppression inspired him to write, and his reputation was based on provocative honesty.

He managed to finish the first draft of *Down and Out*, his moving account of social outcasts, before he began teaching, and his difficulty in placing the book forced him to take a job at The Hawthorns. In the fall of 1930, about a year after he returned from Paris, he sent a much shorter version of the book to Jonathan Cape. They said it was too short and fragmentary, but saw some promise in it and asked for a longer version. He expanded the book and they rejected it again. In December 1931 he sent the book to T.S. Eliot at

Faber & Faber. Two months later, Eliot identified its weak structure (a problem that would plague many of Orwell's works) and also rejected it: "I regret
to say that it does not appear to me possible as a publishing venture. It is
decidedly too short, and particularly for a book of such length it seems to me
too loosely constructed, as the French and English episodes fall into two parts
with very little to connect them."[7]

Deeply discouraged and overwhelmed by failure, he gave the typescript
to Mabel Fierz and told her to burn it and keep the paper clips. He could
have burned it himself, but knew that Mabel believed he had talent, perhaps
even genius. She took it to the only literary agent she knew and, using her
formidable powers of persuasion, forced him to read it. Leonard Moore
(1879–1959), who became Orwell's lifelong agent and most voluminous correspondent, and played an important role in his career, has always remained
a shadowy figure.

Born in London, he went to the City of London School, began his career
with the dynamic literary agent J.B. Pinker, joined the publisher Cassell in
1908 and four years later formed a partnership with Gerald Christy, owner
of The Lecture Agency. Moore was commissioned in 1915, fought in France
and in 1920 lost a leg from trench fever. Married but with no children, he
owned a large country house and garden in Gerrard's Cross,
Buckinghamshire, near Uxbridge. Orwell sometimes motorbiked over to the
house for Sunday lunch. Friends described Moore as "a spare, upright man
of military bearing, about six feet in height, with a boldly dominant face, a
very fresh complexion, wide, high forehead, hooked, prominent nose and
piercing eyes." Fredric Warburg, who found him a tough negotiator, characterized Moore in the 1940s as "obstinate and exceedingly deaf"—or at least
unwilling to hear a publisher's low offer. In 1947 Orwell described Christy
& Moore—whose clients included Leo Amery, General Sir John Glubb,
Ernest Seton Thompson and Georgette Heyer—as "partly lecturing agents,
and somewhat lowbrow in tendency, but [they] do a certain amount of high-
class business."[8]

Despite his artificial leg, Moore was a keen athlete, continued to play a
gentle game of tennis and belonged to the same north London tennis club
as Francis Fierz. Mabel insisted that Moore take on the typescript (along with
the paper clips), and in June 1932 he offered it to Victor Gollancz, who
expressed interest in the book. Orwell then met Gollancz and agreed to deal
with questions of obscenity, blasphemy and libel, to change names and alter
Charlie's story in Chapter II ("the only good bit of writing in the book"). He

then assured Moore, worried about the naiveté of his budding author who tended to run down his own work, that he "did not say anything about the book having no commercial value." Gollancz rather tetchily told his colleagues that Orwell, who may have resisted some changes, "seems to have great difficulty grasping either what constitutes libel in this country, even when the legal position had been clearly explained to him, or the very real dangers involved." But in August he agreed to publish the book, with an advance of £40, and expeditiously brought it out (while the author was still teaching at The Hawthorns) in January 1933.

Victor Gollancz (1893–1967), Orwell's principal publisher until 1945, was born into an Orthodox Jewish family, but later described himself as a Christian Socialist. Educated at Oxford, he taught at Repton School before going into publishing and founding his own firm in 1928. Four years later, a journalist described him as "thirty-nine, but looks forty-nine, burly head dominated by its bald dome, eyes brown, rather small, humorous, shrewd. Likes to smoke a pipe and pace about while he talks." Fredric Warburg, who was also Jewish and replaced Gollancz when he refused on political grounds to publish *Animal Farm*, sharply portrayed him as "founder of the Left Book Club, king-pin of the cultural and political activities of the [pro-Communist] United Front, a demon of energy, capable, trustworthy, and possessed of so overwhelming a belief in the righteousness of his opinions as to bear a recognizable resemblance to the ancient Hebrew prophets." [9]

Unwilling to embarrass his family and wanting to establish a respectable professional image, Blair decided to publish his book under a pseudonym. He considered the rather colorless P.S. Burton, the martial Kenneth Miles ("soldier" in Latin) and H. Louis Allways, which was close to his final choice, but might have provoked jests about his inconsistencies. He considered nearby place-names, but George Walberswick wouldn't do at all. Rejecting the names of rivers on the Suffolk coast near Southwold—the Blythe, Alde, Deben and Stour (too close to "sour")—he finally chose the solid-sounding Orwell, which flows from Ipswich into the North Sea and is also the name of a village near Cambridge. Anthony Powell once asked the elusive Orwell "if he had ever thought of legally adopting his *nom de guerre*. 'Well, I have,' he said slowly, 'but then, of course, I'd have to *write* under another name if I did.' " By abandoning the name of Eric Blair, Orwell did not become a new person, but distanced himself from his family, St. Cyprian's, Eton, Burma, and all the unpleasant associations of his past life.[10]

III

IN JANUARY 1933—six long years after he declared he'd be a writer—his first book, *Down and Out in Paris and London*, was published by Gollancz in London and by Harper in New York. The first printing was a modest 1,500 copies, but another 1,500 copies were called for that month.

Reviewing a book on a French penal colony in December 1930, Orwell noted that "some of [its] incidents are almost certainly exaggerated, but one can accept the book as a genuine document," and in his own journey to the lower depths he heightened reality to achieve dramatic effects. The book's episodic structure and mixed genre helps to explain why he had difficulty placing it. Combining sociology, anthropology, politics and travelogue, it describes poverty, degrading work and unemployment, but also tells the story of Orwell's adventures. It covers the last few weeks of his two years in Paris (when his English lessons came to an end and his money was stolen), his search for work, his job as a dishwasher, his return to England, and tramping in and around London.

The Chaucerian epigraph—"O scathful harm, condicion of poverte!"— suggests some parallels with *The Canterbury Tales*. The narrative is freely interrupted with digressions—anecdotes, stories-within-the-story, character studies and observations—and Orwell's bistro tales come from the oral traditions of illiterate workers. Two of his eccentric types are Communists: Furex, who becomes a French patriot as soon as he's drunk; and Jules, the Magyar waiter, whose politics demand he does as little work as possible. By contrast, the waiters, snobs to a man, delight in servility. Orwell also uses literary models. He quotes a Villon poem on hunger, invokes the name of Zola when describing the hellish kitchen and recalls Baudelaire's *jeune squelette* as he lies in bed hungry all day. As a temporary dweller in poverty, he tells his middle-class readers about that unexplored country.

The book opens abruptly and dramatically on the rue Coq d'Or as a landlady screams abuse at a tenant. With sharp social analysis and in vigorous prose, Orwell gives an economic profile of the quarter, and shows how he fits into it. "All the houses were hotels and packed to the tiles with lodgers, mostly Poles, Arabs and Italians" and as a poor foreigner he's at the bottom of the heap. Yet there are gradations of poverty and each level profits from the one below: "amid the noise and dirt lived the usual respectable French shopkeepers, bakers and laundresses and the like, keeping themselves to themselves and quietly piling up small fortunes."

Orwell is fascinated with the details of poverty, the grey linen, the particular smells and sounds in a room where the walls are as thin as matchwood and the layers of wallpaper house innumerable bugs. In a passage omitted from the published book he recalled the squalid sexual habits of his teenage neighbors. Every evening, when the boy returned from work, he'd first kiss the girl and then, using a slop-bucket, have a loud and long piss. Immediately afterwards came "the creaking of a bed followed by groans."

He's equally obsessed with how to survive on six francs a day. When he discovers one of his coins is Belgian, he has to slink out of a shop without a purchase, and must conceal bread in his pockets as he slips past the *patron* of the hotel. The narrator, a rather naive, trusting and inexpert comic character, needs his mentors, Boris, the Russian waiter, and Paddy, the Irish tramp, to guide him through the marginal world. Boris inks the skin that shows through the holes in his socks, and tells him to lie to the boss; Paddy steers him away from the worst spikes.

Some scenes have a Chaplinesque humor and slapstick quality. Boris contrives to keep the *patron* talking about sport while Orwell, shielded by Boris' wide shoulders, escapes to a pawnshop with a suitcase full of clothes; the cramped kitchen in the Russian restaurant has piles of greasy plates and slippery vegetable peelings underfoot, and the big-buttocked cook bursts into tears when the going gets rough. All this would be funny, except that Boris and Orwell are starving, and the cook works sixteen hours a day to support an invalid husband. Like Chaplin, Orwell pushes comedy to the edge of misery and suffering.

The chapters on the luxurious hotel, the most effective in the book, combine analysis of the social hierarchy with Dickensian descriptions of the laborers. The hotel is like an ocean liner, where the passengers live in splendor while the workers toil in the infernal regions: "there were the same heat and cramped space and warm reek of food, and a humming, whirring noise (it came from the kitchen furnaces) just like the whir of engines." The hellish heat is matched by the raging abuse that pours in torrents from the cooks and waiters, who have to serve hundreds of people at the same time.

Orwell delights in pulling the curtain aside to contrast the elegant façade with the disgusting mess that lies behind the scenes: "It was amusing to look round the filthy little scullery and think that only a double door was between us and the dining-room. There sat the customers in all their splendour." An Italian waiter hurled insults at an apprentice in the filthy kitchen before he entered the dining room and "sailed across it dish in hand, graceful as a swan.

Ten seconds later he was bowing reverently to a customer." The class system in society is replicated in the hierarchy of employees, which naturally inspires resentment and provokes revenge. The cook routinely spits in the soup, the waiters dip their greasy fingers in the gravy. "Roughly speaking," Orwell writes, in the kind of shocking epigram he came to perfect in his later work, "the more one pays for food, the more sweat and spittle one is obliged to eat with it."[11]

Though he works like a slave from seven in the morning until 9:15 at night, he finds—oddly enough—that the job suits him. It needs no skill, is extremely exhausting, has no interest and no future, but it produces a heavy contentment. Having done the work himself, instead of simply observing it, Orwell gains deeper insight into the mentality of workers and the rhythm of their lives. He admires the spirit of people who put up with endless drudgery and take pride in their ability to *débrouiller*, to deal with anything. "What keeps a hotel going," he argues, "is the fact that the employees take a genuine pride in their work, beastly and silly though it is." At the end of the week, the intensity of their work makes their pleasure in the bistro all the sweeter.

Orwell makes the transition to the last third of the book, on tramping and begging in England, by reverting to his travel-writer's mode and contrasting his impressions of Paris and London: "[London] was so much cleaner and quieter and drearier. One missed the scream of the trams, and the noisy festering life of the back streets, and the armed men clattering through the squares. The crowds were better dressed and the faces comelier and milder and more alike, without the fierce individuality and malice of the French. . . . It was the land of the tea urn and the Labour Exchange, as Paris is the land of the *bistro* and the sweatshop."

The tone of *Down and Out* suggests that Orwell was happier as a *plongeur* than as an English tramp. It was easier to be déclassé outside his own country, and in Paris he could enjoy the freedom to be eccentric and the stupefying animal contentment of work and sleep. The first section describes the social organization of work; the second follows Orwell's wanderings. In England he observes men degraded by unemployment and homelessness, reduced to a spineless condition by hunger and malnutrition. Tramps, forced to move from one shelter to another, are cut off from women by extreme poverty. In Paris the kitchen slaves work till they drop, in England the tramps live in soul-destroying "enforced idleness."

A major theme in the book is the desirability and dignity of work. Boris walks miles in search of a job despite his bad leg; Paddy, a veteran who once had a good job, is now homeless and can never again belong to the world of work. Orwell—energetic and skillful in many kinds of work—attacks the system that keeps men like Paddy in this boring subworld. "The evil of poverty," he says, "is not so much that it makes a man suffer as that it rots him physically and spiritually." He differentiates among the tramps and shows compassion for the men as individuals: the elderly man crying over his stolen food; the young man, tense with hunger and close to hysteria. Orwell's detailed description of Bozo the pavement artist and the two organ grinders reveals the complexity of their daily struggles with weather and equipment, sickness and pain, and the hideous irony that begging, in fact, is hard work.

One comic set-piece in the London section, an enforced church service attended by a hundred tramps in exchange for a free meal, matches the Parisian scenes. They gather like kites round a dead buffalo, wolf down the food and then sit in the gallery jeering at the service below. The minister and congregation are intimidated, and the humiliated men get revenge. Orwell ends by summarizing what he's learned: "I shall never again think that all tramps are drunken scoundrels, nor expect a beggar to be grateful when I give him a penny, nor be surprised if men out of work lack energy, nor subscribe to the Salvation Army, nor pawn my clothes, nor refuse a handbill, nor enjoy a meal in a smart restaurant." Aware of how easy it is to fall into destitution, he reminds us that "here is the world that awaits you if you are ever penniless."[12]

Down and Out was well received. Though Orwell had started tramping in the late 1920s, his book gained significance during the Depression, when unemployment and poverty were crucial issues for millions of people. His contrast between the luxury of the grand hotel and the exploitation of the workers, his firsthand analysis of the psychology of poverty met the demand for social realism in the 1930s. Reviewers praised his honesty, his sensitive social conscience, his practical suggestions for the alleviation of poverty, and his portrayal of the differences in national temperament in the sections on Paris and London. The poet Cecil Day-Lewis responded to the vividly presented tour of the underworld by stating: "if you wish to eat a meal in a big hotel without acute nausea, you had better skip pp. 107–109." Herbert Gorman noticed Orwell's masochism and shrewdly observed that he "rather enjoys being down and out."

But a restaurateur with the unlikely name of Humbert Possenti, writing from the Hotel Splendide in Piccadilly, vigorously defended high-class restaurants in a letter to the *Times*: "Such a disgusting state of things as he describes in such places is inconceivable. The kitchens of large and smart restaurants have to be clean . . . are cleaner than those of most private houses." Ignoring the fact that he generalized about all luxury hotels from his experiences in one, Orwell took the offensive and replied: "The passages objected to in my book did not refer to Paris hotels in general, but to one particular hotel. And as M. Possenti does not know which hotel this was he has no means of testing the truth of my statements. So I am afraid that, in spite of his 40 years' experience, my evidence in this case is worth more than his."[13]

In his introduction to the French edition, *La Vache enragée* (*manger la vache enragée* means "to have a rough time"), Orwell took pains to mollify his French audience and wrote: "Since all the personal scenes and events have something repulsive about them, it is quite possible that I have unconsciously portrayed Paris and London as abominable cities." But, he disingenuously added, he would be hurt if Parisian readers "believed I feel the least hostility toward a city that is very dear to me." In an enthusiastic letter of August 1936, Henry Miller, another connoisseur of Parisian low-life, told Orwell: "It's almost fantastic; it's so incredibly true! How you ever held out for so long is beyond me. . . . Did you get to China? It's a pity you couldn't have had another section on down and out in Shanghai. That would be the coup de grace!" In a *Paris Review* interview of 1962, Miller said: "I was crazy about his book *Down and Out in Paris and London*; I think it's a classic. For me it's still his best book." Miller would have been pleased to know that *Down and Out* was the most popular work in the library of Dartmoor Prison.

Mabel—his friend, patron, lover, adviser and agent—was delighted by the success of the book, and pleased to receive a presentation copy (now in the possession of her son) with the deceptively formal inscription: "To Mr. and Mrs. Fierz, with best wishes & many thanks for their great help in getting this book published. Eric A. Blair." By contrast, his own family was as shocked and horrified by the provocative sexual episodes (though toned down by Gollancz) as they had been by his experiences as a tramp. Avril later told Jacintha Buddicom: "although no hint of sex ever appeared in his conversation, his books were often quite lewd. This [personal reticence] may have been a left over Victorianism inherited from our parents who never mentioned sex either."[14]

IV

AFTER LEAVING Uxbridge Hospital in January 1934 and recuperating from pneumonia in his parents' house, Orwell stayed on with them for the next nine months and completed his second novel, A *Clergyman's Daughter*. In August he told Brenda Salkeld about his comical, though decidedly chilly clash with the town's conventional respectability: "I nearly died of the cold the other day when bathing, because I had walked out to Easton Broad not intending to bathe, & then the water looked so nice that I took off my clothes & went in, & then about 50 people came up & rooted themselves to the spot. I wouldn't have minded that, but among them was a coastguard who could have had me up for bathing naked, so I had to swim up & down for the best part of half an hour, pretending to like it."

He grew weary of living with his parents and struggling to finish his novel, and was depressed by the political situation in Europe. After the Roehm purge, Hitler took absolute power in Germany, and Mosley's Fascists were active in England. In September Orwell compared himself to an Old Testament prophet: "You complain about the gloominess of my letters. . . . This age makes me so sick that sometimes I am almost impelled to stop at a corner and start calling down curses from Heaven like Jeremiah or Ezra."

After finishing his novel, he got a job through his Aunt Nellie as a half-time assistant in Booklovers' Corner in Hampstead. The owner, Francis Westrope, had been a conscientious objector in the war and belonged to the Independent Labour Party; his wife, Myfanwy, had been active in the women's rights movement. In October 1934 Orwell moved back to London and lodged in the Westropes' flat. On the fourth floor, above the bookshop at the corner of Pond Street and South End Road, it had a fine view of London. Jon Kimche, who later worked with Orwell on the *Tribune*, also lived at the Westropes' and shared the work in the bookshop.

Orwell always worked tremendously hard, rarely took any time off and— except when he was ill or during the war—began his next book as soon as he'd finished his last one. In another letter to Brenda, Orwell described his strict military timetable: "7 am get up, dress etc, cook & eat breakfast. 8.45 go down & open the shop, & I am usually kept there till about 9.45. Then come home, do out my room, light the fire etc. 10.30 am–1 pm I do some writing. 1 pm get lunch & eat it. 2 pm–6.30 pm I am at the shop. Then I come home, get my supper, do the washing up & after that do about an hour's work."[15] He resented the tedium of the shop and complained to Geoffrey

Gorer that "in a grocer's shop people come in to buy something, in a book-shop they come in to make a nuisance of themselves."

Orwell described the place in *Keep the Aspidistra Flying* and his essay "Bookshop Memories" (both 1936). In addition to used books, the shop sold old typewriters and old stamps, sixpenny horoscopes, children's remainders and Christmas cards, and also had a twopenny lending library. Jon Kimche and Kay Welton Ekevall, whom he met there, both emphasized that it was *not* a dreadful place and that Orwell exaggerated the horrors for dramatic effect. In his essay Orwell says that the shop attracted more aimless and moth-eaten nuisances than genuine lovers of books: "[In] London there are always plenty of not quite certifiable lunatics walking the streets, and they tend to gravitate towards bookshops, because a bookshop is one of the few places you can hang about for a long time without spending any money." Instead of buy-ing serious Victorian or modern writers, the dotty clientele went in for the less demanding works of Ethel M. Dell and Warwick Deeping. Orwell's fif-teen months in the shop gave him a distaste for books—"Seen in the mass, five or ten thousand at a time, books were boring and even slightly sicken-ing"—and they were forever associated in his mind with paranoid customers and dead bluebottles.[16]

In April 1935, while Orwell was still working at the bookshop, Mabel found him a larger, more comfortable room (sharing the kitchen and bath) in the flat of her friend Rosalind Obermeyer at 77 Parliament Hill. Born in South Africa in 1895, Rosalind had come to England in the 1920s. She was divorced and studying for a master's degree in Psychology at University College, London. The third tenant, a medical student named Janet Gimson, found Orwell's room as filthy and chaotic as Roger Beadon had found his house in Insein. Without servants to clean up after him, he tended to sweep things under the carpet or throw them in a corner. Half-finished biscuits, lying on the floor, were eaten by mice, who scurried noisily about at night. The flatmates respected each other's privacy and mainly kept to themselves, but when one of them had guests for drinks or dinner, the others were usu-ally included.

In the spring of 1935 Orwell invited two young writers, Rayner Heppenstall and Michael Sayers, whom he had met through Richard Rees, to dine in Rosalind's flat. Heppenstall was impressed by his skill as a chef and his knowledge of wine: "He cooked for us himself. He gave us very good steak, and we drank beer out of tree-pattern mugs, which he was collecting. I had also met him in restaurants. There he would order red wine, feeling the bottle and then sending it away to have the chill taken off, a proceeding by which I was greatly impressed."

In August, at Mabel's suggestion, the nomadic Orwell moved to a flat with his two new friends at 50 Lawford Road in Kentish Town—a much less fashionable part of north London. The ex-*plongeur* of the Hotel Lotti made breakfast, did most of the cooking and cleared his worktable for their meals. Sayers, a shabby Jewish Dubliner, was short, dark, good-looking and very witty. His wealthy father gave him an allowance and he lived at home, using his room in the flat for romantic assignations. He wrote poems and short stories, and was drama critic for the *New English Weekly*. He later married an American heiress, moved to the United States and worked for the theatrical producer Norman Bel Geddes.

Heppenstall, born in Yorkshire in 1911, was a minor poet, novelist and balletomane. He fetched the beer from the local pub, but slacked off on household duties and was always late with the rent. Disappointed in his own career and envious of Orwell's success in the mid-1940s, he later published a rather caustic yet patronizing portrait of him as an old eccentric—prejudiced against Scots, Catholics, bishops, civil servants, psychiatrists, wealthy bohemians, Socialist cranks, Wyndham Lewis and John Middleton Murry. Heppenstall thought he had "a curious mind, satirically attached to everything traditionally English, always full of interesting and out-of-the-way information like *Tit-Bits*, but arid, colorless, devoid of poetry, derisive, yet darkly obsessed."

For most of his life Orwell had a tendency to violence, settling scores with his fists at school, kicking his servants in Burma, holding his own in the rough Paris kitchens and using the cane freely on unruly schoolboys. Quarreling with an elderly but contentious taxi-driver in Paris, en route to Spain in 1936, he exclaimed: "You think you're too old for me to smash your face in. Don't be too sure!" Heppenstall, in a notorious incident, also suffered at Orwell's hands.

When Heppenstall came home drunk in the middle of the night, woke him up and took a swing at him, Orwell punched him in the face and knocked him out. Ten minutes later Heppenstall came to, sitting on the floor and covered in blood. The fight continued when Orwell locked him in a room, Heppenstall kicked his foot through the door and Orwell—very much the Burma policeman—suddenly pulled it open. "There stood Orwell," Heppenstall wrote, "armed with his shooting-stick. With this he pushed me back, poking the aluminium point into my stomach. I pushed it aside, and sprang at him. He fetched me a dreadful crack across the legs and then raised the shooting-stick over his head. I looked at his face. Through my private mist I saw in it a curious blend of fear and sadistic exaltation." In Heppenstall's story, Orwell pokes him in the stomach, as he did the boys at The Hawthorns, and then raises his stick to deliver a deadly blow, as he reportedly did to the student at the train station in Burma. Heppenstall then blocked the stick with a chair and the fight came to an end. It's fair to note, however, that in all these cases Orwell did not start the violence, but responded to serious provocations.

Despite this brutal incident, the two men, both politically Left wing, patched up their friendship. After Heppenstall married, his wife Margaret recalled, Orwell would come round for a drink and a talk: "He didn't seem at all extraordinary. He was one of us, very hard-up, trying to write." Heppenstall, writing in a more friendly fashion, said that when Orwell spent a night in their flat in 1937–38, "Margaret opened her eyes and saw Orwell, stark naked, wandering about the room. With exquisite politeness but no sign of embarrassment, he apologised for waking her and explained that he was trying to find his way out to the lavatory."[17]

V

WHEN ORWELL first moved into his Pond Street flat Mrs. Westrope had asked him what he particularly wanted and he said, "The thing I most want is freedom." "Do you want to have women up here all night?" she asked. Playing the respectable lodger, he at first said "no"—to which she tolerantly replied, "I only meant that I didn't mind whether you do or not." Despite his diffidence, he took full advantage of his escape from his parents in Southwold and enjoyed his new-found freedom. Though he disliked working in the shop, it was a useful place to meet women.

Orwell met Sally Jerome in the fall of 1934, around the time he published *Burmese Days*. Two years younger than Orwell, with an American mother and a South African father, she was brought up middle-class in the south of England and had been to boarding school. Though not exceptionally fit (she recently recalled), he seemed to have recovered from his bout of pneumonia. She thought they were both anti-establishment, temperamentally "odd people out," shared the same general views, and talked about life in general, politics, "attitudes and platitudes." Like Rosemary in *Keep the Aspidistra*

Flying, she worked in an advertising agency; like Gordon, he always complained about not having enough money, but wouldn't allow her to share expenses.

Sally, who felt Orwell didn't understand her, did not find him particularly attractive and refused to sleep with him. When she discovered that he was secretly seeing two other women, she was (and still is) furious. She later became a lifelong member of the Communist Party, and followed his career with critical disdain. She did not consider him a genuine Socialist, disliked on ideological grounds his "attacks on the working-class" in *The Road to Wigan Pier* and loathed his condemnation of the Communists in *Homage to Catalonia.*

Sally's rival Kay Welton, born in 1911, had a very different personality: calm, open, jolly, warmhearted. Mabel, who took a keen interest in Orwell's love affairs, noted that Kay had "a good figure, useful for sex." Kay thought Orwell, who towered over her and could conveniently reach the top of bookcases, more interesting than attractive. He was good company and a stimulating companion, and they had lively arguments about books, plays and politics. Obsessed by money, but wearing tailor-made clothes and not nearly as poor as he professed to be, he liked to perpetuate the idea that he was hard done by. He disliked the Scots and refused to meet Kay's friend, the poet Edwin Muir. Orwell was gloomy (as he'd confessed to Brenda), always saw the black side of things and didn't think anyone (including himself) was much good.

Kay, who worked in a secretarial agency and would fall "madly in love" with Heppenstall, was Orwell's girlfriend for about nine months in 1934–35. They got on well and it was all very pleasant, but she did not become seriously involved. There was no great romantic passion: Orwell wasn't that sort of man. He didn't open up with her, never really let go — even when they made love. Like Brenda, Kay felt he didn't understand women and was rather careless with them. He never seemed to think about *her* feelings or what she wanted. They promised to tell each other honestly if they fell in love with someone else, and he kept that promise when he met his future wife, Eileen O'Shaughnessy. Kay concluded that Orwell "was too prickly to be nice, too cynical, too perverse, too contradictory, too paradoxical, a strange mix of shyness and assertiveness, endowed with a fundamental honesty and common sense that she never questioned, along with small-minded envies and prejudices that she did not hesitate to call into question."[18]

Orwell's relations with Sally, Kay and Eileen repeated his earlier triangle with Brenda (who would not sleep with him), Eleanor and Mabel (who would). Three of the women were somewhat exotic: Eleanor had a Huguenot background, Mabel was born in Brazil, Sally was partly South African. Both Sally and Kay met him in Booklover's Corner and said he complained about having no money. Though middle-class, both were unconventional, professional women, who became Communists and criticized his political views.[19] Sally, perhaps more emotionally involved with Orwell than Kay, refused to sleep with him and still feels angry about his "betrayal" with other women. Kay became his lover, but didn't fall in love with him or care about her rivals, and now feels quite friendly toward him.

V I

IN A well-known but often misunderstood passage in The Road to Wigan Pier, Orwell wrote that "the landscapes of Burma, which, when I was among them, so appalled me as to assume the qualities of a nightmare, afterwards stayed so hauntingly in my mind that I was obliged to write a novel about them to get rid of them." But in the novel the hero, Flory, loves the Burmese landscape. He often escapes from his misery to find solace in the jungle, and while there achieves his most intimate moment with Elizabeth, the newly arrived English girl who does not return his love. The scenery probably took on a nightmarish tinge during one of Orwell's bouts of dengue fever. They haunted his mind and partly inspired his fiction-as-exorcism. But writing Burmese Days did not get rid of them, and memories of Burma remained intense for the rest of his life. He also wrote the novel to earn money and advance his career, to make use of his exotic experience and show the evils of imperialism.

In "Why I Write" Orwell suggested the limitations of his first work of fiction. Influenced by his favorite nineteenth-century authors, he "wanted to write enormous naturalistic novels with unhappy endings, full of detailed descriptions and arresting similes, and also full of purple passages in which words were used partly for the sake of their sound. And in fact my first completed novel, Burmese Days, which I wrote when I was thirty [and teaching school] but projected much earlier, is rather that kind of book." This self-consciously arty novel is filled with biblical, classical and literary allusions (see Appendix II). Gollancz rejected the book when colonial officials complained it would give offense in India and Burma, but after Harper had published it in New York in October 1934, he changed his mind and brought out the English edition the following year.

The ironic title suggests the genial memoirs of an old colonial hand writing in *Blackwood's Magazine*; and this bitter, nightmarish book could more accurately be called *Burmese Daze*. Profoundly ambivalent about Burma, Orwell let the expatriate Flory extol the virtues of the scenery and the people, and made Elizabeth, the visitor from Europe, express all his negative feelings about the country. He's fascinated by their visit to the *pwe*—"a festival, feast, celebration, ceremony, gathering or public performance . . . [which] consists of acting, singing, dancing and clowning, takes place in the open air and lasts all night"—and she's revolted by it. Feeling uneasy, Elizabeth perceives "that Flory, when he spoke of the 'natives,' spoke nearly always *in favour* of them. He was forever praising Burmese customs and the Burmese character; he even went so far as to contrast them favourably with the English."[20]

The setting is based on Katha (pronounced Ka-táh), Orwell's last post in Burma, and he drew a map showing the roads, bazaar, jail, *maidan* (or common), bungalows, church, cemetery and club that lie between the jungle and the river. The novel takes place during the hot and rainy season, April–June 1926, when Flory (twelve years older than Orwell) is thirty-five. *Burmese Days* was strongly influenced by E.M. Forster's *A Passage to India*, published in 1924 when Orwell was serving in Burma. Both novels concern an Englishman's friendship with an Indian doctor, and a girl who goes out to the colonies, gets engaged and then breaks it off. Both use Club scenes to reveal a depressing sample of colonial society, and measure the personality and moral value of the characters by their racial attitudes. The themes of cultural misunderstanding and difficulties of friendship between the English and the natives, the physical decay and spiritual corruption of the whites in the tropics, are sounded by Forster and echo through Orwell's novel. But *Burmese Days*, in which official failures are not redeemed by meaningful personal relations, is a far more pessimistic book. There are no redemptive characters, like Fielding and Mrs. Moore, who prevail against the overwhelming insensitivity of the English and maintain a civilized standard of behavior. Unlike Forster's Indians, Orwell's Burmese are greedy and malevolent.

His characters, though one-dimensional, are vivid and moving. In Katha in Orwell's time the magistrate, like his fictional U Po Kyin, was Burmese.[21] The judge was, unfortunately, typical of his profession, for a historian reported that "only 50 Class I judges in all of Burma were incorruptible and that the other 600 judges frequently accepted gratuities from litigants," which often equaled ten times their annual salary. Despite Orwell's unremitting attack on British rule, a sahib is the hero and the Burmese—the corrupt U Po Kyin and the extortionate Ma Hla May—the real villains. U Po Kyin slanders the Deputy Commissioner Macgregor, ruins the Indian Dr. Veraswami, incites a rebellion in which two men are killed and, by manipulating May, drives Flory to suicide. His career is a devastating condemnation of his British superiors, who have misjudged his character, promoted him to magistrate and recommended him as an official candidate for the Club. British rule permits him to gouge the people who appear in his court and flourish on the proceeds. U Po Kyin seems to strengthen Dr. Veraswami's arguments about the superiority of a British rather than a Burmese government.[22]

In his review of *Burmese Days* in the *Spectator*, the Irish novelist Sean O'Faolain observed that Orwell tilted the scale against poor Flory, as well as all the other characters, who hadn't "a dog's chance against his author." Besides Flory, the English colony consists of the bigoted and malicious Ellis; the drunken fornicator Lackersteen; his snobbish and scheming wife, who (like Grandmother Limouzin) lived for many years in Burma without learning a word of the language; the stupid and bloodthirsty Westfield; the innocent and inoffensive murder victim Maxwell; and the cruel and arrogant Verrall (named after Dr. A.W. Verrall, the editor of hated Latin and Greek textbooks).

Orwell's vitriolic portrayal of Verrall, the youngest son of a peer, is masterly and convincing. Flory both loathes and envies his antithesis and romantic rival: the reckless, caddish, self-assured aristocrat who performs perfectly and despises everyone. He's an expert horseman, polo player and military commander. He humiliates Flory and intimidates Ellis by exclaiming: "if anyone gives me lip I kick his bottom. Do you want me to kick yours?" He snubs Mrs. Lackersteen, charms and seduces Elizabeth, and deftly disappears without paying the two Indian merchants left wailing, with Elizabeth, at the train station.

Flory, like many of Conrad's characters, is isolated and desperately lonely in a remote Eastern outpost. He naively imagines that the shallow and selfish Elizabeth (who's visiting the Lackersteens, her uncle and aunt) will somehow save him from his Burmese misery. Their hunting trip allows Elizabeth to share his love of Burma and enables him to impress her by shooting some pigeons and a leopard. The earthquake that prevents Flory from proposing to Elizabeth is absurd. But the big scenes—the riotous attack on the club and May's denunciation of Flory in church—are well done. Orwell liked the Victorian method of tying up loose strands at the end of the novel; and his conclusion, which describes the fate of all his characters, gives the tradition an ironic twist. This sad, strangely moving novel reveals how bitterly unhappy Orwell had been, how he hated his work and his colleagues, how he was forced "to live inwardly, secretly, in books and secret thoughts that could not be uttered" and how he was saved, not by a woman's love, but by quitting his job and leaving the country.

The novel was not just a personal exorcism. Orwell attacked imperialism in *Burmese Days* as he would attack capitalism in *The Road to Wigan Pier*, Fascism in *Homage to Catalonia*, Communism in *Animal Farm* and *Nineteen Eighty-Four*. As Flory tells Veraswami while he rants against hypocrisy in one of their eternal arguments: "the lie [is] that we're here to uplift our poor black brothers instead of to rob them. . . . We Anglo-Indians could be almost bearable if we'd only admit that we're thieves and go on thieving without any humbug. . . . The official holds the Burman down while the businessman goes through his pockets. . . . The British Empire is simply a device for giving trade monopolies to the English. . . . I don't deny . . . that we modernise this country in certain ways. We can't help doing so. In fact, before we've finished we'll have wrecked the whole Burmese national culture."

Like Conrad and Forster, Orwell shows the destructive psychological effects of imperialism on the men who run the Empire. The central political principle comes from Montesquieu, who wrote in *The Spirit of the Laws*: "If a democratic republic subdues a nation in order to govern them as subjects, it exposes its own liberty." The connection, Flory notes, between political oppression and private guilt was described by Nietzsche, who observed: "Political superiority without any real human superiority is most harmful. One must seek to make amends for political superiority. To be *ashamed* of one's power."[23] Though these principles are valid, there was no effective system of government to replace the British. Once they left Burma, the U Po Kyins would move into the political vacuum and seize power.

As Orwell intended, the novel gave great offense in Burma. His colleague Roger Beadon remembers hearing that the Scottish superintendent of the Police Training School in Mandalay, Clyne Stewart, whom Blair considered an oaf, "went livid and said that if he ever met that young man he was going to horse-whip him." But most response was favorable and the reviewers, like Victor Gollancz, recognized that his first novel, though flawed, had considerable power. Geoffrey Gorer, a Cambridge-educated anthropologist with extensive experience in foreign cultures, called the novel "an absolutely admirable statement of fact told as vividly and with as little bitterness as possible." He arranged to meet Orwell and they became good friends. Compton Mackenzie, one of Orwell's boyhood heroes, also commended the book: "I thought *Burmese Days* a work of altogether exceptional insight and masterly execution." Cyril Connolly, reviewing the novel in the *New Statesman and Nation*, recommended it "to anyone who enjoys a spate of efficient indignation, graphic description, excellent narrative, excitement, and irony tempered with vitriol."[24]

7

—

Eileen and Wigan Pier,
1935–1937

I

In *Down and Out* and the essays of the 1930s Orwell discovered his painstaking, passionate genius for non-fiction. Yet he wanted above all to be an entertaining and socially influential novelist, a modern Dickens or Wells, with some Lawrencean passion and Joycean brilliance thrown in. "One difficulty I have never solved," he later wrote, "is that one has masses of experience which one passionately wants to write about . . . and no way of using them up except by disguising them as a novel." In *A Clergyman's Daughter* (1935) he tried to convert the tramping and jail material (already used more effectively in his essays) into fiction. He came up with a thoroughly drab heroine—the pale, shy, repressed and overworked Dorothy Hare—and a depressing and episodic plot. The spinsterly Dorothy escapes from her father and the rectory, goes hop-picking, sleeps rough in Trafalgar Square and gets a job schoolteaching. Finally, she returns to the daily round, the common task, unable to believe in God, but equally unable to replace belief with an acceptable alternative. Orwell does, however, pay off one or two scores. He based the setting, Knype Hill, on Southwold, where he wrote the novel while living at home. Mrs. Creevy, Dorothy's employer in the wretched private school, the last station in her *via dolorosa*, is a grotesque version of the tight-fisted, unscrupulous proprietor of The Hawthorns in Hayes.

The style is as wobbly as the structure. It shifts from straightforward accounts of hop-picking in an Orwellian voice, and Lawrencean descriptions of Dorothy communing with nature or fending off the attentions of an older admirer, Mr. Warburton, to the "scenario" section, set among the tramps in Trafalgar Square, a feeble imitation of of the "Nighttown" chapter in Joyce's *Ulysses*. In Joyce's novel, for example, the Honourable Mrs. Mervyn Talboys excites Bloom by threatening to whip him; in Orwell's, the scandalous Reverend Tallboys recites the Lord's Prayer backwards like a naughty school-boy. No wonder Orwell said that when he read *Ulysses* and then came back to his own work, he felt "like a eunuch who has taken a course in voice pro-duction and can pass himself off fairly well as a bass or baritone, but if you listen closely you can hear the good old squeak just the same as ever."

Orwell knew that the friendship between the frigid and spinsterish Dorothy and the hearty, rakish Warburton was improbable. He ineffectually tried to make their relationship more meaningful by stating, rather than showing, "that the pious and the immoral drift naturally together." Gollancz also forced Orwell to weaken the novel with extensive alterations. He had to change "[Warburton] tried to rape Dorothy" to "[he began] making love to her, violently, outrageously, even brutally," which makes her final rejection of him less convincing.[1]

Gollancz's reader, Norman Collins, though critical of the flaws in *A Clergyman's Daughter* and of the bizarre author who deliberately subjected himself to such unpleasant experiences, was nevertheless fascinated—and thought readers would be—by their in-house madman. Collins reported that "it is perfectly clear that he had been through hell, and that he is probably still there. He would certainly be a plum for a practising psycho-analyst. There is in his work, either latent or fully revealed, almost every one of the major aberrations. Indeed the chaotic structure of the book would suggest some kind of mental instability."

In letters to his agent and friends, Orwell defensively condemned his own books. He was aware of their weaknesses and wanted to disarm his critics. Instead of trying to convince Leonard Moore to sell *Down and Out*, he said he "did not think it a good piece of work. . . . Please see that it is published pseudonymously, as I am not proud of it." He told Henry Miller that *Burmese Days* was not "any good qua novel, but the descriptions of scenery aren't bad"—then hastened to add that most readers skipped such passages.[2] He was positively ashamed of *A Clergyman's Daughter*, called it "bollox" and "tripe," and confessed to Moore: "It was a good idea, but I am afraid I have made a muck of it—however, it is as good as I can do for the present. There are bits of it that I don't dislike, but I am afraid that it is very disconnected as a whole, and rather unreal." He also admitted that this novel "was written simply as an exercise and I oughtn't to have published it, but I was desperate for money, ditto when I wrote *Keep the A.* At that time I simply hadn't a book in me, but I was half starved and had to turn out something to bring in £100 or so."

Too harsh about most of his early books, Orwell was accurate about the weaknesses of his second novel. Not nearly as good as *Down and Out* and *Burmese Days, A Clergyman's Daughter* is pretty well unreadable today. Instead of the arresting similes he wanted to use, his imagery is unwittingly funny, solemn and self-pitying. Dorothy feels that "her soul seemed to have withered until it was as forlorn as a dried-up cake of soap in a forgotten soap-dish."[3] He was ill at ease with a dreary female character and, as a non-believer, not seriously interested in spiritual crises and the strains of religious life. Lack of money and loss of respectability were always more important to him than lack of faith.

II

IN MARCH 1935, when Orwell published *A Clergyman's Daughter* and was still working at the Hampstead bookstore, he met Eileen O'Shaughnessy at a party given by her fellow-student, Rosalind Obermeyer. After walking Eileen back to the bus stop, he told Rosalind: "*that* is the kind of girl I would like to marry!" Born in 1905 in South Shields, on the North Sea coast near Newcastle, she was the daughter of a Collector of Customs. She was educated at Sunderland High School, won a scholarship to read English at St. Hugh's College, Oxford, and took her degree in 1927. After university she had a number of jobs: teacher in a girls' school near Maidenhead, social worker among prostitutes, reader to the nearly blind Dame Elizabeth Cadbury (of the chocolate manufacturing dynasty) and owner of a secretarial office in Victoria Street, London.

She also helped her older brother, Laurence, to prepare his work for publication. He was a prominent chest surgeon, with a Harley Street practice, and co-author of the standard textbook, *Pulmonary Tuberculosis.* His wife, Gwen, was also a doctor. Her daughter described Gwen as "a slight woman with a quiet presence, gentle and caring. . . . I can remember her picking up house bound patients and taking them on her rounds to brighten their otherwise dull existence. She was not only their doctor but their friend, mentor, psychologist and adviser. . . . My mother was very open minded and a socialist."

Eileen was prettier than Orwell's other girls (Heppenstall thought her predecessors positively ugly), and the only one who had gone to university. When Orwell met her she was living with her mother in Greenwich and studying for a master's degree in Educational Psychology at University College, London University. According to her close friend Lydia Jackson, a Russian-born fellow-student (who later wrote under the name of Elisaveta Fen), Eileen was careless about her appearance and dressed in good quality but shabby-looking clothes. Lydia wrote that "physically, she was very attractive, though rather gawky in the way she moved. She was tall and slender, and had what is commonly regarded as Irish colouring: dark hair, light-blue eyes and delicate white and pink complexion." When spending the night at Eileen's home, she continued, "I was struck and strangely moved by Eileen's exceptional thinness when I saw her standing in her nightdress before a looking-glass and shivering with cold. I felt sorry for her and wondered what kind of man would lust after a body as ethereal as that."[4]

Lettice Cooper, who worked with Eileen during the war at the Ministry of Food, agreed that she was attractive, and described her slightly vague and dreamy quality: "She was of medium height, a little high-shouldered. She was very pretty, and had what George called a 'cat's face,' blue eyes and near black hair. She moved slowly. She always looked as if she were drifting into a room with no particular purpose. She had small, very shapely hands and feet. I never saw her in a hurry, but her work was always finished up to time." One relative remembers her smoking while making apple pie and absent-mindedly dropping a few ashes in the dough.

Everyone liked Eileen. She was quiet, amusing and nice, had lively interests and a gay, infectious laugh and was sophisticated, fastidious and highly intelligent. Her character shines through her letters: witty, even-tempered, tolerant, self-sacrificial and courageous. In her novel *Black Bethlehem* Lettice Cooper portrayed Eileen as Ann, good-hearted and sympathetic (like Orwell's sister Marjorie): "When you speak to her she generally looks at you for a minute before answering, and then answers very slowly, as though anything you said to her needed careful consideration and was of the greatest importance. . . . Ann attracts crises. Her own friends are constantly ringing up to say that they wish to be divorced, are going to have babies or nervous breakdowns, or have quarrelled with their husbands or lovers." Cyril Connolly found her charming, "very pretty, and totally worthy of him as a wife; he was very proud of her."[5]

Eileen's friends felt Orwell couldn't look after himself properly and needed a woman to take him in hand. To Lydia, he looked rather moth-eaten,
with drab clothes and a tired, unhealthy face. Unlike Heppenstall, she was
not impressed by the cooking at Lawford Road and said his dinner was "hardly edible." But Eileen, who soon took over the cooking, was amused by the
odd things he said and did. She was the only person who ever got very close
to him and even caught the intonation of his voice.

A few weeks after they first met Eileen told Lydia that Orwell had proposed to her.

"What *did* he say?"
"He said he wasn't really eligible but . . ."
"And what did you reply?"
"Nothing. . . . I just let him talk on."
"What are you going to do about it?"
"I don't know. . . . You see, I told myself that when I was thirty, I would
accept the first man who asked me to marry him. Well . . . I shall be thir-
ty next year."

Eileen, who seemed to have had no serious suitors before Orwell and may
have guessed that Lydia was not impressed with him, was defensive and reluctant to admit that she was falling in love. She knew he had no money, was-
n't good-looking and was obviously in poor health. Orwell also disparaged
himself and insisted that he was not really eligible. Eileen pretended that she
was merely accepting her first offer. But she had a deep affinity with him, a
shared idealism, and he brought out the warm, loving, maternal side of her
character. In the fall of 1935, after he'd been seeing her for about six months,
Orwell wrote Heppenstall: "You are right about Eileen. She is the nicest person I have met for a long time. However, at present alas! I can't afford a ring,
except perhaps a Woolworth's one."

Eileen had been working on her graduate degree for the past two years,
had completed all her course and examination requirements, and had chosen her thesis subject: the use of imagination in school essays. But she still
had to do the research, interview school children and write the thesis. She
wanted to earn her degree, become a professional and get a satisfying job.
Eileen must have mentioned the advantages of earning a salary to supplement his meager income. But, traditional in many ways, Orwell did not want
his wife to support him. According to Kay Ekevall, he was generally unaware

of what a woman wanted—his own needs and interests were paramount. He wished to get married and live in the country, and scarcely considered Eileen's career.

In a surge of optimism, Orwell persuaded her to marry on the strength of a £100 advance from Gollancz for *The Road to Wigan Pier*. His books sold an average of 3,000 copies and earned an income of around £150 a year— far less than the sum he considered a comfortable living. But the other part of his plan was to move to a country village—Wallington, Hertfordshire— where they could live cheaply on the earnings from his writing, run a general store, keep animals and grow their own food. He'd prided himself on surviving as a tramp on a few shillings a week, and would now have a great opportunity to indulge his mania for frugal life.

Eileen didn't seem to care about having a Catholic wedding. So Orwell, the religious sceptic, married her at St. Mary's in Wallington, a fourteenth-century Anglican church, on June 9, 1936. In a letter sent that day to his Eton friend King-Farlow, he said: "I am writing this with one eye on the clock & the other on the Prayer Book, which I have been studying for some days past in hopes of steeling myself against the obscenities of the wedding service." Only close relatives were present at the ceremony: Ida and Avril Blair (but not Richard and Marjorie), Mrs. O'Shaughnessy, Laurence and Gwen.

After lunch in the village pub, "George's mother and sister took Eileen upstairs and told her they were very sorry for her, she was taking on something. She knew but she didn't mind." Humphrey Dakin described Eileen as "a good-looking woman of character (not warmth) and assurance. I don't recall that she ever let lack of money worry her unduly and of course she always spoilt Eric."[6] There was no honeymoon, and after the family left they repaired to their cottage. They would look after the garden, the chickens and goats (kept in a stinking shed in back), and tend their tiny shop, while Orwell continued to write his books and essays.

Eileen liked the simple life and didn't fuss about minor inconveniences. But life in Wallington—three miles east of Baldock, where the bus ran only twice a week, and thirty-five from London—proved harsh. The village had about seventy-five people, and its church, manor house, two dozen old cottages and row of ten council houses were surrounded by open fields of wheat and barley.

Orwell's self-punishing instinct for choosing the most primitive and uncomfortable places made living in a cheerful house in an attractive village near a pleasant town out of the question. Their 300-year-old, two-story cottage, called The Stores, was very small and very narrow, a little-ease built of lath and plaster, with a badly fitting front door, low, head-knocking oak beams and an ugly corrugated iron roof that made a terrific racket whenever it rained. There was no electricity; oil lamps provided dim illumination and Calor gas the inadequate heating. The outdoor privy, freezing in winter and none too comfortable at other times, was at the end of the garden.

Lettice Cooper found the cottage almost as unpleasant and hazardous as the London Blitz: "The sink would be blocked. The primus stove wouldn't work. The lavatory plug wouldn't pull. The stairs were very dark . . . and they'd put piles of books on the staircases at odd places, so there were lots of traps, and the place was rather dusty." Eileen told her that there were "battalions of mice, shoulder to shoulder on the shelves, pushing the china off." When offering the cottage rent-free to the working-class *Adelphi* writer Jack Common, in return for looking after the animals, Orwell gave him fair warning about its formidable defects: "It's bloody awful. Still, it's more or less livable. There is one room with a double bed & and one with a single. . . . When there is sudden rain in winter the kitchen tends to flood. . . . The living room fire, you may remember, smokes. . . . There is water laid on, but no hot, of course."[7] Common, though used to hardship, found it pretty rough going. Eileen thought the damp, smoky cottage made Orwell ill. Soon after they married he fell sick and she got stuck with the most disgusting jobs, including cleaning out the whole privy when the cesspool backed up. Orwell enjoyed this hair-shirt existence but Eileen, who did most of the work, suffered terribly.

Despite their Spartan life, when Eileen put a pot of jam on the table Orwell insisted she serve it properly in a dish. Eileen was greatly amused, Lydia said, "as George had warned her that they were going to live like the working class, but she discovered that there were a lot of gentilities that George set great store by." Beneath the leaking roof and near the smoking fire, "there was the family silver; the portrait of an ancestress, Lady Mary Blair; wine with dinner; vegetables and herbs brought in from the garden; old brass candlesticks; the poodle 'Marx.' " Grey-coated, medium-sized and extremely intelligent, Marx liked to sit on the windowsill and watch for the rare passers-by.

Their shop consisted of a counter, a scale, a bacon slicer and some shelves with containers for flour, sugar and other staples. Orwell—a small shopkeeper out of Wells' *The History of Mr. Polly*—learned, rather like the young George Bowling in *Coming Up for Air*, to tie a parcel, "work the bacon slicer, carve ham, put an edge on a knife, sweep the floor, dust eggs without breaking them . . . clean a window, judge a pound of cheese by eye, open a packing-case, whack a slab of butter into shape." Most of his customers, however, were children buying sweets, and his commercial profits amounted to only half a crown a week. Orwell couldn't stock the shop properly and there were too few customers in the small village. Most people shopped on market day in Baldock and went to the cinema as part of their social routine.

Orwell had found another way of abandoning middle-class respectability and refusing to bow down to the money-god, which gave his life at the cottage an idealistic glow. As he nostalgically told Jack Common: "When Eileen and I were first married, when I was writing *Wigan Pier*, we had so little money that sometimes we hardly knew where the next meal was coming from, but we found we could rub along in a remarkable manner with spuds and so forth."[8] Though nearly destitute, they eked out a marginal existence on only £5 a week. They grew some of their own food, got groceries for the shop at a discount and were, at least, precariously independent.

Orwell loved the cottage, and strained the loyalty of friends who barely survived the ordeal of a weekend visit. The extremely narrow house seemed to bulge when guests arrived, and even in June was chillingly cold. The intrepid King-Farlow had won scholarships to Cambridge and Princeton, worked as a wildcatter in the Texas oil fields and had been the third husband of the American heiress Hazel Guggenheim. He visited Wallington just after their wedding, and found the Eton hamster had turned into a scarecrow. He also noted Orwell's diffident manner: "He came out and croaked a warm welcome in that curious voice of his . . . rather bored and slightly apologetic. . . . He was burnt a deep brown and looked terribly weedy, with his loose shabby corduroys and a grey shirt. . . . We had some cold lunch and some very good pickles that Blair and his wife were very proud of."

Mark Benny, another *Adelphi* author, visited Wallington with Richard Rees and found Orwell relishing his monkish poverty. He'd been trying to light the fire, had found the chimney defective, and greeted them covered in coal smuts and surrounded by a cloud of smoke. Some missing bricks had left a hole and caused a downdraft. Rees and Benny carried in some stones to fill the hole, but Orwell shook his head regretfully. The bits of granite were fragments of old tombstones and couldn't possibly be used: "he wouldn't feel right" about the desecration. The fire never got lit, and Benny wondered whether Orwell revered tradition or was slightly mad. Rees, delighted by such fine discrimination, felt they "had witnessed an impressive demonstration of how to be painfully scrupulous while painfully uncomfortable."

Jack Common, who saw a lot of Orwell at Wallington, thought him unusually reticent and noted the Etonian presence in his height, stance, accent and "cool built-in superiority." Despite country life and outdoor work, Orwell was even then very frail, with "deep-furrowed cheeks, pitifully feeble chest" and "flat dead voice, never laughing beyond a sort of wistful half-chuckle." He was known in the village for being a well-educated "clever-Dick" with no real sense about how to run a store or care for animals. He did know enough, however, to advise Common about how to mate Muriel, another of his "Holy Goats": "Whatever happens, don't let her go to that broken-down old wreck of Mr. Nicholls's, who is simply worn out by twenty years of fucking."[9]

In a Wallington photograph, Orwell kneels down in a grassy field to feed the black-and-white-faced Muriel a mashed-up meal in a metal pot, while rather formally dressed in glen-plaid jacket and tie. Wearing baggy trousers, hands on hips, tie outside the buttoned jacket, handkerchief flowing out of his pocket, he also gazes self-consciously into the distance near the tilted gravestones in Wallington churchyard.

Orwell liked to use his hands and was passionate about gardening and carpentry. His other recreation was fishing, from coarse fish in the Thames at Henley and Eton to trout and lobster in the lochs and ocean around Jura. He had traditional taste in food, drink and domestic comforts, preferred to live in the country and disliked modern urban life. In an autobiographical entry for *Twentieth Century Authors*, he wrote: "Outside my work the thing I care most about is gardening, especially vegetable gardening. I like English cookery and English beer, French red wines, Spanish white wines, Indian tea, strong tobacco, coal fires, candle light and comfortable chairs. I dislike big towns, noise, motor cars, the radio, tinned food, central heating and 'modern' furniture. My wife's tastes fit in almost perfectly with my own."

Despite the isolation and hardship, the first six months of his marriage to Eileen was the happiest time of his life. Heppenstall, who usually took a sour view of Orwell, was surprised to find that she'd released his long-pent-up emotions. On his visit, Orwell and Eileen "behaved with conspicuous affection, fondling each other and sitting, if not on each other's knees, at any rate in the same armchair." Geoffrey Gorer observed: "He was fairly well convinced that nobody would like him, which made him prickly. . . . I would have said he was an unhappy man . . . a very lonely man—until he met Eileen."[10]

After their idyll was broken by war and illness, and first Eileen, then Orwell had to stay on alone to tend the animals, they never regained their early intimacy and happiness. Richard Rees, echoing Orwell's girlfriends, said "he was

never inconsiderate but he could be . . . sometimes unaware of other people." Steven Runciman, who remembered Orwell's solitary nature at Eton,
thought that "he must have been a pretty difficult husband. I don't think he
really needed his wife." Lydia Jackson, who adored Eileen and later had reason to dislike Orwell, believed that "he was taking her too much for granted.
Any man, I thought, ought to treasure such a wife—most attractive to look
at, highly intelligent, an amusing and witty talker, an excellent cook." Lydia
thought Eileen felt lonely and intellectually isolated because "Orwell did not
need her help with his work, nor showed any inclination to discuss it with
her. Eric was quite unlike her brother, who had come to depend on her help."
Lettice Cooper thought Orwell's self-absorption and their constant concern
about *his* weak chest made them ignore Eileen's delicate health. Doctors
feared he might infect her and "she was always being tested for T.B. but the
tests were always negative. She needed a good deal of care and George was
incapable of giving it."[11]

Like Ida and Avril, Mabel noted that Orwell was not a particularly good
catch. She remembered Eileen remarking (oddly, since Mabel had been his
mistress) that "she thought Orwell had had too much sex before marriage."
She presumably meant that after a time he'd become jaded and unresponsive. An extraordinarily bitter and revealing entry in Orwell's "Last Literary
Notebook," written in the third person and when he was dying, throws considerable light on Eileen's statement and on the sexual side of their marriage:

> There were two great facts about women which . . . you could only learn
> by getting married, & which flatly contradicted the picture of themselves
> that women had managed to impose upon the world. One was their incor-
> rigible dirtiness & untidiness. The other was their terrible, devouring sex-
> uality. . . . Within any marriage or regular love affair, he suspected that it
> was always the woman who was the sexually insistent partner. In his expe-
> rience women were quite insatiable, & never seemed fatigued by no mat-
> ter how much love-making. . . . In any marriage of more than a year or
> two's standing, intercourse was thought of as a duty, a service owed by the
> man to the woman. And he suspected that in every marriage the struggle
> was always the same—the man trying to escape from sexual intercourse,
> to do it only when he felt like it (or with other women), the woman
> demanding it more & more, & more & more consciously despising her
> husband for his lack of virility."[12]

It's strange that Orwell, willing to live in the most squalid conditions and known more for the mess of his household than its shipshape neatness, should criticize women for dirtiness and untidiness. It's also strange that the man who begged Brenda and Sally to sleep with him, and pleaded with Eleanor for another sexual encounter in the woods, should accuse women of being sexually insistent and insatiable. His observations not only reverse common assumptions about men and women's sexuality, but also fly in the face of his own experience. It's clear from this revelation, which is surely a reflection on his own marriage, and not all others, that Eileen's sexual urge was greater than his own and he felt, as he grew weaker from lung disease, that he could not meet her sexual expectations and sexual needs. When very ill himself, he retrospectively blamed Eileen for his own moral and sexual shortcomings.

Eileen loved Orwell, but she must have been disappointed in some aspects of her marriage. She lost the satisfaction of her own professional career, and had to endure harsh living conditions, boring work with the animals, tedium in the shop and isolation in the village, while he was constantly absorbed in his writing. Eileen did not have enough intellectual and emotional satisfaction. As Orwell became bored with their sexual life—though he genuinely loved her—and she became sexually more insistent to bind him to her, he began to pursue other women.

I I I

IN FEBRUARY 1935, while working in the Hampstead bookshop, Orwell began writing his third novel, *Keep the Aspidistra Flying* (1936). He finished it in January 1936, ten months after meeting Eileen, while living in Lawford Road, and poured a great deal of his immediate experience into it. Avril's tea shop in Southwold is the model for the tea shop where Gordon Comstock's long-suffering sister Julia works as a waitress. Richard Rees and the *Adelphi* appear thinly disguised as Ravelston and the *Antichrist*. Orwell based Gordon's family on his own, and Gordon toils in a grim version of Booklover's Corner. Sally Jerome's ad agency becomes the New Albion. Gordon is a satiric self-portrait, and Orwell gave him many of his own ideas and habits: his resentment of literary careerists, complaints about not having money and refusal to let his women pay their share of expenses. His sexual expeditions to the country with Eleanor Jaques—and later with Eileen—inspired Gordon's uneasy rural jaunts with Rosemary.

Like *A Clergyman's Daughter*, the pattern of the novel is circular (Gordon departs from and returns to the advertising office). His life falls into two phases: before and after his drunken spree and imprisonment—the nadir of his experience. The book is also structured by a series of ironic contrasts: his work in McKechnie and Cheeseman's bookshops; his lodging with Mrs. Wisbeach and Mrs. Meakin; his friendships with Flaxman and Ravelston; his love for his sister and his girl; and his sad sexual encounters with Rosemary in the country and the city. Gordon is perverse—he prefers the worse job and dingier room; he is closer to Ravelston and Rosemary, but finds it easier to accept help from Flaxman and Julia. The lyrical seduction scene fails for want of a contraceptive while the squalid one (as in a Victorian novel, the girl gets pregnant during her first sexual encounter) is all too successful.

Gordon Comstock, the mouse-haired hero and author of *Mice* (250 copies printed and remaindered), is a would-be poet. But while trying to compose his satiric poem *London Pleasures*, a condemnation of the money-god that blights all decent life, he's faced with his own imaginative sterility. Gordon's largely futile efforts mock Orwell's own derivative poetry: his patriotic schoolboy verse imitated Kipling; "On a Ruined Farm near the His Master's Voice Gramophone Factory" was a bleak urban version of Gray's "Elegy in a Country Churchyard"; "A happy vicar I might have been" followed the satiric political song "The Vicar of Bray" (1734); and Gordon's poem in the novel is a weaker version of Housman's disillusioned quatrains and Eliot's vision of disintegration and decay.

Gordon also lacks integrity and honor, and his envy and self-pity, his sense of social, artistic and sexual failure, tend to alienate the reader. He's selfish and unfair to Rosemary; hopelessly parasitic with Julia and Ravelston; cowardly with waiters and servants; improvident and lecherous, callous and cold-blooded, without self-respect or moral principles. Orwell seems to use the novel to exorcise the worst side of his character.

The obsessively repetitive theme ("Money, money, always money") suggests Orwell's own superior attitude about materialism and his disdain for a money-based society. But it's irritating to hear Gordon constantly whine about not having money when he could earn a good salary but refuses to do so. If T.S. Eliot could continue to write poems and maintain his artistic integrity while working first at Lloyd's Bank and then at Faber & Faber, why can't Gordon condescend to write advertising copy? We feel he's right, at the end, to get married and rejoin the agency. He'll certainly be no great loss to poetry.

With all its faults the novel is disarmingly honest, and Gordon's love affair is strangely moving. When Rosemary is about to surrender to him ("But in her heart she was still frightened" imitates D.H. Lawrence), he himself, equating poverty with unworthiness if not impotence, draws back: "And at heart he too was half reluctant. It dismayed him to find how little, at this moment, he really wanted her. The money-business still unnerved him." Despite all his bitterness, Gordon moves from a dying to a flying aspidistra (an almost indestructible houseplant) and the conclusion of the novel is meant to be affirmative. Faced with a choice between the New Albion, the fungus of decaying capitalism, or an abortion for Rosemary, he's secretly relieved to commit himself to a "decent, fully human life"—as Orwell did with Eileen.

Orwell (like Graham Greene) suppressed his second and third novels and would not allow them to be reissued. As he wrote Leonard Moore, equating *Keep the Aspidistra Flying* with his weaker novel, when he was desperate for money: "I don't think I can allow this book to be reprinted, or *A Clergyman's Daughter* either. They are both thoroughly bad books and I would much rather see them go out of print." (*Aspidistra* was not published in America until 1956.) He was thinking of these two novels when he insisted, in "Why I Write": "it is invariably where I lacked a *political* purpose that I wrote life-less books and was betrayed into purple passages, sentences without meaning, decorative adjectives and humbug generally."

Despite Orwell's criticism of the novel and its savage self-portrait, the reviewers were surprisingly sympathetic and respectful. What we now see as witty satire, they read as somber realism. Richard Rees mentioned the influence of Dickens, Butler, Joyce and Lawrence, enthusiastically praised its "consistent seriousness and real vigour," and thought Orwell was "fundamentally honest" about Gordon's flawed character. The novelist William Plomer remarked that Orwell "spares us none of the horrors of sordid loneliness and a hypertrophied inferiority complex." Cyril Connolly, whom Orwell called "almost the only novel-reviewer in England who does not make me sick," loyally called the self-pitying novel "a completely harrowing and stark account of poverty, and poverty as a squalid and all-pervading influence. . . . It is written in clear and violent language, at times making the reader feel he is sitting in a dentist's chair with the drill whirring."[13]

The private response was even more gratifying. Connolly advised Orwell that the novel "needed more colour to relieve the total gloom of the hero's circumstances & self-hatred—there must be jam if people are to swallow the pill. . . . It has left a deep impression on me." But Orwell was uncompromising: his readers (however few) had to swallow the bitter pill without the jam. On May 18, 1936, Anthony Powell praised *Keep the Aspidistra Flying*, which he liked better than *Burmese Days* and *Down and Out*, "altho' the latter stands alone as a document," and referred to the "extraordinary imbecility of most of the reviews I have seen." Orwell agreed that "the reviewers are awful, so much so that in a general way I prefer the ones who lose their temper & call me names to the silly asses who mean so well & never bother to discover what you are writing about." Geoffrey Gorer wrote to Orwell about this novel, as he had about *Burmese Days*. Referring to the biblical symbol of the money-god, Gorer said that "since Swift I do not think any book has been so certain to make 99% of its readers uncomfortably guilty. You have committed the supreme blasphemy—you have mocked Our Lord the golden calf."

As Orwell's books began to make his name known in literary and Socialist circles he received a few invitations to give public lectures at the Adelphi Summer School and local literary societies. In October 1935 he spoke on "Confessions of a Down and Out" in South Woodford, north of London, and was astonished to find a huge crowd of four or five hundred people. Many of them were probably unemployed and, with nothing else to do, were glad to have a warm refuge and hear a free talk. A local newspaper reported that Orwell told the responsive audience that the down and outs "were human beings like the rest of the community, driven by force of circumstances to lead this wretched life."[14]

IV

IN JANUARY 1936, while courting Eileen and after completing *Keep the Aspidistra Flying*, Orwell gave up his job in the Hampstead bookshop. He spent the next two months gathering material for his report on working-class conditions in the north of England, *The Road to Wigan Pier*. The journey to Wigan was a continuation of his tramping expeditions. Once again, he wore old clothes to try to fit into the squalid scene, walked part of the way north, lived among the poor, sought out the worst possible places, endured the most excruciating experiences and retreated to a bourgeois refuge between forays.

He took the train to Coventry on January 31, and for the next four days continued by foot and bus to Birmingham, Wolverhampton and Manchester, where he spent five days. He was in Wigan for the rest of February and rented a room above a revolting tripe shop, owned by a family immortalized in the book as the gloriously squalid Brookers. Their filth became too much even for Orwell. The shop window was decorated with dead bluebottles, and the inside of the house swarmed with black beetles. One morning he saw a full chamber pot beneath the breakfast table. Orwell did not exaggerate—a Wigan man commented that it was indeed "a right filthy hole, a specially filthy hole," and another visitor remembered that the table had "a dozen layers of the local evening newspaper, sodden with tea and greasy with tripe, serving as a tablecloth."

In the 1930s coal "was by far the single largest industry, the only one employing more than a million workers. It had always been the symbol of the class struggle."[15] Wigan Pier, in fact, marked the end of the wagon way or railway line that stretched from the coal mines to the canal, where the coal was tipped into barges. Not at all a seaside spa with a pleasure pier, Wigan, a hideous industrial town, became the butt of turn-of-the-century music-hall jokes. In the 1920s the pits closed down, and the pier was dismantled and sold for scrap. Orwell's road to Wigan Pier is the road to nowhere: it represents a dead end, an economic disaster. The canal that runs by the old pier is, even today, sluggish, muddy and dirty. He went down his first coal mine in Wigan, which completely exhausted him, and descended twice more, at Wentworth and Grimethorpe.

This arduous trip took its toll, and by the time he'd reached Liverpool at the end of February—after two weeks of tripe shop lodgings and three descents into the mines—his frail health broke down. May Deiner, to whom he had an introduction through the *Adelphi* and the Independent Labour Party, vividly recalled:

> Very early morning . . . a horrible morning in February, all frosty and fog, he stood at the door, and he was a strange figure. No overcoat, no hat, no bag and a threadbare coat. Standing there and shivering, he was actually shivering from head to foot. Well, he collapsed, well not quite collapsed, but as near as made no matter. So my husband and I we got him to bed as quickly as we could, and he was really very ill. But he wouldn't have a doctor. So we did the best we could in those circumstances. We gave him hot lemon. Anyway, he got better later on. You see, he was really ill.

While nursing Orwell, she found him very withdrawn, but sensitive and appealing.

After recovering in Liverpool, he moved on to Sheffield and Leeds (where he stayed with the Dakins), and spent two more weeks in Barnsley. Passed on from one useful working-class contact to the next, he visited homes and factories and went to public meetings. In Barnsley he saw Oswald Mosley harangue a crowd and got a horrifying look at British Fascism.

In 1937 W.H. Auden (whom Orwell in *Wigan Pier* called "a sort of gutless Kipling") wrote that the grim industrial landscapes of the north were more beautiful to him than the highest peak in England. The dismal view from Birmingham to Wolverhampton was stamped on his heart, and he found that slagheaps and infernal machinery were, in fact, his ideal scenery. Auden's witty poetic paradox deliberately ignored the human cost of mining and the devastating effects of industrial pollution on the air and natural landscape. As Orwell's train pulled out of Wigan he saw nothing but "slag-heaps, belching chimneys, blast-furnaces, canals and gasometers" that surround the urban slums and deluge them with sulfurous smoke. Sheffield, the ugliest town in Europe, "seemed a world from which vegetation had been banished; nothing existed except smoke, shale, ice, mud, ashes and foul water." His description of the helpless and hopeless woman kneeling "in the bitter cold, on the slimy stones of a slum backyard, poking a stick up a foul drain-pipe" and of the "worn skull-like face" of another woman, who had "a look of intolerable misery and degradation," reveals the human effects of living in such an environment.[16] Orwell returned to London at the end of March. He wrote Connolly that he would have liked to stay in the north for six months or a year, but didn't want to leave Eileen for such a long time.

Orwell had read about these northern industrial towns in books on the condition-of-England question. A century earlier, in his essay "Chartism" (1839), Carlyle had condemned middle-class ignorance of working conditions in industrial areas and posed some essential questions: "Why are the Working Classes discontented: what is their condition, economical, moral, in their houses and their hearts?" "Chartism" was followed by *The Condition of the Working Class in England in 1844* (1845) by Friedrich Engels, who ran his father's factory in Manchester, by Benjamin Disraeli's *Sybil, or The Two Nations* (1845), and by Charles Dickens' *Hard Times* (1854), with its horrifying description of Coketown. All these works argued that the working class in England was cruelly exploited, and Orwell's book continued their tradition of social protest.

Orwell explains that miners have to buy their own tools and are not paid for their arduous underground traveling time from the pit head to the coal face. He describes the earthiness and physical power of "the line of bowed, kneeling figures, sooty black all over, driving their huge shovels under the coal with stupendous force and speed." His geological evocation of the earth, Swiftian ability to isolate the significant detail of grazing cows and description of a mountain supported only by a prop, make his readers see mining— as well as the weight of class oppression—in a strikingly original way: "you have a tolerable-sized mountain on top of you; hundreds of yards of solid rock, bones of extinct beasts, subsoil, flints, roots of growing things, green grass and cows grazing on it—all this suspended over your head and held back only by wooden props as thick as the calf of your leg."[17]

The Road to Wigan Pier (1937), like *Down and Out*, is divided into two loosely connected parts. The first section (bolstered by statistics) is a personal account of the ghastly social and economic conditions of industrial workers during the Depression. The second and far more interesting autobiographical section—for Orwell was always at his best when writing directly about himself—describes how he took the road from Mandalay to Wigan, discusses his background, family, education, his unhappiness in Burma and reasons for tramping, and analyzes the development of his class attitudes and political beliefs. It then offers a lively critique of Socialism (which aroused great hostility and made him many enemies on the Left) as well as some practical recommendations for improving the conditions of the workers.

In his chapters on Socialism Orwell nostalgically idealizes the manners, temperament, stoicism and democracy of the working class, and glorifies the "warm, decent, deeply human atmosphere" of their homes—if (as in his own childhood) the father is steadily employed:

> Especially on winter evenings after tea, when the fire glows in the open range and dances mirrored in the steel fender, when Father, in shirt-sleeves, sits in the rocking-chair on one side of the fire reading the racing finals, and Mother sits on the other with her sewing, and the children are happy with their pennorth of mint humbugs, and the dog lolls roasting himself on the rag mat.

This picture of happy domesticity, difficult to achieve during the Depression, is implicitly contrasted to the grimy photographs, particularly one called "Overcrowding," in the Left Book Club Edition of the book.

Orwell's aim is to unite the extremes of the Labour Party and bring the highbrow theoreticians into closer contact with the workers, yet he deliberately sets out to provoke his readers. In his attack on intellectual Socialists he says the middle class believes that "the *lower classes smell*" (this statement was often distorted by hostile readers to mean that *Orwell* thought the lower classes smell). He slays a few sacred cows, revered by the Left, by calling the Socialist propagandists—William Morris, Bernard Shaw, Henri Barbusse, Upton Sinclair and Waldo Frank—"dull, empty windbags," and by criticizing Beatrice Webb, whose investigative methods were the opposite of his own, as a "high-minded Socialist slum-visitor."

Orwell could not resist lashing out, in a hilariously exaggerated broadside, against his particular *bêtes noires*—the creepy eunuchs in "pansy-left circles" who followed the crankish crusader, Edward Carpenter (1844–1929). Social reformer, pioneer of return to rural simplicity, homosexual propagandist and author of works like *The Intermediate Sex* (1908), Carpenter had a significant influence on both E.M. Forster and D.H. Lawrence. Orwell summons up the instantly recognizable image of the ludicrous intellectual Socialist, with his frizzy hair and Marxist quotations, whom he'd seen in Aunt Nellie's house in Paris, in the Westropes' circle in Hampstead and in the *Adelphi* summer schools. In one of his most notorious passages, he pours vitriol on "all that dreary tribe of high-minded women and sandal-wearers and bearded fruit-juice drinkers who come flocking towards the smell of 'progress' like blue-bottles to a dead cat. . . . If only the sandals and the pistachio-coloured shirts could be put in a pile and burnt, and every vegetarian, teetotaller and creeping Jesus sent home to Welwyn Garden City to do his yoga exercises quietly!"[18] Was the Socialist cause really harmed by eating vegetables? Orwell believed that it was. Instead of working to improve society, the food-crank, obsessed with adding a few miserable years to his life, cut himself off from ordinary humanity. Early on Orwell identified, and despised, what we'd call the "me" generation.

In the crucial autobiographical passage in *Wigan Pier*, Orwell explains why he went down and out, and why, in the north, he lived above the tripe shop instead of in decent lodgings, traveled in winter without an overcoat or hat, and collapsed on a stranger's doorstep:

> I wanted to submerge myself, to get right down among the oppressed, to be one of them and on their side against their tyrants. . . . I could go among these people, see what their lives were like and feel myself temporarily part of their world. Once I had been among them and accepted by them, I

should have touched bottom, and—this is what I felt: I was aware even then that it was irrational—part of my guilt would drop from me.

These are Orwell's most characteristic impulses: his desire to experience conditions from the inside instead of from a purely theoretical standpoint, to extinguish the sense of social class, to fight on the side of the oppressed and agonize over their sufferings. He was thrilled by a *sortie* to the lower depths, and felt the anxiety, relief and guilt-annihilating euphoria of going to the dogs and knowing he could bear it.

Charles Dickens and T.E. Lawrence throw some light on Orwell's motives for wanting to hit bottom. In *Little Dorrit* (1857) Doctor Haggage, imprisoned in the Marshalsea, tries to relieve William Dorrit's anxiety by explaining: "Elsewhere, people are restless, worried, hurried about, anxious respecting one thing, anxious respecting another. Nothing of the kind here, sir. We have done all that—we know the worst of it; we have got to the bottom, we can't fall, and what have we found? Peace." And in *Seven Pillars of Wisdom* Lawrence confesses: "I liked the things underneath me and took my pleasures and adventures downwards. There seemed a certainty in degradation, a final safety. Man could rise to any height, but there was an animal level beneath which he could not fall. It was a satisfaction on which to rest." Like Lawrence, Orwell thought these penitential experiences conveyed a kind of literary virtue, that authentic writing was not possible without them.

This willful suffering and expiation, this desire to cure the ills of the world, gave him a kind of religious mission. St. John of the Cross, the sixteenth-century Spanish mystic, wrote of the path to spiritual truth in terms that seem to define Orwell's arduous approach to life:

> Strive always to prefer, not that which is easiest, but that which is
>   most difficult;
> Not that which is most delectable, but that which is most
>   unpleasing;
> Not that which gives most pleasure, but rather that which gives
>   the least;
> Not that which is restful, but that which is wearisome.[19]

V.S. Pritchett caught this aspect of Orwell when he called him "a kind of saint."

Victor Gollancz gamely published the book on March 8, 1937, in an edition of 2,150 copies. But he added a Foreword to the Left Book Club Edition that drew the venom from Orwell's sting, dissociated Socialism from sodomy and soothed the outraged feelings of the members of the Club. (Orwell was never forgiven in Wigan and Sheffield.) Gollancz praised Orwell's "burning indignation against poverty and oppression," but was appalled when he described Socialists as "a stupid, offensive and insincere lot." Gollancz blindly refused to recognize that Stalin used brutal methods to achieve industrialization, and condemned his own author for committing "the curious indiscretion of referring to Russian commissars as 'half-gramophones, half-gangsters.' "

The Left Book Club Edition, with Gollancz's strictures, sold more than 44,000 copies (about twenty times more than the trade edition) and for the first time made Orwell's name widely known. As proud of this book as he was ashamed of his previous ones, he had copies sent to his parents, Aunt Nellie, Laurence O'Shaughnessy and his closest friends: Mabel Fierz, Richard Rees, Dennis Collings, Geoffrey Gorer—and his admirer in Paris, Henry Miller.

The reviews tended to divide along party lines. Harold Laski, on the editorial board of the Left Book Club, noted the influence of *Hard Times* and Émile Zola's coal-mining novel *Germinal* (1885), and dismissed Orwell's "propaganda" as "an emotional plea for Socialism addressed to comfortable people." But to Douglas Goldring, "this brilliant, disturbing book" explained why the Socialist party "has been steadily losing ground during the past ten years." In 1939 Geoffrey Gorer sent Edith Sitwell a copy of the book. She became an unexpected admirer and particularly praised Orwell's description of the tripe shop: "The horror of the beginning is unsurpassable. He seems to be doing for the modern world what Engels did for the world of 1840–50. But with this difference. That Orwell is a born writer."

In 1937 the historian Arthur Bryant attacked *The Road to Wigan Pier* from a conservative point of view in his Preface to the autobiography of a coal miner, G.A.W. Tomlinson. Bryant summarized the book in a condescending tone, and mocked Orwell's call for revolutionary change: "It was written by a young literary man of refined tastes who at some apparent inconvenience to himself had 'roughed it' for a few weeks at Wigan and Sheffield. The impression left by the first part of this book is that Wigan and Sheffield are Hell: the corollary, worked out with great skill in the second part, that every decent-hearted man and woman, sooner than allow such conditions to endure a day longer, should at once enroll in the ranks of those who are seeking change by revolutionary methods." Bryant went on to foresee the limits of Orwell's view: "'The weakness of the argument lies in the fact that revolutionary change, whatever it may hope to achieve, involves not only a bloodbath . . . but the loss of individual freedom of choice and the end of democratic government: the experience of Russia and Spain proves this."[20] This would become, in Orwell's later work, the anti-Stalinist theme of the "revolution betrayed." *Wigan Pier* was the high point of Orwell's belief in a Socialist revolution.

When the first American edition of *The Road to Wigan Pier* came out in 1958, two substantial reviews placed the book in its historical perspective. Philip Toynbee said that it "reads like a report brought back by some humane anthropologist who has just returned from studying the conditions of an oppressed tribe in Borneo," and called Orwell the best reporter of his generation. Toynbee also criticized his literary persona, and argued that he saw "himself too consciously as the tough and honest man who has really found out the truth instead of simply dealing in high-minded abstractions." In a valuable review in the *New Yorker* Dwight Macdonald, who'd published Orwell's wartime essays in his journal *Politics*, compared him to Engels, Henry Mayhew, Jack London and Leon Trotsky, and called his book "the best sociological reporting I know." He particularly praised the exuberant "rhetoric of abuse" that "combines indignation with specificity" as well as his "emotional identification with the people he lives among." The posthumous reviews recognized that Orwell was a better reporter than novelist, and shifted the emphasis from the current political issues to the committed man, from the Socialist squabbles of the Thirties to Orwell's idealism and vivid self-portrayal.

Richard Rees wrote that when Orwell returned—transformed—from Wigan and began to write his book "It was almost as if there'd been a kind of fire smouldering in him all his life which suddenly broke into flame, at that time." Orwell became, as he said of his hero Dickens, "a man who is always fighting against something, but who fights in the open and is not frightened . . . who is *generously angry.*"[21] Between 1935 and 1937 Orwell stirred up controversy and reached a wide audience. He found an effective way to join the personal and the political, discovered his distinctive voice, and created an original and influential book of reportage. He carried the mode of *Down and Out*—suffering through experience—to a much higher level, and made a tremendous leap from minor novelist to major social critic.

8

Fighting for Spain,
1937

I

ON JULY 19, 1936—while Orwell was writing *The Road to Wigan Pier* in Wallington—the Spanish Fascists, under General Francisco Franco, rose up against the democratically elected Republican government in a Rightist coup. This revolt provoked the civil war that became an ideological battleground for all of Europe and a prelude to World War II. The military rising did not succeed in taking over the entire country, and the Republicans, backed by an armed working class, maintained control of two-thirds of Spain, including Madrid, Bilbao, Barcelona and Valencia. Battle lines were drawn between the Republicans (or Loyalists), chiefly made up of peasants and workers and led by the Communists, and the Fascists (or Nationalists), supported by the army, the landowners and the Catholic Church and led by Franco.

As the war progressed, Orwell later wrote, Hitler's Germany and Mussolini's Italy "intervened in order to crush Spanish democracy, to seize a strategic keypoint for the coming war, and, incidentally, to try out their bombing planes on helpless populations. The Russians doled out a small quantity of weapons and extorted the maximum political control in return. The British and French simply looked the other way while their enemies triumphed and their friends were destroyed." It soon became clear that the Republicans—though helped by Russian technicians and advisers, and by volunteers in the International Brigades—could not win the war unless England, France and America abandoned their policy of neutrality, and supported the Left as actively as Germany and Italy supported the Right. Though the Republicans were outnumbered and outgunned, they fought the Fascist armies for three years.

Orwell soon became one of the thousands of international volunteers who risked their lives to help the Spanish Republicans. The novelist Alan Judd described him as "a brave soldier, an effective if reluctant colonial policeman, emotionally reserved but honest, a radical critic, a rider of motorbikes, and a scorner of illness and overcoats. In short, he was manly." He was also newly married, living happily if uncomfortably in the country and writing the first of his books to reach a wide audience. His health was poor and he passionately wanted to have children. But he was willing to sacrifice everything for a foreign cause in a distant land. If he was killed he'd have nothing to leave Eileen. When he left for Barcelona after finishing his book in late December, his brother-in-law, Laurence O'Shaughnessy, remarked that Orwell had "a warrior's cast of mind."[1]

Orwell tried to reassure his wife, family and friends by telling them that he was going to Spain as an observer and journalist, but he always intended to fight. Philip Mairet, his editor at the *New English Weekly*, remembered him forcefully saying: "This fascism, somebody's got to stop it." He joined the militia right after he arrived in Barcelona, as if to cancel out his policeman's job and work off some of the guilt he'd acquired in Burma.

In contrast to Connolly, Auden and Spender, who cruised through Spain for a few weeks before returning safely home, Orwell planned to stay for the duration. Adept at languages, he prepared for the trip by starting to learn Spanish before he left England. Recommending himself as a translator as early as January 1932 and exaggerating his knowledge of Spanish, he told Leonard Moore: "I know French thoroughly & Spanish pretty well." In fact, according to an English doctor who knew him in Spain, "Orwell's knowledge of Spanish was primitive—certainly his spoken Spanish was the bare minimum for use with a café waiter."[2] Still, he also learned some Catalan and managed to scrape along with what he knew.

He was committed to fight in Spain, but getting there was difficult. He was rejected as politically unreliable by Harry Pollitt, Secretary of the British Communist Party, who controlled English volunteers for the International Brigades. Pollitt probably had advance warning from Victor Gollancz about the attacks on the Left in *The Road to Wigan Pier*. Orwell then turned to the

Independent Labour Party, though he was not affiliated with them. The ILP had been founded in 1873 by Keir Hardie, a Scottish labor leader and M.P., after he'd severed connection with the Liberals. For the next forty years it maintained a volatile alliance with the Labour Party, but refused to ally itself with the Communists or join the Comintern. Bernard Crick described the ILP of the mid-1930s as "Left-wing, egalitarian, a strange English mixture of secularised evangelism and non-Communist Marxism." In other words, after the Great War it represented the extreme Left wing of the Labour Party. By 1935 it had drifted, wrote the historian of the Party, "to a position of almost total isolation in Britain." Its weekly paper, the *New Leader*, had denounced the 1936 Russian Purge Trials "as a fraud and was promptly condemned by the Communist Party as a fascist journal." The ILP gave Orwell the necessary credentials as well as an introduction to the POUM—the Unified Marxist Workers' Party—its closest ally in Spain. In a nice symbolic gesture, he pawned his portion of the Blair family silver to equip himself for war. When Ida came to tea, Eileen had to say they'd sent it out to be engraved.

Orwell had been corresponding with the American expatriate Henry Miller, whose early novels he'd praised, and stopped to see him in Paris on his way south. In "Inside the Whale" (1940), his essay on Miller, Orwell recorded the reaction of the apolitical, insular, hedonistic Miller to his own ideological commitment: "he felt no interest in the Spanish war whatever. He merely told me in forcible terms that to go to Spain at that moment was the act of an idiot. He could understand anyone going there from purely self-ish motives, out of curiosity, for instance, but to mix oneself up in such things *from a sense of obligation* was sheer stupidity." Miller later recalled: "Though he was a wonderful chap in his way, Orwell, in the end I thought him stupid. He was like so many English people, an idealist, and, it seemed to me, a fool-ish idealist." Nevertheless, Miller wished him well and gave him a leather jacket, which was useful at the front. Orwell was shocked and, in a strange way, impressed by Miller's completely selfish attitude, and their meeting helped him define his own aims as a writer. He felt that his books, in con-trast to Miller's, had to be politically engaged. His own beliefs were confirmed as the "Red" train from the Gare d'Austerlitz, packed with foreign volunteers, crawled through southern France. Though there couldn't have been many laborers toiling in the hard soil at Christmas-time, "every peasant working in the fields turned round, stood solemnly upright and gave the anti-Fascist salute. They were like a guard of honour, greeting the train mile after mile."[3]

The Spanish border was open and Orwell crossed without trouble. As soon as he arrived in Barcelona he reported to the POUM headquarters. Noted for its revolutionary zeal and romantic utopianism, the POUM "was a combination of anti-Stalinist Communist dissidents and Trotskyists who united in 1935 in an effort to create a bolshevist vanguard party." It had 40,000 members, but had failed to attract most of the urban unions, whose support was essential. Their aim was first to complete the revolution, then win the war. According to historians, "the party, which had been in existence for only ten months at the start of the war, had not had time to develop. Lacking a real base except in Catalonia [in northeast Spain], its political influence on a national scale" was limited. "Dubbed Trotskyist by its [Stalinist] opponents, disowned and vigorously criticized by Leon Trotsky and his friends, the POUM . . . had barely more than 3,000 militants in July 1936."

The Communists, who criticized the POUM and were then the largest and most popular force on the Left, wanted to win the war first and defeat Fascism *before*—instead of after—completing the revolution. They feared that the revolution, with its expropriation of property, would antagonize the middle classes, the foreign ministers, and the British and French governments. "The POUM 'line,' " wrote the historian Raymond Carr, "if implemented—and it is hard to see how such a small party could have hoped to implement anything—would have brought [military] disaster." In fact, according to one English volunteer, "military sense was not even present inside the POUM."[4]

When Orwell joined the POUM militia (not the regular army), he had very little idea of what it stood for. Like other volunteers, he assumed their common goal was to defeat Franco, and was completely unaware of the violent hostility of the splintered factions on the Spanish Left. Though attracted to the hopeless individuality of the undisciplined and ill-armed troops, he accidentally joined what soon became a defeated faction of the defeated side. As a result he had firsthand experience of the Communists' murderous persecution of their political enemies. As he later wrote of his ironic situation: "It was chance that I was serving in the POUM militia and not another, and I largely disagreed with the POUM 'line' and told its leaders so freely, but when they were afterwards accused of pro-Fascist activities I defended them as best I could." Conversely, the Party was as ignorant of Orwell as he was of it. According to the POUM historian Victor Alba, "the leaders of the POUM were not aware of Orwell as a special 'case.' He was just another English volunteer. I believe this was just the reason he was able to see, understand and explain so much about the war."[5]

II

JUST AS Orwell had deliberately kept out of expatriate circles in Paris, so he also remained an outsider in Spain. He did not attend literary conferences; he did not meet other writers like Hemingway and Martha Gellhorn, Pablo Neruda and Rafael Alberti, who gathered at the Hotel Florida on the Gran Vía in Madrid; he did not join the more glamorous units, like Malraux's Escadre España or the International Brigades, which attracted most foreign fighters. But Orwell experienced the same exhilaration as Cyril Connolly, who'd spent a few weeks in Barcelona and wrote: "The pervading sense of freedom, of intelligence, justice, and companionship, the enormous upthrust in backward and penniless people of the desire for liberty and education, are things that have to be seen to be understood."

In Barcelona, as the trade unions took control, the long-dreamed-of Socialist revolution seemed to have arrived. The dining rooms of luxury hotels were turned into canteens for the militia. Bourgeois ties and hats, tipping in bars and restaurants, in barber shops and shoeshine stands, along with the formal third-person mode of address, suddenly disappeared. Nightclubs and brothels were shut down. Willy Brandt, the future chancellor of West Germany, found the hardship and austerity of the city at war balanced by a bracing egalitarianism: "You soon got used to having hardly anything to eat, and taking the edge off your hunger with red wine or at best with olives; you quickly found that it was not good manners to give tips or summon waiters by clapping your hands." Jason Gurney, an English volunteer in the International Brigades, was also deeply moved by the pervasive idealism: "what was exciting was the glorious feeling of optimism; the conviction that anything that was not right with society would assuredly be put right in the new world of universal equality and freedom which lay ahead." Despite the shocking desecration of the churches, the persecution and murder of priests and nuns, Orwell was intoxicated by the atmosphere of Barcelona. He told Connolly that Spain was the great turning point of his life: "I have seen wonderful things & at last really believe in Socialism, which I never did before."[6] For the rest of his life he cherished this vision of social equality and human dignity.

The ILP representative in Barcelona and Orwell's liaison with the POUM was John McNair. Born in Newcastle, a dedicated Socialist from a working-class background, about fifteen years older than Orwell, he'd been in business in France for many years and spoke both French and Spanish. Both

McNair and Jennie Lee, an M.P. from Scotland, remembered Orwell saying he'd come to Spain to join the militia. He told them he was ready to drive a car or do anything else, had been a policeman and knew how to handle a rifle. Making the most of his shop in Wallington, he disguised himself on the company roll as "Eric Blair: grocer." But in February 1937 the POUM's English-language newspaper, the *Spanish Revolution*, quoted Orwell's statement: "I have decided that I can be of most use to the workers as a fighter at the front." A few months later, this bit of newspaper publicity—and photographs of Orwell in the POUM publications—made him a marked man.

Just as the French peasants had saluted the train, so enthusiastic crowds greeted the Republican volunteers in Barcelona. But most of the young men had no military experience. After a few hours of elementary training, they formed into units and were quickly sent into battle against experienced Fascist troops. In a retrospective essay that recalled the romance of defeat, Orwell described the physical hardships that united the comrades-in-arms of the Lenin Division: "the huge cavalry barracks in Barcelona with its draughty stables and cobbled yards, the icy cold of the pump where one washed, the filthy meals made tolerable by pannikans of wine, the trousered militiawomen chopping firewood, and the roll-call in the early mornings." The Spaniards were at first so unused to foreigners that they thought the English drilling in the Lenin Barracks were Russians. Three thousand British volunteers fought in the Spanish war; half were seriously wounded and 300 were killed.

Accustomed to a certain amount of deference as an Etonian and policeman, equipped with rudimentary Spanish, and at thirty-three older by a decade than most volunteers, Orwell naturally assumed command. McNair, impressed by Orwell's experience and skill, noted that

> he was an immediate success at the barracks. He spoke fair Castilian and sufficient French to understood a good deal of Catalan. . . . In the barrack square [he was] training about fifty young recruits. He had them running and marching. Teaching them rifle and bayonet drill without weapons, simply using sticks. . . . George ran and marched with the best of them. When they said they were tired (discipline was very slack until he tightened it up), he allowed them five minutes rest and no smoking. This staggered them, but George was adamant.

One of the English said: "We did the British military training of advancing, throwing yourself down and firing, and running forward and throwing your-

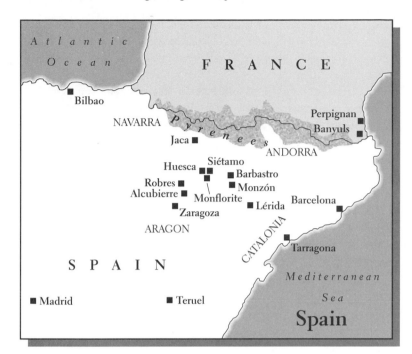

self down again. This highly amused the Spanish. They said, 'You don't lay down and fire, you stand up and fire.' " The divisional commander, observing Orwell train the Spanish boys, optimistically declared: "If we had a hundred men like him we would win the war."[7]

In early 1937, after only seven days in Barcelona, Orwell was sent to Alcubierre, on the Aragón front in northeast Spain. Given the rank of corporal, he commanded twelve men. After three fairly quiet weeks, he joined the English ILP group—which had arrived after him and had just finished training in Barcelona—at Monte Oscuro, overlooking Zaragoza. Ilya Ehrenburg, friend of Stalin and Soviet war correspondent for *Izvestiya*, visited the front at about the same time, and described the scenery and climate of the harsh, impoverished region:

> The stony red desert of Aragón stretched before one's eyes. Small groups of dusty olive trees dotted the landscape. In summer the heat was intolerable; in winter icy winds blew. Occasionally a peasant would come riding along the empty twisting road on a diminutive donkey. Hungry goats nuzzled among the stones in search of a blade of grass sheltered from the blaz-

ing sun. The villages clung to the bare mountain-slopes; the houses were of the same colour as the hills and their blind walls turned towards the road made them look as though they had been abandoned.

The revolution had spread, in a promising way, to the agrarian collectives that helped supply the militia in Aragón. Raymond Carr wrote that "money was 'abolished,' retail trade suppressed, coffee, alcohol and prostitution frowned on; at long last the heavenly city of anarchism was a reality." But military success "hinged on two factors: first, and most important, the degree and effectiveness of outside support in arms, and, to a lesser extent, in trained personnel; secondly, the relative rapidity with which the two sides trained an efficient combat force. In both respects the Nationalists, by 1937, had come out on top."

The POUM militia was anarchistically inefficient and inadequately equipped with archaic and sometimes disastrous rifles and ammunition. Most of the men had long German Mausers, made in 1890, which had been obsolete at the start of the Great War. Hugh Thomas wrote that on the Aragón front "uniforms were still non-existent, though everyone wore corduroy knee breeches and a zipper jacket. Training continued to be rudimentary since all the rifles were at the front; and even these continued, except for parts of the Madrid front, to be old and unreliable, while artillery was everywhere scarce. Grenades were still as liable to explode in the hands of the thrower as upon the enemy. In many places there were no maps, range-finders, periscopes, field-glasses, or cleaning materials."[8] Orwell recorded the tedium, not the excitement, of life at the front, "the boredom and animal hunger of trench life, the squalid intrigues over scraps of food, the mean, nagging quarrels which people exhausted by lack of sleep indulge in." Like all soldiers, he treasured the rare moments of relative peace and comfort: "one of those nights when you had good straw to sleep on, dry feet, several hours rest ahead of you, and the sound of distant gunfire, which acts as a soporific provided it *is* distant."

In this phase of the war, despite frequent efforts to press forward, the shortage of ammunition caused a stalemate at the front. Both sides held strong positions on the mountain ridges and, without artillery or bombers, the fighting was limited to occasional raids and clashes between patrols. Bob Edwards (later on, a Labour M.P.) sent propagandistic dispatches back to the *New Leader*, the ILP paper in London. To attract more volunteers and inspire support of the Republican cause, Edwards adopted an unrealistically heroic tone: "We took part in a number of offensives against strongly-held Franco positions, we spent many hours together on patrol inside the Fascist lines, we made a raid or two on loosely-held outlying Fascist farms and we talk incessantly of the political situation in Spain." But Harry Milton, the only American fighting with the British, was more grimly accurate: "Our sector of the front was as quiet as a graveyard. We were miserably armed. The majority of the regiment was a bunch of kids. They were shooting at each other accidentally. And we had only one real go at the enemy. It was the first time we went into action. It was a hellish business: the whole thing was botched up. I never expected to survive the Spanish experience."[9]

Orwell himself implied that the military commanders hadn't learned much from the last major conflict, and described the fighting as "a bad copy of 1914–18, a positional war of trenches, artillery, raids, snipers, mud, barbed wire, lice and stagnation." Unnerved by the rats in the trenches, Orwell also suffered horribly from the bitter cold in the Spanish mountains and from continuous attacks of bronchitis. He shaved regularly—sometimes using wine, more plentiful than water. Edwards recalled his eccentric appearance: "He came striding towards me—all six foot three of him—dressed in a grotesque mixture of clothing—corduroy riding breeches, khaki puttees and huge boots caked with mud, a yellow pigskin jerkin, a chocolate-coloured balaclava helmet with a knitted khaki scarf of immeasurable length wrapped round and round his neck and face up to his ears, an old-fashioned German rifle over his shoulder and two hand-grenades hanging from his belt."

To pass the time on sentry duty during the freezing nights, Orwell would recite over and over to himself Gerard Manley Hopkins' "Felix Randal," an elegy for a "big-boned and hardy-handsome" blacksmith, which he called "the best short poem in the English language." The poem poignantly concludes:

> This seeing the sick endears them to us, us too it endears.
> My tongue had taught thee comfort, touch had quenched thy tears,
> Thy tears that touched my heart, child, Felix, poor Felix Randal;
>
> How far from then forethought of, all thy more boisterous years,
> When thou at the random grim forge, powerful amidst peers,
> Didst fettle for the great grey drayhorse, his bright and battering sandal!

Why, of all poems, did "Felix Randal" comfort Orwell in wartime? In a 1944 review of a book on Hopkins, he wrote: "Art arises out of suffering, and it is clear that Hopkins was unhappy, and not merely because he was of poor health, neglected as a poet and condemned to unsympathetic work in dreary places." In a dreary place himself, Orwell identified with the Jesuit poet.

Inspired, perhaps, by his nocturnal musings on this poem, Orwell also tried to inspire his comrades. Stafford Cottman, an English teenager, saw him as " 'different from the rest of us,' in part because he wrote each day after breakfast, in part because of his Eton accent. But Cottman admitted that he 'was a person capable of influencing' his comrades, that he possessed the 'common touch' "—which he'd shown with tramps and miners. "He was a natural leader," said Cottman. "You had respect for him. He knew what he was talking about." Bob Edwards added that "he was absolutely fearless."[10]

Edwards' report in the *New Leader* of April 30, 1937, reads like an adventure story in the boys' weeklies that fascinated Orwell: " 'Charge,' shouted Blair. . . . In front of the parapet was Eric Blair's tall figure, coolly strolling forward through the storm of fire. He leapt at the parapet, then stumbled. Hell, had they got him? No, he was over." (Whew!) Benjamin Lewinski, another British militiaman, said "he was very clever, very logical, and [had] much courage, but I was afraid for him. He was so tall and always standing." He refused to take cover, was recklessly brave and seemed to feel invulnerable.

In late March Orwell got blood poisoning from a badly infected cut. His hand had to be lanced and he spent ten days in hospital at Monflorite, just behind the front. While he was there, two big bombs dropped near Huesca, about two miles away. They made a terrific roar, shook the houses and made all the panicky patients flee their beds. During his stay the *practicantes*, or nursing aides, in a comradely gesture, stole his camera, photographs and most of his valuables.

Given leave in Barcelona and frustrated by the stagnant Aragón front, Orwell thought—for the second time—of joining the Communist-controlled International Brigades and taking part in the serious fighting around Madrid. In a review of July 1937, he called the Brigades "a thin line of suffering and often ill-armed human beings standing between barbarism and at least comparative decency." But he did not realize that this attempt to join the Brigades, as naive and futile as his interview with Harry Pollitt, would be doomed by his association with the Anarchists. A police report of his request, dated April 30, 1937, and now in the Moscow Central Party Archives, suggests that he was still unaware of the hostility among the political factions of the Left, that the Communists suspected he was trying to infiltrate their ranks and that he'd unwittingly alerted the authorities who would soon turn violently against the

POUM: "Blair enquired whether his association with the POUM would be likely to prejudice his chances of enlisting in the International Brigades. He wishes to fight on the Madrid front and stated that in a few days he will formally apply to us for enlistment when his discharge from the POUM has been regularised."[11] If he had managed to join them, he would certainly have been shot as "politically unreliable."

III

ORWELL'S COMMANDER in Spain, Georges Kopp, became a close friend and hero of *Homage to Catalonia*. His father was a doctor with contacts all over Europe; his mother, *née* Neumann, came from Odessa; and Georges, their only child, was born in St. Petersburg in 1902. Ten years later, the family emigrated to Brussels. Georges spoke eight languages, was trained as a civil engineer in Belgium and Switzerland, but left the university without earning his degree. (He later invented a successful technique for cutting coal.) He did national service, but had no great military expertise. He met and married his first wife, the Belgian Germaine Warnotte, in 1925, and they had four boys and a girl. He was divorced in 1934, and his wife took custody of the children.

Like many adventurers and soldiers of fortune (Malraux is the most notorious example), Kopp enhanced reality by constructing an elaborate myth about his past. A Dutch journalist, Bert Govaerts, has recently discovered that "instead of being a Belgian engineer with prior military experience, Kopp's true nationality was Russian and he had never served in the military (i.e., as a reserve officer in the Belgian army). In addition, he was neither a graduate engineer nor a devoted husband and father as Orwell believed. It would also appear that Kopp's claim that he was forced to flee Belgium because he was fabricating illegal munitions for the Spanish Republic was also false." Govaerts concluded, after studying Kopp's career: "All in all, Orwell's famous gift for observation was grotesquely beaten by this very very curious man." But Orwell, while fighting alongside Kopp in Spain, had no way to find out the truth about his background. In any case, the myth Kopp created makes absolutely no difference to his impressive heroism — in action and in prison — in both the Spanish Civil War and the French Resistance in World War II.

Photographs and descriptions of the colorful, larger-than-life Kopp portray a six-feet-tall, heavy-set, fat-necked, red-faced bull of a man: formidable, alarming and fierce. They also reveal that he was the physical model for the dynamic and devastating O'Brien in *Nineteen Eighty-Four*: "In spite of the bulkiness of his body there was a remarkable grace in his movements. . . . A wave of admiration, almost of worship, flowed out from Winston towards O'Brien. . . . When you looked at O'Brien's powerful shoulders and his blunt-featured face, so ugly and yet so civilised, it was impossible to believe that he could be defeated."[12]

In February 1937, while Orwell was fighting under Kopp's command, Eileen came to Barcelona to work as McNair's secretary in the ILP office. Though some idealists served as nurses, journalists and typists, foreign women were extremely rare in Spain. Stafford Cottman described Eileen as "a remarkably even-tempered young Englishwoman, 'like a pleasant young school-mistress,' as she efficiently handled the affairs and finances of half a dozen members of the ILP contingent." Another English volunteer, commenting on her relationship to Orwell, called her "a mousy kind of girl, and she worshipped the ground he walked on. She'd do anything for him." In mid-March she was allowed to visit her husband for three days in the front line trenches. As she told Leonard Moore the following month, while she was there "the Fascists threw in a small bombardment and quite a lot of machine-gun fire." Excited rather than frightened by the attack, she found it "quite an interesting visit—indeed, I never enjoyed anything more."[13]

A series of blurry snapshots offer a glimpse of their life in Spain. In January 1937, at the end of a scraggly military column, Orwell (a head taller than his comrades) marches out of the cobblestoned courtyard of the Lenin Barracks in Barcelona. He's also seated on a bench below the barred window of a whitewashed house near the front. His comrades, facing the camera, eat out of metal plates while Orwell (with boots off and cigarette in hand) turns aside to engage in a heated discussion. During the siege of Huesca he sits in a wide plowed field, near a solitary tree, and shares a steaming pot of stew with three soldiers. During Eileen's visit, his comrades (some helmeted, others bare-headed) line up behind a parapet of sandbags. They've mounted a machine gun on a tripod and aimed it at the enemy. Orwell, face blurred in an over-exposed photograph, wears the leather jacket Henry Miller gave him and towers above the others as the dark-haired, pale-faced, dark-clad Eileen sits at his feet.

1. Eric Blair in a sailor suit, 1906. The miniature image of a solid British tar, coddled and content.

2. Ida and Richard Blair (in uniform), with Eric and Avril, 1916. Father looked smart posing with his family in military uniform. Ida had dark eyes, thin features and an acute mind.

3. Eric, with Prosper and Guinever Buddicom, 1917. In jacket, tie and long trousers, he stands at ease with a croquet mallet.

4. Eric, with Guinever and another girl, fishing, 1917. "The great fish were gliding round the pool behind Binfield House."

6. Eric, studio portrait while at Eton, 1921. With his hair neatly combed and parted, he's dressed in a three-piece flannel suit.

5. Cicely Wilkes. A stocky, square-built woman with prominent brows and deepset suspicious eyes.

7. Police Training School, Mandalay, 1923. Rather pale and wearing a uniform, Eric (*standing third from the left*) holds his solar topee.

8. Sir Richard Rees. "A tall distinguished figure, aristocratically shabby, his eye rather moody."

9. Francis and Mabel Fierz, with their daughter Fay, at the seaside, 1937. "She was a woman of great energy, activated by transient enthusiasms."

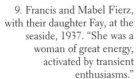

10. Orwell in Fierzes' garden, c. 1930. Forcing a rather wan smile, he tenderly holds the family's pet rabbit.

11. Orwell on Southwold beach, 1934. The gusty wind blows his tie across his shoulder.

12. Eileen O'Shaughnessy, mid-1930s. *"That is the kind of girl I would like to marry!"*

13. Dr. Laurence O'Shaughnessy, 1930s. A prominent chest surgeon, with a Harley Street Practice.

14. Dr. Gwen O'Shaughnessy, 1930s. "A slight woman with a quiet presence, gentle and caring."

15. Eileen visits Orwell at the Huesca front, March 1937. "The Fascists threw in a small bombardment and quite a lot of machine-gun fire.

16. Georges Kopp, holding his nephew, London, 1938. A six-feet tall, heavy-set, fat-necked, red-faced bull of a man.

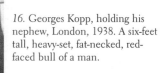

17. Majorie Blair Dakin, Henry Dakin and Ida Blair, Bristol, 1937. Majorie was a sympathetic listener who invited confidences.

18. Lydia Jackson, 1926. A dark attractive woman, exuberant and experienced.

19. Cyril Connolly. Fatally weakened by sloth, self-pity and an inordinate taste for luxury.

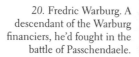

20. Fredric Warburg. A descendant of the Warburg financiers, he'd fought in the battle of Passchendaele.

21. Sonia Brownell (*left*) in the *Horizon* office, 1949. She had "rich golden hair, brilliant eyes, a fine oval face, and voluptuous figure."

22. Inez Holden. "She was a torrential talker, an accomplished mimic, excellent company."

23. Arthur Koestler, 1940s. "Hungry for experience, politically engaged, and racked by despair."

24. Anthony Powell, 1940s. "Tony is the only Tory I have ever liked."

25. David Astor, 1940s. He battled "on behalf of the oppressed, of minorities and of the persecuted."

26. Barnhill, 1948. A cross between Wuthering Heights and Cold Comfort Farm.

27. Orwell, Canonbury Square, 1946. "The wintry conscience of a generation."

28. Susan Watson, 1940s. A pretty blonde with an ingenuous expression and childlike manner.

29. Celia Paget, c. 1940. Stunningly beautiful, highly cultivated and frequently photographed.

30. Anne Popham, in motorcylcle uniform, 1943. Orwell said: "It's scandalous that a person like me should make advances to a person like you."

31. Bill Dunn and Avril Blair, 1948–49. Bill, a penniless ex-army officer, had a fierce temper. Avril was tall and thin, with deep grooves in her face.

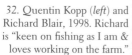

32. Quentin Kopp (*left*) and Richard Blair, 1998. Richard is "keen on fishing as I am & loves working on the farm."

I V

ORWELL COULD not have known, of course, that in December 1936, even before he left for Spain, Stalin had ordered the Communist leaders in Catalonia to destroy the POUM. Its Secretary, Andrés Nin, once associated with Stalin's archenemy Leon Trotsky, had become his most coveted prey in Spain. Though the POUM did not follow Trotsky, it was denounced as a Trotskyist party. Its paper, *La Batalla*, also earned Stalin's undying hatred by relentlessly exposing the brutalities of his Purge Trials. They began in 1935 and were reenacted in Spain, with the POUM as the victims, by agents of the Soviet secret police. Stalin's biographer explained his aims and his failure: "He dispatched to Spain, together with military instructors, agents of his political police, experts at heresy-hunting and purging, who established their own reign of terror in the ranks of the Republicans." Stalin wanted to crush the Anarchist revolution in order "to avoid antagonizing the British and French Governments. He saved nobody's respectability and he antagonized everybody."

When Orwell went on leave in late April, the month after Eileen's visit to the front, conditions were fairly normal, and the Communists and the POUM were still allies. On May 1 Eileen told her brother that the normally austere Orwell, after four months of privation, had been gorging en route to Barcelona: "George is here on leave. He arrived completely ragged, almost barefoot, a little lousy, dark brown and looking very well. In the previous twelve hours he has been in trains consuming anis, muscatel out of anis bottles, brandies and chocolate."

On May 3, while he was still on leave in Barcelona, fighting erupted between the Communists and the Anarchists. The Telephone Exchange was held by the Confederación Nacional de Trabajo (CNT), an Anarchist-Syndicalist union loosely connected with the POUM. The Communist-controlled Civil Guards, dissatisfied with how the Exchange was being run, tried to take control. When the Anarchists refused to give it up and opened fire on the invaders, the fighting quickly spread through Barcelona and touched off a full-scale battle that paralyzed the city. The Communists had a much stronger force and were armed with machine guns. The POUM, few in number and with only sixty rifles between them, were forced into the fight to support the Anarchists. While defending the party headquarters, Orwell spent three nerve-racking days on the roof of the Poliorama cinema. In a newspaper article, "Eye-Witness in Barcelona" (August 1937), he explained the confused and desperate situation: "We thought, all of us, that we were simply defending ourselves against an attempted *coup d'état* by the Civil Guards, who had forcibly seized the Telephone Exchange and might seize some more of the workers' buildings if we did not show ourselves willing to fight."

Willy Brandt explained how this war within a war led to the persecution and eventual extermination of the POUM:

An additional and crazy civil war began on 3 May, claiming hundreds of victims within a few days. The regional Government, now run by the Communists, took over the *telefónica*, the telephone and telegraph switchboards, run by the syndicalists, and with it control of the city of Barcelona. People who did not go along with this arrangement were slandered, persecuted and murdered. They included members of the POUM, at the time allied with the anarchists; their leaders, such as Andrés Nin, were now at the top of the Soviet secret police's blacklist. Albert Camus called the torture and murder of Nin "a milestone in the tragedy of the twentieth century."

Burnett Bolloten, a leading historian of the Spanish Civil War, described how the Communists, following Stalin's orders, attacked their enemies: "In the weeks and months following the May events, the story of Catalonia—the former power center of the CNT-FAI [the ultra-Left Spanish Anarchist party] and the POUM—was one of arbitrary arrests, of detentions in clandestine jails, of tortures, kidnappings and assassinations, as well as of the destruction of agricultural collectives. The spontaneous, undirected terror of the CNT and FAI during the height of the Revolution had now given way to the more sophisticated, centrally directed, and, hence, more fearful terror of the Communists." Frank Frankford, one of the ILP volunteers, tried to justify the Communist persecution by falsely claiming that the POUM was secretly helping the Fascists in Aragón (see Appendix III).

In early May 1937 Orwell met the American novelist John Dos Passos, who was making a documentary film for the Republicans. Dos Passos wrote that Orwell's "face had a sick drawn look," that he "was already suffering from the tuberculosis that later killed him." As the two discussed the political terror raging around them, Dos Passos was struck by Orwell's dispassionate grasp of the situation. "Orwell referred without overemphasis to things we both knew to be true. . . . 'It's complicated . . . in Bellver our people want to know whether to move against the anarchists. In some other places they are with them. . . . You know Spain.' Orwell seemed to understand the entire situation. Perhaps he was still a little afraid of how much he knew."

After five days of fighting—during which 1,000 people were wounded and 400 killed—security forces from the Republican government in Valencia restored order in Barcelona. By August, wrote the disillusioned Jason Gurney, the social revolution had been crushed and the idealism that Orwell had witnessed the previous December was completely extinguished: "There were far fewer people in the street. The parades with bands and banners had all gone. The euphoric revolutionary enthusiasm had disappeared and everybody seemed to be minding their own business. Most of the shops and restaurants were closed and even the night life had become subdued."[14]

On May 10, before the political implications of the struggle became clear, Orwell returned to the Huesca front. Promoted to second lieutenant, he now commanded a half-English, half-Spanish group of thirty men. Ten days later, at 5 A.M. on May 20, he was shot through the throat by a sniper's bullet. Georges Kopp sent a scientifically exact description of the wound, accompanied by a precise diagram, to Eileen's brother, Dr. Laurence O'Shaughnessy:

> The bullet entered the neck just under the larynx, slightly at the left side of its vertical axis, and went out at the dorsal right side of the neck's base. It was a normal 7mm bore, copper-plated, Spanish Mauser bullet, shot from a distance of some 175 yards. At this range it still had a velocity of some 600 feet per second and a cauterising temperature. Under the impact, Eric fell on his back. The hemorrhaging was insignificant. . . . No essential organ had been touched; the bullet went right through, between trachea and the carotid [artery].

Harry Milton, who caught Orwell when he was shot, noted that "the speed of the bullet had seared the entrance of the wound. I put his head in my arms, and when I put my hand under his neck there was a puddle of blood."[15] He was taken to the divisional hospital at Barbastro and then, when out of danger, by train through Lérida and Tarragona to the Sanatorium Maurín in the suburbs of Barcelona.

"I have been nastily wounded," he coolly wrote Connolly from the hospital on June 8, "not really a very bad wound, a bullet through the throat which of course ought to have killed me but has merely given me nervous pains in the right arm & robbed me of most of my voice." According to Kopp,

a week after his vocal chords were damaged "Eric was able to utter any artic-
ulate sound but feebly and with the characteristic, grinding, noise of the
brakes of a Model T, very antiquated, Ford; his speech was inaudible outside
a range of two yards." Orwell was told that his larynx was "broken" and he
had permanently lost his voice. By June 10, Eileen informed her brother, he
had regained some voice and appetite, but was saddened by the end of his
military career and by the disastrous change in the political situation in
Barcelona: "Eric is I think much better, though he cannot be brought to
admit any improvement. His voice certainly improves very *slowly*, but he uses
his arm much more frequently though it is still very painful at times. He eats
as much as anyone else & can walk about & do ordinary things quite effectively for a short time. He is *violently* depressed, which I think encouraging."
In a strange twist to this incident, the poet Roy Campbell, a passionate supporter of the Spanish Fascists, claimed, in a "curious fantasy that it was he,
Campbell, who shot 'George Orwell' through the neck, during the Spanish
war, with, of all things, an orange-wood bow."[16]

V

WHILE ORWELL was recovering from his wound, the POUM was being
hunted down by the Soviet Police. Richard Rees, driving an ambulance in
Spain, saw Eileen in Barcelona in May and was shocked by her visible fear:
"She did not come out to lunch with me, because it would be too dangerous for me to be seen in public with her. . . . In Eileen Blair I had seen for
the first time the symptoms of a human being living under political terror."
Eileen had good reason to be frightened, for her association with Orwell put
her own life in danger. Partly to throw the police off his trail, she had
remained in the Hotel Continental. On June 18 her room was searched by
the Spanish Communists, who took away many of Orwell's papers. But, too
prudish or chivalrous to order a foreign woman out of bed, they failed to discover, under her mattress, the most crucial documents. Eileen remained
remarkably cool throughout this ordeal.

The incriminating diaries stolen by Communist agents from Eileen's hotel
room formed the basis of the NKVD "Report to the Tribunal for Espionage
and High Treason" in Valencia on July 13, 1937—three weeks after Orwell's
escape from Spain. According to this Report, which summarized his activities in Spain and would have been used by interrogators if he'd been cap-

tured, Eric and Eileen Blair both belonged to the ILP. Eric, a liaison with the ILP in England, was asked to send news of party members. As an ILP agent of the POUM, he fought with the POUM at the Huesca front. Using a "credential" of the POUM executive committee signed by Kopp, Eileen visited the front on March 13. Both Blairs used to live in the POUM's Hotel Falcón; and Eric took part in the events of May, when the POUM fought the Communists. Most damaging of all was the false statement that both Blairs were "rabid Trotskyists."

Another report, dated July 7, 1937, and now in the Central Party Archives in Moscow, alludes to *The Road to Wigan Pier* (published on March 8 while Orwell was in Spain) and reveals that he was well known to the Communists: " 'the leading personality and most respected man in the [ILP] contingent at present is Eric Blair. This man is a Novelist who has written some books [on] proletarian life in England.' But 'he has little political understanding.' " The historian James Hopkins concludes that the Report "charges that he had played an active role in the Barcelona fighting in May. This contradicts his account in *Homage to Catalonia*, in which he describes himself as a passive and troubled bystander who was not drawn into the actual fighting. . . . By labeling him as a Trotskyist, the Communists had in effect signed his death warrant if he remained in Spain. . . . Within a short time every follower of the POUM was either dead, in prison, or, like the wounded Orwell, on the run."[17]

Orwell now found himself once again attacked by his former allies and caught up in the fighting behind the front lines. After being released from the Sanatorium Maurín, collecting his discharge papers from the hospital at Monzón and visiting the front around Barbastro (where the commander had to sign his papers), he returned to Barcelona on June 20 to find that the POUM had been declared illegal. Its leaders had been arrested and all its members were being hunted by the police. For the next three days, though still weak from his wound, he went into hiding and slept in ruined buildings.

Shocked by the imprisonment and execution of many of his comrades, he told McNair: "This is bloody awful . . . these buggers (the police) are shooting our chaps in the back." The Communists even seized the POUM men who were wounded; and when visiting the jail Orwell saw a ten-year-old boy and two men with amputated legs. Referring to his experiences in Spain as well as in Burma in "Inside the Whale," he exclaimed: "I have seen the bodies of numbers of murdered men—I don't mean killed in battle, I mean murdered."[18]

While Orwell and Eileen were themselves in danger of arrest and execution, they discovered that Kopp had been seized on June 20. In an effort to get him out of prison, they risked their lives by visiting him, and even went to police headquarters to retrieve a document that might save him. As Kopp gratefully told Eileen, more than a year later: "I really do admire you [and Eric] for what you did when you were in hiding, approaching Major Fenech's Secretary, the Police headquarters and those Assault Guards in the [Café] Moka; it was daring and it would have been 100% nice if it had succeeded in keeping me out of trouble. In any case, it was awfully brave and heroical." Arrested on the very day that Orwell returned to Barcelona (and the day Andrés Nin was murdered), Kopp was cruelly treated. During his eighteen months in prison the Communists did everything but actually kill him. He suffered scurvy and blood poisoning, was tortured and lost ninety-eight pounds in weight. The *Independent News* of August 11, 1939, described the brutal treatment that had failed to break his spirit:

> When Georges Kopp came to Spain he was a robust strapping young man, radiantly healthy and strong. Today he has emerged from his long calvary, thin, feeble and bent, walking slowly with the aid of a cane. His body is covered with scabs and bruises, the marks of the diseases he had contracted in the subterranean dungeons of the stalinist "checas," in the damp, airless holds of the prison ships, and in the Forced Labor Camps. . . . When Kopp refused to sign [a confession] he was put in a coal bin without light, air, or food where enormous rats ran in and out of his legs. For 12 days he remained in the black pit, seeing no one, hearing no one until one day a voice called out, "Tonight we're going to shoot you!" . . . He fought [his] last battle only seven days before his arrest. At that time he was Major in the Popular Army and had occupied commanding posts in the 29th Division.

On December 18, 1938, Kopp telegraphed from Toulon, France: "Saved but sort of half dead—Georges." Orwell greatly admired his toughness and laconic stoicism. If Orwell, weakened by his wound, had been arrested and tortured, he would certainly have died in prison.

Their experience in Spain made both men bitterly disillusioned with Communism. "It is very hard of course to have risked one's life," Kopp wrote, "and have suffered what I got in Spain for a cause in which one has ceased to believe." Orwell, in a letter to Heppenstall, described his own ignominious escape: "we started off by being heroic defenders of democracy and ended by slipping over the border with the police panting on our heels."[19] On June 23, after three days in hiding, Orwell, Eileen, John McNair and Stafford Cottman obtained travel documents from the British consulate and boarded the train to France. Lounging in the restaurant car as if they were ordinary tourists, they escaped detection when two agents went through the train looking for suspicious foreigners. When they crossed the border they joyfully embraced each other, and Orwell and Eileen spent three restful days on the French coast at Banyuls.

But this time there was no peasant salute. Orwell had seen the Communists betray the Anarchists. He would see Franco's army, aided by German and Italian troops and weapons, defeat the Republicans. The most depressing and disillusioning aspect of his Spanish experience was that the Communists had persuaded the workers to betray their allies for ideological reasons and then spread lies about the POUM, which were believed by Leftist intellectuals in England and America. This enraged him, and he resolved to do everything in his power to expose the Communists' treachery.

VI

WHEN ORWELL returned from Spain as a wounded fighter his legend began to take hold. He'd made a name for himself and now had a well-defined role in English intellectual life. He kept up with Old Etonians and upper-class friends but, as if to maintain his connection with the miners and workers, developed a working-class persona. He wore his habitual battered tweed jacket with leather patches at the elbows, dark shirt, hairy tie and baggy flannel trousers. He became an eccentric "character," whose personality was identified with a political position, and cultivated this image in a dour, ironically self-aware sort of way.

Orwell offered his dress and manner, his hand-rolled cigarettes and proletarian appearance, as an alternative not only to the nudists and homosexuals on the Socialist fringe, but also to bourgeois clothing and comfortable surroundings. His personal style became an acceptable norm for Left-wing intellectuals, and was widely imitated in British schools and universities. His obsessions could be mocked, even parodied, as when Connolly remarked that Orwell "could not blow his nose without moralising on conditions in the handkerchief industry." But his persona was a genuine attempt to reach out to and achieve solidarity with the workers. And his scruffy asceticism, his idealism, self-sacrifice, honesty and independence, eventually became identified with his literary work. His friend Peter Quennell noted that Orwell, though sensitive to the political connotations of dress, was also good-humored about it:

> We met one evening at Cyril Connolly's house; and, since I was bound, later that night, for a more ceremonious occasion, I happened to be wearing a black tie. This attracted the Socialist prophet's notice. "So you *still* wear the uniform of the class enemy!" he observed with a faintly teasing smile. . . . Orwell's lengthy, hollow-cheeked face reflected the essential kindness of his nature. A thin military moustache bordered his tight-lipped mouth. He had a beaky, distinguished nose, rather large ears, a big, irregularly prominent chin and a broad and deeply wrinkled forehead.[20]

Malcolm Muggeridge observed that Orwell's "proletarian fancy dress" highlighted his eccentric personality: the "punctilious rolling of his cigarettes, his rusty laugh and woebegone expression and kindly disposition." John Morris, one of the few people who disliked Orwell, failed to recognize his warmth. Morris said his eyes combined "benevolence and fanaticism," and emphasized the saintly, sacrificial aspect, reinforced by his gaunt physique, that would become a prominent part of the legend: "Orwell always reminded me of one of those figures on the front of Chartres Cathedral; there was a sort of pinched Gothic quality about his tall thin frame. He laughed often, but in repose his lined face suggested the grey asceticism of a medieval saint carved in stone and very weathered." Yet he had a patrician accent, an unmistakable Eton drawl and, wrote Julian Symons, "his talk, like his journalistic writing, was a mixture of brilliant perception, common sense and wild assertion."[21]

Noel Annan, reinforcing the saintly image, said that Orwell "remained a biting, bleak, self-critical, self-denying man of the idealist left. . . . [He] spoke with the voice of ethical socialism. . . . He was the first saint of Our Age, quirky, fierce, independent and beholden to none." Muggeridge, in a famous formulation, noted that after Spain, "he loved the past, hated the present and dreaded the future." Orwell never could—perhaps never wanted to—resolve the contradictions in his elusive character: Etonian prole, anti-colonial policeman, bourgeois bum, Tory Anarchist, Leftist critic of the Left, puritanical lecher, kindly autocrat.

Orwell found the cottage at Wallington, rented in his absence by Aunt

Nellie, had become terribly run-down. He immediately began to put things in order and to write about Spain. Connolly, who'd been making his name in London journalism and been corresponding with him, now sought him out and invited him to lunch. They had not met since Eton, and Connolly was shocked by the changes made by the last fifteen years. Three bouts of pneumonia, dengue fever, blood poisoning and a bullet wound had transformed the chubby schoolboy into a gaunt, lined and weatherbeaten figure: "his greeting was typical, a long but not unfriendly stare and his characteristic wheezy laugh. 'Well, Connolly, I can see that you've worn a good deal better than I have.' I could say nothing, for I was appalled by the ravaged grooves that ran down from cheek to chin. My fat cigar-smoking persona must have been a surprise to him." Orwell had the effect of making Connolly feel slightly guilty about his soft, self-indulgent life.

Though Orwell remained shy and awkward, and felt he was unattractive, he had a powerful impact on the ladies. "He came along," Connolly said, "looking gaunt and shaggy, shabby, aloof, and he had this extraordinary magical effect on these women. They all wanted to meet him and started talking to him, and their fur coats shook with pleasure. They were totally unprepared for anyone like that and they responded to something . . . this sort of John the Baptist figure coming in from the wilderness."[22]

The charming and well-connected Connolly introduced Orwell to several people who became important in his life: Stephen Spender, John Lehmann, editor of *Penguin New Writing*, David Astor, editor of the *Observer*, and Sonia Brownell, his attractive assistant. Connolly favorably reviewed *Keep the Aspidistra Flying* and *Animal Farm*, and published many of Orwell's best essays in his magazine *Horizon*. Orwell in turn reviewed Connolly's books, but was, as always, quite honest about their defects. He'd opened Connolly's first novel, *The Rock-Pool* (1936) with lively interest, found the treatment mature and skillful, but the subject matter tiresome. Then, in a finely turned sentence, he defined the moral chasm between himself and his old friend: "even to want to write about so-called artists who spend on sodomy what they have gained by sponging betrays a kind of spiritual inadequacy." He called *The Condemned Playground: Essays, 1927–1944* (1945) "an intelligent and amusing book," and mentioned "the urbane hedonism which makes him so readable a writer." Reviewing *The Unquiet Grave* (1944), published under a transparent pseudonym, Orwell again noted their sharp difference in outlook: "With his background of classical culture, religious scepticism, travel, leisure, country houses, and civilised meals, 'Palinurus' naturally contemplates the modern world without enthusiasm and even, at moments, sheer aristocratic disdain."[23] The portly Connolly, he felt, had been fatally weakened by sloth, self-pity and an inordinate taste for luxury.

VII

ORWELL'S HALF-YEAR in Spain was the most important experience of his life. It deepened his understanding of politics and sharpened his hostility to Catholics and Communists. The bitter experience intensified his commitment to Socialism, inspired his finest book, *Homage to Catalonia*, and pointed the way toward his last and most influential political works. As he said in a famous passage in "Why I Write" (1946): "Every line of serious work that I have written since 1936 has been written, directly or indirectly, *against* totalitarianism and *for* democratic Socialism. . . . What I have most wanted to do throughout the past ten years is to make political writing into an art. My starting point is always a feeling of partisanship, a sense of injustice."

Spain left a spiritual wound much greater than the sniper's bullet. When he returned to England he was, for all his courage, depressed about the future, gloomier than ever and profoundly sceptical about the nature of political activity. "It is heart-breaking," he told Connolly in October 1937, when the war already seemed lost, "to see the way things have gone, nearly a million men dead in all, they say, and obviously it is all going to be all for nothing." But he had a mission. If he'd been captured and killed—and he very nearly was—no one else would have had the knowledge, skill and authority to tell the truth about the Communist betrayal in Spain. Camus eloquently explained what that experience meant to idealists like Orwell: "It was in Spain that men learned that one can be right and yet be beaten, that force can vanquish spirit, that there are times when courage is not its own recompense. It is this, doubtless, which explains why so many men, the world over, regard the Spanish drama as a personal tragedy."[24]

Juan Negrín, Prime Minister of the Spanish Republic from 1937 to 1939, went into exile at the end of the war. He met Orwell in London and provided (in this stilted translation) a rare Spanish view of his weaknesses and strengths. He considered Orwell

> a decent and righteous gentleman, biased by a too rigid, puritanical frame,
> gifted with a candor bordering on naiveté, highly critical but blindly cred-

ulous, morbidly individualistic (an Englishman!) but submitting lazily and without discernment to the atmosphere of the gregarious community in which he voluntarily and instinctively anchors himself, and so supremely honest and self-denying that he would not hesitate to change his mind once he perceived himself to be wrong.

This was the man who revealed the truth about the Spanish war when the British Left was sadly deluded by Communist propaganda.

The English intellectuals' worshipful attitude toward the Communists was expressed in a 1935 poem by Cecil Day-Lewis which asked: "why do we all, seeing a Red, feel small?" Ralph Bates, an English novelist who had fought in Spain, did not admit until the 1990s "that he had been misinformed by his wife, a devout Stalinist, concerning the activities of the POUM." Most writers on the Left, reacting against social and economic injustice in England, fell for the Communist party line and lent prestige to a far worse kind of hierarchy. Orwell made a clear distinction between the Communist ideals of the Russian Revolution and the betrayal of these ideals by the forcible collectivization of agriculture, the Purge Trials, the extermination of opposition parties in Spain and, later on, the Hitler-Stalin Pact. To illustrate how the faithful blindly followed Stalin's disastrous policies, Orwell told the story of a Communist hard-liner who went to the toilet during a meeting, returned to cast his loyal vote and was shocked to find that in his absence the party line had suddenly changed. Intellectuals desperately wanted to believe that the Russian Communists were the absolute antithesis of the German Nazis. Referring to the year Hitler took power, in his essay on Arthur Koestler, Orwell wrote that "The sin of nearly all leftwingers from 1933 onwards is that they have wanted to be anti-Fascist without being anti-totalitarian."[25]

Getting down to work as soon as he returned to Wallington, for he hadn't earned any money in the last six months, Orwell described the suppression of the POUM in "Spilling the Spanish Beans." He submitted it to the *New Statesman*, the leading Left-wing journal in England, but the editor, Kingsley Martin—in what the historian of the journal called "an appalling misjudgment"—rejected it. Martin then asked him to review Franz Borkenau's *The Spanish Cockpit*, an account of the civil war that was also based on firsthand experience. Orwell agreed with Borkenau's view that the Communists were an anti-revolutionary force in Spain, "using every possible method, fair and foul, to stamp out what was left of the revolution." Martin twisted the knife by also rejecting the review. Admitting, later on, that he'd underestimated the Communist atrocities which Orwell had described, Martin still defended his decision. He argued that it was expedient to back the Party since the Anarchists had no chance of winning the war and Russia was the only country that supported the Republicans.

Orwell was disgusted at the way the liberal press in England tried to cover up the atrocities. In August 1937 he told his French translator Yvonne Davet: "They all think that to win the war you must hide the real facts of what is going on in Spain."[26] Later on, eating with Muggeridge at a Greek restaurant on Percy Street, Orwell asked him to change places. He'd been looking "straight at Kingsley lunching at an adjoining table; the sight of so corrupt a face, he said, would spoil his luncheon." Furious about the *New Statesman*'s attempt to suppress the truth, in the next six months Orwell published three more articles, three more reviews and a public letter in five different journals.

He also blasted Nancy Cunard, daughter of the shipping magnate, who repeatedly sent Orwell a fashionably trendy and insincere request to contribute to her generally pro-Republican pamphlet *Authors Take Sides on the Spanish War*. In an uncharacteristically rude reply he expressed his extreme bitterness and anger:

> Will you please stop sending me this bloody rubbish. . . . I am not one of your fashionable pansies like Auden and Spender. I was six months in Spain, most of the time fighting, I have a bullet-hole in me at present and I'm not going to write blah about defending democracy or gallant little anybody. . . . Chances are that you . . . have money and are well-informed . . . and have deliberately joined in the defence of 'democracy' (i.e. capitalism) racket in order to aid in crushing the Spanish working class and thus indirectly defend your dirty little dividends.

After his experience with the *New Statesman*, Orwell knew that Gollancz, a strong Communist supporter, would never publish a book by someone who'd been associated with the POUM and seen the May riots in Barcelona, so he took his new book to Fredric Warburg. Born in 1898, a descendant of the Swedish branch of the Warburg financiers, Warburg had been educated at Westminster School and Christ Church, Oxford, and had fought as a lieutenant in the battle of Passchendaele in World War I. In 1936 he'd borrowed £5,000 from a rich uncle to buy out Martin Secker and form his new firm, Secker & Warburg. He became a close friend as well as Orwell's publisher.

In a BBC interview Warburg frankly described Orwell's appearance (the first two sentences were deleted from the broadcast), mentioned the contradiction between his personal reserve and the autobiographical revelations in his writing, and ended with an acute allusion to *Homage to Catalonia*:

> He was very tall, with piercing blue eyes, a bony face and a bulging forehead. Slovenly and not overclean clothes covered his thin, his pitifully thin frame. . . . He was a lonely man. He very rarely revealed anything personal about himself, although his personal life, transmuted, was put into his books. . . . He was rather a chilly character, and I don't think he exuded warmth and I don't think he received warmth returned from his friends. . . . Orwell never liked being associated with anything that was too powerful or successful. . . . He wrote without regard to being popular and without fear of being detested.[27]

VIII

STAFFORD COTTMAN remembered Orwell writing every day before breakfast, when it was relatively quiet on the front lines. According to Warburg, he began *Homage to Catalonia* (1938) in the trenches in February 1937 and sent his notes, written on scraps of paper and on the backs of envelopes, to McNair's office in Barcelona, where Eileen typed them up. These papers were stolen from Eileen's hotel room by the Communist police. Nevertheless, writing this material helped relieve boredom, recorded his immediate impressions and got him started on the book.

He composed *Homage to Catalonia*—"the best [book] I have written"—in a state of white-hot anger. Disgusted by the lies he read in the English newspapers, he was determined to reveal the truth about what had really happened in Spain. Unlike the Great War novelists—Hemingway, Aldington and Remarque (the model for his own memoir)—Orwell did not wait ten years to publish his book. Like Malraux with *Man's Hope* (1937), he wrote it with astonishing clarity and insight while the war was still raging. As he explained in "Why I Write": "I happened to know, what very few people in England had been allowed to know, that innocent men were being falsely accused. If I had not been angry about that I should never have written the book."[28]

As in his earlier works, Orwell is sustained by physical contact with a work-ing-class comrade. In *Down and Out* he "helped a hawker pick up a barrow that he had upset. 'Thanks, mate,' he said with a grin. No one had called me mate before in my life." In *Wigan Pier*, "going into the dark doorway of that common lodging-house seemed to me like going down into some dreadful subterranean place—a sewer full of rats, for instance." But a drunken steve-dore flung his arms round his neck and tearfully cried: " 'Ave a cup of tea, chum!" And on the first page of *Homage to Catalonia*, an Italian militiaman "stepped across the room and gripped my hand very hard. Queer, the affec-tion you can feel for a stranger! It was as though his spirit and mine had momentarily succeeded in bridging the gulf of language and tradition and meeting in utter intimacy."[29] These were the emotional rewards of commit-ment and solidarity.

A historian has recently argued that the workers in Catalonia were not very enthusiastic about the revolution and that in his opening chapter "Orwell provided a questionable image of a working-class paradise. . . . Orwell told us more about his conception of the working class and of work itself than about Barcelona workers in the first months of the revolution." But many aspects of his supposedly "idealized" Barcelona foreshadow aspects of *Nineteen Eighty-Four* and suggest, even in the early days, that danger lurked beneath the surface. Workers wear rough overalls, political posters are every-where and loudspeakers blast out propaganda. The buildings are run-down, the streets dimly lit, the shops shabby and half empty. Meat, sugar, milk and bread as well as coal and gasoline are either in short supply or completely unavailable. Rats, "great bloated brutes" that fed on corpses and horrified Orwell, squirm, crawl and run through the book. When he returns from the front Orwell, like Winston Smith after torture, looks like a scarecrow. During the purge of the POUM police spies lurk everywhere and people fear that friends will denounce them. And Orwell, again like Winston, receives (when treated in hospital) a series of electrical shocks. Worst of all is the official sup-pression of truth and the triumph of lies. Orwell believed that "good war books are nearly always written from the angle of a *victim*," and the narrator-victim is more emotional and naive, less capable and courageous than the real Orwell.

The hero of the book is not Orwell, but the resolute, daring and heroic Georges Kopp, who calls the war "a comic opera with an occasional death," and pays "no attention to the bullets that streamed over the low parapet and cracked close to his head." First seen riding a black horse at the head of a column, Kopp represents the ideal military leader and reappears at moments of intense crisis and action—at the successful assault on the parapet, the attack on the Café Moka and throughout the hunt for the POUM in Barcelona. During the chaotic street fighting he walks "unarmed, up to men who were frightened out of their wits and had loaded guns in their hands," and prevents bloodshed by ordering his men to detonate the unexploded bombs. After Kopp's arrest, Orwell gives a proud résumé of his life and character: "He was my personal friend, I had served under him for months, I had been under fire with him, and I knew his history. He was a man who had sacrificed everything—family, nationality, livelihood—simply to come to Spain and fight against Fascism. . . . He had been in the line since October 1936, had worked his way up from militiaman to major, had been in action I do not know how many times, had been wounded."[30]

In *Homage to Catalonia* Orwell compares an attack to the thrill of stalking a wild animal and describes how he lunged at a man with his bayonet without managing to stab him. But in an essay on the Spanish war he also recalled how a man "jumped out of the trench and ran along the top of the parapet in full view. He was half-dressed and holding up his trousers with both hands as he ran. I refrained from shooting at him. . . . I had come here to shoot at 'Fascists'; but a man who is holding up his trousers isn't a 'Fascist,' he is visibly a fellow creature, similar to yourself, and you don't feel like shooting at him." Orwell knew quite well that humane considerations were irrelevant in battle and that he had to kill the enemy in order to win the war. But he couldn't help adding an element of fairness and decency (one of his favorite words), which was so notably absent in the Fascists and, too often, in his own side as well. He truly believed that "the real objective of Socialism is human brotherhood." In Spain this was symbolized by the clenched fists of the peasants, the beltless man he didn't kill and the "crystal spirit" of the Italian militiaman who shook his hand in the guardroom. As Malraux wrote of his own fictional hero: "What he liked about war was the masculine comradeship, the irrevocable commitments that courage imposes."

Kopp's parapet attack and Orwell's wound climax his two stays at the front. When shot, he offers a detached, almost "posthumous" reflection in the midst of the ghastly experience. He felt he was "*at the centre* of an explosion." There was a bang, a flash, a shock—but, strangely enough, no pain. He felt weak and shriveled, as if jolted by an electrical terminal; then he crumpled up, fell down and banged his head.[31] Few soldiers have survived such a wound and given such a precise account of how it feels to be shot.

Orwell's political message was not well received by the English Left. *Homage to Catalonia* sold only 600 copies in the first twelve years after publication and did not in his lifetime earn the modest advance of £150. The reviews of the book (several of them by Orwell's friends) were inevitably influenced by the writers' politics. Geoffrey Gorer recognized Orwell's "personal and political protestant integrity," praised his description of the "emotional atmosphere of a revolutionary militia" and commended the book as "a work of first-class importance." John McNair's propagandistic review emphasized the spirit of comradeship and confirmed the reliability of his political reporting. Philip Mairet agreed with Gorer that "the book is likely to stand as one of the best contemporary documents of the struggle" (a view that still prevails) and noted Orwell's political naiveté, "the heart of innocence that lies in revolution." The *Manchester Guardian* reviewer found Orwell's "defence of the Trotskyist POUM convincing" and realized that the conflict on the Left—later portrayed in *Animal Farm*—was between the Trotskyites who wanted immediate revolution and the Stalinists who wanted to win the war. In the end, of course, they achieved neither revolution nor victory.

Douglas Woodruff, writing in the conservative, Catholic *Tablet*, called Orwell a romantic who did not understand the Fascist point of view, but nevertheless "reached the conclusion that the one thing at stake in Spain is certainly not Democracy, but a choice of dictatorships." V.S. Pritchett, writing in the *New Statesman* and following the editor's party line, stated "there are many strong arguments for keeping creative writers out of politics and Mr. George Orwell is one of them," and concluded that his "appetite for the unvarnished truth was 'perverse.' " (Pritchett later called Orwell "the wintry conscience of a generation," but in 1938 he seemed to lack a political conscience of his own.) Stephen Spender had forgiven Orwell's cracks about the "pansy Left" and had renounced Communism as "the god that failed." Though Spender felt the book contained both common sense and crankiness, he called it "one of the most serious indictments of Communism which has been written."

Homage to Catalonia was first published in America in 1952, during the Korean War. In sharp contrast to the 1930s, Orwell's anti-Communism now seemed persuasive and was warmly received. T.R. Fyvel called Orwell a "romantic, typically English figure" and attributed the book's poor sales to "Communist machinations" instead of to the unpopular point of view that had antagonized both the Left and the Right. The historian Hugh Thomas thought the book was the best firsthand account of the Spanish Civil War, but noted that it is limited to Barcelona and the Aragón front, and gives only the POUM point of view. In a brilliant summary, Thomas explained why the POUM, despite the noble idealism that inspired Orwell's book, was doomed to defeat:

> If the Republicans were to have a hope of winning the civil war, the only policy was to centralize war production, delay the revolutionary process (to avoid antagonizing the peasants), establish a regular army in place of the militias and—as long as England and France continued with Non-Intervention—make certain of a regular supply of Russian arms. It was communist support for all these policies that led to their dominance of the Republican cause. The anarchists and the POUM, through greater idealism, were unable to swallow such realistic stuff and their stars declined as inevitably as that of the communists rose.[32]

9

Morocco and *Coming Up for Air,*

1938–1939

I

In late December 1937, when Orwell was completing *Homage to Catalonia*, he received an offer from Desmond Young, the editor of the *Pioneer* newspaper in Lucknow, northern India. Impressed by Orwell's colonial background and "excellent" novels, he wanted him to write editorials and book reviews. Young wrote: "If by any chance you want a job which will add to [your income], leave you some leisure in which to write & perhaps give you some material, I wonder if you would care to consider coming out here as a leader-writer?" He explained that the British-owned paper, which supported "landlord and vested interests," was politically moderate. It agreed with the Congress Party's demand for Indian self-government—but only in the distant future.

Orwell was tempted. Lucknow was only 250 miles west of Motihari, where he was born. The job offered a regular salary of £360 a year, enough to live comfortably there with Eileen. It would bring him back to India in a very different role, and give him the chance to attack British imperialism and press for Indian independence. He'd be able to find new material for the English papers. The job also had a romantic attraction: he knew that Kipling had worked for the Allahabad *Pioneer* in the 1880s. In "The Man Who Would Be King" Kipling had described putting the paper to bed on a broiling night: "It was a shade cooler in the press-room than the office, so I sat there, while the type ticked and clicked, and the night-jars hooted at the windows, and the all but naked compositors wiped the sweat from their foreheads, and called for water."

In January Young wrote to Alec Joyce of the India Office, who would have to vet Orwell's candidacy, to find out more about Orwell and obtain permission to appoint him. On February 12, 1938, Orwell told Joyce that "my object in going to India is, apart from the work on the *Pioneer*, to try and get a clearer idea of political and social conditions. . . . I shall no doubt write some book on the subject afterwards." Young was attracted to Orwell's original and independent-minded writing, but the *Pioneer* also required a journalist who would toe the line. In February Joyce interviewed Orwell and, in a shrewd estimate of his character, told Young that he'd be hard to handle and ought to be discouraged: "Blair keen for twelve months. Leadering ability undoubted but probably temperamental, unbusinesslike. . . . Probably an extremist outlook, plus definite strength of character [would make] for difficulties when there is a conflict of views."

Orwell also thought about the negative side of the offer. The pay was only half his salary in Burma (though double what he was earning in England) and the stifling climate would be bad for his health. He'd spent considerable time and energy getting Wallington back in running order and, after all his persistence and hard work, was at last in demand as a writer and reviewer. It seemed the wrong time to leave England. He told Jack Common about his conflicted feelings: "It is a frightful bore and I have seldom wanted to do anything less, but I feel that it is an opportunity to see interesting things and that I should afterwards curse myself if I didn't go."[1]

The question was settled by a dramatic event that suddenly made India impossible. Orwell had always neglected his health. He worked compulsively, ate poorly, lived austerely, refused to wear a hat and overcoat in winter, and was reluctant to see a doctor. On March 8 his three bouts of pneumonia and wounds in Spain finally caught up with him, when he began to hemorrhage and blood from an old lesion in his lung poured out of his mouth. Eileen was terrified, for "the bleeding seemed prepared to go on for ever." Orwell, who may not have been informed about the gravity of his illness, played it down. A week later he told Connolly: "I've been spitting blood again, it always turns out to be not serious, but it's alarming when it happens & I am going to a Sanatorium in Kent to be X-rayed. . . . It's a good excuse for not going to India, which I never wanted to."

Laurence O'Shaughnessy examined Orwell and decided to send him by ambulance to Preston Hall Sanatorium in Aylesford, Kent, where Laurence was a Consulting and Thoracic Surgeon. It was run by the British Legion for ex-servicemen, and the wings were named after military heroes. On March 15 Eileen wrote, "everyone agreed that Eric must be taken somewhere where really active steps could be taken if necessary—artificial pneumothorax to stop the blood or transfusion to replace it. . . . Everyone was nervous of being responsible for the immediate risk of the journey, but we supported each other."

Though he was almost six feet, three inches tall, Orwell was now extremely thin and weighed only 159 pounds. X-rays revealed "irregular and widespread shadows which often occur from aspiration of blood into otherwise healthy areas of lung." In June Eileen wrote Denys King-Farlow: "he of course has never believed that he was 'ill,' but for the first two months or so he appeared to have phthisis [tuberculosis] in both lungs, which could have been pretty hopeless." One diagnosis was "bronchiectasis of the Left lung, with nonspecific fibrosis of the Right lung." Though less serious than tuberculosis, bronchiectasis—a chronic viral infection of the bronchial tubes—limited the capacity to breathe and could lead to lung disease or cerebral abscess. But there seemed to be some doubt about this, and Orwell may well have had *both* diseases. He mentioned the "old lesion in one lung which has been there at any rate 10 years & was never discovered before," and told both Stephen Spender and Yvonne Davet that he had tuberculosis. His medical report clearly stated: "T.B. confirmed."[2]

The treatment consisted of little more than complete rest and injections of calcium and vitamins. Until Selman Waksman discovered streptomycin in 1944, there was no effective treatment of tuberculosis. Doctors might try to keep the truth from their patients, or be brutally honest, but they could only palliate the disease, not prevent or cure it. In the 1930s patients still followed the strict regimen described in Thomas Mann's *The Magic Mountain* (1924): rest cure, proper diet and fresh air. Sanatoria prevented patients from infecting other people, taught them hygienic discipline, decreased their mental and physical strain, and allowed doctors to study the disease. But, as the standard textbook (of which Laurence O'Shaughnessy was a co-author) later stated, prolonged rest, special diets and change in climate made no significant difference: "No locality or climate specifically prevented the development of tuberculosis or caused its cure." A contemporary study reported that it was often healthier to stay out of the hospital: "a damaging survey of sanatoria, home and untreated patients found that 54 per cent of non-sanatoria stage I cases were 'cured' at four years after diagnosis, compared with 31 per cent of sanatoria cases."[3]

Orwell's illness inevitably put a great strain on Eileen, who was always in danger of becoming infected. She had to manage the cottage and battle with the animals, all on her own. Every two weeks she made the slow, difficult and expensive trip from the village, through London to Aylesford, just north of Maidstone, in the Kentish countryside. "Depressed about being in an institution devised for murder, but otherwise remarkably well," Orwell remained there for five-and-a-half months. He passed the time studying botany and doing crossword puzzles. As he got stronger he was allowed to walk in the spacious grounds, do some gentle fishing, and even take bus trips to Rochester and Maidstone.

He had some interesting visitors. John Sceats, a Socialist writer, saw him at Aylesford soon after the publication of *Homage to Catalonia* in April 1938 and left an account of Orwell's deeply pessimistic political views and strong opposition to war with Germany:

> As he saw things then, it was a matter of months before either Fascism or War landed him in the Concentration Camp (British) [for opposing the war]; whatever the future held he could not believe it would allow him to go on writing. He was of course anti-Nazi, but could not (at the time) stomach the idea of an anti-German war: in fact, talking to Max Plowman (who called in the afternoon) he implied that he would join him in opposition to such a war with whatever underground measures might be appropriate.

An important friendship began when Reginald Reynolds (1905–58), whom Orwell had probably met in ILP circles, came to see him. Though Reynolds was a pacifist, his character and political views were strikingly similar to Orwell's. An ILP Socialist, he was a passionate advocate of Indian independence, a supporter of the non-Communist Republicans in Spain and strongly opposed the coming war with Germany. Like Orwell, Reynolds "was always tearing comfortable conventions to tatters and replacing them with something new, simply because he cared deeply." He also combined personal reserve with fanatical idealism, and "was not easy to know and understand, wrapped up as he was in himself and so sure of the righteousness of his causes." Though Reynolds seemed healthy at the time, he too developed tuberculosis. Writing from his own hospital bed in August 1945, he told Orwell: "I had to come here suddenly on Monday night, as I was gargling my own blood."[4]

They were also alike in their personal eccentricities. Orwell satirized

Reynolds' self-consciously Socialist outfit (all too apparent at the ILP summer schools)—"sockless, dressed in sandals, well-worn corduroys and a vivid open-necked shirt"—both in *The Road to Wigan Pier* and in *Coming Up for Air* (1939), where his hero George Bowling scorns the freaky types who believe in "vegetarianism, simple life, poetry, Nature-worship, roll in the dew before breakfast." These passages were good-humoredly appropriated by Reynolds' wife, the novelist Ethel Mannin, who dedicated her next novel, *Rolling in the Dew* (1940), "to George Orwell, who so abominates the bearded fruit-juice drinking sandal-wearers of the roll-in-the-dew-before-breakfast school." Reynolds did not let Orwell have all the running. He pointed out that Orwell "had his own conscientious pose, which was to live down his class origin by identifying himself with his own (not very accurate) conception of the manual worker. . . . [This] made him appear shabby and unkempt."

They clearly had a great deal to talk about. Reynolds confirmed Sceats' account of Orwell's political views, darkened by his disease as well as by the inexorable approach of war, and emphasized his disillusionment and gloom: "A realist without a streak of that *mystique* which enables the fanatic to work hopefully . . . for apparently hopeless causes, Orwell already saw the world through tired eyes. . . . Many of the 'amusing' things about people and the times in which we lived were regarded by him only as indications of the general corruption of both. . . . He was, in short, the most hopeless person I ever met and probably the most unhappy." As the biographer James Boswell wrote of his tormented subject, Samuel Johnson: "He was afflicted with a bodily disease, which made him often restless and fretful; and with a constitutional melancholy, the clouds of which darkened the brightness of his fancy and gave a gloomy cast to his whole course of thinking."[5]

The friendship continued until Orwell's death. In March 1942, while working at the BBC, Orwell tactfully turned aside Reynolds' proposal for a radio talk. "I know how important the subject of soil fertility and conservation of sewage is," Orwell said, "but I am doubtful about being able to fit it into any schedule." They did, however, collaborate on an anthology, *British Pamphleteers* (1948), while Orwell was writing *Nineteen Eighty-Four*. "[He was] too busy to do much work on the job," Reynolds wrote. "It fell to me to select and edit the pamphlets, with historical notes and explanations, to find suitable political cartoons, and deal with proofs and other drudge work. He contributed a characteristic and provocative introduction of about 5,000 words to the first volume, which covered the time of Queen Elizabeth to the French Revolution."[6]

II

To AVOID another flare-up of his illness, Orwell was advised to spend the winter in a warm, dry climate. In the summer of 1938 Max Plowman's wife told the wealthy novelist L.H. Myers, who had visited Orwell in the sanatorium, that he would be released on September 1. Like Richard Rees, Myers felt guilty about his unearned income and, through Dorothy Plowman, gave Orwell an anonymous gift of £300. He and Eileen spent the winter in French Morocco, and Jack Common looked after the cottage while they were abroad.

Arnold Bennett described Myers as "a thin dark man, *silencieux, un peu précieux*, but apparently of a benevolent mind." Fond of Myers, Orwell thought he was "a lovable man and a delicate and scrupulous writer, but he lacked vitality." He sometimes stayed at his friend's country house in Hampshire, and later described Myers' political beliefs and generous character:

> He spoke with the utmost bitterness of the British ruling class and said that he considered that many of them were actually treacherous in their [sympathetic] attitude towards Germany. . . . His instincts were those of a Liberal but he felt it his duty to support the USSR and therefore repudiate Liberalism. I think part of his uncertainty was due to his having inherited a large income. Undoubtedly in a way he was ashamed of this. He lived fairly simply and gave his money away with both hands . . . a sweet-natured and open-minded man.[7]

After leaving the sanatorium Orwell spent only one day in London. He and Eileen then went straight to Southampton to board the P & O liner *Stratheden* (the Spanish Civil War was still raging and they had to go by ship to avoid the Iberian peninsula). They booked second-class passage to Gibraltar, crossed the Strait to Tangier, took a train to Marrakech and arrived on September 14. After a week in the Majestic Hotel and a month lodging with a Madame Vellet, they rented the Villa Simont, three miles north of town, on the edge of a huge date-palm plantation.

Marrakech, a crossroads for caravan routes across North Africa, had a perfect climate and was supposed to be the most attractive place in Morocco. The Koutoubia Mosque and its 200-foot-high minaret dominated the town, the museums, the royal palaces, the gardens and the maze of *souks*. The towering Atlas Mountains, snowcapped in winter, provided a stunning background for the palm trees, pink buildings and high mud ramparts. The living center of town, the vast Djmaa el Fna square, was filled with food sellers, storytellers, letter writers, witch doctors, dentists, mystics, acrobats, drummers and dancers.

Eileen told her mother that their villa was "entirely isolated except for a few Arabs who live in the outbuildings to tend the orange grove that surrounds it. . . . There is a large sitting room, two bedrooms, a bathroom & a kitchen." As in Wallington, there was "no provision for cooking but we'll have some little pots with charcoal in them & a Primus." Both Orwell and Eileen were tired and weak, unhappy and ill. After her harrowing experiences in Spain, Eileen looks pale and exhausted in the photo on her French identity card. In a Marrakech photo that Eileen probably took, the emaciated Orwell—wearing a short-sleeved shirt with flies settled on it (a local touch), a signet ring on his little finger and a cigarette dangling from his mouth— sits at a desk on a straw-bottomed chair, softened by a pillow, head down and writing away on his next novel, *Coming Up for Air*. He took time off to milk one of his black goats with white marks on its face—he always had to have goats—chained up and held by a white-robed African with a shaved head.

Orwell was not interested in the picturesque, touristic aspects of Morocco, but in the social and economic conditions, agricultural methods and urban poverty. He was disgusted by what he saw. His months in Marrakech enabled him to evaluate British and French colonialism, and he felt that compared to Morocco, Burma seemed like paradise. The villagers lived in miserable little straw huts, surrounded by mud walls. The old Arab quarter of town had labyrinthine bazaars full of camels and donkeys, very exotic, but degraded by dirt and poverty. The decadent colonial milieu and threat of a major European war filled him with gloom. He had the novelist's instinct for atmosphere, and knew what was going to happen.

Eileen also found Marrakech "dreadful to live in. There are beautiful arches with vile smells coming out of them & adorable children covered in ringworm & flies." As they watched the sun go down behind a graveyard, Orwell morbidly insisted that the place was "dominated by invisible worms" and they left without seeing the sunset. He dwelled on impending bombs, famine and concentration camps, and depressed Eileen with his dark mood. Orwell got to know some Foreign Legionnaires stationed nearby, who surprised him by showing no interest in the impending European crisis.

Eileen nervously wrote Mary Common that "he has been worse here than I've ever seen him. The country is, or was anyway, almost intolerably depressing." Elisaveta Fen explained that "it was not too good a choice: the dry, hot climate with much sand dust in the air acted as an irritant on George's lungs. . . . Neither of them was stronger or better in health when they returned to England in the spring of 1939."

In late January, to escape the heat and dust and give Orwell a break from writing the novel, they spent a week in Taddert. The village, about sixty-five miles southeast of Marrakech, was 5,000-feet high in the Atlas Mountains. The road soared upward from the desert, between slopes dotted with olean-ders and scrub oaks, to a picturesque setting with fine views, mountain streams and a modest inn. "It's wonderful country," Orwell wrote to Geoffrey Gorer, "enormous limestone gorges & ravines full of frozen snow, & little Berber villages of mud huts with flat tops."[8]

But in Taddert the couple encountered a different kind of problem. Eileen's friend Lettice Cooper once said, "I don't think George was the kind of person who likes being married all the time." He was absorbed in his own work, needed an unusual amount of privacy and independence, and also wanted the freedom to have other women. He was strongly attracted to the readily available and unusually pretty Berbers, whom he described in his "Morocco Diary" as "exceedingly striking. In general they are rather fair, sometimes fair enough to have red in their cheeks, with black hair and remarkable eyes. None are veiled. . . . All the women have tattooing on their chins and sometimes down each cheek. Their manner is much less timid than that of most Arab women."

His encounters with Berber women while living with Eileen and recu-perating from lung disease might seem improbable. But he was invigorated by the cold mountain air, and later told two different people about his liai-son. Harold Acton, whom he'd spoken to about the sweetness of Burmese women, gave a rare glimpse of the sensual side of Orwell's character: "this cadaverous ascetic whom one scarcely connected with fleshly gratification admitted that he had seldom tasted such bliss as with certain Moroccan girls," and praised their naturalness, grace and candid sensuality. Orwell's close friend Tosco Fyvel wrote that "he found himself increasingly attracted by the young Arab girls and the moment came when he told Eileen that he had to have one of these girls, on just one occasion. Eileen agreed and so he had his Arab girl." Eileen may have allowed Orwell to go with a prostitute, but it must have made her unhappy and hurt their marriage.

In December 1938 Orwell told Connolly why he disliked Morocco: "[It] seems to me a beastly dull country, no forests and literally no wild animals, and the people anywhere near a big town utterly debauched by the tourist racket and their poverty combined, which turn them into a race of beggars and curio-sellers." His essay "Marrakech" (1939) contains a series of vivid impressions: fly-blown funerals, starving Arabs, squalid Jews, hopeless farmers, aged porters, brutalized donkeys and wretched soldiers. These brief scenes illuminate the desperate economic conditions of the French colony and reinforce his attack on colonialism, which reduces its subjects to moral, social and political insignificance: "when you see how people live, and still more how easily they die, it is always difficult to believe you are walking among human beings. . . . People with brown skins are next door to invisible."[9]

Toward the end of March they sailed from Casablanca on the S.S. *Yasukuni-maru*, despite the Japanese invasion of China and Japan's support of Nazi Germany, for the £6.10s fare was much lower than on the P & O line. When they reached London on March 30, they learned that Franco had won the civil war and taken control of Spain. Thousands of Republicans had fled the country, and thousands of those who remained were arrested and executed. The news confirmed Orwell's worst fears about the future of Europe.

III

ORWELL'S INTEREST in other women continued when he returned to England. While he was in the sanatorium in 1938, Eileen, knowing he was lonely, had urged her friend Lydia Jiburtovich Jackson to visit him. Born in Russia in 1899 and educated at Leningrad University, Lydia had come to England in 1925, married a Cambridge law lecturer four years later and divorced him in 1935. She studied psychology with Eileen at University College, and became a child therapist. She wrote under the name of Elisaveta Fen, and in 1951 translated and introduced a Penguin edition of Chekhov's plays. A dark, attractive woman, Lydia wore her hair pulled straight back like a ballerina. More exuberant and experienced than Eileen, she was an expert fencer, skier and rider.

In her autobiography, *A Russian's England* (1976), Lydia wrote that Orwell had placed her in an awkward situation, as they sat on the grass, by suddenly embracing her. She was loyal to Eileen and not at all attracted to Orwell—"his ill-health even aroused in me a slight feeling of repulsion"—and she

·might also have been afraid of getting infected. But she knew that he was unhappy, depressed and separated from his wife, which made it difficult for her to repulse him and hurt his feelings. Not wanting to behave like a prude or make too much of the incident by pushing him away, she took a civilized approach and allowed him to embrace and kiss her. She thought little of it at the time: "I was convinced that he was very fond of Eileen and that I was in no sense a rival to her."

By trying to be kind, Lydia misled Orwell about her feelings. On March 1 he secretly wrote to her from Marrakech to prepare her for his return to England: "I have thought of you so often—have you thought about me, I wonder? I know it's indiscreet to write such things in letters, but you'll be clever & burn this, won't you? I am so looking forward to seeing you." After convalescing in Morocco he seemed to feel better and have a greater sexual urge. On the morning he reached London he delivered the manuscript of *Coming Up for Air* to Leonard Moore, then went straight over to Lydia's flat and found that she was out. He left a note asking her to stay home the next morning, but she again managed to elude him. Exasperated and confused, he said in another reproachful note: "You were mean not to stay at home this morning like I asked you. . . . I rang up 3 times. Are you angry with me? I did write to you twice from Morocco & I don't think you wrote to me. . . . [Perhaps] we can arrange to meet—unless you don't want to."

Orwell persisted and, after he'd been to Southwold, they finally met in April. Lydia's annoyance was extinguished by compassion and she could not bring herself to be "unpleasant" to him. Once again, as she tried to be kind, he misinterpreted her feelings and pressed her to sleep with him. Still loyal to Eileen, she refused to become his lover. "He, no doubt, chose to think that I let him kiss me because I liked it. I did not. . . .[He was] a sick man, losing confidence in his attactiveness to women, needing reassurance, needing comforting. . . . That was how I saw his insistence on treating our relationship as an amorous affair, though I resisted throughout it becoming a love affair."

Eileen guessed he was seeing another woman. Not suspecting Lydia, she thought the guilty party was Brenda Salkeld. Eileen came to Lydia's flat "in a state of great frustration and anger against her husband." She told Lydia that after returning from Morocco "their relationship had been unusually harmonious," but had then gone seriously wrong. The cause, Eileen believed, was "a schoolmistress, or something. The village people saw him meeting her. This affair goes on because she wouldn't sleep with him. If she had, it would have been finished long ago. " Relieved that she was not suspected, but horrified at the thought of hurting Eileen, Lydia broke off relations with Orwell. In May 1948, when he was in another sanatorium, sicker and lonelier than ever, he wrote to Lydia and exclaimed: "I would love to see you again. The other night I was wishing very much that you were with me." This time, however, she evaded all entanglements.[10]

Between furtive visits to Lydia, Orwell went to Southwold to see his family and comfort his father, who was suffering from agonizing intestinal cancer. "My father's dying, poor old man," he told Jack Common, using a cricket metaphor and mentioning the effect on himself, "he's 81, so he'd had a pretty good innings, but what a hole it seems to leave when someone you have known since childhood goes." The following month Eileen, dashing over from Wallington when the whole family became sick, had to deal with another medical crisis: "E[ric]'s father is permanently & very ill, his mother got ill with phlebitis [inflammation of a vein], I came down all in a rush as they say to do a bit of filial-by-law nursing & was met at the doorstep by Eric with a temperature of about 102." Richard Blair died, at the age of eighty-two, on June 28.

Orwell rarely saw his father in childhood and didn't get to know him until after he returned from Burma. They were estranged during his tramping years and never became close after that. But, as Mabel Fierz wrote, Orwell "always wanted his father to be proud of him. . . . That was a great sorrow to him, that he never came up to his father's expectations." Like a set-piece in a Victorian novel, or the parable of the Prodigal Son, Orwell won his father's approval in a brief but gratifying deathbed reconciliation. On June 25, in a glowing review entitled "Mr. George Orwell's Success," Ralph Straus called *Coming Up for Air* "a brilliant novel." Orwell told Leonard Moore that old Mr. Blair had died just after hearing this news: "I am very glad that latterly he had not been so disappointed in me as before. Curiously enough his last moment of consciousness was hearing that review I had in the *Sunday Times.* . . . My sister took it in and read it to him, and a little later he lost consciousness for the last time." Orwell told Richard Rees "that he himself had closed his father's eyes in the traditional way by placing pennies upon the eyelids," but added a typically frank and ironic twist to the tale. "After the funeral he had been embarrassed to know what to do with the pennies. 'In the end I walked down to the sea and threw them in. Do you think some people would have put them back in their pocket?' "[11]

IV

LIKE HIS current novel, *Coming Up for Air*, the final paragraph of *Homage to Catalonia* contrasts the horrors of war with the peaceful, green and pleasant Thames Valley of his early years:

> Down here it was still the England I had known in my childhood: the railway cuttings smothered in wild flowers, the deep meadows where the great shining horses browse and meditate, the slow-moving streams bordered by willows, the green bosoms of the elms, the larkspurs in the cottage gardens . . . all sleeping the deep, deep sleep of England, from which I sometimes fear that we shall never wake till we are jerked out of it by the roar of bombs.

Orwell said the phrase, a "sleep-walking people," coined by Hitler to describe the Germans, "would have been better applied to the English." This idea resonates through the novel as Orwell hammers home his thesis: the good old life of England has disappeared and been replaced by a streamlined, efficient, yet tasteless and ugly mass civilization; we are paralyzed by inertia and complacency, but war is inevitable and will destroy all vestiges of the past. George Bowling, the first-person narrator, predicts: "*It's all going to happen.* All the things you've got at the back of your mind, the things you're terrified of, the things you tell yourself are just a nightmare or only happen in foreign countries. The bombs, the food-queues, the rubber truncheons, the barbed wire, the coloured shirts, the slogans, the enormous faces, the machine-guns squirting out of bedroom windows. It's all going to happen. . . . There's no escape."

Bowling, his first deliberate effort to create a representative man, is Orwell's most engaging hero. He chose a lower-middle-class insurance agent: a fat, chatty, brazen character who gets on well with people in pubs and could never be confused with Orwell himself. He lives with a nagging, money-obsessed wife and two irritating children in a shoddy house in a dreary London suburb. The novel begins on a January morning as he decides not to tell his wife about the money he's won on a horse race. At forty-five Bowling feels trapped and resentful, but as he goes about his business his private anger gives way to a general sense of foreboding, "a kind of prophetic mood, the mood in which you foresee the end of the world and get a certain kick out of it." Despite the bustle of traffic and people, he seems to be "the only person awake in a city of sleepwalkers."

In March he decides to spend the money on a trip to Lower Binfield, where he spent an idyllic childhood before the Great War. In June he breaks loose for a week but, severely disillusioned, lamely returns home. Frustrated in the present, caught between the vanished past and the destructive future, Bowling tries to escape the modern age, but finds his Eden lost forever. On one level, Orwell taps a universal theme, the aching regret of Villon's *"Où sont les neiges d'antan?"* (Where are the snows of yesteryear?). On another, the book is a political "state-of-England" novel, a call for the sleepers to wake up, to stop the destruction of the countryside, the decay of society and the impending war.

The novel's confident style and consistent tone mark a distinct departure from Orwell's earlier books. Bowling's extended meditation is cast in an artful speaking voice. His thoughts appear to ramble in all directions, yet they all revolve around certain obsessive ideas: he's trapped in his job and dissatisfied with his marriage. Unattractive and aging, fat and with false teeth, he's sadly convinced that no woman will ever look at him again.

Bowling sets up a series of contrasts: the traffic and sprawl of today against the stillness of the river in the past; the disgusting ersatz sausage he eats in the snack bar against the homely food his mother once made; himself then and himself now. Bowling thinks the world has changed as he has changed, both for the worse, but that he still remains the same young person, full of potential: "I'm vulgar, I'm insensitive, and I fit in with my environment. . . . But also I've got something else inside me, chiefly a hangover from the past. . . . I'm fat, but I'm thin inside."[12]

Though Orwell drew on recollections of playing near the river with the Buddicom children, Bowling's evocation of a secure and idyllic childhood in his father's grain shop was inspired by the novels of H.G. Wells. Orwell said that Wells' greatest gift "was his power to convey the atmosphere of the golden years between 1890 and 1914," and confessed that *Coming Up for Air* "was bound to suggest Wells watered down. I have a great admiration for Wells, i.e. as a writer, and he was a very early influence on me."

The structure and style of the novel, however, owe more to Joyce's *Ulysses*. Bowling is Orwell's Bloom, an average sensual man, with the genial personality and self-deprecating humor of a stand-up comedian. Like Joyce, Orwell uses recurring motifs to tie the novel together: Bowling's three thwarted attempts to go fishing; his past sexual encounters and present failure to be unfaithful to his wife; the gory newspaper reports of severed legs, and the body parts of the bombing victims; the black planes that constantly fly overhead and finally bomb the marketplace in Lower Binfield. Bowling's thoughts are full of images of drowning—swimming in fear, coming up for air, choking in pollution—and these watery themes also unify the novel.

Bowling's voice, especially in the nostalgic childhood passages, sounds very like Orwell's intimate, quirky, persuasive tone in his "As I Please" column and essays on English popular culture. In "The Art of Donald McGill" (1940), Orwell lists the conventions of comic postcard jokes—all women plot marriage, which only benefits women; all husbands are henpecked; middle-aged men are drunkards; nudism is comical; air raid precautions are ludicrous; illegitimate babies and old maids are funny—and Bowling believes in nearly all of them.

These stereotypical prejudices help delineate Bowling's character, but they also come close to Orwell's own ideas. *The Road to Wigan Pier* satirized many of the same subjects: drab and soulless estate housing, the difficulty of finding live fish in unpolluted streams, mild and mindless Socialists, and the crankish swarm of vegetarians, health-food addicts, fruit-juice drinkers, sandal-wearers, nudists and homosexuals. Bowling's prophetic mood is identical to Orwell's, and his misogyny—all the women in the novel are mean-spirited or decrepit, cold or indifferent—betrays Orwell's own dissatisfactions with marriage, his guilt about his infidelities and remorse about Eileen's unhappiness. In this context Bowling's fatness seems to be a metaphor for Orwell's illness. Bowling says of his wife, Hilda: "Sometimes the way she caught me out would have made me believe in telepathy. . . . I'm more or less permanently under suspicion, though, God knows, in the last few years . . . I've been innocent enough. You have to be, when you're as fat as I am." His self-pity hints at Orwell's vain pursuit of Lydia.

The descriptions of Bowling's wound and his long period of reading at a deserted depot in World War I recall Orwell's experiences in Spain and Burma. Bowling's keen eye for the lyrical detail, his memory for church smells and noises, his sense of the cruel, the macabre and the disgusting, his loathing of the fake and pretentious, all belong to Orwell. When Julian Symons noted that, for all Orwell's imaginative efforts, Bowling came a little too close to his creator, Orwell responded: "Of course you are perfectly right about my own character constantly intruding on that of the narrator." Recognizing that the novel was a polemic, he added: "I am not a real novelist anyway, and that particular vice is inherent in writing a novel in the first person, which one should never do."[13]

Coming Up for Air, a transitional work, gathers the themes Orwell had explored in the poverty books of the Thirties and anticipates the political satires of the next decade. The location and central motif of the novel appear as early as *Down and Out*, when he describes tramping in Lower Binfield and fishing in the Seine. *Keep the Aspidistra Flying* has many similarities: Gordon Comstock's belief that our civilization is dying and the whole world will soon be blown up; his fulminations against marriage and vision of a million fearful slaves groveling before the throne of money. Gordon's fellow-lodger, the traveling salesman Flaxman, has the same good humor, stout physique and mild vanity of Bowling, and he too uses some extra money to escape from his wife. The dead-alive Comstocks resemble Hilda Bowling's fossilized Anglo-Indian family. Like Bowling's friend the Oxford don Porteous, they live entirely in the past. They've withdrawn from politics and been replaced by the rabid Left Book Club lecturer. Listening to his jargon-ridden speech that stirs up hatred against the Germans, Bowling reflects that "all the decent people are paralysed. Dead men and live gorillas. Doesn't seem to be anything between." He tells a young man at the meeting that the last war "was just a bloody mess. If it comes again, you keep out of it."

D.H. Lawrence had written despairingly in the midst of the Great War: "I am so sad, for my country, for this great wave of civilisation, 2000 years, which is now collapsing, that it is hard to live. So much beauty and pathos of old things passing away and no new things coming . . . the winter stretches ahead, where all vision is lost and all memory dies out." *Coming Up for Air*, written just before the next and even more destructive world war, developed Lawrence's apocalyptic themes to include an overtly political prediction. Though Bowling feels things cracking and collapsing under his feet, decent people in the momentarily peaceful backwater of England are completely passive. "What about the new kind of men from eastern Europe, the stream-lined men who think in slogans and talk in bullets?" he warns. "They're on our track. Not long before they catch up with us."[14]

Bertrand Russell remarked that people born after 1914 "are incapable of happiness." Bowling's search for the past poignantly recreates that time of utter security and connects it with making love to Elsie Waters in the woods. She is "curiously soft, curiously feminine. As soon as you saw her you knew that you could take her in your arms and do what you wanted with her. She was really deeply feminine, very gentle, very submissive." He remembers how it felt to walk with her in the dusk: "1913! My God! 1913! The stillness, the green water, the rushing of the weir! It'll never come again. I don't mean that 1913 will never come again. I mean the feeling inside you, the feeling of not being in a hurry and not being frightened, the feeling you've either had and don't need to be told about, or haven't had and won't ever have the chance to learn." Later, as Bowling stands over his parents' grave, a bomber flying overhead casts a sudden and alarming shadow, which symbolizes the novel's main theme: the dead past and threatening future.

The English reviewers were respectful, and the *Times Literary Supplement* critic praised *Coming Up for Air* as a "cautionary tale" with "an impassioned and ruthless honesty of imagination." It was not published in America until just after Orwell's death in 1950 and, overshadowed by the impact of *Animal Farm* and *Nineteen Eighty-Four*, was not fully appreciated. Forgetting when it was written, Irving Howe called it "completely predictable." He argued that Orwell did not possess "the creativity of the true novelist," and was best in essays and reportage. Edmund Fuller called Orwell misanthropic: he "did not just dislike the human race; he downright despised it." But the Irish author James Stern praised Orwell's concern for the common man and considered *Coming Up for Air* "a masterpiece of characterization, an astonishing *tour de force*."

Misled perhaps by Bowling's lighthearted tone, Isaac Rosenfeld thought the book "failed to catch the anxiety of pre-war days"—though it is hard to imagine a more anxious, even panic-stricken novel. But he made the acute and influential observation that Orwell was "a radical in politics and a conservative in feeling," a paradoxical attitude he expressed in *Coming Up for Air*. Though this novel is full of yearning for the past, Orwell was intellectually convinced of the need for revolution, and his wartime journalism looked forward to the radical changes that would be made by a Socialist government.

Coming Up for Air opposed the idea of England going to war with Germany. But when war broke out three months after the novel appeared, Orwell changed his mind. On October 30 the novelist Ethel Mannin—married to Reginald Reynolds, and a lifelong pacifist—was outraged by Orwell's support of the war in a letter he'd written to her: "Dear Eric Blair (since you sign yourself that way) I was staggered by the last paragraph of your letter. . . . You wished you were fit enough to get into uniform and help smash Hitler and Fascism and all the rest of it. . . . After all you wrote in *Coming Up for Air*, I don't understand."[15] For Orwell the patriotic defense of his endangered country was more important than prewar principles. He had fought for Spain and would fight, if he could, for England.

10

London in the Blitz,
1939–1941

I

WHEN THE long-expected war broke out in September 1939 Eileen, seizing the chance to join the war effort and escape the austerities of Wallington, moved to London and got a job at the Censorship Department in Whitehall. It was bureaucratic and clerical work, but more suited to her abilities than tending the village shop. She lived with her mother and sister-in-law in their comfortable house in Greenwich (where she often sought refuge from her harsh life in the country), and spent every other weekend at the cottage. Her brother Laurence left the family to join the Royal Army Medical Corps. Orwell, still attached to Wallington, stayed on alone.

By April 1940, however, he became worried about Eileen and tired of his lonely life among the chickens and the goats. "I want her to get out of it," he wrote Geoffrey Gorer, "as they are simply working her to death, besides its making it impossible for us to be together." Jack Common saw him that month and was struck by the contrast between his desire for military toughness and his own poor physique: "He was standing with a hoe, looking very frail, deep-furrowed cheeks and pitifully feeble chest. His strong cord trousers gave a massivity to his legs oddly in contrast to his emaciated torso. . . . He [talked] in that flat dead voice of his, never laughing beyond a sort of wistful half-chuckle, a weariness in all he said. Again his theme is hardness—curious for his physique denies that this is his need. Hardness and action! That reiterated when all the while it saddens me to see how obviously he needs love and repose." Orwell's marriage had been twice disrupted by war and illness, and he and Eileen did not seem entirely compatible. Most of his work had been done under intense stress, and there was often no time for love and repose.

In early June 1940, Laurence O'Shaughnessy, treating the wounded during the retreat from Dunkirk, was killed by a shrapnel wound in the chest. This tragic event cast another shadow over Orwell's marriage. Deeply attached to her older brother and relying on his rock-like solidity, Eileen was shattered. In the first shock of grief, she could not help comparing her brother's love with her husband's. "If we were at the opposite ends of the world and I sent him a telegram saying 'Come at once,' he would come," she told Lydia. "George would not do that. For him his work comes before anybody." Friends noticed that Eileen fell into a deep depression. "After her brother's death," Lydia said, "she seemed to have less energy. Less sparkle. She seemed to me always tired. She neglected her health. There was perhaps some form of anemia." Tosco Fyvel, who met the Orwells earlier that year, recalled that "she seemed to sit in the garden sunk in unmoving silence while we talked. . . . Eileen not only looked tired and drawn but was drably and untidily dressed. Trying in vain to involve Eileen in conversation, Mary [Fyvel] said that she seemed to have become completely withdrawn."[1]

Eileen also seemed to welcome the dramatic chaos of war, which freed her from the oppressive responsibilities of Wallington and could sometimes jolt her out of her depression. In her novel *Black Bethlehem* Lettice Cooper wrote of the hard-working, sacrificial character, based on Eileen: "You feel about Ann that she is not only used to actual war, but is fundamentally used to the idea of war. . . . Ann and Christopher have the standards of comfort of soldiers on the march. Something to eat and somewhere to lie, and a share of anything they've got for any fellow-campaigner." Ann always stays late to finish her office work. "She cooks and cleans for her brilliant, erratic husband and their friends, [and] is generally washing up at midnight."

In January 1940 Orwell told Geoffrey Gorer: "now that we are in this bloody war we have to win it & I would like to lend a hand." But he was declared medically unfit for the army and found it difficult to get any kind of official work. In May, when the end of the static "phony war" and the German invasion of Norway posed a serious threat to London, many people left the capital to seek safety in the country. Orwell—always going against the grain—left Wallington and moved to the city, where he and Eileen lived in a series of uncomfortable flats. (Lydia Jackson and her friend rented the cottage.) It was his way of participating in the war—of sharing its dangers. As he told Julian Symons: "You've got to stay here while the war's on. You can't leave when people are being bombed to hell."[2] In his war diary that October, a year after the war had begun, Orwell registered his weariness and gloom. It was now clear that they were in for a long haul, and he noted "the unspeakable depression of lighting the fires every morning with papers of a year ago, and getting glimpses of optimistic headlines as they go up in smoke."

But the austerities of war suited his character. Several friends noted his vaguely military look as he strolled around London, hatless, in a pair of gumboots, a huge trench coat, large gauntlet gloves and a long woolen scarf. He took delight in the dreadful wartime food, which allowed him to suffer with the soldiers at the front and the civilians at home. The more wretched the dish, the more cheerful he became. He'd gobble up over-boiled cod with bitter turnip tops and annoy his companions by masochistically remarking: "I'd never have thought they'd have gone so well together!" He even ate boiled eels that Eileen had left for the cat and found them quite tasty. Stephen Spender, who visited him at Preston Hall Sanatorium with Cyril Connolly, remembered his "rather drizzly voice. Listening to one of Orwell's monologues, with all its rambling speculations, was very English in a way. It was like walking through a drizzly street." Humphrey Slater tersely summed him up as "grisly old George."[3]

Orwell believed, or hoped, that the upheavals of war would lead to the kind of social revolution he had glimpsed on his first visit to Barcelona, and spoke of Red militias billeted at the Ritz. According to V.S. Pritchett, Orwell "rather liked the war, for he saw it as a fight against the governing class as well as a fight against the Nazis. . . . He had the strange lonely detachment and fevered half-laughing energy of the sick." Connolly agreed that "he felt enormously at home in the Blitz, among the bombs, the bravery, the rubble, the shortages, the homeless, the signs of rising revolutionary temper."

Though deeply committed to the struggle, he could also take aesthetic pleasure—as his prophecies were grimly fulfilled—in the destruction all around him. In his "War Diary" he compared destroying an enemy plane to shooting a game bird, and recorded the dramatic spectacle of London burning:

This morning, for the first time, saw an aeroplane shot down. It fell slowly out of the clouds, nose foremost, just like a snipe that has been shot overhead.

Sitting in Connolly's top-floor flat and watching the enormous fires beyond St. Paul's, and the great plume of smoke from an oil drum somewhere down the river, and [Humphrey] Slater sitting in the window and saying, "It's just like Madrid—quite nostalgic." . . . [I] was chiefly struck by the size and beauty of the flames.[4]

As paper and publishing were drastically cut during the war and little magazines closed down, it became increasingly difficult to bring out books. Since Gollancz paid an advance of only £20 for *Inside the Whale*, Orwell had to work harder than ever on essays and reviews (he wrote seventy-five articles in 1940) to earn only £5 a week. From 1941 to 1946 he wrote a "London Letter" for the Left-wing anti-Stalinist *Partisan Review* in New York, turned out many pieces for the Socialist *Tribune* and wrote some of his best long essays for Connolly's *Horizon*. When dunned by Inland Revenue, he never even bothered to open the envelopes. "What's the good?" he asked Fyvel. "You can't get blood from a stone."

The serious shortage of funds meant that Orwell could—indeed, had to—indulge his peculiar relish for personal discomfort. In May 1940, when he moved to London, he and Eileen rented a dark, miserable two-room flat, above some shops, in 18 Dorset Chambers, Chagford Street, near Baker Street. There was no elevator to the fourth floor and they had to share a bathroom with the other tenants. But they hung the treasured portrait of Lady Mary Blair amidst their tattered possessions and cheap secondhand furniture.

Orwell, like Chekhov, was idealistic in his character and his work. Endearingly cranky and eccentric, he had exemplary courage and compassion. Both he and Eileen gave up part of their rations so that others—people they didn't know—would have more to eat. "She and George were always hard up," wrote Lettice Cooper, "always bombed out, and always in difficulties, but always helping somebody else, and never really ruffled by their difficulties."

They had a strange affinity for bombs, but never paid much attention to them unless they actually struck the house. As in Spain Eileen (like Orwell) was indifferent to danger, even excited by it. In his "War Diary" he noted: "A lot of bombs at Greenwich, one of them while I was talking to E. over the phone. A sudden pause in the conversation and a tinkling sound: I. 'What's that?' E. 'Only the windows falling in.' " Whenever a bomb came right over them, he felt Eileen's heart beating faster against him as they lay in bed. He depended on Eileen and referred to her as a "good old stick," which was, from him, high praise. In June 1940, aware, as always, of his poor health and the dangers of war, he still felt positive about the purpose of his life: "I have so much to live for, in spite of poor health and having no children."[5]

II

THE HAZARDS of war put great strains on their marriage: separation, shortages of essential food and goods, lack of money, poor housing, arduous work, the shock of the Blitz, bad health and, for Eileen, the deaths of her brother in 1940 and her mother in 1941. The novelist Anthony Powell, who became a friend toward the end of the war, observed that Eileen, though capable, "always appeared a little overwhelmed by the strain of keeping the household going, which could never have been easy. Possibly she was by temperament a shade serious for Orwell, falling in too easily with his own tendency to gloom."

In this wartime atmosphere Londoners led a precarious existence, lived in a heightened emotional state and felt quite free to have love affairs. Orwell told Celia Goodman (who became a close friend in 1945) that during the war both he and Eileen had been unfaithful. He seemed to have a *laissez-faire* attitude towards her affairs, but she could be jealous of his. He had affairs with secretaries at the BBC and the *Tribune*. There's no clear evidence about Eileen's lovers, but two candidates, Karl Schnetzler and Georges Kopp, were Europeans. Schnetzler, a German refugee, was interned until 1943 and then continued to work as an electrical engineer. He met Eileen at her brother's house in Greenwich, sometimes visited Wallington and went with her to see Orwell at the sanatorium. Lydia thought he was in love with Eileen, but David Astor, who knew him well, believed they were only friends.[6]

Georges Kopp, who was clearly fond of Eileen and drove her to the Aragón front to visit Orwell, had written to her after he'd escaped—half-dead—from a Fascist prison. After convalescing in Toulon, he joined the Foreign Legion and had another heroic war. In a long letter to Eileen on September 8, 1940, Kopp gave a detailed (and perhaps exaggerated) account of his adventures: "You remember you wished me a 'good war'—well, I got it. I was on the Aisne, on the Marne, on the Seine, on the Yonne, where eventually I was wounded and made prisoner. You have no doubt heard, probably, about the fate of the poor French infantry, betrayed, tankless and planeless, fighting, one against thirty, a hopeless battle."

On June 15, according to Kopp, he'd shot at a German to warn the French that trucks and tanks were approaching their barricade. In retaliation he was shot through the left forearm and lung, and eventually lost his thumb and the use of two fingers. He was taken to a French first-aid center, where, under horrific conditions, the 700 patients were soon reduced to 300. He described the crude method of stunning patients with a kick to the solar plexus ("it will interest Eric") so that doctors could operate without anesthesia. After escaping from the hospital, Kopp made his way to Lyon, where he was demobilized. He bitterly remarked that the victorious Germans now got all the girls: "*la femme est la récompense du vainqueur.*"

Thinking of Eileen, Kopp's letter turned lyrical. A real trencherman, he described the luscious melons, anchovy pies and *brioches au chocolat* that he knew she would love, and the French landscape, filled with umbrella pines, that reminded him of the road from Barcelona to Monserrat. He told her "I would like to come here some day with you to show you around." He planned to go to England to join the Free French under de Gaulle, and emotionally concluded: "Must I tell you what joy it will be for me to see and hear you, and see everybody in the Family, who I hope are all well? You know all that. You even know what sort of *pensées choisies* I am sending you. With love, George." In this moving, intimate letter, written in a style more continental than English, Kopp poured out his heart to Eileen. His strong feelings for her were partly inspired by their old comradeship and by his loneliness and suffering in two wars. We don't know if her feelings for him ever went beyond warm friendship.

After recovering from his wounds the indestructible Kopp worked as a consulting engineer with the French Ministry of Industrial Production. He resurfaced in July 1943 to hint that "it is not a full time job and does not prevent me from performing my other duties; far from it." These secret duties involved slipping behind enemy lines (by clinging—Ulysses-like—to the underside of a train) and spying on the Germans for British Naval Intelligence. Betrayed to the Gestapo, he was flown out of France by the British in 1943. Orwell had told him, "if you get out of France, call us"; Kopp, taking up the invitation, stayed with the O'Shaughnessys in Greenwich.[7]

Orwell could never hope to match Kopp's heroic record. But he joined the Home Guard just after it was created in June 1940 and served for three years in St. John's Wood, north London, until his medical discharge in November 1943. Keen to fight, he told the poet William Empson: "I hold what half the men in this country would give their balls to have, a yellow ticket [of exemption] . . . but I don't want it." When he heard that Evelyn Waugh (also born in 1903 and rather old for combat) was serving with a Commando unit, he asked the Tory Anthony Powell, "Why can't someone on the Left ever do something like that?" He wanted, above all, to "die *fighting* and have the satisfaction of killing somebody else first."

The Home Guard did not offer much opportunity to kill. Its main function was "to take over guard duties and release regular soldiers to fight invading Germans or to carry on the war overseas." The new force began unpropitiously. There were innumerable volunteers, but "no organization, no facilities for training, and, above all, no weapons. . . . For the first months of their existence the Home Guard looked and felt absurd, as they drilled with wooden rifles or practised street-fighting with non-existent Sten guns." In July 1941 "the first big call-out of the Home Guard in London District exposed alarming deficiencies in transport and 'total ignorance of elementary military principles.' "[8] Everyone knew they'd be slaughtered if they met German soldiers in combat.

Orwell was savage about the appalling leaders who marched to imaginary battle under the Old School Tie. The officers, mainly antiquated Blimps in their sixties, were fixated on static trench warfare. When the men were addressed by a general, Orwell said, "the usual senile imbecile, actually decrepit, made one of the most uninspiring speeches I ever heard." Worse still, the commander of his own platoon was a former member of Oswald Mosley's Fascist Blackshirts. When the Home Guard first started out as eager amateurs, they doctored shotgun cartridges with candle-grease and practiced grenade-throwing with lumps of concrete. Two years later, during a surprise call-out, they were still hopelessly unprepared: "It took 4½ hours to assemble the Company and dish out ammunition, and would have taken another hour to get them into their battle positions. This mainly due to the bottleneck caused by refusing to distribute ammunition but making each man come to HQ to be issued with it there."

The ill-armed and ill-trained Home Guard must have reminded Orwell of the POUM volunteers drilling in the Lenin Barracks, and he naively hoped that his unit would become a revolutionary militia. He took a course at Osterley Park, taught by Tom Wintringham and Humphrey Slater (who'd both fought in Spain), on street fighting, hand-to-hand combat, ambushing tanks, hit-and-run raids and guerrilla tactics. Promoted to sergeant, Orwell commanded twenty men, including his publisher Fredric Warburg.

Orwell had always loved explosives and had experimented with them since childhood. One of Eileen's friends exclaimed: "He made bombs, you know. Probably Molotov cocktails," and quoted her exasperated comment: "I can put up with bombs on the mantlepiece, but I will not have a machine gun under the bed." The Home Guard gave him a great opportunity to achieve the biggest blast of his life. According to Warburg, their spigot-mortar, an excellent anti-tank weapon, "was designed to hurl a 50 lb. plastic bomb with very considerable accuracy up to a distance of 400 yards." When Orwell loaded the wrong kind of bomb and gave the order to fire, the man holding the mortar lost all his front teeth and another was knocked unconscious for twenty-four hours.[9] Sergeant Orwell was clearly a greater danger to his men than to the invisible enemy.

III

ALWAYS PRESSED for money and willing to try any kind of journalism, in the ten months between October 1940 and August 1941 Orwell wrote twenty-six film reviews for *Time and Tide*, a politically independent weekly edited by Lady Rhondda, the daughter of a Welsh coal magnate. He was too intellectually serious to enjoy popular movies, and film criticism—which he abandoned when he joined the BBC in August 1941—was not his *métier*. In *Keep the Aspidistra Flying* Gordon had objected to sitting "on the padded seat in the warm smoke-scented darkness, letting the flickering drivel on the screen gradually overwhelm you." And in "Confessions of a Book Reviewer" (1946), Orwell complained that "the film critic cannot even do his work at home, but has to attend trade shows at eleven in the morning and, with one or two notable exceptions, is expected to sell his honour for a glass of inferior sherry."

Orwell reviewed films—a little-known aspect of his career—through a prism of anxiety about the massive defeats of the Allied armies during 1939–41. The Nazi invasion of Poland; the occupation of Norway, Denmark, Belgium, Holland and France; the evacuation of Dunkirk and (beginning August 1940) the air raids on England; the conquest of Yugoslavia and Greece; the destruction of shipping by U-boats and the siege of Leningrad—these events placed all of Europe under Hitler's domination and threatened the very existence of Britain. America had not yet entered the war; the victories at Stalingrad and Alamein, which turned the tide in the Allies' favor in November 1942, were distant and difficult to imagine. Orwell's film reviews specifically mentioned the *Athenia*, torpedoed with 1,400 people aboard two days after the war began, Russian tank battles, and General Wavell's first bright triumphs in Libya and Abyssinia in February 1941. In no mood to appreciate the modest virtues of morale-building escapist entertainment, he loathed *One Night in Lisbon* and angrily exclaimed: "What rot it all is! What sickly, enervating rubbish! How dare anyone present the war in these colours when thousands of tanks are battling on the plains of Poland and tired aircraft workers are slinking into the tobacconist's shop to plead humbly for a small Woodbine?"

Orwell was not interested in film as an art form, and unlike his contemporaries Graham Greene and James Agee, rarely even mentioned the directors. He was mainly concerned with the political, social and moral content of films, their propaganda value, the way they reflected the progress of the war, and the difference between English and American cinema. Orwell mainly reviewed films of poor quality, and his reviews were generally short and formulaic: an opening comment, discussion of the plot, snap judgment on the film and remarks on the cast, with particular praise for veteran English character actors. He enjoyed sneering about the technical deficiencies of the new medium, and remarked that the horrible early Technicolor in Noël Coward's *Bitter Sweet* made the actors' faces "marzipan pink . . . garish magenta and poisonous green." As in *Coming Up for Air*, Orwell was openly contemptuous of American popular culture and its influence on British life. George Cukor's *The Gay Mrs. Trexel*, which lacked "any decent, intelligent vision of life," disgusted and offended him.[10]

He was so repelled by the gratuitous violence in American culture, which he later discussed in his essay on detective novels, "Raffles and Miss Blandish," that he failed to recognize a good movie when he saw one. To Orwell, the Raoul Walsh gangster film *High Sierra* represented the essence of sadism, bully worship and gunplay, repugnantly combined with sentimentality and perverse morality. He wrote: "Bogart is the Big Shot who smashes people in the face with the butt of his pistol and watches his fellow gangsters burn to death with the casual comment, 'They were only small-town guys,' but is kind to dogs and is supposed to be deeply touching when he is smitten with a 'pure' affection for a crippled girl who knows nothing of his past. In the end he is killed, but we are evidently expected to sympathize with him and even to admire him." Forgetting his own propensity to violence and desire to kill a few Buddhist monks and Nazi soldiers before he died, Orwell ignored Bogart's fine performance and emotionally complex character—a criminal with integrity and a code of honor.

Charlie Chaplin's *The Great Dictator* challenged Orwell's prejudice against Hollywood, and he was impressed by the way Chaplin presented serious ideas through absurd comedy. He praised the "glorious scenes of fights against the Storm Troopers which are not less, perhaps actually *more* moving because the tragedy of wrecked Jewish households is mixed up with [slapstick] humour." He described how the little Jewish barber is mistaken for Hynkel, the Dictator of Tomania, and said the great moment of the film occurred when the barber is surrounded by Nazi dignitaries, waiting to hear his triumphant oration: "Instead of making the speech that is expected of him, Charlie makes a powerful fighting speech in favour of democracy, tolerance, and common decency . . . one of the strongest pieces of propaganda I have heard for a long time."

Though Orwell believed the film was technically weak, had no more unity than a pantomime and gave the "impression of being tied together with bits of string," he found it deeply moving because he identified with Chaplin's peculiar gift: "his power to stand for a sort of concentrated essence of the common man, for the ineradicable belief in decency that exists in the hearts of ordinary people, at any rate in the West. We live in a period in which democracy is almost everywhere in retreat, supermen in control of three-quarters of the world, liberty explained away by sleek professors, Jew-baiting defended by pacifists. . . . Chaplin's appeal lies in his power to reassert the fact, overlaid by Fascism and, ironically enough, by Socialism, that *vox populi* is *vox Dei* and giants are vermin."[11]

IV

IN HIS "War Diary" Orwell contrasted his dashing off reviews at one sitting with the painstaking work he did on his books. He usually rewrote his major works at least three times and revised individual passages as many as ten times. At the beginning of the war he brought out two short books of masterly exposition and criticism. *Inside the Whale*, published by Gollancz in March 1940, contained three essays: on Charles Dickens, on boys' weeklies and the title piece on Henry Miller. *The Lion and the Unicorn*, published by Secker & Warburg in February 1941, was an extended essay on his hopes for a Socialist society in Britain. He defined the national character in the opening section, "England, Your England."

Though Orwell's essay is one of the earliest critical studies of Dickens, it is still valuable for its freshness, breadth and suggestiveness. Lucid, lively and utterly free of jargon, it manages to say a great deal in a short space. A passionate reader of all kinds of novels, Orwell had an impressive grasp of Dickens' life and work, and of the social and political history of his time. His essay (like the other two in the book) touches on key issues: what is the "message" of fiction? How does it relate to the author's life? How does it reflect its political context? Should a novelist have a political purpose? All three essays are subtly autobiographical, exploring aspects of Orwell's life and reading, staking out and defining his own purpose as an author.

Orwell begins with the striking idea that Dickens is a writer "well worth stealing." He's been appropriated by the Right and the Left, but belongs to neither. Orwell then asks the crucial question: "where exactly does he stand, socially, morally and politically?" Dickens has no political program. His central characters are drawn mainly from the urban lower-middle class to which he belonged, his aristocratic characters are caricatures and his lower classes criminal or comic. He never writes about work, and his heroes' ideal is a static, safe domesticity. Why then, is Dickens a great writer?

Orwell states that there are two possible approaches to social inequalities: the revolutionary or the moralist. The revolutionary supposes that you can improve human nature by changing the system; the moralist, like Dickens, believes the world will change only when men have a change of heart. Orwell cites A Tale of Two Cities to show that Dickens feared mob hysteria and understood that revolution always results in a new abuse of power. "There is always a new tyrant," Orwell wrote, "waiting to take over from the old—generally not quite so bad, but still a tyrant"—an idea which became the dominant theme of Animal Farm and Nineteen Eighty-Four. Orwell insists that Dickens ought to have a political purpose and lists Dickens' shortcomings as a thinker, but then reverses his own argument. These apparent defects are actually virtues: "Dickens is not in the accepted sense a revolutionary writer. But it is not at all certain that a merely moral criticism of society may not be just as 'revolutionary'—and revolution, after all, means turning things upside down."

Orwell phrases his insights in memorable epigrams. Dickens' infinite elaboration is "all fragments, all details—rotten architecture, but wonderful gargoyles—and never better than when he is building up some character who will later on be forced to act inconsistently." Dickens is a moralist who "is always preaching a sermon, and that is the final secret of his inventiveness," for "you can only create if you can care." Orwell's self-reflective concluding sentence brings Dickens to life and makes us see that his spirit is continuous with our own: "It is the face of a man who is always fighting against something, but who fights in the open and is not frightened, the face of a man who is *generously* angry—in other words, of a nineteenth-century liberal, a free intelligence, a type hated with equal hatred by all the smelly little orthodoxies which are now contending for our souls."

To Orwell, Dickens was a great deal more than a novelist. He notes that Dickens developed the theme of the child as victim, describes Dickens's childhood trauma of working in the blacking-factory and deals at some length with his two most autobiographical novels, *David Copperfield* and *Great Expectations*. He vividly recalls reading *David Copperfield* at the age of nine, and thinking a child must have written it. These novels influenced the way he remembered his prep-school days when he came to write "Such, Such Were the Joys." He, too, had been forced into a harsh and humiliating environment, and threatened with disgrace and failure. Orwell's Winston Smith begins life as an orphaned and traumatized child, and he falls under O'Brien's spell partly because he's never had a father.

In "Boys' Weeklies," an amusing sociological analysis, Orwell returns to another kind of childhood reading—magazines like *Gem* and *Magnet*—which had been popular with boys for more than thirty years. He first defined the essential conventions of the stories: the boys never grow older, sex is completely taboo, snob appeal is shameless, all foreigners are funny, England is always right and always wins. He then condemned the subtle and hitherto unnoticed strain of propaganda. Their young readers "get what they are looking for, but they get it wrapped up in the illusions which their future employers think suitable for them . . . : the conviction that the major problems of our time do not exist, that there is nothing wrong with *laissez-faire* capitalism, that foreigners are unimportant comics and that the British Empire is a sort of charity-concern which will last forever." In these illusory Right-wing stories the clock has deliberately stopped at 1910: "Britannia rules the waves, and no one has heard of slumps, booms, unemployment, dictatorships, purges or concentration camps."

True enough, but Orwell overstates his argument. The magazines were meant to entertain, and few boys would want to read about economic cycles or political oppression. Nevertheless, his innovative approach to popular culture opened the field to serious study and was extremely influential. The novelist and critic David Lodge, for example, has recently said that as a student he was fascinated by "essays that discussed topics like saucy postcards and boys' comics and pulp fiction in a way that was intelligent, accessible and free of cant. I would like to think that Orwell influenced the way I tried to write criticism."[12]

In "Inside the Whale" Orwell defined his own place in contemporary literature by means of a sympathetic contrast to Henry Miller and to the main literary traditions of the Twenties and Thirties. Though Miller's *Tropic of Cancer* (1931) seems to be the very antithesis of Orwell's work, it's set in the same proletarian Paris of the 1920s that he described in *Down and Out*. Like Miller, Orwell had no connection with the brilliant literary and artistic world of Paris before the crash; and *Tropic of Cancer*, for all its obscenity and amorality, represents the kind of novel Orwell might have written about Parisian squalor. Orwell felt Miller's whole atmosphere was deeply familiar. As you read the novel, he said, "you have all the while the feeling that these things are happening to *you*." Defending Miller against the charge of obscenity, he remarks that "if there were easy money to made out of dirty words, a lot more people would be making it." (Ironically enough, Orwell's copy, illegal in England, was seized by two detectives who suddenly arrived in Wallington as he was writing about it.)

Miller differs from Orwell and from most of the writers of the 1930s in his passive, non-political attitude, his apathetic though realistic acceptance of the world as it is. In the second part of the essay Orwell explains Miller's escape from current literary engagement by discussing the "message" of the major English writers since the Great War. A.E. Housman's cynical strain and bitter paganism, his implied sexual revolt and personal grievance against God, made him the most influential postwar poet. But he was soon eclipsed by the more experimental writers of the 1920s—Joyce, Eliot, Pound and Lawrence—who replaced the Georgian poets' nature-worship with a tragic sense of life. Both schools, in different ways, were escapist. Housman and the Georgians evoked the thatched roofs and muscular smiths in the villages of pre-industrial England, while the more avant-garde writers looked "to Rome, to Byzantium, to Montparnasse, to Mexico, to the Etruscans, to the Subconscious, to the solar plexus—to everywhere except the places where things are actually happening."

The Auden-Spender school of the 1930s revolted against the pessimistic and reactionary outlook of their predecessors and introduced a serious purpose into literature. By 1930 traditional values like religion, family, patriotism and the Empire had lost their significance. During the struggle against Fascism, English intellectuals came under the influence of Communist ideology. These writers, growing up in the land of liberalism and habeas corpus, accepted and even condoned "the purge-and-Ogpu [secret police] side of the Russian régime and the horrors of the first Five-Year Plan," in which hundreds of thousands of people were killed, because they were incapable of understanding what it meant. The phrase "necessary murder" from Auden's poem "Spain" "could only be written by a person to whom murder is at most a *word*. . . . Auden's brand of amoralism is only possible if you are the kind of person who is always somewhere else when the trigger is pulled."

According to his biographer, "Auden himself said of the line: 'I was not excusing totalitarian crimes but only trying to say what, surely, every decent person thinks if he finds himself unable to adopt the absolute pacifist position. . . . If there is such a thing as a just war, then murder can be necessary for the sake of justice.' However, possibly as a result of Orwell's criticism, he changed the line to 'The conscious acceptance of guilt in the fact of murder.' "

In the final section Orwell returns to Miller, who shares his own sense of the impending ruin of modern civilization, but doesn't care to do anything about it. Orwell agrees that remaining metaphorically inside the whale is an attractive declaration of irresponsibility, and even tolerates this attitude, which after all expressed the feelings of most people. But he cannot adopt this position himself because, as he warned when foreshadowing the theme of *Nineteen Eighty-Four*, "we are moving into an age of totalitarian dictatorships—an age in which freedom of thought will be at first a deadly sin and later on a meaningless abstraction. The autonomous individual is going to be stamped out of existence."[13]

Critics responded favorably to Orwell's blend of political and literary analysis, and praised his sanity and sharpness. Philip Mairet noted the influence of Marx and described him as "too sincere to write except when he is interested and too active in temperament to be interested in anything without doing something more than write about it." V.S. Pritchett praised the "lucid revelation of a mind that is alive, individual and nonconforming." Queenie Leavis, in *Scrutiny*, was one of the first critics to draw attention to the distinctive qualities of Orwell's criticism, and recognized the value of his personal experience: "He has lived an active life among all classes and in several countries, he isn't the usual parlour-Bolshevik seeing literature through political glasses."

The propagandistic *The Lion and the Unicorn: Socialism and the English Genius* was the first in a series of Searchlight booklets which offered socialistic solutions to wartime problems: nationalization of major industries, limitation of incomes, reform of education, Dominion status for India,

representation of colored peoples on the Imperial General Council and formal alliance with all victims of Fascist powers. Many of these ideas were
implemented when the Labour government was elected in 1945.

"England Your England" (1941), the opening section of this book, was
later reprinted separately and stands as an independent work. The title comes
from W.E. Henley's patriotic poem, "For England's Sake" (1892):

> *What have I done for you,*
> *England, my England?*
> *What is there I would not do,*
> *England my own?*

Orwell's essay analyzed the distinctive cultural characteristics and class structure of England, and contrasted the English belief in justice and objective
truth to the power-worship and terrorism of the Fascist enemies. As in "Inside
the Whale," he implicitly suggested his own character and ideals through his
definition of the positive and negative aspects of English life.

As in *Down and Out* and *Homage to Catalonia*, Orwell began with a brilliant synthesis of the sounds, smells and surfaces of things one notices when
returning to England from abroad: "The beer is bitterer, the coins are heav-
ier, the grass is greener, the advertisements are more blatant. The crowds in
the big towns, with their mild knobbly faces, their bad teeth and gentle manners, are different from a European crowd." He then revealed the differences
from other countries by generalizing about the English. They are not gifted
in music or the visual arts, dislike abstract thought, are snobbish, xenopho-
bic and hypocritical, value privacy and individual liberty, and, though their
religious belief is weak, have a deep respect for morality and legality. Their
gentleness is manifested in a hatred of war and militarism, and a tendency
to support the weaker side. Just as artistic insensibility is balanced by great
literature and a lack of intellectuality by a gift for instinctive action, so gentleness is compounded with barbarities like flogging and hanging, individual liberty with class distinctions and a gross inequality of wealth and privilege.

Orwell wanted to encourage his compatriots in wartime by celebrating
their distinctness and their virtues as a nation, and at the same time to attack
the political system from a Socialist point of view. He suggested that England
was not engaged in war because of historical inevitability or the aggressive
policy of dictators, but because of the decay of the English ruling class and
their disastrous appeasement in the 1930s. Just as the English writers of that

decade refused to see the Russian reality and supported Communism because it opposed Fascism, so the English statesmen of the time accepted Fascism because it was hostile to Communism. England (and France), by remaining strictly neutral during the Spanish Civil War, allowed Germany and Italy to help Franco win the war. The ruling class were morally sound but, "tossed to and fro between their incomes and their principles," they made "the worst of both worlds." Orwell, unlike most writers of his time, recognized that both Fascism *and* Communism were opposed to democracy.

While the imperialists declined with the stagnation of the Empire, the intelligentsia took their ideas from Europe and were ashamed of their own nationality. Orwell belonged to both these groups, and remained isolated within each of them. He understood that the Empire was doomed and welcomed the independence of the colonies, but his contact with imperial, economic and military facts protected him from "the emotional shallowness of people who live in a world of ideas and have little contact with physical reality." Unlike the philistine Blimps and the snobbish intellectuals, Orwell was proud of his country's culture. He makes a strong case for intelligence *and* patriotism.

In May 1941, three months after the book appeared, the Democratic-Socialist Club invited him to speak at Oxford University. The poet Philip Larkin recalled that "we took Dylan Thomas to the Randolph and George Orwell to the not-so-good hotel. I suppose it was my first essay in practical criticism."[14]

V

Just as Orwell's circle of friends widened considerably when he moved from provincial Southwold to London in the early 1930s and met Rees, Plowman and *Adelphi* writers like Heppenstall and Sayers, so he again made important new friends—Tosco Fyvel, David Astor and Arthur Koestler—when he moved from the isolation of Wallington to London a decade later. The bombardment of London drew people together and established a wartime camaraderie.

The kind, gentle, loyal Fyvel (1907–85), born in Cologne, was educated in Switzerland and at Cambridge, and emigrated to Palestine with his Zionist parents in the 1930s. During the war he engaged in psychological warfare in North Africa and Italy. In 1945 he succeeded Orwell as literary editor of the *Tribune*, and then worked for the BBC. He met Orwell through Warburg in

January 1940 when they began to edit the Searchlight series, and found they shared many literary and political interests. Fyvel came to know him well, wrote a perceptive memoir of him and—like Runciman and Heppenstall—felt Orwell helped create his own legend as a small-scale farmer, urban proletarian and sacrificial idealist. He vividly recalled meeting Orwell at his small mews-flat on Chagford Street, "a rather poverty-stricken affair of one or two rather bare, austere rooms with second-hand furniture. I saw an extremely tall, thin man, looking more than his years, with gentle eyes and deep lines that hinted at suffering on his face. The word 'saint' was used by one of his friends and critics [V.S. Pritchett] after his death, and—well—perhaps he had a touch of this quality. Certainly there was nothing of the fierce pamphleteer in his personal manner. He was awkward, almost excessively mild. Both about him and his wife . . . there was something strangely unphysical."

David Astor is the younger son of the 2nd Viscount Astor, who owned the *Observer* and was a Conservative M.P. for Plymouth, and of the American-born Nancy Astor, who was the first woman to be elected to the House of Commons and succeeded her husband as M.P. in 1919. Born in 1912, David was educated at Eton and Balliol College, Oxford. He served during the war in the Royal Marines, and was editor of the *Observer* from 1948 to 1975. Though he grew up in great luxury on the family estate in Cliveden, Buckinghamshire, he made the *Observer* "the most radical liberal newspaper in modern British journalism, battling on behalf of the oppressed, of minorities and of the persecuted in Britain and around the world."

He and Orwell met in about December 1941 after Astor had asked Connolly to recommend someone who was "good on politics." The two lunched at a hotel near the BBC and established immediate rapport. Astor found him direct, informal, easy to get on with. "We got right down to it," Astor recalled. "I found him a kindred spirit and could talk to him at once." They discussed what Orwell could do for the *Observer*, and he was passionate about independence for India. He became Astor's close friend and political mentor, and made him "aware of the postwar problem of decolonization in Africa." Astor distributed copies of Orwell's "Politics and the English Language"—a model for clear thinking and writing—to the entire staff of the newspaper. "Stick to Orwell," Koestler advised, "he'll never let you down"—and he never did. Astor said: "I really adored him. He was very likeable: honest, straightforward and truthful."[15] Overcoming all obstacles, including Orwell's unwillingness to ask for help, Astor became the benefactor of his last years, as Rees had been at the start of his career.

Orwell's friendship with Koestler was a union of opposites, firmly cemented by Left-wing anti-Stalinism, based on their near-fatal experiences in Spain. Koestler was central European, Jewish, ex-Communist, cosmopolitan, hedonist, unscrupulous with women, a demonic worker, heavy drinker and restless traveler. He was born in Budapest in 1905, studied engineering and psychology in Vienna, and became the science correspondent for the Ullstein chain of newspapers in Germany. He joined the Communists in 1931, spent a year in Russia and left the Party in 1938. During the Spanish Civil War, as correspondent for the London *News-Chronicle*, he was imprisoned for several months when the Fascists captured Málaga. He heard the bursts of rifle fire each night as groups of Republicans were executed and was himself in constant danger of being shot. Reviewing *The Spanish Testament*, which described these experiences, Orwell wrote in February 1938: "It is of the greatest psychological interest—probably one of the most honest and unusual documents that have been produced by the Spanish war."

When World War II broke out Koestler escaped from a French detention camp and made his way to England, where he was jailed for the third time. (He said Pentonville was his favorite prison.) In 1940 he published his masterpiece, *Darkness at Noon*, about the psychological effects of the Moscow Purge Trials on its victims. Reviewing the book in January 1941, the month before he met Koestler, Orwell wrote: "Brilliant as this book is as a novel, and a piece of prison literature, it is probably most valuable as an interpretation of the Moscow 'confessions' by someone with an inner knowledge of totalitarian methods." Koestler knew the meaning of exile and persecution, and understood—like Orwell, but few others in England—that revolutionary idealism was inevitably destroyed by the corrupting effects of power. As the novelist John Banville observed, Koestler was "the classic Mitteleuropean sensibility: deracinated, sophisticated, ambitious, self-doubting, hungry for experience, politically engaged, and racked by despair."[16]

The two men met through Fredric Warburg in mid-February 1941. Impressed by Koestler's profound understanding of Spanish politics and European dictatorships, Orwell reviewed his books, worked with him on several political projects and, when he left for Jura, arranged for Koestler to take over his work at the *Observer* and the *Partisan Review*. Orwell was always scrupulously impartial when reviewing his friends' books. In November 1945 he wrote of Koestler's play, *Twilight Bar*: "The dialogue is mediocre, and, in general, the play demonstrates the gap that lies between having an idea and working it up into dramatic shape." When Orwell visited him the following month, Koestler admitted the play was pretty poor but asked why Orwell hadn't softened his criticism a bit. Placing the blame squarely on Koestler, Orwell first said that had never occurred to him, but later conceded that he might have been too severe. In his 1941 essay on Koestler's works, Orwell identified the crucial weakness in his writing (as well as in Connolly's): "Men can only be happy when they do not assume that the object of life is happiness. It is most unlikely, however, that Koestler would accept this. There is a well-marked hedonistic strain" in Koestler, which explained "his failure to find a political position after breaking with Stalinism." Despite their profound temperamental differences, Orwell shared Koestler's passionate anti-totalitarian views. In March 1946 they tried to arrange the publication of a Polish pamphlet which revealed that in 1940 more than 15,000 Polish soldiers had been murdered and buried in mass graves in the Russian forest of Katyn, near Smolensk. According to Warburg, "the only man he discussed his work with was Arthur Koestler."[17]

Unlike Astor, Koestler found Orwell rather intimidating at their first meeting. Reducing his rank, he described him as "rather cold, a real Burmah police sergeant." He would never have guessed he was an Old Etonian and thought he looked more like a Borstal Boy. But once he got to know him, Orwell "was one of the very few Englishmen for whom Koestler—the hard-edged Continental intellectual—felt affection and admiration in equal measure." He used to see Orwell at weekly lunches in the Elysée with Fyvel, Julian Symons and Malcolm Muggeridge. Since they were both pessimists, Koestler found it more stimulating than depressing to be with him. He remembered Orwell saying "how lovely it was to be in a hot bath and dream of the tortures one is inflicting (in fantasy) on one's enemies."[18] Contrasting their characters, he later wrote that Orwell's "chronic illness made him irritable and short-tempered with fools but he had an enormous store of kindness and even tenderness in him, which I admired and sometimes envied." At a 1941 PEN luncheon with Connolly and Stevie Smith, Koestler shrewdly "bet five bottles of burgundy that in five years' time Orwell would be a best seller"—and of course won his bet. Connolly, imitating Koestler's strong Hungarian accent, liked to ask: "The great question is: 'Who vill vin ze desert var? Wavell, Fyvel or Orvell?' "[19]

11

Wartime Propagandist,
1941–1943

I

THOUGH *Burmese Days* had been banned in India, Orwell finally found war work in August 1941 as a Talks Producer on the Eastern Service of the BBC. In addition to his modest income from writing in 1942 (£60 for eighteen articles and £6 for *Keep the Aspidistra Flying*) he now earned a salary of £640 a year. For the first time since 1925 he made more money than he had as a policeman in Burma. The job was demanding: nine hours on weekdays and three on Saturday mornings. He had to provide news commentaries as well as cultural, educational and political programs that would persuade intellectual Indians to support the British in the war. This propaganda became more important after the fall of Burma in January 1942 when there was a strong possibility that the Japanese would invade India.

In August he attended a two-week crash course at Bedford College in Regent's Park on war propaganda. At the "Liars' School," the new employees, including the poets William Empson and Louis MacNeice, went to lectures, demonstrations and practical classes, and received "instruction in Programme Techniques, accompanied by sketches of the main Engineering and Administrative processes." The dour Sir John Reith, Director-General from 1927 to 1938, had given the BBC a reputation for accuracy and rectitude, but had also made it a puritanical organization, and his moral influence lasted well into the 1940s. Announcers wore evening dress to broadcast the news, racing and gambling were forbidden subjects, and employees could be fired if they divorced. The war brought a great many bohemian writers into this rather prim atmosphere.

Just as Eileen's work in the Censorship Department influenced Orwell's portrayal of the Ministry of Truth, so many aspects of the BBC went straight into *Nineteen Eighty-Four*. Room 101 at 55 Portland Place, where the Eastern Service held compulsory—and apparently boring—committee meetings, became the room in which Winston was tortured and broken. The army of charwomen, who (Orwell wrote) "sit in the reception hall waiting for their brooms to be issued to them and making as much noise as a parrot house, and then have wonderful choruses, all singing together as they sweep the passages," became the red-armed prole woman who sings while hanging her washing on the line: "Her voice floated upward with the sweet summer air, very tuneful, charged with a sort of happy melancholy."[1]

In June 1942, the BBC expanded and Orwell moved to its temporary headquarters at the Peter Robinson department store at 200 Oxford Street. According to Martin Esslin, who also worked there, the vast rooms had been subdivided "into a honeycomb of small cubicles, separated from each other by flimsy hardboard partitions. In the basement were studios and the canteen," which had horrid food, dented cups and grubby waitresses. "The old-maid secretaries seemed to be members of the Anti-Sex League." Esslin added that on the ground floor "the large plate-glass shop windows . . . were bricked up, those on the upper floors covered with dingy blackout curtains. A drearier, more dismal environment could hardly be imagined." The wartime BBC canteen became, virtually unchanged, the canteen in the novel: "A low-ceilinged, crowded room, its walls grimy from the contact of innumerable bodies; battered metal tables and chairs, placed so close together that you sat with elbows touching; bent spoons, dented trays, coarse white mugs; all surfaces greasy, grime in every crack; and a sourish, composite smell of bad gin and bad coffee and metallic stew and dirty clothes."[2] Orwell would demonstrate his proletarian manners by pouring his tea into his saucer and drinking it with a loud slurping noise.

Orwell's increasingly eccentric character made a strong impression on colleagues, including William Empson and John Morris, who wrote essays about his time at the BBC. Orwell was extremely conscientious and turned out an enormous amount of work: 220 news commentaries in addition to essays, stories, imaginary interviews and radio adaptations of works by Hans Andersen, Anatole France, Oscar Wilde, H.G. Wells and Ignazio Silone. His secretary Elisabeth Knight recalled that "he couldn't have been better to work for. He was very organised, but relaxed. He never told me off and never put pressure on me, no last minute demands. He was quiet, but not withdrawn. His eyes were lively and watchful"—and often watched her.

The Eastern Service, with its grim setting but characteristic ambiance, reminded Orwell of the Orient. "When I listen to the high-pitched Indian voices in the office," he said, "as I look out the window I am surprised not to see palm trees waving." Problems were often solved in the eastern way. When the Secret Service discovered that Kothari, who translated the newsletters into Marathi, was or had been a Communist, the BBC had to sack him. Since Jatha, his replacement, couldn't write the language, Kothari secretly kept his old job by ghosting for him. Orwell noted that "wherever Indians are to be found, this kind of thing will be happening." But he actually admired the ingenious solution that dodged the bureaucratic obstacles, completed the job and helped the workers. Arguing with one of his colleagues and adopting a self-consciously cockney accent, Orwell could be heard through the thin partition saying: "The FACK that you're black . . . and that I'm white, has *nudding whatever to do wiv it*."[3] Curiously enough, his invisible Indian colleague did not reply "But I'm *not* black!"

To an Indian colleague, Bahadur Singh, who didn't know him as well as Elisabeth did, he appeared "withdrawn and preoccupied." His work was all the more impressive since he gave the "impression of being generally bored. . . . He was doing a job of work without having his heart in it and with not much enthusiasm." Malcolm Muggeridge noted that when Orwell recalled the many absurdities of the BBC "he began to chuckle; a dry, rusty, growly sort of chuckle, deep in his throat, very characteristic of him and very endearing." Sunday Wilshin, who often met him in the canteen and took over his job when he left the BBC, agreed with Koestler that "he was rather forbidding in his approach to people, but at the same time you could feel this inner warmth in him." The art critic Herbert Read, who made several wartime broadcasts, declared: "my God, Orwell is a gloomy bird!"[4]

Orwell used his literary contacts, and his appeal to patriotic duty, to recruit a number of distinguished literary figures to broadcast for the BBC: T.S. Eliot, E.M. Forster, Dylan Thomas, Connolly, Spender, Lehmann, Read and Pritchett. He tried to get official clearance for the eighty-seven-year-old Bernard Shaw to talk on Ibsen, arguing that "his chances of making undesirable remarks are not very great in a programme of this type." But his supervisors were nervous about inviting that loose cannon, and Shaw himself felt he was "getting past that sort of thing." Orwell lunched with Eliot a number of times. In January 1943 he invited Eliot to dinner and suggested he stay the night to avoid traveling home during the blackout and air raids.

In a BBC photograph of 1942, Orwell and Empson stand next to a group of broadcasters to India. Eliot and several Indians, including the Ceylonese poet Tambimuttu, are seated around a table, scripts in hand, and below a hanging microphone in a recording studio. Orwell also appears on his own, in a well-known photo, seated before a black microphone that's solidly planted on a shiny desk. His hair is high in front, close cut at the sides. He wears a grey flannel shirt and sweater, with a thick woolen jacket, a hairy (never an old-school) tie and a handkerchief flowing out of his breast pocket like a rumpled flower. His mustache is clipped, his face is thin and deeply grooved, but his eyes are bright and lively.

Orwell tested his ideas at the BBC. His talks on Edmund Blunden, Jack London and Jonathan Swift were early versions of his review of Blunden's *Cricket Country*, his introduction to London's *Love of Life* and his essay on *Gulliver's Travels*, which meant more to him "than any other book ever written." But all his material had to be simplified for Indian audiences and makes pretty dull reading today. Some of his radio discussions were absurd ("*Orwell*: The second poem is . . . more like a ballad. *Empson*: Actually, it's a savage attack on militaristic sentiment. *Orwell*: Possibly, but as I was saying. . . .") Others were unintentionally funny: "It's a pity [Wilfred Owen] isn't here to read it. He was killed. But we've got Edmund Blunden here today."[5]

Orwell needed all the help he could get. His friend George Woodcock thought he "had a very rudimentary idea of radio production, and his own voice [weakened by the bullet wound] was too thin to make him an effective broadcaster." John Morris agreed that "he was a poor and halting speaker; even in private conversation he expressed himself badly and would often fumble for the right word. His weekly broadcasts were beautifully written, but he delivered them in a dull and monotonous voice." When Laurence Brander was sent to India in September 1943 to find out who was listening to the programs and which broadcasters were most popular, Orwell did poorly on the approval ratings. Wickham Steed, former editor of the *Times*, got 76 percent, the novelist J.B. Priestley 68 percent, Forster 52 percent, Lady Grigg (who threw her weight around and caused a lot of trouble) 20 percent, and Orwell himself tied with his old enemy Kingsley Martin at 16 percent.

Even if Orwell's voice had been dazzling, Brander discovered, virtually no one heard him or anyone else. Of the 300 million Indians, only 121,000 owned radios (a minuscule .04 percent) and only a few thousand actually tuned in. The broadcasts were aimed at a small number of students and intellectuals, who were generally anti-British, hostile to their propaganda and not even interested in programs of light entertainment. In any case, as Brander depressingly reported, the programs "could hardly be heard because the signal was so weak. Very few students had access to wireless sets. Impressive processions of literary men and professors were hurrying through the B.B.C. broadcasting to India, where practically nobody was listening or able to listen."[6]

Since the BBC personnel files are still closed, we don't know how his superiors evaluated Orwell. But he described the atmosphere as "something half way between a girls' school and a lunatic asylum" and, after great efforts were made and nothing was achieved, claimed that "all we are doing at present is useless, or slightly worse than useless." He complained about the desperate search for suitable subjects, lamented the poor quality of the transmissions ("it was a complete muck-up, owing to some technical hitch, and consisted largely of scratching noises") and regretted that he was forced to lie for propagandistic purposes. Still, the BBC was not all bad. During the war it continued to pay Hitler royalties, through neutral Sweden, for excerpts from *Mein Kampf*.

In fact, Orwell hated propaganda and hated his job as much as Winston Smith does in *Nineteen Eighty-Four*. In *Homage to Catalonia* he had bitterly observed that "one of the most horrible features of war is that all the war-propaganda, all the screaming and lies and hatred, comes invariably from people who are not fighting." In April 1942, disgusted with wartime propaganda on both sides, he wrote a scathing passage in his diary: "You can go on and on telling lies, and the most palpable lies at that, and even if they are not actually believed, there is no strong revulsion. We are all drowning in filth. . . . I feel that intellectual honesty and balanced judgement have simply disappeared from the face of the earth. . . . Is there no one who has both firm opinions and a balanced outlook? Actually there are plenty, but they are powerless. All power is in the hands of paranoiacs."[7]

In the summer of 1942, on a rare fishing holiday, he stayed on a farm near the River Severn at Callow End, Worcestershire. Struck by the quiet, the isolation from war and the bountiful food, he wrote: "no noise except aeroplanes, birds and the mowers cutting the hay. No mention of war except with reference to the Italian prisoners who are working on some of the farms. . . . In spite of the feeding difficulties, plenty of pigs, poultry, geese and turkeys about. Cream for every meal."

In August 1943, frustrated by the impossibility of getting anything done at the BBC, Orwell told Heppenstall: "I am definitely leaving, probably in about 3 months. Then, by some time in 1944, I might be near-human again & be able to write something serious. At present I'm just an orange that's been trodden on by a very dirty boot"—a brutal image that recurred in his essays and in *Nineteen Eighty-Four*. He was far too independent and out-spoken for this essential but soul-destroying war work in a huge bureaucratic organization. Though he felt he'd managed to keep "our propaganda slightly less disgusting than it might otherwise have been," at the BBC, as in Burma, he moved from from idealism to disillusionment.[8]

II

KIND AND gentle in his personal relations, Orwell was passionate about politics and fiercely combative in his polemical writings.[9] He was always surprised when sensitive authors like Koestler were hurt by his attacks, and never quite understood why vicious in-fighting should interfere with—or pre-clude—friendships. He also had the uncanny ability to become close friends with people he had attacked in print. Heppenstall had resumed their friend-ship after Orwell punched him in the nose. Stephen Spender, Alex Comfort, George Woodcock and (later on) Julian Symons all established warm personal relations after receiving a metaphorical punch.

Orwell had taken a few pokes at Spender for belonging to what he considered a precious literary coterie. In his raging letter to Nancy Cunard about the Spanish Civil War, he ordered her to "tell your pansy friend Spender that I am preserving specimens of his war-heroics and that when the time comes when he squirms for shame at having written it . . . I shall rub it in good and hard." Baffled and surprised by his sudden change after Spender had visited him in the sanatorium, Spender wrote in April 1938: "I've never read any of your attacks on me, but I am puzzled as to why when knowing nothing of me you should have attacked me; and equally puzzled as to why when still knowing nothing of me, but having met me once or twice, you should have withdrawn these attacks."

Orwell began his most virulent controversy in his "London Letter" to the *Partisan Review* in January 1942. He charged that "pacifism is objectively pro-Fascist" because it weakens the Allied side and helps the enemy. He specifically lashed out at contributors to the little anti-war paper, *Now*. He called

Alex Comfort—poet, novelist and medical biologist, later famous for *The Joy of Sex* (1972)—"a 'pure' pacifist of the other-cheek school" and said Julian Symons wrote "in a vaguely Fascist strain." In the "Pacifism and War" controversy that followed in the September *Partisan Review*, Alex Comfort replied with moderation and calm. Alluding to Orwell's role in the Spanish Civil War and calling him "the preacher of a doctrine of Physical Courage as an Asset to the left wing intellectual," he accused him of "intellectual hunting" and of finding that "almost every writer under thirty in [England] has his feet already on the slippery slope to Fascism." Orwell roughly replied that the pacifist, or Fascifist, gang wrote "mentally dishonest propaganda and degraded literary criticism to mutual arse-licking."

The controversy spilled into the pages of the Socialist *Tribune* in June 1943 when Comfort and Orwell cut and thrust at each other in satiric verse. Orwell, suddenly but characteristically, switched from abusive to charming. In a personal letter to Comfort, he apologized for his harsh anti-pacifism and praised Comfort's poem, which seems to have impressed him: "I'm afraid I was rather rude to you in our *Tribune* set-to, but you yourself weren't altogether polite to certain people. I was only making a *political* and perhaps moral reply, and as a piece of verse your contribution was immensely better."[10]

Orwell followed precisely the same pattern in his vitriolic exchange with George Woodcock. Anarchist, critic and editor of *Now*, Woodcock was born in Canada in 1912, grew up in England and after the war returned to Canada to teach. In his *Partisan Review* response, he accused Orwell of renouncing his old ideas and former friends: the imperial police officer now opposed the Empire, yet returned to his "imperialist allegiances . . . to fox the Indian masses" with British propaganda, the war resister now turned against his pacifist colleagues, the POUM militiaman attacked his Anarchist friends. Orwell convincingly defended himself against Woodcock's attempt to discredit him and concluded by asking: "Why not try to find out what I am doing [at the BBC] before accusing my good faith?"

Orwell was a chivalrous opponent, and his sense of fair play and fundamental decency led him to recant accusations that he realized were unfair. "I'm afraid I answered rather roughly in the *Partisan Review* controversy," he told Woodcock in December 1942. "I always do when I am attacked—however, no malice on either side, I hope." Woodcock, who had met Orwell at the BBC earlier that year, described how his face reflected his character:

Orwell was a tall, thin, angular man, with worn Gothic features accentuated by the deep vertical furrows that ran down the cheeks and across the corners of the mouth. The thinness of his lips was emphasized by a very narrow line of dark moustache; it seemed a hard, almost cruel mouth until he smiled, and then an expression of unexpected kindliness would irradiate his whole face. The general gauntness of his looks was accentuated by the deep sockets from which his eyes looked out, always rather sadly.[11]

While Orwell worked at the BBC and engaged in political polemics, and Eileen shifted in the spring of 1942 from the Censorship Department to the Ministry of Food, they continued to move restlessly around wartime London. In April 1941 the lease expired on the grim little Chagford Street flat and they moved to a nicer place, with an elevator, on the fifth floor of a modern building at 111 Langford Court, near Abbey Road in St. John's Wood, where his Home Guard unit was stationed. In the summer of 1942, about fifteen months later, they moved again to a larger—but very cold—flat on the ground floor and basement of 10A Mortimer Crescent, near Kilburn High Street, in Maida Vale. He had a carpentry shop in the basement and kept chickens in the backyard.

Orwell's teenage nephew Henry Dakin visited them at Mortimer Crescent. He remembered that Eileen was terribly untidy and wore an old black coat splattered with cigarette ash. She gave him a warm welcome, was gentle and sweet, and he liked her very much. She and Orwell seemed very fond of each other. Orwell never relaxed after work. He'd either bolt his dinner and disappear into his basement study or spruce himself up in his uniform and go on duty with the Home Guard.

On June 28, 1944, after two years at Mortimer Crescent, they were bombed out of the building and Inez Holden lent them her flat at 106 George Street, near Baker Street. Orwell and Inez belonged to the same artistic circles of wartime London. Born into an upper-class family in 1904, Inez met Orwell through Fredric Warburg in 1940, when the two writers planned to bring out their wartime diaries in one volume. Anthony Powell, who published her stories in the 1950s when he was literary editor of *Punch*, called her "very pretty, with the fashionable type of beauty. . . . [She] was a torrential talker, an accomplished mimic, her gossip of a high and fantastical category, excellent company." Once a society beauty and, for a time, one of Augustus John's many mistresses, after a disastrous operation in 1933 she put on a lot of weight and lost her good looks. In the 1940s she had a long, unhappy love affair with

Humphrey Slater, whom Celia Paget Goodman (Koestler's sister-in-law and Inez's cousin) described as "good-looking, intellectual and exceptionally intelligent." He'd been an officer in the International Brigades in Spain, was a captain in the Home Guard and became editor of the highbrow *Polemic* (with Celia Paget as his assistant), to which Orwell contributed five important essays. Reviewing Inez's *To the Boating* in October 1945, Orwell called her an uneven writer, but thought she was "at the top of her form in several of her stories," which had "accurate detail and remarkably lifelike dialogue."[12]

In 1940 Inez introduced Orwell to the poet and novelist Stevie Smith, an eccentric and endearing woman who worked as a secretary and lived with an aunt in a north London suburb. In her novel *The Holiday* (1949), Stevie portrayed Inez as Lopez; and later described her as "rather off the handle nice, and really funny. . . . So amusing, and not groupy at all, she always made me laugh so much." In the wartime novel Lopez has a party, and Orwell appears as Basil Tait, a Left-wing Old Etonian who's fought in Spain and revolts against middle-class values. Stevie probably exaggerated when she told the editor Norah Smallwood that she'd had "an intimate relationship" with Orwell. Muggeridge spread the rumor that Orwell had slept with Stevie in a park, but (according to Powell) "that was a misunderstanding. George tried to have her, but unable to bring it off (too well endowed)."

Orwell's work at the BBC and widening circle of friends in London gave him more opportunity for sexual adventures. He made a pass at Inez, but she was involved with Slater.[13] Rumors circulated at the BBC about a brief affair with a secretary. This might have been Elisabeth Knight, who admired and worked closely with him, or the attractive Sunday Wilshin, who often met him in the canteen and took over his job when he left. An appropriate candidate would have been another secretary, Winifred Bedwell. (She sounds like Barbara Bedworthy, the author of *Almost a Virgin*, an imaginary novelist in *Keep the Aspidistra Flying*.) Later on he had a more serious affair with his secretary at the *Tribune*, Sally McEwan, about whom Eileen made "a fiendish row."

After a drunken party at William Empson's house in Hampstead in June 1944, Orwell left with an acquaintance from the BBC. When they couldn't find a taxi, he "insisted, very much against her inclination, as she was young and was nervous of him, on walking her home and then trying, while crossing the [dark and empty] Heath, to make love to her far too persistently, somewhat violently even." After she failed to keep their rendezvous in London, he reproached her in a letter (now lost) and tried to make her feel guilty about breaking the appointment.[14]

In August 1941 Inez Holden got caught in the crossfire during Orwell's notorious public quarrel with H.G. Wells. In *Horizon* that month Orwell published an essay, "Wells, Hitler and the World State," in which he attacked Wells' *Guide to the New World* (1941) for drastically underestimating the power of Hitler, for naively imagining that his own idealistic World State could come into being and for falsely equating Science with common sense. In short, Wells had been "squandering his talents [since 1920] in slaying paper dragons" and was completely out of touch with the brutal realities of the modern world. As if to soften what he called his "parricide" (a rare Freudian phrase), he also paid a handsome tribute to Wells' innovative work. When your parents were "systematically warping your sexual life, and your dull-witted schoolmasters sniggering over their Latin tags, here was this wonderful man who could tell you about the inhabitants of the planets and the bottom of the sea."

To patch things up, Orwell invited Wells to dinner at Langford Court, along with his colleague William Empson and Inez Holden (who was living in a flat attached to Wells' house in Hanover Terrace). The "God-awful row" began when Wells slapped down a copy of *Horizon*, which he'd brought along for the occasion, and said "I want to have this out with Orwell." Orwell thought Wells' belief that the Nazis would easily be defeated undermined the war effort; Wells accused Orwell of being defeatist, though he withdrew that charge when Empson pointed out that Orwell had done some pretty tough fighting in Spain. "Orwell had put some whiskey and snuff between them," Inez recorded, and "tried to keep it on as friendly as possible a footing. He never got rude or impertinent, although it was agreed that his manners were not as good on paper. H.G. enjoyed the evening." He stayed quite late and told Empson it had been amusing. According to Michael Meyer, who heard Orwell's version of the dispute, things got sticky when Wells first said he couldn't eat anything rich, then tucked into a huge meal, ending up with plum cake. A week later Wells wrote furiously: "You knew I was ill and on a diet, [but] you deliberately plied me with food and drink."[15] Nevertheless, both writers enjoyed squaring off and the flames seemed to die down.

Orwell reignited the fire when his BBC talk "The Re-discovery of Europe" was published in the *Listener* on March 19, 1942. In this essay he revived the criticism that Wells had thought false and now considered treacherous.

Quoting *Hamlet,* Orwell wrote that "his basic 'message,' to use an expression I don't like, is that Science can solve all the ills that humanity is heir to, but that man is at present too blind to see the possibility of his own powers." On March 27 Wells responded violently in a personal letter, calling Orwell "a Trotskyist with big feet" and exclaiming, "I don't say that at all — read my early works, you shit." In a public letter to the *Listener* of April 9, Wells objected more temperately to Orwell's "foolish generalisations" and complained that he'd been "informing your readers that I belong to a despicable generation of parochially-minded writers who believed that the world would be saved from its gathering distresses by 'science.' From my very earliest book to the present time I have been reiterating that unless mankind adapted its social and political institutions to the changes invention and discovery were bringing about, mankind would be destroyed." Wells' biographers, without admitting the truth of Orwell's attack, wrote that "Orwell had undoubtedly misrepresented him at a time when he was unwell, and more than usually sensitive to suggestions that his ideas were out-moded, wrong-headed and inconsistent." Wells and Orwell were quite different in their styles of argument: Wells was ruder in private, Orwell in public.

In the summer of 1942 Ida and Avril Blair had moved from Southwold to London. Avril got a job in a sheet-metal factory and Ida became a saleswoman in Selfridge's department store. On March 19, 1943, the sixty-seven-year-old Ida died of a heart attack in New End Hospital, Hampstead. As with his father, Orwell was present at her deathbed. She left a modest estate of £560.

The following month, Michael Meyer, twenty-two years old and just down from Oxford, met Orwell at the Czardas restaurant on Dean Street (Koestler's favorite). Meyer noticed the deep carved furrows on Orwell's cheeks, the languid drawl, the ostentatiously rough dress, the plebeian haircut, the weak high-pitched voice (which made it difficult for him to get a word in during noisy lunches with the talkative Malcolm Muggeridge) and the strained breathing after a brisk walk.

Orwell, always hospitable, served cakes, buns and strong tea filled with floating tea leaves. His instinctive courtesy put Meyer at ease and made him forget their difference in age. Independent and lucid, Orwell talked as brilliantly about politics as Koestler and Rebecca West. He had great integrity, and his "luminous" quality seemed to embody the crystal spirit he'd described in his poem on Spain. Excited by their friendship, Meyer introduced Orwell to Graham Greene. Both Left-wing novelists had gone to public schools, but Greene was Catholic and Communist. By carefully avoiding contentious subjects, the two modest and likable men talked about books and literary life, got on tremendously well and stayed drinking in the pub from after dinner until closing time. Greene, then working at Eyre & Spottiswoode, asked Orwell to write a preface to Leonard Merrick's now-forgotten novel *The Position of Penny Harper* (1911). But Greene left the firm, the series ended and the book was never reissued. When Orwell reviewed Greene's novel *The Heart of the Matter* (whose hero is a colonial policeman) for the *New Yorker* in July 1948, he put his finger on its fatal flaw: "If [Scobie] believed in Hell, he would not risk going there merely to spare the feelings of a couple of neurotic women."[16]

III

ON SEPTEMBER 24, 1943, giving two months' notice, Orwell resigned from the BBC. He made clear that he had no grievance and did not disagree with BBC policy. Indeed, he felt he'd been treated generously and allowed considerable latitude. He was leaving because he felt he was wasting his own time and the public's money on a hopeless task that produced no results. Ivor Brown of the *Observer*, hearing he'd soon be free, offered him a job as war correspondent in Algiers and Sicily. But, as with the Lucknow *Pioneer*, his poor health prevented him from accepting. In late November, after two wasted years at the BBC, he became literary editor of the weekly Socialist newspaper, the *Tribune*. He joined the National Union of Journalists and in the photo on his membership card looks rather scruffy and badly in need of a shave. He earned £500 a year (£140 less than at the BBC) but worked there only three days a week, and used his new freedom to write *Animal Farm*.

The *Tribune*, with offices in the Strand, was aimed at middle-class readers, emphasized foreign policy and took its tone from the fiery editor Aneurin Bevan, who led the dissident wing of the Labour Party. Born in 1897, the son of a Welsh coal miner, Bevan left school at thirteen and went to work in the pit. He "thinks and feels as a working man," Orwell wrote in a profile for the *Observer*, is "naturally genial but capable of sudden anger and rough speech." Though Orwell got along well with Bevan, and was glad to get a good job during the war, he had no natural affinity with the paper. He'd consistently attacked the Left in *The Road to Wigan Pier* and *Homage to Catalonia*, and mocked the Left Book Club in *Coming Up for Air*. His colleagues Jon Kimche (a friend from the Hampstead bookshop), Tosco Fyvel and Evelyn

Anderson (a German refugee, married to an Englishman) were all Jewish and, like Bevan, pro-Zionist. Orwell, by contrast, thought the Zionist movement was unfair to the Arabs.

Orwell's outspoken columns and reviews offended many readers, and some prominent authors wrote letters of protest. The novelist Antonia White, objecting to his (long-standing) criticism of Catholicism, maintained that many people *did* believe in personal immortality. Gerald Brenan—who'd won an M.C. in the Great War and written *The Spanish Labyrinth* (1943)— felt civilians like Orwell, who lived in safety but criticized jingoism, wanted soldiers to act out their own violent and sometimes sadistic impulses.[17]

As at the BBC, Orwell attracted a number of distinguished writers and published articles by Forster, Connolly, Spender and Herbert Read. When he took over as literary editor at the *Tribune*, he found his desk drawers "stuffed with letters and manuscripts which ought to have been dealt with weeks earlier, and hurriedly shut it up again." He had a fatal tendency to accept manuscripts which he knew very well could never be printed, but didn't have the heart to send back. He must have remembered Gordon Comstock's bitter rage when his verse was rejected: "why be so bloody mealy-mouthed about it? Why not say outright, 'We don't want your bloody poems. We only take poems from chaps we were at Cambridge with. You proletarians keep your distance'?"

Orwell's eighty idiosyncratic, humane, strikingly original and consistently acute "As I Please" columns, written between December 1943 and April 1947, were his greatest contribution to the *Tribune*. He wrote that "if you climb to the top of the hill in Greenwich Park, you can have the mild thrill of standing exactly on longitude 0°, and you can also examine the ugliest building in the world, Greenwich Observatory"; observed that ads for spouses in personal columns demonstrated "the atrocious loneliness of people living in big towns";[18] took a crack at the upper classes by noting, as he looked through photographs in the New Year's Honours List, "the quite exceptional ugliness and vulgarity of the faces displayed there"; and remarked that rabid nationalists like Napoleon, Hitler (and Stalin) "tend not to belong to the nation that they idealise"; condemned the "mean and cowardly attitude adopted by the British press towards the recent rising [against the Nazis] in Warsaw"; yet advocated forgiveness rather than punishment after the war.

Describing the sexual habits of amphibians in one of his most charming *Tribune* essays, "Some Thoughts on the Common Toad," he combined close observation and unusual facts with tenderness for a repulsive creature, and ended with a comical twist: "All he knows, at least if he is a male toad, is that he wants to get his arms round something, and if you offer him a stick, or even your finger, he will cling to it with surprising strength and take a long time to discover that it is not a female toad."[19]

Orwell often tried out his ideas in conversation before he wrote them, and impressed Woodcock by completing an almost perfect piece straight on the typewriter. His columns transformed a humble genre into significant literary works. He not only promoted Socialist ideas and put contemporary political events in historical perspective, but also (gloomy as he was) cheered people up with entertaining subjects and — in an intimate tone of voice — combined public issues with personal feelings. After his release from bondage at the BBC and with victory at least in sight, Orwell tried out this new kind of humor. It had occasionally surfaced in *Coming Up for Air* and would add enormously to the appeal of *Animal Farm*.

12

Fatherhood and Eileen's Death,
1944–1945

I

When Margaret Heppenstall gave birth to a daughter in April 1940, Orwell congratulated Rayner: "What a wonderful thing to have a kid of one's own, I've always wanted one so." Eileen had a very different attitude. She'd planned to write her thesis on the use of imagination in children's writing, but her interest was purely academic, and she'd told Lydia that she couldn't think of anything more boring than playing with children. Though in poor health and exhausted by her work at the Ministry of Food, as well as by looking after Orwell, she wanted to keep her job.

They were, in any case, unable to have children. Orwell believed he was biologically sterile, though he never actually took the test, which he thought would be "disgusting." He had a similar distaste for condoms and seems not to have used them. When he told Kay Welton that he didn't think he could have children and she asked why, Orwell replied: "Well, I've never had any." Eileen told Lettice Cooper that their failure to have a baby had nothing to do with her. But she herself, as it turned out, had medical problems that probably hindered conception.

After eight years of marriage, it seemed clear that they were not going to have a child of their own and Orwell finally persuaded Eileen to adopt one. Gwen O'Shaughnessy, who'd already adopted a little girl, knew a patient who'd had a baby boy. He was born in May 1944, the result of a wartime affair with a Canadian soldier, and his mother wanted to give him up for adoption. In early June, Eileen brought a nightgown and shawl to the hospital, dressed him and carried him home to Mortimer Crescent. Orwell burned out the names of the baby's parents from the birth certificate, but one of Eileen's letters reveals that his real name was Robertson.

Three weeks later their flat was bombed, though no one was hurt and they managed to rescue their possessions. Since Inez Holden was living in the country, they moved into her pleasant flat near Baker Street. Her journal for July 1944 described a rather sad Orwellian scene: "He had been planning to get his books up from the country [Wallington] for some time. At last he managed it, but now his house has been broken up by the blast. The place is no longer habitable, but he goes each day to rummage in the rubble to recover as many books as possible and wheel them away in a wheel-barrow. He makes the journey from Fleet St. during his lunch hour." Inez probably exaggerated. The *Tribune* offices were on the Strand, not Fleet Street, and it is almost four miles each way to Mortimer Crescent. Though it took at least three hours to make the trip, he did return several times to retrieve his books.

Orwell told Heppenstall that people always grow up to resemble their names and that it took him thirty years (till he adopted his pseudonym) "to work off the effects of being called Eric." They named the child Richard Horatio Blair, after one of his ancestors, a captain in the Royal Navy who died in 1875 and was buried in Weymouth, on the Dorset coast. Richard was also the name of his father and of his close friend, Richard Rees. The adoption enabled Eileen to leave her job and take care of the baby at home instead of putting him in a day nursery. She quickly overcame doubts that she would not be able to love an adopted child and became an adoring mother.

In early October they moved to what would be Orwell's last London flat, 27B Canonbury Square, Islington, where he kept a goat, once again, to provide milk for Richard. When rationing continued after the war and he had trouble getting enough protein for the baby, he bought a hen—which laid eggs without shells. (Stevie Smith suggested that he set the hen directly on the frying pan.) Responding to Richard and learning to care for him allowed the normally inhibited Orwell to be tender and affectionate. When Fyvel admired the way he looked after the child, Orwell remarked: "Yes. You see, I've always been good with animals."

Since Richard took a long time to speak, Orwell invited Geoffrey Gorer to see if the child had reached the same stage of development as the chimpanzees Gorer studied, and was reassured to learn that he'd actually surpassed them. Concerned about Richard's education (since he knew he might not be around to supervise it), he recalled a conversation with the Communist John Strachey in 1936. Strachey said he'd just had a son and was putting him down for Eton. Orwell asked, "how can you do that?" and he replied that " 'given our existing society it was the best education.' Actually, I doubt whether it is the best, but in principle I don't feel sure he was wrong."[1] Orwell thought Eton needed to be reformed. As a compromise, he put Richard down as a day-boy at Westminster, where, he was glad to hear, the boys no longer wore top hats.

Even when he could afford them, Orwell wanted very few material things in life. He dearly wanted Richard to have a handsome white perambulator with wavy gold lines on the sides, which usually goes with a uniformed nanny in Kensington Gardens, but they were hard to find during the war. Instead, he steered Richard around the seedy streets of Islington in a rickety no-frills push-chair with a wicker grocery-basket hanging behind. In a series of photographs taken by Vernon Richards in 1946, Orwell tenderly holds the big-eared, wide-eyed, open-mouthed baby, dresses him, feeds him, walks him and plays with him. Though Orwell was nearly forty-one when he adopted Richard—rather late to become a father and change his habits—he was remarkably flexible and adept at caring for him.

In other Islington photos a pensive Orwell deftly rolls a cigarette, examines a long Burmese sword, practices woodwork with his chisel and lathe, talks while holding a cigarette and mug of tea, types in front of a long white row of books. One moving photo shows him dressed in his usual grubby tweeds, standing in front of a white wall. With furrowed brow and wistful expression, he gazes into the distance—aware, it seems, that he hasn't long to live.

II

From October 1944 to December 1948, with long absences in Jura and in hospital, Orwell lived in Canonbury Square—a bleak tenement in a down-at-heel area. The flat was in a row of rather uncomfortable eighteenth-century houses. The two front rooms looked out onto the square, and two other rooms and a kitchen were at the back. Fyvel, a frequent visitor, remarked on "the utter cheerlessness of the awkwardly built flat. . . . It looked as if every door had a slice of the bottom sawn off so that cold draughts could whistle through the entire" place.

As with the canteen and charwomen at the BBC, certain aspects of the flat went straight into *Nineteen Eighty-Four*. In one of his "As I Please" columns he mentioned that "accumulations of snow have caused water to pour through the roof and bring down plaster from the ceilings." In Winston Smith's flat, "the plaster flaked constantly from ceilings and walls, the pipes burst in every hard frost, the roof leaked whenever there was snow." The long climb up six flights of the stone staircase to the top floor—the most dangerous place to live when the bombs began to fall—was not easy for a tubercular invalid who often had to carry groceries, coal buckets and a heavy infant. Woodcock, Meyer and other friends noticed that Orwell was wheezing and gasping for breath by the time he reached the door. In the novel, Winston always has a violent coughing fit when he wakes up, and when climbing to the top floor he always "went slowly, resting several times on the way."[2]

In a rare interview of September 1946 a reporter from the style-conscious *Vogue* magazine, boldly venturing into darkest Islington, noted that "the stuff around his rooms—a Burmese sword, a Spanish peasant lamp, the Staffordshire figures—show something of his foreign life, his strong English solidity." The centerpiece of the living room was a huge screen, which also kept out drafts, covered with shellacked pictures he'd cut out of magazines. (It appears in three photos by Vernon Richards.) Orwell proudly described the screen, "all too rare nowadays," that was pasted over with colored scraps to make more or less coherent pictures: "In one corner of my own scrap screen, Cézanne's card-players with a black bottle between them are impinging on a street scene in medieval Florence, while on the other side of the street one of Gauguin's South Sea islanders is sitting beside an English lake where a lady in leg-of-mutton sleeves is paddling a canoe." Woodcock agreed with Fyvel that "it was a dark and almost dingy place, with a curiously Dickensian atmosphere. In the living room stood . . . a collection of china mugs, celebrating various popular nineteenth-century festivals, crowded on top of the crammed bookshelves. . . . By the fireplace stood a high-backed wicker armchair of an austerely angular shape . . . and here Orwell himself would always sit, like a Gothic saint in his niche. The small room which he called his study looked like a workshop, with its carpenter's bench, its rack of chisels and its smell of newly cut wood."[3]

The furniture and food went perfectly with the decor. As Orwell wrote in his description of the ideal pub, "everything has the solid, comfortable ugliness of the nineteenth century"—except that in his flat things were uncomfortable as well as ugly. He loved to work with his hands, but was not very good at manual jobs and quite helpless with machinery. He'd made a chair and would offer it to guests, but it was torture to sit in no matter what position one took. During the war he wanted to make bookshelves and Meyer managed to get some wood through his father. The finished product, according to Meyer, was awful beyond belief. He'd made shelves without proper supports that sagged like hammocks, then whitewashed the lovely cherry-wood in a "criminal way." On the shelves, Orwell admitted, were ten books that he'd borrowed and not returned.

He kept the proletarian habits of rolling his own cigarettes from Nosegay Black Shag (a strong tobacco that stained his teeth) as well as pouring tea in his saucer and blowing on it. The desperately poor, half-starved Canadian Paul Potts—who printed and sold his own poems in pubs—painted an idealized picture of high-tea with Orwell on a winter's evening: "a huge fire, the table crowded with marvelous things, Gentleman's Relish and various jams, kippers, crumpets and toast." But Koestler, who'd been brought up on Continental cuisine, agreed with Lydia Jackson that the man who loved boiled cod with bitter turnips "had no taste in food." His housekeeper filled in the gory details: "He liked northern English cooking. Kippers were a prime favorite or black pudding boiled first, then fried with onions and served on a bed of creamy mashed potatoes. Then there would be Gentleman's Relish on toast, or brown bread and butter or home-made scones with jam." His niece added a vivid observation: he would "make a highly satisfied sort of squeaky whine, rather like a puppy, if he was eating pudding that he really enjoyed!"[4] His pleasures were simple: long walks on Hampstead Heath, and lively talks with writer-friends at home, in pubs like the Wheatsheaf in Rathbone Place, or the Bodega, Akropolis, Czardas and Elysée restaurants in Soho.

III

THE POET Ruth Pitter had been shocked by Orwell's emaciation, waxen pallor and slow, careful movements when they met again in 1942, and he'd been unable to accept the *Observer*'s offer to go to North Africa in the fall of 1943. But in 1945 his medical exam was apparently waived. He gave up the *Tribune* job and accepted David Astor's invitation to become a war correspondent for the *Observer* and the *Manchester Evening News*. Between February 15 and

May 24 he sent eighteen despatches about the effect of war on the civilian population in liberated Paris, in occupied Cologne, Nuremberg and Stuttgart, and in Salzburg, Austria.

Momentous events took place while Orwell was in Europe and the victorious Allied armies fought their way into Germany. Cologne was captured, the British crossed the Rhine, the Russians crossed the Austrian frontier, Danzig was captured, the Americans took Osnabrück, the Allies entered Arnheim, the Russians reached Berlin, the Allies reached the Po River, American and Russian troops met at the Elbe, Mussolini was killed by the partisans, Hitler committed suicide, Berlin was captured, the Third Reich collapsed, V.E. Day was declared on May 8 and the Russians took Prague. (In July the Labour Party won a landslide victory in Britain and Clement Attlee replaced Churchill as Prime Minister.)

Orwell did not witness the great events: the frontline battles, the liberation of the concentration camps and (later on) the war-crimes trials. He did see the massive destruction of Germany and the desperate plight of French and German civilians. Reporting from Cologne in late March and early April, he wrote: "To walk through the ruined cities of Germany is to feel an actual doubt about the continuity of civilization. . . . The whole central part of the city, once famous for its romanesque churches and its museums, is simply a chaos of jagged walls, overturned trams, shattered statues, and enormous piles of rubble out of which iron girders thrust themselves." He also noted the extreme suffering of Allied prisoners of war: "A British prisoner described how on his arrival he and his companions had thrown some soap over the wire to the Russians, and the starving Russians had promptly eaten it. Another told me of a camp in Silesia [now in Poland] where, when a Russian prisoner died, his comrades would cover his body with a blanket and pretend that he was merely ill so that they could go on drawing his soup ration for a few days longer." His curiously flat, lifeless and impersonal despatches disappointed David Astor. Orwell may have been too horrified to comprehend and capture conditions during the last months of the war, and needed more time to absorb the impact of what he'd seen.

Orwell spent most of his time at the Hôtel Scribe in Paris, was struck by the tribe of American reporters with their glittering uniforms and stupendous salaries, and met a number of eminent writers. Harold Acton, whom he astonished with stories about his sexual adventures in Burma and Morocco, "was impressed by his mournful dignity. . . . He mentioned his lung trouble as if it were something to be ashamed of." Orwell also had a strong effect on another Old Etonian, the Oxford philosophy don A.J. Ayer, who was in Paris in the spring of 1945. "His moral integrity made him hard upon himself and sometimes harsh in his judgement of other people," Ayer wrote, "but he was no enemy to pleasure. He appreciated good food and drink, enjoyed gossip, and when not oppressed by ill-health was very good company." Both Acton and Ayer noted how ill he was. Though willing, indeed eager, to eat ghastly food in the BBC canteen, he also liked fine meals and was equally at home when invited to posh restaurants like Boulestin's or Rules.

He also had some contact with French writers who shared his political views and had worked in the Resistance. He arranged to have lunch with Albert Camus at the Deux Magots, but he was even more ill than Orwell and couldn't come. He met Malraux, an adviser to de Gaulle, and found him very friendly. When Kopp's introduction to the French edition of *Homage to Catalonia* was deemed unsuitable, Malraux planned to write one but never did. Ayer, in a suggestive comparison, described their political affinity: "Both were individualists, and each of them combined left-wing sympathies with the conservative values of patriotism, self-reliance and discipline in action. I suppose that Orwell was the more puritanical, though in personal relations neither priggish nor arrogant, perhaps also the more romantic and the more keenly aware that power corrupts. Malraux seems to have been more of an adventurer. It is to their credit that Marx would have seen them both as sentimental socialists."[5]

Hemingway, who'd "liberated" the Ritz hotel in August 1944, told an interviewer that he'd met Orwell (both men were in Paris between February 15 and March 6). Offering rare praise for a contemporary writer, he called *Homage to Catalonia* a first-rate book and Orwell a first-rate man, and regretted he had not been able to spend more time with him. He thought his own politics were quite close to Orwell's, and was sorry that Orwell had fought for the weak POUM Anarchists instead of the more effective International Brigades. Orwell, who would publish *Animal Farm* a few months later, in August 1945, told Hemingway he was afraid of being killed by the Russians, who'd hunted him in Spain and still considered him a dangerous enemy. When the Germans were defeated and the Communists emerged from underground, a lot of people were shot. He asked to borrow a pistol, and Hemingway lent him a Colt .32.

In *True at First Light* (1999) Hemingway confirmed the story. He patronized Orwell, while doubting he was in danger, but offered to protect him:

the last time I had seen [Orwell] in Paris in 1945 after the Bulge fight . . .
he had come in what looked like civilian clothes to Room 117 of the Ritz
where there was still a small arsenal to borrow a pistol because "They" were
after him. . . .

He was very gaunt and looked in bad shape and I asked him if he would
not stay and eat. But he had to go. I told him I could give him a couple of
people who would look after him if "They" were after him. That my characters were familiar with the local "They" who would never bother him
nor intrude on him. He said no, that the pistol was all he needed. We asked
about a few mutual friends and he left.

Orwell never mentioned this encounter and left no record of their conversation.[6]

A meeting with the popular English humorist P.G. Wodehouse led to one
of Orwell's important essays. In 1940, when the Germans occupied France,
Wodehouse was interned. The following year he gave a radio interview in
Berlin, and the Germans broadcast it to the United States. Through flattery
they persuaded him to give five talks about his experiences as an internee, to
be broadcast to Britain and America. His naive comments on Germany, seen
as pro-Axis propaganda, had caused an uproar and he was accused of being
a traitor. Orwell took him to lunch at a good restaurant near les Halles in
Paris, and in July 1945 published "In Defence of P.G. Wodehouse." He
argued that "the events of 1941 do not convict Wodehouse of anything worse
than stupidity. The really interesting question is how and why he could be
so stupid." He concluded that "the wretched Wodehouse—just because success and expatriation had allowed him to remain mentally in the Edwardian
age—became the *corpus vile* in a propaganda experiment."

Immensely grateful for Orwell's chivalrous defense—not guilty by reason
of stupidity—Wodehouse abjectly thanked him for the superb lunch and the
uncannily accurate literary analysis: "It was extraordinarily kind of you to
write like that when you did not know me, and I shall never forget it. . . . I
have been re-reading the article a number of times and am more than ever
struck by the excellence of its criticism. It was a masterly bit of work and I
agree with every word of it." After Orwell's death, when Wodehouse was out
of danger and his gratitude had considerably subsided, he described the essay
as "practically one long roast of your correspondent. Don't you hate the way
these critics falsify the facts in order to make a point?"[7]

IV

JUST AS Orwell had reassured Eileen by telling her that he did not intend to enlist in Spain, so she—not wanting to prevent him from reporting the European war—didn't tell him that she was seriously ill. Even close friends like Lydia Jackson believed she needed only a simple operation to arrest the decline of red corpuscles in her blood. In fact, she had tumors in her uterus, suffered internal bleeding and had to have a hysterectomy. Eileen, and several of her friends, suspected it was cancer. Demoralized by harsh conditions and hard work in Wallington, by the manhunt and mortal danger in Spain, by the deaths of her brother and mother, by inadequate food, four years of demanding jobs and bombing during the London Blitz, she now had an insidious disease. After collapsing in London and seeing a specialist, she took Richard by bus to Gwen's house in Stockton-on-Tees and arranged to have the operation in Newcastle. Georges Kopp saw them off at King's Cross.

On March 23 Eileen wrote Lettice from Stockton: "It's a mercy George is away—in Cologne at the moment. George visiting the sick is a sight infinitely sadder than any disease-ridden wretch in the world." Her last, unbearably sad letters to Orwell, written on March 21 and 29, were mainly concerned with making things easy for him. Better than anything else written by or about her, they reveal her appealing, selfless character and explain why she'd been willing to put up with such discomfort, even hardship, during their marriage.

Eileen realized that she couldn't "just go on having a tumour or rather several rapidly growing tumours." But she was (rather perversely) more worried about the "outrageous" expense of the surgery than about her own health and survival. She compared the price of the operation with the cost of a long-drawn-out disease and concluded: "I really don't think I'm worth the money. On the other hand of course this thing will take a longish time to kill me if left alone and it will be costing some money the whole time." She added, with morbid irony, that she was sure the surgeon, Dr. Harvey Evers, "will finish me off as quickly as anyone in England . . . so he may well come cheaper in the end." She knew Orwell disapproved of the removal of her uterus, which meant she could never have children, and had a "hysterical" desire to please him. Unwilling to worry him and fearing her poor health might prevent the adoption of Richard, she did not see the doctor until they'd taken possession of the baby "in case it was cancer."

In an unnerving passage that suggests severe psychological distress and was undoubtedly influenced by fear of the impending operation, she tried to convey her horror of urban life and (in a sentence that recalls the most repulsive episodes of *Down and Out*) her disgust with the filthy food and asphyxiating atmosphere of a big city:

> I don't think you understand what a nightmare the London life is to me. I know it is to you, but you often talk as though I *liked* it. I don't like even the things that you do. I can't stand having people all over the place, every meal makes me feel sick because every food has been handled by twenty dirty hands and I practically can't bear to eat anything that hasn't been boiled to clean it. I can't breathe the air, I can't think any more clearly than one would expect to in the moment of being smothered, everything that bores me happens all the time in London and the things that interest me most don't happen at all.

Eileen felt so repelled by London that, even when recalling the revolting sewage problems in Wallington, she was "not actually frightened as I should have been of living a primitive life again."[8] To Eileen, worn down by the war, conditions in both city and country had become quite intolerable.

Eileen's last, unfinished letter was written on March 29, only an hour before her surgery. Trying to be positive and reassuring, and portraying herself as protectively swaddled in cotton, she explained that the surgeon—in the high-handed manner of those days—hadn't told her exactly what kind of operation she was going to have. Nevertheless, she was resigned, even hopeful (despite her fears) as she was about to be cut open and fell into morphia-induced unconsciousness:

> Dearest, I'm just going to have the operation, already enema'ed, injected (with morphia in the *right* arm, which is a nuisance), cleaned & packed up like a precious image in cotton wool & bandages. When it's over I'll add a note to this & it can get off quickly. Judging by my fellow patients it will be a *short* note. They've all had their operations. Annoying—I shall never have a chance to feel superior.
>
> I haven't seen Harvey Evers since arrival & apparently Gwen didn't communicate with him & no one knows what operation I am having! They don't believe that Harvey Evers really left it to me to decide—he always "does what he thinks best"! He will of course. But I must say I feel irritated though I'm being a *model* patient. They think I'm wonderful, so placid

& happy they say. As indeed I am once I can hand myself over to someone else to deal with.

Eileen died of heart failure, just after the anesthetic was applied and before
the operation had even begun. She was only thirty-nine. Gwen
O'Shaughnessy "had a premonition that Eileen would not make it and asked
her pharmacist to let her know immediately when the call came through. It
did in the middle of a crowded surgery." The coroner's inquest concluded
that the doctors were not responsible and reported the cause of death as "car-
diac failure whilst under anaesthetic of ether and chloroform skilfully and
properly administered for operation for removal of uterus."[9]

At the same time, Orwell's own health had broken down while he was traveling in war-ravaged Europe. As Eileen entered the hospital in Newcastle,
he went into hospital in Cologne with a flare-up of lung disease, possibly
even a hemorrhage. Referring to this period, he later told Fyvel: "I thought
at one time it was all up with me." He'd returned to Paris and telegraphed
his consent to Eileen's operation, and was horribly shocked to receive another telegram from the *Observer*, the very next day, announcing that she was
dead. He got on a military plane—his first flight—arrived in London on
March 31 and went straight to Inez Holden.

Orwell was devastated but stoically hid his feelings. He tersely told Julian
Symons, in schoolboy slang: "My wife died last week. I'm very cut up about
it." On April 1, before he'd seen the coroner's report and still under the
impression that the surgery was minor, he explained to Lydia: "I do not know
whether you will have heard from anyone else the very bad news. Eileen is
dead. As you know she has been ill for some time past and it was finally diagnosed that she had a growth which must be removed. The operation was not
supposed to be a very serious one, but she seems to have died as soon as she
was given the anesthetic, and, apparently as a result of the anesthetic. . . . It
was a dreadful shock and a very cruel thing to happen, because she had
become so devoted to Richard." Ten days later he wrote Anthony Powell that
Eileen had been ill for a long time: "It was a most horrible thing to happen
because she had had five really miserable years of bad health and overwork,"
and—when they adopted the baby and she quit her job—things were just
starting to improve.[10] Eileen did not live to see Richard grow up, nor enjoy
the hard-won wealth and fame of Orwell's last years.

When he went to Wallington for the first time after Eileen's death, he
"expected it to be horribly upsetting but actually it wasn't so bad except when

I kept coming on old letters." Recalling the poverty and suffering they had endured, the idealism and danger they'd shared in Spain, Orwell confessed: "What matters is being faithful in an emotional and intellectual sense. I was sometimes unfaithful to Eileen, and I also treated her very badly, and I think she treated me badly too at times, but it was a real marriage in the sense that we had been through awful struggles together and she understood all about my work." Eileen not only knew what his work meant, but also what it meant to him; that though he loved her, it came before everything else.

Losing her so suddenly and unexpectedly, in particularly distressing circumstances, overwhelmed the guilt-ridden Orwell with the most intense grief and guilt of his entire life. Bitterly and harshly reproaching himself, he now felt sorry that he'd encouraged her to give up her promising career and subjected her to an unusually difficult existence. He'd remained absorbed in his own work, left her alone when he went to Spain, couldn't meet her emotional and sexual desires, and was occasionally unfaithful. He'd neglected her health while she looked after him, didn't realize she was seriously ill, worried about the cost of her treatment, was opposed to a hysterectomy and was not by her side to comfort her before the operation. His greatest regret, he told Koestler after Eileen's death, was that he'd "left so much unsaid."

Orwell arranged the funeral in Newcastle and found a temporary home for Richard with Georges and Doreen Kopp, who also lived in Canonbury Square. Then—disoriented and desperate for distraction—he returned to Europe, from April 8 to May 24, to be on the move as a war correspondent. Recalling the emotional difficulties of adoption, the bombing of Mortimer Crescent, his own absence abroad, Eileen's death and Richard's temporary stay with the Kopps, Orwell was relieved to find that Richard didn't seem to be harmed by "the many changes in his short life."[11] He knew it would be difficult for a hard-pressed writer with no experience of children to look after an infant, and most friends expected him to give up the child. But he was determined to keep the beloved boy, his precious link to Eileen, and became a devoted, capable father.

V

THE YEAR following Eileen's tragic death was the most bizarre period of Orwell's life. Fearing he hadn't long to live and desperate to complete his final work, racked by guilt and loneliness, he was eager to find a woman to take care of Richard as well as himself. He impulsively proposed marriage to several attractive younger women whom he scarcely knew. He told one of them, Celia Paget (then seeking a divorce from her husband), "if I could choose, I should like to be irresistible to women." Still shy and awkward, and looking much older than a man of forty-two, he was not a promising candidate. They all rejected him.

The stunningly beautiful, highly cultivated and frequently photographed Paget twins, Celia and Mamaine, were cousins of Inez Holden, and thirteen years younger than Orwell. Their mother had died a week after their birth and their father, a clergyman, died when they were twelve. They had been educated first by a village schoolmaster in Suffolk and then at boarding schools in England and Lausanne, where they learned perfect French. They became the leading debutantes of the 1930s, and after their presentation at Court they often appeared, dressed alike and with the same hairstyles, in gossip columns and glossy magazines. But they were not merely beautiful. Mamaine married Arthur Koestler, and Celia played a lively part in the circle of intellectuals who contributed to Humphrey Slater's *Polemic*.

At Christmas 1945 Orwell and Celia were invited to spend a week at the Koestlers' house in North Wales. Celia first saw him when he arrived at the railway station with a suitcase in one hand and Richard under one arm. Father and son were closely attached to one another; whenever Orwell went out, Richard would look for him in every room. The English novelist Storm Jameson, who was not there at the time and must have got the story from Koestler, wrote that "he had George Orwell staying with him in the farmhouse he rented in the hills behind the hotel: ill, exhausted by the journey, Orwell was sleeping heavily in the same room as his baby son: the child woke early, and to keep him quiet, so that Orwell could sleep on, Arthur sat beside the cot for an hour and amused him by silently pulling faces." Koestler often told flattering stories about himself, and this dubious episode is quite out of character. Orwell rarely slept late, Koestler hated children and an hour's a very long time to spend pulling faces. On another occasion, when Richard clambered all over Koestler and actually peed on him, he was extremely annoyed that Orwell failed to discipline the child.

Jameson's story does suggest, however, that the hedonistic Koestler revered his Spartan friend. According to Celia, he believed that of all contemporary writers, Orwell was most likely to survive, that it was not disillusioning to meet Orwell, who was exactly like his books. Koestler later mentioned a paradoxical quality in the character he had so closely studied: "His uncompromising intellectual honesty . . . made him appear almost inhuman at times. There was an emanation of austere harshness around him which diminished only in proportion to distance, as it were: he was merciless towards himself, severe upon his friends, unresponsive to admirers, full of understanding for those on the remote periphery."[12]

Talking over drinks, he surprised Koestler by remarking that he was desperately lonely. Unused to such frankness from the normally reticent Orwell, Koestler remarked: "the closer one came to him, the more there seemed to be a barrier against warmth and personal contact." Koestler urged Celia to smarten up Orwell and get him a dinner jacket. After he'd heard about Orwell's proposal—"Would she marry him, or at least have an affair?"— Koestler "practically went on his knees and implored me to marry George," Celia said, "because he simply loved George, and he would have loved to have George as a brother-in-law. He thought that was a wonderful idea."

Celia found Orwell amused by life and amusing about it, easy to get on with. A tremendously masculine person who liked and needed women, he was not very romantic or physically attractive to her, and seemed far too old. She later observed of their relations: "if I call it love (as I do) it might give the impression that I was in love with him, but it was just because I wasn't that I didn't agree to marry him or have an affair with him."[13] Celia emphasized that he "expressed great concern for *my* happiness. He always seemed to feel that he wasn't a good bet for me, both because he was quite a lot older . . . and because of his poor health."

An extraordinary letter from Orwell to Celia, which has never been published, revealed his strong sexual feelings. It was inspired, she explained, by an incident that took place in early 1946. Rodney Phillips and his wife Anna (financial backers of *Polemic*), as well as Humphrey Slater, Orwell and Celia

all went to dinner in Greek restaurant in Percy Street, and afterwards we piled into a taxi to go on to some friends of Humphrey's. As there wasn't room for us all on the seats, and as I was the smallest of us and George the largest, I sat on his knees for this short ride. . . . It must be remembered that George had been "living on ice" (I imagine) for quite a time . . . before I met him. So the reaction he mentions in the letter was very understandable.

Excited by embracing Celia, Orwell confessed that when they rode in the taxi and she sat on his lap in her fur coat, the passion went through him like an electric shock.[14]

Anne Popham, another prospective wife, was the daughter of A.E. Popham, Keeper of Prints and Drawings at the British Museum. The same age as Celia, she was trained as an art historian at the Courtauld Institute in London, and (like Eileen) had worked for the Ministry of Information during the war. After being bombed out, she moved to Canonbury Square. After the war, she was sent to Germany to trace and recover stolen art. Later on, she worked for the Arts Council of Great Britain, married Quentin Bell and edited Virginia Woolf's *Diaries*.

While living in Canonbury Square, Anne and her flatmate gave a dinner party for Orwell and Victor Pritchett, where the men, engrossed in their own conversation, showed no interest in the ladies. Anne liked what she called Orwell's "practical side"—his apparent ability to fix things, and to take care of Richard. She found him amiable, though a bit frightened of and imperceptive about women. She knew he was a distinguished man, but couldn't see the greatness of the lonely intellectual who looked so much older than his age. And Anne, like Celia, did not find him physically attractive. She thought his mustache was mannered, affected, even ridiculous. Only Frenchmen wore mustaches, which were simply "not on in that period."

Orwell invited Anne to tea, dismissed Richard and his nursemaid with "Go along, now," and told her: "Come and sit here. It will be more comfortable on the bed in the corner." Though he hardly knew her, he kissed and embraced her, and asked, "Do you think you could care for me?" Since there was absolutely no courtship, wooing or getting to know him, Anne was deeply embarrassed and shocked by his proposal. It came out of the blue, and seemed both precipitate and calculating. Feeling intensely uncomfortable, she wriggled out of his arms and rejected his offer as gently as possible. Despite her negative reaction, he didn't completely give up hope and asked: "Were you shocked? Can I write to you? To persuade you?"

On April 18, after Anne had left for Germany, Orwell wrote his most intimate and revealing letter:

> I wonder if I committed a sort of crime in approaching you. In a way it's scandalous that a person like me should make advances to a person like you, and yet I thought from your appearance that you were not only lonely and unhappy, but also a person who lived chiefly through the intellect and might become interested in a man who was much older and not much good physically. . . . What I am really asking you is whether you would like to be the widow of a literary man. If things remain more or less as they are

there is a certain amount of fun in this, as you would probably get royalties coming in and you might find it interesting to edit unpublished stuff. . . .

Several times in the past I have been supposed to be about to die, but I always lived on just to spite them. . . . I am also sterile I think—at any rate I have never had a child, though I have never undergone the examination because it is so disgusting. On the other hand if you wanted children of your own by someone else it wouldn't bother me, because I have very little phys-ical jealousy. . . . You are young and healthy, and you deserve somebody better than me: on the other hand if you don't find such a person, and if you think of yourself as essentially a widow, then you might do worse—i.e. supposing I am not actually disgusting to you. If I can live another ten years I think I have another three worth-while books in me . . . but I want peace and quiet and someone to be fond of me. . . .

There isn't really anything left in my life except my work and seeing that Richard gets a good start. It is only that I feel so desperately alone some-times. I have hundreds of friends, but no woman who takes an interest in me and can encourage me.

Orwell emphasized his age and poor health and practically promised to die as soon as possible. He offered widowhood rather than marriage and the chance to edit his works. He also confessed, to put the topping on the cake, that he was sterile (though he didn't know for sure) and had been unfaithful to Eileen. And he made a Clifford Chatterley-like offer to let his would-be fiancée breed with another man. This strange, abject, thoroughly unappeal-ing declaration is reminscent of Franz Kafka's anguished letters to his fiancée, Felice Bauer—he too was tubercular and close to death—in which he assumed a pathetic posture, confessed the worst about himself and tested her ability to endure him: "I should want to drag you . . . down to the dreadful decrepitude that I represent. . . . In spite of everything [do] you want to take up the cross? . . . I am prostrate before you and implore you to push me aside: anything else means ruin for us both."[15]

Considering his abrupt proposals, bleak accounts of his prospects and dis-couraging attempts to persuade, it is not surprising that Orwell failed to find a wife. But during this emotional chaos his life was changed by the sudden and unexpected success of *Animal Farm*.

13

Animal Farm and Fame,

1945

I

THE ADOPTION of Richard, the tragic death of Eileen, the decline in his own health and the unexpected success of *Animal Farm*—published in August 1945—completely transformed Orwell's life within a few months. After Eileen died, Orwell clung tenaciously to Richard as the living bond between them. It was difficult to find a nursemaid-housekeeper during the war, but in July 1945 he met Susan Watson, who'd been recommended by the Heppenstalls and the Empsons. Susan and Orwell liked each other instantly. She thought he was a very lonely man, and admired him for keeping the baby. He watched her bathe Richard and asked, "you will let him play with his thingummy, won't you?" When she assured him she'd be appropriately permissive, he hired her at the generous wage of £7 a week, though he did not mention that he had tuberculosis. Susan took care of Richard and did the shopping and cooking, and he also had a cleaning woman to "do" for them.

Susan was not an ordinary domestic servant. Her mother, Wyn Henderson, was an arty literary editor and friend of Wyndham Lewis. The twenty-seven-year-old Susan (two years younger than Celia Paget and Anne Popham) was a pretty blonde with an ingenuous expression and childlike manner. These traits were accentuated by her lameness from cerebral palsy, which made it hard for her to climb the six flights of stairs up to the flat. She was getting divorced from a Cambridge mathematician (who'd introduced her to Wittgenstein), had a seven-year-old daughter in boarding school (who was welcome at Canonbury Square during holidays) and had been working at an international nursery.

Susan lived in Orwell's household for fifteen months, observed him closely, and was perceptive about his tastes, habits and eccentric character. He loved strong pots of Ceylon tea and roast beef and potatoes. "Your hands need never be cold in the winter," he told her, "you can always put a baked potato in each pocket and put your hands in." When she served the food, he'd say to Richard: "Gosh, boys, this looks good!"

Susan sometimes found it necessary to practice benign deceit on Orwell, who was rather naive about household affairs. He loved steamed pudding, which was difficult to make, so Susan bought a tin of it in a shop and served it as if it were homemade. Orwell was taken in and asked her: "How do you manage to get such a beautiful shape?" He liked everything to be clean, hated dirty diapers and urged Susan to be firmer with Richard about toilet training. When Richard pooped on the carpet, Susan cleaned up the mess with a copy of the *Tribune* and put it into the potty. Pleased with the results, Orwell remarked: "You see, I told you it only needed perseverence." When he asked her about the missing *Tribune*, she pretended she didn't know where it was.

Susan thought Orwell was slightly Victorian and moralistic, domineering and sometimes repressive. He liked to be the head of the household and was rigid about the routine of domestic life. He worked from nine to one, went out for lunch, returned for dinner at six and often typed until three in the morning. Susan got so used to the sound of his typing that she'd wake up when he stopped. He'd sometimes take a break to do some carpentry, with Richard, his "mate," handing him the nails. Whenever they had a disagreement in the evening, he'd tell Susan: "I think it's time you went to bed." She found him "a conflicting mixture of emotional inhibition and intellectual expansiveness." He behaved very properly, if rather stiffly, towards her, as if unsure about "whether to treat her as a trusty old housekeeper-nurse or as a young daughter." But she had her own emotional life and there was never any question of marriage to Orwell.

Susan was a friend of Randall Swingler, poet and editor of the *Left Review*, who wanted to meet Orwell. Though reluctant at first, Orwell finally agreed to a meeting and afterwards said: "What a nice chap. Pity he's a Communist." After Swingler's attack in the September 1946 issue in *Polemic*, Orwell hated him passionately, refused to shake his hand and always kept a weather eye open to avoid running into him in a pub. In this case, at least, he did not generously forgive his opponents.

Susan recalled that Orwell still had terrifying dreams from the Spanish Civil War. His diary described a nightmare in which he was exposed under fire: "I had a very disagreeable dream of a bomb dropping near me and frightening me out of my wits. Cf. the dream I used to have towards the end of our time in Spain, of being on a grass bank with no cover and mortar shells dropping round me." A more serious incident occurred in February 1946 when he suddenly began to hemorrhage from his lungs. He remained calm, however, and merely told Susan to bring an ice pack to put on his head. This traditional remedy, according to one of his doctors, did no good at all, except to comfort the patient, but at least did no harm. Orwell refused to call a physician, but had to spend two weeks in bed.[1] No wonder he looked the worse for wear when he proposed marriage to Celia and to Anne.

I I

Animal Farm became a great literary and financial success after a very long struggle to get into print. This book—like *Down and Out, Burmese Days* and *Homage to Catalonia*—went against the current political grain and was rejected by five publishers before it finally appeared. Orwell began writing it, during his free days at the *Tribune,* in November 1943. He completed it in February 1944, after Stalingrad and before Normandy, when the Allies first became victorious and there was a strong feeling of solidarity with the Russians, who, even in defeat, had deflected Hitler from England. Instead of waiting until the war was over, Orwell believed the best time to expose the corrupt nature of the Soviet state was when the Russians were at the height of their popularity. He foresaw how depressing it would be to defeat Hitler and then find Europe dominated by Stalin. As he wrote in his illuminating Preface to the Ukrainian edition (1947): "Nothing has contributed so much to the corruption of the original idea of Socialism as the belief that Russia is a Socialist country and that every act of its rulers must be excused, if not imitated. And so for the past ten years I have been convinced that the destruction of the Soviet myth was essential if we wanted a revival of the Socialist movement."

Gollancz had returned to the Communist fold after Hitler's invasion of Russia in June 1941. Orwell knew that for political reasons he would never publish the book, and told him so. But Gollancz, enforcing his option on Orwell's next work of fiction, insisted on reading it and tried to defend his position by claiming: "I suppose I ought rather to pat myself on the back that you apparently regard me as a Stalinist stooge, whereas I have been banned from the Soviet embassy for three years as an anti-Stalinist." Despite this show of impartiality, Gollancz, as Orwell predicted, "felt immediately that to publish so savage an attack on Russia at a time when we were fighting for our existence side by side with her could not be justified." Orwell was pleased to be free at last. In July 1945 he told Leonard Moore: "I have no quarrel with him personally, he has treated me generously and published my work when no one else would, but it is obviously unsatisfactory to be tied to a publisher who accepts or refuses books partly on political grounds and whose own political views are constantly changing."[2]

After a quick refusal for the same reason by Nicholson & Watson, Moore submitted the book to Jonathan Cape, who'd rejected *Down and Out* in 1931. Cape's reader reported: "This is a kind of fable, entertaining in itself, and satirically enjoyable as a satire on the Soviets," and recommended publication. Cape wanted to bring out the book; but he had some doubts and submitted it to a senior official in the Ministry of Information. He appealed to Cape's patriotism and advised him not to disturb Britain's relations with its Russian ally. (The government, it's worth noting, was far more perceptive than the publisher about the potential impact of the book.) Following official advice, Cape changed his mind, wrote Moore that it was "highly ill-advised" to publish the book during the war and drew attention to Orwell's troublesome porkers: "It would be less offensive if the predominant caste in the fable were not pigs. I think the choice of pigs as the ruling caste will no doubt give offence to many people, and particularly to anyone who is a bit touchy, as undoubtedly the Russians are." Orwell, by now quite furious, described the censorship as "no bribes, no threats, no penalties—just a nod and a wink and the thing is done." He mocked Cape's concern that Stalin might not like the book, telling Inez Holden: "Imagine old Joe (who doesn't know one word of any European language) sitting in the Kremlin reading *Animal Farm* and saying 'I don't like this.' "[3]

Michael Meyer reported that the book was also refused by William Collins, "the meanest of Glasgow Scots," who cared nothing about the political aspects, but didn't think he could sell so short a book. The manuscript then went to T.S. Eliot at Faber & Faber, who'd also turned down *Down and Out* at the start of Orwell's career. His perverse misreading of the book—the pigs, once again, were a sticky point—and grave misjudgment were the English equivalent of André Gide's notorious rejection of Proust's *Remembrance of Things Past*:

> We agree that it is a distinguished piece of writing; that the fable is very skilfully handled, and that the narrative keeps one's interest on its own plane—and that is something very few authors have achieved since *Gulliver*. On the other hand, we have no conviction . . . that this is the right point of view from which to criticise the political situation at the present time. . . .
>
> My own dissatisfaction with this apologue is that the effect is simply one of negation. It ought to excite some sympathy with what the author wants, as well as sympathy with his objections to something: and the positive point of view, which I take to be generally Trotskyite, is not convincing. I think you split your vote, without getting any compensating strong adhesion from either party—i.e. those who criticise Russian tendencies from the point of view of a purer communism, and those who, from a very different point of view, are alarmed about the future of small nations. And after all, your pigs are far more intellectual than the other animals, and therefore the best qualified to run the farm—in fact, there couldn't have been an Animal Farm at all without them: so that what was needed (someone might argue), was not more communism but more public spirited pigs.

Eliot willfully ignored the crucial passage—inspired perhaps by Orwell's first exhilarating visit to revolutionary Barcelona—in which he wrote that after they drove out Farmer Jones and *before* the pigs took over, "the work of the farm went like clockwork. The animals were happy as they had never conceived it possible to be." Having been shot down by the Communist Gollancz and the Ministry of Information, the book was then refused by the conservative Eliot. At least Eliot saw its merits as satire and justly compared it to Swift, but objected to what he misread as a Trotskyite point of view. Dial Press in New York missed the point entirely and rejected it because "it was impossible to sell animal stories in the USA."[4]

In desperation, Orwell thought of publishing it with a small Anarchist press (which happened to have some paper, still in very short supply during the war) or even bringing it out himself. David Astor offered to back the project with a loan of £200. But he finally turned to Secker & Warburg—then a much smaller and less influential firm than the others—which had published *Homage to Catalonia* and were very keen to get *Animal Farm*. This book, and *Nineteen Eighty-Four*, put the firm on the map, and Warburg reaped all the benefits of Gollancz's earlier investment in Orwell.

When Warburg asked him about the plot of the book, Orwell, as self-deprecating as ever and never very good at describing his work in progress, fobbed him off by saying: "it's all about animals, and very anti-Russian! I'm afraid you're not going to like it." But he described the real imaginative spark of the tale in his Preface: "I saw a little boy, perhaps ten years old, driving a huge cart-horse along a narrow path, whipping it whenever it tried to turn. It struck me that if only such animals became aware of their strength we should have no power over them, and that men exploit animals in much the same way as the rich exploit the proletariat."

Some aspects of the fable were based on Orwell's experience. He liked animals in general, but was hostile to pigs and told David Astor: "They are most annoying destructive animals, and hard to keep out of anywhere because they are so strong and cunning." In *Animal Farm* the pigs, like the bureaucrats at the BBC, "had to expend enormous labours every day upon mysterious things called 'files,' 'reports,' 'minutes' and 'memoranda.' " When the self-sacrificial horse Boxer collapses from overwork, he suffers, like Orwell, a tubercular hemorrhage: "A thin stream of blood had trickled out of his mouth. . . . 'It's my lung,' said Boxer in a weak voice."[5]

Orwell's lucid, witty and ironic style was perfectly suited to his satiric fable. In "Why I Write," he echoed Eliot's pronouncement, "The progress of the artist is . . . a continual extinction of personality," by stating: "one constantly struggles to efface one's own personality. Good prose is like a window pane." He also achieved his most transparently brilliant effects by adapting literary tradition to his own individual talent. The most famous phrase in *Animal Farm* (enunciated by the self-serving pigs)—"ALL ANIMALS ARE EQUAL, BUT SOME ANIMALS ARE MORE EQUAL THAN OTHERS"—combined Jefferson's fundamental concept in the Declaration of Independence, "all men are created equal," with Eve's self-destructive command to the Serpent in Milton's *Paradise Lost* (9.823–25): "render me more equal, and perhaps, / A thing not undesirable, sometime / Superior."[6]

The familiar and affectionate tone of the story and its careful attention to detail allowed the unpopular theme to be pleasantly convincing, and satirized the Soviet myth in a subtle fashion that could still be readily understood. Orwell fused his artistic and political purpose so well that the animals are completely convincing on the literal level. The pigs' solemn burial of some hams that hang in the kitchen is wonderfully effective.

Virtually every detail has political significance in this allegory of corruption, betrayal and tyranny in Communist Russia. The human beings are capitalists, the animals are Communists, the wild creatures who could not be tamed are the peasants, the pigs are the Bolsheviks, the Rebellion is the October Revolution, the neighboring farmers are the Western armies who attempted to support the Czarists against the Reds, the waves of rebelliousness that ran through the countryside afterwards are the abortive revolutions in Hungary and Germany in 1919 and 1923, the hoof and horn is the hammer and sickle, the Spontaneous Demonstration is the May Day Celebration, the Order of the Green Banner is the Order of Lenin, the special pig committee presided over by Napoleon is the Politburo, the revolt of the hens— the first rebellion since the expulsion of Jones (the Czar)—is the sailors' rebellion at the Kronstadt naval base in 1921, Napoleon's dealings with Whymper and the Willingdon markets represent the Treaty of Rapallo, signed with Germany in 1922, which ended the capitalists' boycott of Soviet Russia, and the final meeting of the pigs and human beings is the Teheran Conference of 1943. Orwell allegorizes three crucial political events: the disastrous results of Stalin's forced collectivization (1929–33), the Great Purge Trials (1936–38) and the cynical diplomacy with Germany that terminated with Hitler's invasion of Russia in 1941.

The principal pigs, Napoleon (Stalin) and Snowball (Trotsky), are constantly fighting each other, and the novel also portrays their two most significant battles. Trotsky fought for the priority of manufacturing over agriculture, and his ideas about the expansion of the Socialist sector of the economy were eventually adopted in Stalin's first Five-Year Plan of 1928, which called for collectivization of farms *and* for industrialization. In their central ideological conflict—which had spilled over into the battle between the POUM and the Communists in Spain—Trotsky defended his idea of Permanent Revolution, with its faith in the revolutionary proletariat of the West, against Stalin's theory of Socialism in One Country, with its glorification of Russia's unique Socialist destiny. Though Trotsky was Stalin's victim, Orwell thought he was potentially as great a villain as Stalin and that *both* men had betrayed the Revolution: "Trotsky, in exile, denounces the Russian dictatorship, but he is probably as much responsible for it as any man now living, and there is no certainty that as a dictator he would be preferable to Stalin, though undoubtedly he has a much more interesting mind."

Throughout the fable Orwell parodies the style and thought of Karl Marx.

Squealer's ingenious gloss on "Four legs good, two legs bad" is a witty and ironic example of specious Marxist reasoning: "A bird's wing, comrades . . . is an organ of propulsion and not of manipulation. It should therefore be regarded as a leg." The last sentence of the book—"The creatures outside looked from pig to man, and from man to pig, and from pig to man again: but already it was impossible to say which was which"—echoes Marx's *Economic and Philosophic Manuscripts of 1844*: "[The worker] in his human functions no longer feels himself to be anything but an animal. What is animal becomes human and what is human becomes animal."

The idea that the victors in every revolution of the Left become corrupted by power and inevitably set up a tyranny of their own was bitterly expressed as early as 1911 by Joseph Conrad, the son of a Polish patriot and failed revolutionary, in *Under Western Eyes*: "The scrupulous and the just, the noble, humane, and devoted natures; the unselfish and the intelligent may begin a movement—but it passes away from them. They are not the leaders of a revolution. They are its victims: the victims of disgust, of disenchantment—often of remorse. Hopes grotesquely betrayed, ideals caricatured—that is the definition of revolutionary success."[7]

Animal Farm was finally published in August 1945—eighteen months after Orwell finished writing it—at a crucial moment in world history. In the previous four months, Roosevelt had died, Mussolini had been killed and Hitler committed suicide. Churchill had been voted out of office, Germany had surrendered and, on August 6, the atomic bomb had exploded over Hiroshima. Of the Big Three, only Stalin was still in power. Orwell's friend William Empson, author of *Seven Types of Ambiguity* (1930), praised the book, yet presciently warned that its political meaning would be misinterpreted: "The danger of this kind of perfection is that it means very different things to different readers. . . . You must expect to be 'misunderstood' on a large scale." Indeed, Orwell had dashed around the bookshops, just after publication, moving it from the children's to the adults' section.

Orwell also had great difficulty publishing the book in America. According to Peter Viereck, writing in 1952 (in a journal edited by a promising academic called Henry Kissinger) there was a Communist conspiracy to prevent publication: "Some 18 to 20 publishers, almost all the leading ones, turned down the best anti-Soviet satire of our time. In view of its wit, its readability, its saleability, and its democratic outlook, the most likely motive for these rejections is the brilliantly successful infiltration (then, not now) of Stalinoid sympathizers in the book world." The fable was finally brought out by

Harcourt, Brace after their editor Frank Morley saw its great success in London and immediately bought the rights. The first U.S. printing was 50,000 copies.

The evaluations of *Animal Farm* were inevitably influenced by the politics of the reviewers and their attitude toward Stalinist Russia. Graham Greene described Orwell's difficulty in publishing the satire in the face of wartime appeasement and prophesied the animated cartoon of the book that appeared in 1955. The "Stalinoid" Kingsley Martin, who'd refused to publish Orwell's reports from Spain, distorted Orwell's political views by claiming that his criticism of the Soviet Union (which in fact began with *The Road to Wigan Pier*) was a recent development. Like Eliot, Martin called Orwell a Trotskyist (the derogatory name for anyone who opposed Stalin), claimed that he'd "lost faith in mankind" and concluded that his satire "is historically false and neglectful of the complex truth about Russia."

Cyril Connolly described Orwell as "a revolutionary who is in love with 1910" and painted a brighter picture of Stalinist Russia than Orwell would have allowed. Arthur Schlesinger, Jr., writing on the front page of the *New York Times Book Review*, linked Orwell with Koestler and Silone as political novelists. He called the satire "the most compact and witty expression of the left-wing British reaction to Soviet Communism" and "a wise, compassionate and illuminating fable for our times."[8]

Edmund Wilson, who mentioned Orwell's difficulty in publishing *Burmese Days* in England, expressed unqualified enthusiasm. In a rare accolade, Wilson called the book "absolutely first-rate," compared Orwell with Voltaire and Swift, and thought he was "likely to emerge as one of the ablest and most interesting writers that the English have produced" in the last decade. Wilson's influential *New Yorker* review praised Orwell's literary qualities just as Schlesinger had praised his political insight, and these two authoritative estimates helped solidify his reputation in America.

Orwell responded to the enthusiastic reviewers by calling them "grudging swine . . . not one of them said it's a beautiful book." A few months later the Queen herself sent to Secker & Warburg for the book, which was completely sold out. Orwell was greatly amused to hear that the Royal Messenger, in ceremonial garb, had to buy one from an Anarchist bookshop on Red Lion Street. Its engaging style and satiric wit enabled *Animal Farm* to reach an astonishingly wide audience, from peasants to royalty. It was translated into thirty-two languages, including Maltese, Gujurati and Vietnamese, and has been used throughout the world as a standard text for teaching English. In the French edition, to avoid giving offense, Napoleon was quietly renamed César.[9]

Orwell received a modest advance of £100 and the first printing of the English edition was only 4,500 copies. But when it was accepted by the American Book-of-the-Month Club the number of copies soared. Frank Morley told Orwell:

> This insures a minimum circulation of between 400,000 and 500,000 copies in this country, quite apart from the distribution through book stores. . . . They pay a royalty of twenty cents a copy, with an advance of seventy thousand dollars against that royalty. The money is paid to us, and we share it with you on a fifty-fifty basis. Your share will be, as a minimum, thirty-five thousand dollars, less the income tax of thirty percent.

Orwell used the first royalty check to repay half the anonymous loan from L.H. Myers for the trip to Morocco, and to support worthy causes and indigent writers. Remembering how Eileen had contributed to the humor of the book, which he'd read to her in bed at night as he composed it during the cold winter, he told Dorothy Plowman: "It was a terrible shame that Eileen didn't live to see the publication of *Animal Farm*, which she was particularly fond of and even helped me in the planning of."[10]

III

Toward the end of the war Orwell met his last group of intellectual friends. Julian Symons was introduced to Orwell at the *Tribune* offices in 1944. Born in 1912, he was the younger brother of A.J.A. Symons, author of the innovative biography *The Quest for Corvo*. A self-proclaimed Trotskyist, Julian had edited *Twentieth Century Verse*, served in the war, worked in advertising and began writing crime novels in 1945. After meeting Symons, Orwell publicly apologized for claiming that Symons " 'writes in a vaguely Fascist strain' — a quite unjustified statement based on a single article which I probably misunderstood."

Symons — who admired him but found him a remote character and permanent outsider — used to lunch regularly with Orwell, Anthony Powell and Malcolm Muggeridge after the war, to discuss books as well as the day-to-day military and political events. Powell then worked at the *Times Literary*

Supplement, Muggeridge at the *Daily Telegraph* and Symons at an ad agency off the Strand. When Orwell gave up his weekly reviews at the *Manchester Evening News* in November 1946, he arranged for Symons to replace him (as Koestler had replaced him at the *Observer*). This important boost helped Symons to leave advertising and become a professional writer.

Anthony Powell, the handsome son of an army colonel, was a younger contemporary at Eton and went up to Balliol College, Oxford. He worked in journalism and publishing, brought out his first novel in 1931 and served in the Intelligence Corps in the war. He sent Orwell a fan letter in 1936 and met him briefly, through Inez Holden, at the Café Royal in 1941. But they didn't become friends until Powell returned from the war. Powell found him "very assured but also very diffident." Orwell, explaining that personal affinity prevailed over political differences, told Symons that "Tony is the only Tory I have ever liked." In Powell's series of novels, *A Dance to the Music of Time*, Orwell appears as Alf, Viscount Erridge, an artistic and high-minded social revolutionary, who wears an old corduroy jacket, lives in squalor and supports a great many Left-wing spongers.[11]

Powell's wife, Violet, who sometimes looked after young Richard, wrote that "Muggeridge, in the mid-1940s, asked Powell to introduce him to Orwell. Powell asked if Orwell would agree. Orwell said, 'Yes, but I shall probably sock him.' Muggeridge and Orwell became friends, and remained so until Orwell's death." Born in 1903, the son of a Socialist politician, Muggeridge was educated at Cambridge and married the niece of Beatrice Webb. He was an anti-imperialist teacher in India and Egypt, a disenchanted Communist in Moscow, a journalist in Calcutta and London, an unsuccessful novelist, author of *The Thirties* (1940), ebullient paterfamilias and sexual philanderer. During the war he was an intelligence officer in Mozambique and, as a liaison officer with the French after the liberation, ran into Orwell in Paris. Orwell would have disapproved of Muggeridge's later, self-promoting roles as scourging editor of *Punch*, provocative television personality and (mocked as "the Blessed Mugg") proselytizing Catholic convert.

Reviewing *The Thirties*, a history of the decade, Orwell noted his anti-Stalinism and wrote that Muggeridge, like himself, "is not loved in 'left' circles, is often labelled 'reactionary' or even 'Fascist.' " Muggeridge recalled in *The Thirties* that Orwell, observing the fading of the old order, "was liable to break off a conversation to make statements like: 'Eton's doomed,' or, 'Soon there won't be any more state openings of Parliament.' " Muggeridge respected Orwell's ramrod honesty and battered idealism, but was also aware of his faults. Lively and amusing himself, he recalled that Orwell "was a gauche, ungainly sort of person; more lovable than likable, and not particularly good company. One loved to be with him for quite other reasons than the charm of his presence or the pleasure of his conversation"[12]—which Muggeridge often interrupted.

The American writer who had the most in common with Orwell, and who enjoyed a position in the American literary world comparable to Orwell's in England, was Edmund Wilson. Both had spent years in poverty before achieving success toward the end of their lives. These wide-ranging men of letters were essentially autobiographical writers, best at non-fiction, excellent reporters and experienced travelers to exotic countries. As Socialists who criticized Communism from the Left, they were deeply concerned about the falsification of history in Soviet Russia. As foreign correspondents in the spring of 1945—for the *Observer* and the *New Yorker*—they considered the moral problems of vengeance against the Germans and the proper treatment of a defeated enemy.

They were both interested in popular culture and what Orwell called "good bad books." They tried to promote clear and vivid English, free of cant, and had a direct, straightforward prose style. They approached literature from a historical and ideological point of view, and combined incisive literary criticism with a shrewd political analysis. They shared an interest in Dickens, Kipling and Yeats, and wrote major essays on the first two at about the same time. Wilson and Orwell were hostile to religion, but longed for the lost world of their childhood. They shared high principles, personal integrity and a sympathy for the oppressed.

Reviewing *The Wound and the Bow* in May 1942, Orwell said that Wilson had written "the best essay on Dickens that has appeared for some time" and had thrown "brilliant flashes of light on some very dark places" of the writer's psyche. He called Wilson "one of the very few literary critics of our day who gives the impression of being grown up, and of having digested Marx's teachings instead of merely rejecting them or swallowing them whole"—a description that fits Orwell himself.

The two writers met through Cyril Connolly in the summer of 1945—just before *Animal Farm* made Orwell wealthy and famous. Eileen had suddenly died in March, and Wilson, who'd been through a similar experience with the accidental death of his second wife, was especially sympathetic. In *The English People* (1947) Orwell claimed that "if we really intended to model our language upon American, we should have, for instance, to lump the lady-bird . . . and scores of other insects all together under the inexpressive name of *bug*." When they met, Wilson insisted on straightening out this misconception.

Wilson's brief acquaintance increased his admiration for Orwell's work. Reviewing *Dickens, Dali and Others* (1946), he praised him as "the only contemporary master" of sociological criticism and identified his quintessential strengths: his "readiness to think for himself, courage to speak his mind, the tendency to deal with concrete realities rather than theoretical positions, and a prose style that is both downright and disciplined." Stressing Orwell's unique and paradoxical qualities in his notice of the posthumously published *Shooting an Elephant* (1950), Wilson placed him in the tradition of "middle-class British liberalism that depended on common sense and plain-speaking."

Most writers, after struggling for fifteen years to achieve literary success, would have remained in London to be lionized and enjoy their celebrity. But Orwell, immune to the effects of wealth and fame, couldn't endure his success: it didn't match his idea of himself. Desperately tired and jaded in the spring of 1946, he complained to Koestler that "everyone keeps coming at me wanting me to lecture, to write commissioned booklets, to join this and that, etc.—you don't know how I pine to get free of it all and have time to think again."[13] *Nineteen Eighty-Four* was beginning to take shape in his mind, and he wanted to rest for two months and allow the idea to germinate. Quite unexpectedly, the man who hated Scotland took off for the remote island of Jura in the Inner Hebrides.

14

Escape to Jura,

1946–1947

I

"Thinking always of my island in the Hebrides," Orwell wrote in his "War Diary" as early as June 1940—perhaps recalling the tumultuous lines in James Thomson's *The Seasons* (1730):

> *Or where the Northern ocean, in vast whirls,*
> *Boils round the naked melancholy isles*
> *Of farthest Thulè, and th' Atlantic surge*
> *Pours in among the stormy Hebrides.*

The dream became reality—and began Orwell's "Jurassic" period—when David Astor told him about the deer-shooting lodge that his family owned on Jura, sixteen miles off the west coast of Scotland. The hardship, bleakness and isolation appealed to him. "If the Atomic bomb falls on Glasgow," he grimly told Astor, "there'll be only two tidal waves." Jura, he thought, would be the last place to be affected by the regime he was planning for *Nineteen Eighty-Four*. He'd discussed his plan with Eileen, who'd naturally been sceptical about retreating to one of the most unappealing and inaccessible places in the British Isles. In September 1945, after the war ended, he spent two weeks arranging to rent and repair an abandoned house on the northern end of the island.

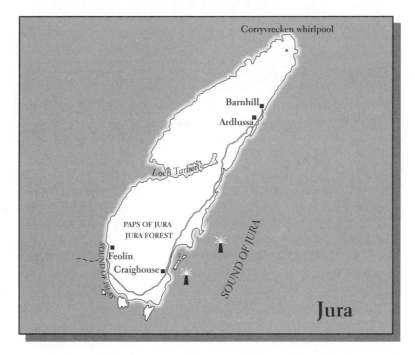

He'd always disliked the Scottish name of Blair and the cult of Scotland that Flip had preached at St. Cyprian's. The national dish was awful enough to appeal to him: "there is the famous Scottish haggis [he wrote], in which liver, oatmeal, onions and other ingredients are minced up and cooked inside the stomach of a sheep." He'd called the Scots "whiskey-swilling bastards," and had refused to meet Edwin Muir in Hampstead. But in many ways Orwell's austere and dour, Spartan and ascetic character as well as his tall, gangly figure were more Scottish than English. His compulsion to live an arduous and exhausting existence on the wet bog and windy moorland of Jura, in the country of Calvinism and oatcakes that he professed to dislike, was typically perverse—even suicidal. But, far from medical assistance, he followed what he called "the *internal* necessity that drives men into seemingly meaningless actions."[1]

The western side of the narrow island was as empty as the Empty Quarter of Arabia. The only road ran for thirty miles along the east coast from the tiny villages of Feolin and Craighouse in the south to Ardlussa in the north. A modern travel book notes that "Ardlussa marks a great change in the character of Jura. Southward all is high moorland; northward, low and gently swelling, is pleasing to the eye by way of change." Crofting and raising high-land cattle were the main occupations, but Jura was in economic decline and the local farmers were dying out. The population had peaked at 1,320 in 1841, but in Orwell's time had shrunk to about 250 people and 4,000 deer.

The journey from London to Barnhill, Orwell's house on Jura—by train to Glasgow, bus to the west coast, boat to Kintyre, bus across Kintyre, boat to Jura, and taxi from Craighouse to Ardlussa—took forty-eight hours. The last seven miles—along a grueling, badly rutted cart-track, full of enormous pot-holes—had to be negotiated on foot. During the winter Jura was sometimes cut off from the mainland for weeks by stormy seas. The only shop on the island was twenty-five miles away. When Richard fell off a chair and gashed his forehead, it took six hours to get him to a doctor. If Orwell had suffered a serious hemorrhage on Jura, he would have been (to use his expression) a "goner." "People talk about isolation," one resident said, "but they don't real-ize till they get here what it's like."

The sea-level location, damp climate and arduous life were precisely the opposite of the high altitude, thin dry air and prolonged rest recommended for patients with lung disease. It rained, Orwell admitted, "all the time." The sea was icy, even in summer; the winter, he also conceded, was "pretty bleak . . . dark and gloomy." Richard later described the atmosphere as "cold and wet for two days out of three, the house was always cold and the peat they burned gave out little heat."[2]

Barnhill, which Richard Rees called "the most uninhabitable house in the British Isles," was much larger but just as uncomfortable as the cottage in Wallington. Vacant since 1934, it was a cross between Wuthering Heights and Cold Comfort Farm. Set in the brown moorlands, it looked south across a sloping pasture toward a small bay dotted with islands. The landscape, Richard said, was made up of "heather, bog, peat and snakes." The house had four small bedrooms upstairs, three rooms and a kitchen downstairs. It had a bathroom, but there was no electricity or telephone, and getting food and transportation was extremely difficult. Bill Dunn, who lived at Barnhill and did most of the farm work, noted that Orwell's hermetically sealed work-room made things even worse. He smoked thick black tobacco and "had this black paraffin stove in the middle of the floor, and the window was tight shut and the door was tight shut, and it must have been terribly bad for him."

Orwell spent about six months a year on Jura in 1946, 1947 and 1948. His second strenuous stay sent him straight into a sanatorium. When he emerged seven months later he returned to the island, and every month he had to take a long and tiring journey to see a specialist near Glasgow. After five more months on Jura, he went back into hospital, from which he never emerged. David Astor, who'd merely suggested Barnhill for a summer holiday, never dreamed that Orwell would remain there in winter and make it his permanent home. "I was horrified when I heard this," Astor exclaimed. "It was an extremely uncomfortable place to live. . . . For a person in delicate health, it was a crazy place to go." Sonia Brownell, who became Orwell's second wife, refused to visit him there, despite his fervent if daunting invitations. She agreed with Astor that "it was a very bad idea; it killed him in the end."[3] Though safe from the atomic bomb, Orwell fell victim to his own self-destructive impulse.

I I

ROBIN FLETCHER, who'd been a housemaster at Eton, had inherited the 20,000-acre Ardlussa Estate. It included Barnhill, and he was Orwell's landlord. His wife, Margaret, remembered her first encounter with the fiercely independent writer. She thought he was a

> sad, lonely man when he arrived on the island. I felt extremely anxious as to how he could manage on his own because he appeared really ill. I offered to help with food supplies, which were still rationed and difficult to obtain. He said he would be all right and preferred to manage himself. I had the impression he was content as long as he had a roof over his head and a loaf of bread to eat.

Like a figure of death, "he carried a scythe . . . to cut his way through the fast-growing rushes that blocked the track" from Ardlussa to Barnhill.

Orwell had many adventures with animals on the wild island. Keeping a pig merely intensified his hatred: "They are really disgusting brutes and we are all longing for the day when he goes to the butcher." Susan Watson recalled that when a truck arrived to pick up a bull, Orwell locked Richard and Susan in the upstairs bedroom and guarded the entrance with a loaded revolver, as ready to shoot a bull as he'd been to shoot an elephant. Bill Dunn described a grisly incident on the island of Scarba, just north of Jura, that recalled Orwell's dissection of the jackdaw at Eton:

We saw a dirty great adder, an enormous thing, and Eric quickly planted his boot right on top of its neck and anchored it to the ground and I fully expected that with the other foot he would grind its head into the ground too . . . but he got out his penknife and quite deliberately opened and proceeded more or less to fillet this wretched creature, he just ripped it right open. . . . It surprised me terribly because he always really struck me as being very gentle to animals.[4]

Richard thrived on Jura and continued to develop faster than Geoffrey Gorer's chimpanzees. Though his boundless energy was sometimes hard to handle, he was given a free rein and allowed to play with Orwell's jackknife and carpentry tools. (He once got a shock from fooling around with a loose wire in the doorbell at Canonbury Square.) When Orwell threw his cigarette ends into the fireplace, Richard picked them up, filled an old pipe and asked for a light. He then tried to smoke it—and was violently sick for the rest of the day.

Georges Kopp, still colorful and larger than life, had also moved from Canonbury Square to Scotland after the war. He became an engineer and farmer near Biggar, south of Edinburgh. Full of inventive ideas but a poor businessman, and with three young children to support, he never settled down to a successful career. In March 1946 he invited Orwell for a weekend visit "with rabbit shooting (legal now)"—though there were plenty of rabbits on Jura—"and any amount of poaching, inclusive trout and salmon in the Tweed." And he added: "you can have a jeep whenever you like."

Orwell bought a dilapidated old Ford truck from Kopp, but was furious when he couldn't drive it off the ferry and had to abandon it on the dock. Kopp, who knew the condition of the truck, might have considered the sale an indirect way of borrowing money from his now prosperous friend. But it caused bad feeling, and there's no record of Kopp visiting Orwell in the sanatorium near Glasgow. In April 1947 Orwell told Gwen O'Shaughnessy that he'd received a note from the Kopps announcing their new baby, but hadn't heard anything else from them. Kopp returned to France, his health undoubtedly weakened by his torture in Spain. He died in Marseille of kidney and heart failure, at the age of forty-nine, in 1951.

Orwell loved Jura, especially in the summer. There was so much work to do at first that he kept his resolution and didn't write for several months. Instead, he occupied himself with building obstinately sagging bookshelves and planting a vegetable garden, looking after the geese and hens, making hay and getting milk for Richard from a neighboring farm, going fishing and setting lobster traps, shooting rabbits and butchering venison, walking the hills and exploring the north coast in his outboard motorboat. He enjoyed a rich diet of lobster, rabbit and deer, and (since there was no beer) had a ration of gin every night. He sent lyrical descriptions of the pristine quality of Jura and tried to tempt Anne Popham to visit by writing: "It would be wonderful walking over to the west side of the island which is quite uninhabited and where there are bays of green water so clear you can see about 20 feet down, with seals swimming about."[5]

Though Orwell liked the isolation, he also needed social life and stimulating talk. Sonia and Anne, younger friends like Rayner Heppenstall, Michael Meyer and Julian Symons couldn't quite face the challenge of the dismal journey and rough life. But a number of other friends, including Brenda Salkeld and Inez Holden, loyally trekked all the way up to Jura. The tall, thin, bearded and balding Richard Rees, a confirmed bachelor then living in Edinburgh, became his financial partner and put up the capital to buy the necessary equipment and run the farm. Young Richard, who was very fond of his namesake, later called him a "super old man" and tried to clarify Rees' sexual attitudes by explaining that he was "a misogynist, not a homosexual." Marjorie's daughters, Jane and Lucy Dakin, described Rees as a perfect gentleman who always wanted to help on the farm, but was pretty hopeless at most practical jobs. When Orwell was away and Rees took care of the house, things became pretty chaotic. Like Orwell, Rees didn't talk down to the girls and listened carefully to what they said. When they spotted a roughly dressed female hiker with a backpack, Rees naively asked: "Tell me, on a holiday like that, how does a lady preserve her personal daintiness?" Rees' painting, *Orwell's Bedroom*, modeled on Van Gogh's *Vincent's Bedroom at Arles* (1889), portrays a simple table, hard chair, iron bed, rough carpet and sloping floor.[6]

Sally McEwan, his secretary at the *Tribune*, came up at the same time as the down-and-out poet Paul Potts. Orwell tactfully described him as "an old friend of mine, a person who has been unfortunate but has gifts which he has not yet been able to use very successfully." In the summer of 1946 Susan, running out of newspaper with which to start the fire, burned some scrap paper that turned out to be Potts' manuscript. Always extremely touchy, he left Barnhill in a fury.

Michel Kopp, Georges' son by his first marriage, visited Jura in the summer of 1947 and found the farmhouse "rather dilapidated." Orwell, Michel recently wrote, was driving himself hard, "working day and night at his book with perhaps the premonition that *Nineteen Eighty-Four* would be the last one and that death was lurking in the background. . . . I used to see him mainly at supper-time. He was looking in poor health, eating little, chain-smoking and drinking a lot of coffee."

Jane and Lucy Dakin, on Jura in the summers of 1946 and 1947, found both Orwell and Avril—who was keeping house for him—remote, detached and self-absorbed. When Lucy finally arrived, thoroughly exhausted after the long and difficult journey from London, he merely said, "Ah, there you are Lu." And there was no hug from Aunt Avril, who gave her a glass of milk with a shot of brandy. Avril, who'd run a tea shop in Southwold, was a good cook. She was practical, Orwell was not; and though he thrived on hardship, he could never have survived on Jura without her. Apart from mealtimes, he typed for most of the day. They ate ghastly Scottish bread, and there always had to be a pudding, which he loved. After dinner he'd take a walk or fish for food. Jane and Lucy helped make hay and fetch the milk for Richard from the neighboring farm. In their spare time they read copies of the exotic *New Yorker*—sent free to Orwell as a valued contributor.[7]

Gwen O'Shaughnessy, with her children Laurence and Catherine, also traveled up to Jura. Catherine, who became a nurse in later life, remembered the difficult approach to the uncomfortable house:

> We were met, in the dead of night, by a horse and cart and taken to a farm-house where we spent the night. We then travelled . . . in this cart along a path they called a road. It was literally a two-wheeled dirt track with great big ruts in it which made the journey long and rough. He was living in an old farmhouse on the edge of the sea. Freezing cold. It pelted with rain, slamming it into the side of the house with such force that I thought it would blow the place down. He chose that place for its isolation and quiet-ness but for a TB patient it couldn't have been worse. It was damp and cold most of the time. Not an ideal place to convalesce.

To Catherine, Orwell seemed "long-suffering, tired looking, immensely thin, but gentle."

A most perceptive guest was the young Cambridge-educated poet and ex–Tank Corps commander, David Holbrook. He had a romantic interest in Susan and came up to see her in September 1946. By his account it was an unfortunate visit. The ship he took across the sound to Jura was buffeted by huge sea swells and stank of oil, sheep's tallow and human vomit. Jurassic speech was hard to understand, but he did hear one man, holding a rooster, exclaim: "Hurry up, Donald. Ma cock's gettin' cold."

On the long walk to Barnhill he was first attacked by a swarm of midges, then had a mysterious encounter with a rugged Wordsworthian shepherd: "He was dressed in a rough grey blanket, which was so filthy it might have been a skin, roughly wound round him toga-wise and tied with a tough cord. His feet were bare, and he carried a staff." Finally, as the Corryvrecken whirlpool swirled and crashed in the distance, he came upon some Monarch-of-the-Glen rutting stags, straight out of a Landseer painting. As they squared-off, he heard "a powerful grunting roar, bellowing round from hill to hill," and "watched the stags, who closed on one another, and then began to clash their antlers together with great force."[8] It was an inauspicious beginning.

Like Michel and Catherine, Holbrook found Barnhill grimy and dismal. On his visit, neither the motorbike nor the old truck were in running order. Orwell and Avril couldn't quite cope with all the difficulties, and seemed to prefer "everything to be inaccessible, broken, beyond repair, unattainable." Orwell shot a goose instead of wringing its neck, and had to extract the buckshot as he plucked the feathers. Avril was scathing about the mess he'd made, and he wore a hangdog look. Hardly up to scratch herself, she burnt the bird so thoroughly that only part of it was edible. The ochre-washed walls of the kitchen, Holbrook wrote, were "blackened with smoke from a large old-fashioned range, once black-leaded, now glum and rusty. The fire in this cooker gleamed out bravely, but could lift no echoing sparkle from the chilly floor of cracked quarry tiles. The ceiling was so low that [Orwell], who was over six foot, had to stoop, which made his long face and posture even more melancholy."

Holbrook had brought good cheese and wine as well as a new outboard motor for the boat, and expected a friendly reception. Greeting him with a mournful expression, without a smile or extended hand, Orwell merely said: "You must be Susan's friend from London." Holbrook had never met Orwell and had no way of knowing that he greeted everyone, even his pretty niece Lucy, that way. Surprised by the lack of warmth and hospitality, Holbrook found "not a word of enquiry into his walk, or what kind of crossing he had, or who he was, or how he knew [Susan]. For [Orwell] and his sister it was somehow as if he might not exist. . . . [He] had expected a kind of comradely warmth—or at least a willingness to share political interests. But instead there was this icy apartness."

Though Orwell was not apparently ill, Holbrook felt, he was certainly not in blooming health. Grouchy and strange, with a whistling noise in his throat, he seemed to be fighting against overwhelming obstacles. Holbrook looked forward to talking about books and politics, but the famous author bored him to death with endless descriptions of the habits of birds. To him Orwell seemed ponderously remote, with an air of lofty superiority. When Robin Fletcher, the Laird of Barnhill, came in for a Sunday morning dram after the hunt, Orwell abandoned his egalitarian principles. Treating Susan like a "below-stairs skivvy," he told her and David to keep out of sight and entertain the beaters in the kitchen. Some visitors, quite clearly, were more equal than others.

Gradually Holbrook realized the reasons for the lack of welcome and his failure to establish rapport with his host. Orwell knew from Susan that he was a Communist, and suspected that Holbrook had been sent by the Party to spy on him. There was also tension in the air because Orwell disapproved and Avril (whom they secretly called "Old Witchy") was jealous of his affair with Susan. David and Susan had no privacy inside the house, and had to take to the moors when they wanted to be alone.[9]

Holbrook was also caught in the crossfire between Avril and Susan. Avril had never married, led a rather empty existence and lived at home until her mother's death in 1943. Unlike the friendly, open, warmhearted Marjorie, Avril was sour, spinsterish and resentful. Like Orwell, she was tall and thin, with deep grooves in her face. After Marjorie's death from kidney disease in May 1946, Orwell became Avril's closest relative. He could now afford to support her, so when he moved to Jura that month, she joined him as cook and companion. When Susan arrived with Richard in July, Avril was already installed as mistress of the house. Susan then had to take orders from two people—who did not always agree on what should be done.

Avril disrupted the congenial routine that Susan had established with Orwell and wanted things run *her* way. Though he often typed until three o'clock in the morning, she insisted that he come down to breakfast promptly at eight. "She was such a sarcastic woman," said Susan. "She had beautiful eyes, but she was always giving me the once over. She was smug and she was sour-faced. She even criticized the way I cleaned the table after meals." She seemed to give Susan all the dirty jobs.

Avril tried to prevent Susan from fishing with Orwell in the evening, which they both enjoyed. When rabbits got into the garden, Avril refused to tell him and Susan had to break the bad news. Richard called Susan "Mummy," which Avril disliked. She said, "You should teach the baby to call you 'Nana,'" a name Susan disliked. So Richard tried to call her "Susie," which came out as "Toosie." When Avril urged her to smack Richard for a trifling offense, Susan replied: "No one but George will smack Richard." To which the ever-critical Avril replied: "You're not to call him 'George.' His proper name is *Eric!*"

Forgetting, or perhaps never really understanding, that Susan was not a professional nanny, Avril also gave Susan "absolute hell about being disabled." She'd exclaim: "Call yourself a nanny and can't even darn neatly. Can't fetch milk because you can't walk properly." She challenged Susan by telling her: "What I want, I fight for." And Susan, poor Cinderella, meekly replied, "I don't fight." When Avril wanted to take over Susan's job and look after the house and Richard, it became clear that Susan would have to go. Orwell—who tried to stay out of the feud, but felt obliged to side with Avril—gave Susan some extra money to soften the blow. Katie Darroch, who lived on the neighboring farm, recalled that Richard was naturally upset when Susan suddenly left them in September: "the poor wee laddie, he cried and he cried."

Given Avril's domineering temperament, it was clear that Susan would eventually be fired. Avril justified the decision by claiming that life at Barnhill was too difficult for a physically handicapped young woman. It was highly ironic that she later married the penniless ex-army officer, Bill Dunn. Thirteen years younger than Avril, and a fierce-tempered heavy drinker, Bill had his leg blown off in the Italian campaign on the same day that Richard was born. This oddly matched, tough and irascible couple would eventually become Richard's parents.[10]

III

ORWELL'S MAIN interests in life were narrowly focused on his ruling passions—literature and politics. After he left teaching, he never played or watched sports, though he liked to fish and occasionally tinkered with carpentry. He almost never went to a museum or art gallery, to a concert, opera or ballet. He occasionally saw movies with his father in Southwold, but hated writing film and theater reviews. He didn't see the cultural sites when he took the train from Marseille to Calais in 1927 nor, of course, when he lived down-and-out in Paris two years later. He recuperated from illness in Morocco, visited Spain, France, Germany and Austria in wartime, but never traveled in Asia or went to Italy or Greece. Apart from three days in Banyuls after escaping from Spain, he never had a holiday abroad.

Orwell's enormous output, despite frequent illness, suggests that he did not take much time off. Shortly before leaving for Jura, he described himself as a journalist who worked hard to produce about 150,000 words a year. He'd had to do a tremendous amount of hack-work in order to survive, and the hundreds of dud books he dealt with rarely inspired great reviews. In February 1946 he published his second collection of substantial essays on subjects that truly interested him. In contrast to the short reviews he *had* to write, these pieces are masterful. His capacity for intense observation, clear thinking and vigorous style made him one of the greatest English essayists.

The essay lacks the glamour and status of drama and poetry, the scope and weight of the novel. But in Orwell's hands it has depth and range, sparkle and seriousness. He could write fierce polemics, literary criticism and tender nature pieces, all with apparent ease. His advice about writing in "Politics and the English Language" recommends fresh, direct language and unambiguous expression. He believed in the writer's power and responsibility to communicate in the clearest way possible. Like Kipling, who advised authors to "leave your work to drain overnight," and like Hemingway, who compared prose to an iceberg that hides most of its substance beneath a deceptively simple surface, Orwell thought writing should be a paring-down process. Though he makes it look artless, it certainly was not, especially when his topics were complicated or morally ambiguous.

Orwell's plain style, the basic weapon in his arsenal, appeals to readers' common sense and persuades them of his honesty and good faith. At the same time his arguments are sophisticated, provocative and entertaining. The striking openings of his major essays, for example, are uncannily effective and immediately hook the reader:

—In Moulmein, in Lower Burma, I was hated by large numbers of people.
—As I write, highly civilised human beings are flying overhead, trying to kill me.
—Saints should always be judged guilty until they are proved innocent.
—Autobiography is only to be trusted when it reveals something disgraceful.[11]

Orwell's mind was drawn to the unexpected and paradoxical. We assume a white policeman in British Burma inspires fear and respect—the essay shows otherwise. In modern war killing people requires an intelligent and skilled elite—we almost long for the good old days when we were killed one at a time. We distrust evil people, but need to be just as sceptical about goodness and honesty. Orwell often makes us test our assumptions against the evidence he offers. He invites us to look at familiar subjects from an unusual point of view ("Shooting an Elephant," "Charles Dickens") or at an unfamiliar subject in the light of commonsensical and humane values.

Gloomy George, the blunt Englishman, could also be the supercilious, witty Etonian. In a review of *The Hamlet* in 1940, the old colonial policeman puts down William Faulkner by describing his characters as if they were a primitive tribe in a remote corner of the earth: "people with supremely hideous names—names like Flem Snopes and Eck Snopes—sit about on the steps of village stores, chewing tobacco, swindling one another in small business deals, and from time to time committing a rape or a murder." He also challenged assumptions about British superiority by mocking the mechanical way he was taught history at school: "in 1499 you were still in the Middle Ages, with knights in plate armour riding at one another with long lances, and then suddenly the clock struck 1500, and you were in something called the Renaissance, and everyone wore ruffs and doublets and was busy robbing treasure ships on the Spanish Main."

Orwell reprinted ten of his liveliest pieces in *Critical Essays* (U.S. title: *Dickens, Dali and Others*). The essays on Dickens, boys' weeklies, Koestler, Wells and Wodehouse have already been discussed. The other five—on Kipling, Yeats, "The Art of Donald McGill," "Raffles and Miss Blandish" and Salvador Dali—are worth noting.

Orwell and Kipling had many things in common, including a sadistic streak, a talent for writing about animals and an ability to add new phrases to the English language. In his essay on Kipling's poetry (1942), Orwell could not resolve the conflict between his disapproval of Kipling's politics and admiration of his art. He immediately conceded that "Kipling *is* a jingo imperialist, he *is* morally insensitive and aesthetically disgusting," and then attempted to "find out why it is that he survives." He pitted his own belief that "an empire is primarily a money-making concern" against Kipling's view that it's "a sort of forcible evangelising." Just as he'd defined England by evoking its essential characteristics, so he extracted from Kipling's poetry (reinforced by his own experience in Burma) a vividly memorable picture of the colonial army: "the sweltering barracks in Gibraltar and Lucknow, the red coats, the pipeclayed belts and the pillbox hats, the beer, the fights, the floggings, hangings and crucifixions, the bugle-calls, the smell of oats and horse-piss, the bellowing sergeants with foot-long moustaches, the bloody skirmishes, invariably mismanaged, the crowded troopships, the cholera-stricken camps, the 'native' concubines, the ultimate death in the work-house." He concluded that Kipling's power as a good-bad poet comes from "his sense of responsibility, which made it possible for him to have a world-view, even though it happened to be a false one."

Yeats was another reactionary writer whom Orwell admired and could quote extensively from memory. Concerned in 1943 with tracing the connection between political tendency and literary style, he noted that "a Socialist would not write like Chesterton or a Tory imperialist like Bernard Shaw." He argued that Yeats' tendency was Fascist and that his political ideas were connected to his interest in the occult. Thinking of Wyndham Lewis, Pound and Eliot, he concluded that the "best writers of our time have been reactionary."[12]

Susan Watson recalled that when Orwell invited Aunt Nellie Limouzin—wrapped in black satin and adorned with jet beads—to tea in Canonbury Square, he'd amuse her with his collection of postcards by Donald McGill. He did not want Susan to see her enjoying these improper cards and told her not to serve tea until Nellie had finished laughing at the jokes. Nellie, a true bohemian, would not have minded at all, but Orwell was slightly shocked by them. In his pioneering sociological essays on popular culture, he favorably compared the static and old-fashioned view expressed in these works with that of their harsher and crueler successors. In "The Art of Donald McGill" (1941) he took comic postcards seriously, and explored the meaning and purpose of the genre. He analyzed the kinds of recurrent jokes about sex, marriage, drunkenness, lavatories and working-class snobbery, and concluded that they mocked traditional values and represented a "harmless rebellion against virtue."

As with comic postcards, Orwell's analysis of crime novels in "Raffles and Miss Blandish" (1944) revealed considerable interest in what appeared to be inconsequential works. He argued that there was an "immense difference in moral atmosphere" between the two novels (*Raffles*, by E.W. Hornung, published in 1900, and *No Orchids for Miss Blandish*, by James Hadley Chase, in 1939) and discussed the "change in the popular attitude that this probably implies." The first had an almost schoolboy atmosphere; the second, full of cruelty and corruption (like the film *High Sierra*), was "a header into the cesspool." There are, however, rather perverse elements in Orwell's condemnation. He loathed Chase's fictional character, "whose sole pleasure in life consists in driving knives into other people's bellies" but, as he himself sadistically wrote in "Shooting an Elephant," he thought the "greatest joy in the world would be to drive a bayonet into a Buddhist priest's guts." He blamed the horrors of James Hadley Chase on the American obsession with violence—though the author was in fact English. Connecting his thesis to wartime politics, Orwell argued that Chase's obsession with the struggle for power and the triumph of the strong over the weak revealed "the interconnection between sadism, success-worship, power-worship, nationalism and totalitarianism."

In "Without Benefit of Clergy" Orwell reviewed Salvador Dali's repulsive autobiography. As in Chase's thriller—which glorifies cruelty, sexual perversion and the power instinct—the moral atmosphere of Dali's book (in which he claims to have eaten a dead bat covered with ants) revealed "the perversion of instinct that has been made possible by the machine age. . . . He is a symptom of the world's illness." Orwell admitted that Dali was a hard worker and brilliant draftsman, but was not willing to overlook the fact that he was a disgusting human being. He would not give him benefit of clergy—based on his status as an artist—to excuse his moral cowardice and exhibitionism, his depiction of sexual perversity and necrophilia.

Orwell used a witty hyperbole from Dali's autobiography—"At seven I wanted to be Napoleon. And my ambition has been growing steadily ever since"—to explain his aberrations. He suggested, given his egoism and talent, that Dali could only escape into wickedness and achieve fame by shocking and wounding people. But this subjective and moralistic explanation is unsatisfactory. Though he saw that Dali's dishonest book was an exaggerated fantasy, he used everything that Dali said as evidence against him and made no distinction between fantasy and reality. He didn't seem to see that Dali's Surrealistic fiction was deliberately designed to attack bourgeois values. He naively rose to Dali's obvious bait, and unleashed his puritanical indignation at the artist who confessed that at the age of five he'd flung another little boy off a bridge. The essential question, which Orwell asked but never answered, was "*why* the rentiers and aristocrats should buy his pictures instead of hunting and making love like their grandfathers."[13] He ignored the possibility that Dali's behavior and art were not a symptom of the world's sickness, but a powerful expression of it.

Orwell tended to be more hyperbolic in political than in literary contro-versy, and one of his most reckless and irresponsible statements brought him into conflict with the formidable Wyndham Lewis. As Julian Symons noted, the two shared the same cross-grained integrity: "Like Orwell [Lewis] main-tained intellectual independence in a time favourable to one or another sort of conformity; like Orwell had an itch for politics; like Orwell was ignored, because of his ideas, by some people in important positions; like Orwell was utterly informal, without a trace of literary or social affectation. Yet although he was easy to talk to Lewis was inhuman, in a way Orwell was not: he was a man devoured by a passion for ideas, which he wished to put to the service of art."

Both *Homage to Catalonia* and Lewis' novel *The Revenge for Love* (1937) attacked the Communists in Spain, were neglected in the 1930s and were not published in America until 1952, at the height of the Cold War and the McCarthy witch-hunts, when their anti-Communism was particularly wel-come. Lewis' *Left Wings Over Europe* (1936), though written from a Right-wing point of view, foreshadowed two important ideas in *Nineteen Eighty-Four*: "Doublethink" and the Dostoyevskian theme of the conflict between freedom and responsibility. Lewis' *The Art of Being Ruled* could have supplied Orwell's novel with a brilliant title. The theme of the revolu-tion betrayed in *Animal Farm* was repeated by Lewis in *Self Condemned* (1954). And Orwell's attack on the English class structure in *Keep the Aspidistra Flying* had many themes in common with Lewis' *The Vulgar Streak* (1941). Lewis asked his editor to send a copy to Orwell, who he thought would be a sympathetic reader.

Orwell took his first jab at Lewis in 1945 when he wrote, "enough talent to set up dozens of ordinary writers has been poured into Wyndham Lewis's so-called novels, such as *Tarr* or *Snooty Baronet*. Yet it would be a very heavy labour to read one of these books right through." In his "London Letter" to the *Partisan Review* the following year, Orwell—often unreliable in his wartime predictions and political judgments of friends and enemies—stated, with absolutely no justification: "Wyndham Lewis, I am credibly informed, has become a Communist or at least a strong sympathiser, and is writing a book in praise of Stalin to balance his previous books in favor of Hitler."[14] Lewis, who had staunchly opposed Stalin when nearly all the intellectuals of the 1930s had thrown themselves at his feet, was justifiably enraged. Orwell's assertion, however improbable, damaged Lewis' already dubious reputation in America. Orwell ignored the radical change in his political beliefs and, even worse, stated that Lewis had written two books in favor of Hitler, when he had actually written a favorable book in 1931 and a hostile one in 1939.

Lewis, remarkably restrained, told Dwight Macdonald, an editor at *Partisan Review*, that Orwell "is a silly billy. He's full of political tittletattle — but he gets it all wrong. He thinks people are always falling in love with political Stars. I am so glad that emotional publicschoolboy has transferred his excitable loyalties to the Partisans." Defending himself against the libel in *Rude Assignment* (1950), Lewis wrote that Orwell "believes it is perfectly in order for people to do any 'smearing' they think fit. . . . The sahib imagined himself in the jungles of Burma, doing a bit of rogue-elephant hunting!"

Lewis then mounted a full-scale counterattack in *The Writer and the Absolute* (1952). He contemptuously opposed the commonly accepted view of Orwell's political ideas and argued that he began as a fashionable Socialist, and was eventually emancipated by anti-Communism. According to Hugh Gordon Porteous, the wild rumor that Lewis had become a Communist originated when Lewis said — as a joke — to the gossipy Roy Campbell: "Tell them I've changed my views and am now writing a book about Stalin." Campbell repeated this in all seriousness to Porteous, who passed it on to Orwell.[15] Delighted with this bit of gossip, Orwell did not check its source, published it in the *Partisan Review* and damaged Lewis' reputation as well as his own.

IV

On AUGUST 19, 1947, while writing *Nineteen Eighty-Four*, Orwell came close to drowning himself and three others. To entertain his summer visitors, he took Richard and two of Marjorie's children camping and fishing on the western side of the island. On the way back he misread the tidal tables and steered his twelve-foot dinghy straight into one of the most perilous whirlpools in Europe. Martin Martin portrayed the place in his classic *Description of the Western Isles of Scotland* (1703):

> Between the north end of Jura and the Isle of Scarba, lies the famous and dangerous gulf, called Cory Vrekan, about a mile in breadth; it yields an impetuous current, not to be matched anywhere about the isle of Britain. The sea begins to boil and ferment with the tide at flood, and resembles the boiling of a pot; and then increases gradually, until it appears in many

whirlpools, which form themselves in sort of pyramids, and immediately after sprout up as high as the mast of a little vessel, and at the same time make a loud report.

A modern cruising manual explains that the gulf can only be crossed with caution and judicious timing: "In calm weather at slack water the whole gulf becomes placid, and gives no hint of its ferocious nature under certain conditions of wind and tide. It is at its most dangerous when an Atlantic swell, having built up after several days of strong Western winds, meets a flood tide. A passage at this time would be unthinkable."[16]

The small boat was bashed around at the edge of the whirlpool and the outboard motor, which Orwell had not secured with a rope or chain, was wrenched off the mounting and fell into the sea. In true Blair fashion, there were no screams of fear and everyone remained curiously calm. At the tiller but too weak to give any help, Orwell made quaint remarks about the local fauna that swam around the boat: "Curious thing about seals, very inquisitive creatures."

Henry Dakin, aged twenty-one and on leave from the army, got out the oars, kept the boat steady and made for the nearest landfall. A long Atlantic swell, rising and falling about twelve feet, pushed them toward a small rocky island. The boat crashed into the rocks and turned over, and they lost most of their equipment. Henry managed to scramble up the rocks on bare feet and pulled the others to safety. Richard Blair later said that "it was very dangerous, and could well have been tragic." Exhausted and soaked by the icy sea, gasping for breath and weaker than ever, Orwell confessed that he thought they were "goners."

They couldn't get off the rocks without engine or oars. Orwell went off to find some food, discovered some baby seagulls, but didn't have the heart to kill them. After a few hours on the barren outcrop, they waved a shirt on a fishing rod and were rescued, with some difficulty, by passing lobstermen. Lucy had lost a shoe and scraped her ankle. Henry, who'd taken off his boots to swim to the rocks, had lost them in the sea. Orwell, who still had *his* boots, was embarrassed by his foolish mistake and by their role as helpless castaways. Wanting to retain his last shred of independence, he infuriated Lucy by refusing the lobstermen's offer to drop them at Barnhill. Casually remarking: "Oh no, it's all right. We'll walk back," he forced them to go barefoot over three miles of rough country.[17]

That evening he still had enough energy to give a detailed description in his diary of his descent into the maelstrom:

On return journey today ran into the whirlpool & were all nearly drowned. Engine sucked off by the sea & went to the bottom. Just managed to keep the boat steady with the oars, & after going through the whirlpool twice, ran into smooth water & . . . so ran in quickly & managed to clamber ashore. H. D. jumped ashore first with the rope, then the boat overturned spilling L. D., R. & myself into the sea. R. trapped under the boat for a moment, but we managed to get him out. Most of the stuff in the boat lost including the oars. . . . Made a fire of dead grass & lumps of dry peat, prised off the surface, at which we dried our clothes. We were taken off about 3 hours later. . . . [We] must have struck Corryvreckan at about 11.30, i.e., when the tide had been ebbing about 3 hours. It appears this was the very worst time. . . . Only serious loss, the engine & 12 blankets.

Already burdened by guilt, Orwell would have been devastated by the death of Henry, Lucy or Richard. As he wrote in his "Last Literary Notebook" in 1949: "Nowadays the death of a child is the worst thing that most people are able to imagine. If one has only *one* child, to recover from losing it would be almost impossible. It would darken the universe, permanently."

Warburg observed that Orwell had risked his life unnecessarily—and often courageously—on duty in Burma, under Fascist fire and when pursued by Communists in Spain, during the Nazi bombing of London, in the whirlpool near Jura and "in his persistent neglect of elementary medical precautions. . . . Obliteration was finally the sole remedy for his overpowering sense of guilt."[18] He had told Richard Rees, his literary executor, to destroy the manuscript of *Nineteen Eighty-Four* if anything happened to him. He was almost killed in Spain before he wrote *Homage to Catalonia*. Now, for the second time, he came close to death before he could finish a book that radically changed our view of the modern world.

15

The Dark Vision of
Nineteen Eighty-Four,
1948

I

ORWELL HAD spent the winter of 1946 in London before returning to Jura in April 1947 and resuming his arduous life on the island. During the unusually cold weather he suffered severe attacks of bronchitis that kept him in bed for weeks at a time. Friends who came round to Canonbury Square found him in pajamas and shaggy bathrobe, looking like a death's head but typing furiously. In his "Last Literary Notebook" he described the manic compulsion to work that helped to kill him:

> There has literally been not one day in which I did not feel that I was idling, that I was behind with the current job, & that my total output was miserably small. Even at the periods when I was working 10 hours a day on a book, or turning out 4 or 5 articles a week, I have never been able to get away from this neurotic feeling that I was wasting time. . . . As soon as a book is finished, I begin, actually from the next day, worrying because the next one is not begun.

He spoke of spending the next winter in a warm climate and had plans to travel abroad. He even thought of living for several months in the American South in order to find out how it felt to be dispossessed and deprived—a kind of down-and-out in Georgia and Alabama. In November 1947 an editor at the *Observer* suggested he spend three months in Africa to cover the ground-nuts scheme in Kenya and the elections in South Africa. But, like the plans to work on the Lucknow *Pioneer* and report on the Sicilian campaign, poor health forced him to withdraw.

On Jura he was seriously ill in September and October. By the end of December he'd lost twenty pounds, seemed to be wasting away and felt death-ly sick all the time. More afraid than ever of infecting Richard with what was now conclusively diagnosed as tuberculosis, he did his best to keep the boy away from him. On December 20, 1947, he entered Hairmyres Hospital in East Kilbride, about twenty miles south of Glasgow, where he remained for the next seven months. Avril took care of Richard; and Orwell, worried that the child would forget him during his long absence, found them a place to live near the sanatorium.

A former patient described the hospital and the kind of treatment it offered: "Hairmyres was built in extensive grounds 580 feet above sea-level, with the idea of combining sanatorium treatment with facilities for training patients in outdoor work. There was a tree nursery, a market garden, pigs, poultry and a herd of Ayrshire cows, and for recreation, a putting green, cro-quet lawn and a football pitch. . . . The theory was that rest in clean country air (whether sunlit or thick with falling snow) and a solid, balanced diet formed the best treatment for tuberculosis." Admitted to Ward 3 of the Thoracic Surgical Unit, Orwell was diagnosed as having "bilateral pul-monary tuberculosis with a large cavitating lesion in one lung and a patch in the other."[1]

He was put under the care of Dr. Bruce Dick, head of the Surgical Unit—a huge fellow, jovial and extroverted, who slapped people on the back and was fond of the bottle—and his assistant Dr. James Williamson. Since Orwell was rather quiet and withdrawn, Dr. Williamson did not find him especially interesting, and did not know that his patient was a famous writer. Doctors did not understand the effects of smoking until after the war, and some even thought the coughing brought on by cigarettes helped bring up sputum. So Orwell was allowed to smoke his powerful Nosegay Shag. Dr. Williamson defined Orwell's illness as a fibrotic, feverish, wasting disease "of a very chron-ic nature. It was confined to the upper part of both lungs, mostly his left lung. . . . There were tubercle bacilli in his sputum, which means he was infec-tious. . . . He was never very ill with severe wasting and drenching night sweats. But he'd probably forgotten, almost, what it was like to feel completely well. . . . His lung would have been tough, like leather. With chronic fibrotic TB you could live for quite a long while. . . . He lived for many years with TB." Orwell had always ignored or denied his condition, but his health was now permanently ruined.

The main treatment (described in 1924 in Thomas Mann's *The Magic Mountain*, and still used at that time) was a phrenic crush. It paralyzed the phrenic nerve and collapsed the affected lung, which was kept out of action for six months in order to close the cavities. Dr. Williamson explained that "you just pull the muscle aside, expose the nerve, and tweak it with a pair of forceps. The patient would get one sudden pain, and the diaphragm would jump, and that was the diaphragm paralysed for three to six months, until the nerve recovered again. Then we pumped air into his abdomen. The diaphragm was pushed up by this, and the lungs were collapsed."

Orwell found the phrenic crush "hellishly painful" and, a week after he arrived, told Gwen O'Shaughnessy: "They first crushed the phrenic nerve, which I gather is what makes the lung expand & contract, & then pumped air into the diaphragm, which I understand is to push the lung into a different position & get it away from some kind of movement which occurs automatically. I have to have 'refills' of air in the diaphragm every few days." Though the needles used to pump in air were not painful if used by an expert, the doctor noted that Orwell disliked them and winced more than most: "he appeared to dread each refill and was quite unable to relax on the table. He never, however, complained or uttered any gasps or exclamations and we all remarked upon his degree of self-control."[2]

As Orwell seemed to make slight progress, he kept friends informed about his treatment. He wrote Woodcock that he felt a bit less like death since entering the hospital. Jollied along by the doctors, he reassured Warburg that his disease wasn't dangerous and that the cure was going quite well. But—knowing that Robert Louis Stevenson, Anton Chekhov and D.H. Lawrence had all died at the age of forty-four—he admitted that tuberculosis was bound to claim him sooner or later. On June 25, 1948, he sadly informed Powell: "It's my birthday to day—45, isn't it awful. I've also got some more false teeth, and, since being here, a lot more grey in my hair." In his personal diary, just before his birthday, he dropped his stoic mask. His description of himself as a ruined old man anticipates his portrayal of Winston Smith after his torture in *Nineteen Eighty-Four*: "Perpetual tired weak feeling in legs, aching knees. Stiffness amounting to pain in small of back & down loins. Discomfort in gums. Chest more or less always constricted. Feeling in the morning of being

almost unable to stand up. Sensation of cold whenever the sun is not shin-
ing. Wind on the stomach. . . . Eyes always watering."[3]

On February 1 Dr. Dick told Orwell about streptomycin, an expensive and
miraculously effective new drug, discovered in 1944 but not yet available in
Britain. David Astor quickly obtained the drug from America and on about
February 20 Orwell began a course of one gram daily for fifty days.
Unfortunately, he had a severe allergic reaction. His nails disintegrated, his
hair fell out and patches of white appeared, the skin flaked off his face, a rash
inflamed his back, a persistent sore throat made it difficult to swallow. He
had ulcers in his throat and blisters in his mouth that burst and bled, and in
the morning his lips were glued together with dried blood. Though the drug
helped his lesions, he had to stop taking it. The doctors, unfamiliar with the
treatment, did not know that if he had been given smaller doses he could
have avoided the side effects and been saved. Orwell gave the rest of the precious medicine to two other patients, who were completely cured.

David Astor, Richard Rees and Bill Dunn visited Orwell at Hairmyres,
and Fredric Warburg saw him just after the streptomycin treatment began.
He found Orwell "sitting bolt upright in bed when I went into his room,
wearing a shirt. He greeted me with a smile that was both welcoming and
wintry. He told me he thought the antibiotic might be doing him a bit of
good, but the actual injections, which seemed to him to be all too frequent,
were exceedingly painful. He showed me his arm which was marked by the
scars of numerous needles." As he began to recover from the treatment,
Orwell also had lively conversations with another patient, who worked for
the Thomson newspaper empire in Dundee and wrote Billy Bunter–type stories for a boys' weekly called *Hotspur*. Dr. Williamson put them in the same
room and they got on well together.

For medical reasons Orwell's right arm had to be put in plaster, which
started a rumor that the doctors had taken extreme measures to prevent him
from writing. According to the history of the hospital, the staff insisted on
complete physical and mental rest and confiscated his typewriter. When
Orwell kept writing with a ballpoint, they put his arm in plaster. "The staff
had the last word. A plausible reason having been given, his writing arm was
immobilised in plaster for several weeks. . . . Orwell's typewriter was returned
to him in May 1948. He spent the remainder of his stay in Hairmyres writing, walking in the grounds and playing croquet. . . [He is remembered] as
a reserved, courteous man who appeared to accept pain and discomfort stoically." Dr. Williamson is certain this story is false. Too weak to work for the

first few months in hospital, Orwell was allowed to write as soon as he was well enough ("there was no point stopping him"). He had tuberculosis, weight loss, high fever and acute pain; his right arm was in plaster; he was bedridden and unable to type. But, driven by his demons, he continued to write.

Released on July 28, 1948, Orwell returned to the discomforts of Jura. In August he told Michael Meyer that he could get out of bed for only half the day, couldn't do anything that required exertion and had to live an invalid's life for at least another year. Avril, who looked after him, thought that if he'd gone into a convalescent home instead of trying to lead a normal life, he probably would have been cured. In mid-September he returned to East Kilbride for a checkup, which coincided with a commercial convention in the city. Fyvel wrote that he "had tramped from one full-up hotel to the next in heavy boots, carrying a suitcase weighted with purchases, finding a bed only when totally ill and exhausted." This debilitating trip caused a relapse and put him back in bed. In October he told Astor: "I am a bit better now but felt very poorly for about a fortnight. It started funnily enough with my going back to Hairmyres to be examined."[4]

Orwell's awareness that death was approaching intensified his emotions and heightened his powers of expression. Once in Jura he resumed writing *Nineteen Eighty-Four*. He explained to Lydia Jackson that he could have taken care of his health when he began to relapse at the end of September (the warning signs were by now unmistakable), but "had to finish the wretched book." He completed the final draft in November and found it too indecipherable to send to a typist. With the help of Moore, Warburg and Astor, he tried desperately to find a woman who'd come to Jura from London, Edinburgh or Glasgow. Miranda Wood, who was subletting his Canonbury Square flat and did occasional work for him, and Sally McEwan, his friend from the *Tribune*, were unavailable. Despite intensive efforts, no one could be found who was willing to go to Jura to help a distinguished author work on his extraordinary manuscript—even at two or three times the going rate of pay.

The exhausted Orwell, anxious to get on with the work and racing against time, decided to type it himself. Sonia Brownell observed that "George was perfectly aware that he could come to London and engage an efficient secretary, but as he saw things, leaving Jura was just not on. It would have meant an upheaval in his whole consciousness of himself which he did not want to face." He'd never admit that he was a permanent invalid, too weak to live on

Jura, and that the whole way of life there had been madness. "Besides," she went on, "all his life he had ignored his illnesses up to the point where they got too bad, when he went to bed and waited to recover as he always did. Perhaps he thought that this time, too, he would recover; or he just refused to think." Fyvel explained that though Orwell was seriously ill, he sat up in bed typing the final copy of the 150,000-word typescript "and then had his final collapse from which he did not recover." The creation of *Nineteen Eighty-Four* virtually killed Orwell, and the novel's vision of the future is correspondingly grim.

Just before Christmas 1948 he left a bitterly cold Jura for the last time. On the way to the ferry, in the early winter darkness, the car got bogged down in the muddy, potholed road. Bill Dunn hobbled back on his wooden leg to get help while Orwell read to Richard in the car. In January he belatedly confessed to Rees: "I think it would be wiser to do as I first intended, when I took the place in 1946, & use it only for the summers."[5] Winter was always a dangerous time for him. On January 9, 1949, a year after he was admitted to Hairmyres, he entered the Cotswold Sanatorium, and a year after that he was dead.

II

Nineteen Eighty-Four, Orwell's last and most ambitious work, was an extraordinary achievement. He'd been thinking about the idea for many years, throughout the Blitz, on his journey to postwar Germany, in his essays and book reviews, and in conversations with Koestler, who'd had direct experience with political repression. In *Coming Up for Air* he'd warned that England was under threat, and in 1944 noted that English people could scarcely imagine "the real totalitarian atmosphere, in which the State endeavours to control people's thoughts as well as their words." His last, anti-utopian novel was designed to reveal the dangers of totalitarian ideas. *Nineteen Eighty-Four* is an inspired piece of anti-Communist propaganda that sums up a lifetime of thinking about politics. It is also deeply personal, imaginative and inventive, bleak and tragic.

The story of Winston Smith, the last thinking man in Europe, takes place in the worst possible state of England. Devastated by atomic bombs, and still at war, the country is now Airstrip One, a grimy, run-down outpost of Oceania, a vast totalitarian system that includes North America and the old British

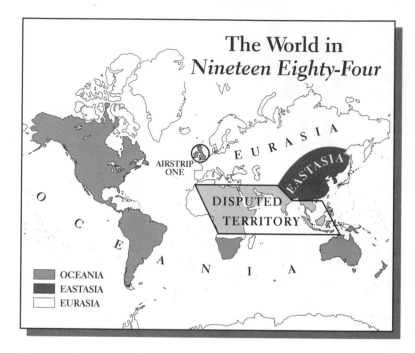

Empire. The world is divided into three power zones—Oceania, Eurasia and
Eastasia—ruled by authoritarian oligarchies. All three possess atomic
weapons and wage perpetual conventional warfare with the others. Winston,
an educated bureaucrat, belongs to the select Outer Party. O'Brien, his inter-
rogator and member of the more elite Inner Party, represents the corrupt
intellectuals who have accepted dictatorship in exchange for extraordinary
power and privilege. Winston's love affair with Julia shows him the moral differences between the trained Party members and the majority of degraded,
slave-like proles. At the peak of his moral awareness he is arrested, imprisoned, tortured and brainwashed.

   Nineteen Eighty-Four breaks fictional conventions and blends science fiction, satire, realism and parody (including fake documents). In Wells' scientific romances, the hero is transported by some fantastic means to a remote
time or place, meets a powerful figure who explains the society to him and
finally either returns to his original world or fights against conditions in the
new. The plot of Orwell's novel is an ironic reversal of the Wellsian pattern.
Winston and Julia exist in the future, try to escape into the atmosphere of
the past and are harshly wrenched back to the future. The evil O'Brien,

whose name Orwell used to suggest the absolute power of the Catholic church, both enlightens and dooms him. The knowledge he gains is devastating, and there is no escape.

Orwell transposes the political terror of Nazi Germany and Stalinist Russia onto the London of the 1940s. Though the landscape of the city has been reduced to rubble and its skyline is dominated by the four massive buildings of Minitrue, Miniluv, Minipax and Miniplenty, Orwell's description of living conditions are close to those of wartime and postwar England under the newly elected Labour government. There was more to eat in England during the war than there was in 1948, when he completed the novel. Bread was first rationed in June 1946 when wheat destined for Britain was diverted to feed the defeated Germans.

Like Winston, Orwell had trouble finding "some really rare object" like a comb or a tin of boot polish, and in October 1948 concluded: "Physically, the average British citizen is probably somewhat worse off than he was three years ago. The housing situation is extremely bad; food, though not actually insufficient, is unbearably dull. The prices of cigarettes, beer, and unrationed food such as vegetables, are fantastic. And clothes rationing is an increasing hardship." In the novel Winston laments "houses falling to pieces, bread dark-coloured, tea a rarity, coffee filthy-tasting, cigarettes insufficient. . . . One's heart sickened at the discomfort and dirt and scarcity, the interminable winters, the stickiness of one's socks, the lifts that never worked, the cold water, the gritty soap, the cigarettes that came to pieces, the food with its strange evil tastes." [6]

Orwell incorporates contemporary events to create an atmosphere of documentary reality, and the power of the novel comes from a realistic use of familiar materials rather than from imaginary speculations about the future. During the war Orwell was horrified by the way "U-boat captains had sunk passenger ships without warning and machine-gunned the survivors." At the beginning of the novel Winston watches a newsreel showing the sinking of a refugee ship. The specific incident that inspired the newsreel took place on September 27, 1940, when the *City of Benares*, carrying ninety children and their nine escorts to Canada, was torpedoed by the Germans and sunk 600 miles out in the Atlantic. Nearly 300 passengers and crew were killed. Only seven children survived. In the novel the newsreel shows the ship being bombed by helicopters in the Mediterranean rather than torpedoed in the Atlantic, but in both cases the passenger ships are defenseless and children the main victims. [7]

III

NONDESCRIPT, SEEDY, thirty-nine years old, Winston Smith is Orwell's last and most poignant self-portrait. As he enters Victory Mansions (where the hallway smells of boiled cabbage), pursued by a vile wind and a swirl of gritty dust, we're on familiar ground. Like Gordon Comstock, he counts his last remaining cigarettes; and he lives among bomb craters and rubble, the aftermath of George Bowling's vision of a universal smashup. Orwell's targets in previous books—the social injustice, sexual repression and xenophobia of England in the1930s—have become the rigid class system, sexual puritanism and permanent state of war in Oceania. Just as Orwell exaggerates certain aspects of normal life to create his setting and atmosphere, so he gives Winston more extreme characteristics of earlier heroes: loneliness, guilt, physical weakness, sexual frustration, alienation from society, desire for spiritual and moral integrity. Comstock and Bowling have to compromise with ordinary life, but Winston is indoctrinated, spied upon and tortured.

Born in the mid-1940s (like Orwell's adopted son), Winston has lost his parents and sister in the purges of the 1950s, and is a product of the new state. The novel opens as he begins to question the nature of society and his role in it, and his attempt to capture a true sense of the past not only reveals his desperate situation, but also structures the entire book. His memories are not of prep school, but of a children's camp where he was indoctrinated with Party ideology; he does not feel snobbish shame about his family, but guilt about having survived starvation or extermination; his wife Katharine's frigidity is considered normal by the Party, his own longings perverse and illegal.

Like Gordon Comstock, Winston expresses his anxiety in his writing, which is now a dangerous act, forbidden as "thoughtcrime" and "ownlife." In his job he alters the records of the past to fit current Party policy. In private, he writes on the creamy paper of an old diary with an old-fashioned pen and ink. The first kind of writing (like Orwell's in the BBC) is mechanical and exhausting, the second (like Orwell's own creative writing) is psychologically liberating, but also sets off disturbing memories and dreams. The first is systematic lying in Newspeak, the second a passionate search for truth in Oldspeak. Orwell contrasts the mindless, bureaucratic attitude Winston needs to do this work with his panic at the blank sheet of paper, his poor handwriting, his mental and emotional confusion when he starts writing for himself. Winston's work forces him to practice "doublethink," the ability to hold simultaneously two contradictory opinions which cancel each other out.

Winston has to believe that he's rectifying errors, yet also knows that he's falsifying information. Each task forces him to find a plausible formula to disguise the truth. Winston is manipulated by the system, and yet, in his role of Outer Party intellectual, he's part of the system that manipulates others.

In his diary Winston relives his past and expiates guilt, and in the dreams stimulated by the effort of writing he recaptures the values of the past. Vaguely aware that his mother in some way had sacrificed herself for his survival, Winston accepts his guilt and gains insight into normal human relationships. He now realizes that her death "had been tragic and sorrowful in a way that was no longer possible. Tragedy, he perceived, belonged to the ancient time, to a time when there were still privacy, love and friendship, and when the members of a family stood by one another without needing to know the reason. . . . Today there were fear, hatred and pain, but no dignity of emotion, no deep or complex sorrows."

When Winston first begins to write he's blocked by the thought that he has no present or future audience, but writing itself becomes a heroic means of staying sane and carrying on the human heritage. Despite its third-person narrative, type-characters and political context, the novel often sounds a note of personal appeal. Winston's salutation, *"To the future or to the past, to a time when thought is free,"* sounds like Orwell's last will and testament.

Like Orwell himself, Winston feels that his sexual life is finished, so that meeting Julia (like Orwell meeting his second wife, Sonia) is tremendously exciting. He reflects that "the sexual act, successfully performed, was rebellion. Desire was thoughtcrime," and Julia allows him to satisfy his longing for love and sexual intimacy. In "Such, Such Were the Joys" Orwell gave the rationale for the lovers' rebellion: "the weak in a world governed by the strong [must] break the rules, or perish. . . . The weak have the right to make a different set of rules for themselves."[8]

Julia and Winston have very different personalities and attitudes. Decisive, assertive, practical and sexually experienced, she initiates the affair and openly delights in outwitting the authorities. In contrast to Winston's middle age, poor health and fearfulness, she's youthful and psychologically tough. He's an idealist, concerned about mankind's future as much as his own; she's a realist, eager to get what she can for herself. Much younger than Winston, she does not remember that things had once been very different. Resourceful and willing to take risks, Julia arranges their rendezvous, procures coffee and sugar, dares to buy lipstick, and dreams of owning a dress and high-heeled shoes. Julia accepts the idea that social change is impossible, and has learned to enjoy life by circumventing the rules rather than by challenging them: "any kind of organised revolt against the Party, which was bound to be a failure, struck her as stupid. The clever thing was to break the rules and stay alive all the same." She yells with the crowd in public and steals her fleeting joys in private. When Winston remarks "we are the dead," anticipating their certain doom, she does not contradict him, but reminds him "we're not dead yet," urging him to enjoy her beauty and her body while he can.

Julia shares Winston's hatred of the system, but startles him with her contemptuous language. Her open sensuality and vulgarity seem natural and healthy to the long-repressed Winston. In one way Julia is the typical athletic girl prefect, complete with school uniform and sash. When Winston reads aloud from Goldstein's Book, she falls asleep (which suggests Orwell's awareness that many readers would skip this part of the novel). Yet, by stating that the war is a complete myth, she reveals that she's far more acute than Winston and more resistant to Party propaganda. Julia arrives at Winston's political insight by following her hedonistic code.

In their first sexual encounter Winston is hesitant and shy, but when Julia assures him that she's promiscuous and corrupt, and positively enjoys sex for its own sake, he's both sexually and politically aroused. It was "above all what he wanted to hear. Not merely the love of one person, but the animal instinct, the simple undifferentiated desire: that was the force that would tear the Party to pieces." Julia's affairs, like Winston's writing, are defiant political acts, and Winston's love affair encourages his intellectual self-assertion. His desire to write and to love are part of the forbidden desire for individual fulfillment.

Amoral and self-indulgent, hostile to other women, vain and sensual, indoctrinated but uneducated, Julia might seem to be a negative character. But like Winston, she is a symbolic figure. When she brings chocolate to their first meeting, the smell of it stirs a troubling memory in Winston. Later, in bed with Julia, he wakes and remembers that the day he stole the family's chocolate ration was the same day that his mother and sister disappeared. The chocolate connects Julia with his lost mother's love and helps relieve his guilt for his mother's death. Julia represents the power of instinctive feeling and the continuity of love.

The sexual drive which animates Julia, despite her regimented upbringing, links her to the proles, the vast swarming underclass who live to work, drink, gamble and reproduce. Party members regard them as less than human; but Winston believes, since they're uncorrupted and outside the Party, that they're the only hope for the future. In prison he sees that prole criminals show contempt for the guards, while political prisoners, implicated by ideology in their own punishment, are silent and cowed with terror.

Winston's love for Julia enables him to see the proles as fully human. The prole woman singing as she hangs out her washing represents the nurturing maternity that he lost when his mother disappeared. He realizes that people of two generations ago must have been governed by private loyalties. The proles "were not loyal to a party or a country or an idea, they were loyal to one another. . . . They had held on to the primitive emotions which he himself had to re-learn by conscious effort." "The proles are human beings," he tells Julia, "We are not human."9

I V

If the proles are the most ignorant and decent people in the novel, O'Brien is the most knowledgeable and evil—the tormentor, protector, inquisitor and friend who's organized Winston's surveillance for seven years and now supervises his reeducation. He's mastered all the political and social arguments against the Party, but dispenses with truth and morality for the sake of power. In the last section of the novel—inspired partly by the Grand Inquisitor chapters of Dostoyevsky's *The Brothers Karamazov*, and partly by contemporary reports of Stalin's purges—Winston and O'Brien engage in an unequal intellectual duel.

Orwell created Winston's state of mind and the perverse intimacy of torturer and victim by intensifying the memories of "Such, Such Were the Joys." In prep school he suffered cold, hunger and discomfort; recalled the painful separation from his parents, feelings of guilt and rejection, shame about his body, conviction that he was a worthless failure; and was indoctrinated into a rigidly hierarchical society. He feared he was watched by the headmaster's army of spies who reported his illicit visits to the sweetshop. Like the young Eric Blair, Winston has no privacy or close friendships, and is so lonely that a stray glance from O'Brien becomes a significant event. In the essay Orwell remembers with horror his hypocritical desire to suck up to the tyrannical Flip; in the novel Winston hero-worships O'Brien, who's compared to a schoolmaster as he questions a promising pupil and makes him suffer. Even under torture Winston longs for his approval, clings to him like a baby, looks at him gratefully when the pain stops and feels that "in some sense that went deeper than friendship, they were intimates." Like Winston in Oceania,

Orwell in St. Cyprian's experienced "a sense of desolate loneliness and help-lessness . . . in a world of good and evil" where it was impossible to keep the rules. Both places are ruled by a capricious power, rather than by a rational code of law, and in both the central character is torn between his desire to rebel and his desperate longing to be part of a community.

Like Dostoyevsky's Grand Inquisitor, O'Brien believes men are incapable of ruling themselves and unworthy of free choice. Winston argues that all men are potentially good, O'Brien maintains the opposite. He wants to break his victims' spirits, not just kill them. Winston realizes there is no escape and no possibility of heroism. O'Brien boasts he will cure Winston, make him per-fect—or perfectly willing to agree that 2+2=5. He even boasts that the Party has transformed the basic principles of social life, for "no one dares trust a wife or a child or a friend any longer." He looks forward to the future, when the sex-instinct will be eradicated and "there will be no loyalty, except loyalty towards the Party. . . . no love, except the love of Big Brother."[10] There will be no science, literature or art, no pleasure save the sadistic thrill of victory.

Orwell's ghastly experiences in Hairmyres Hospital also influenced the torture scenes. He told David Astor that the worst part of his treatment was when they pushed a rod down his throat to look at his lungs: "It was a hideous-ly painful thing, and very frightening. He spoke of this with a fair amount of horror," and it seems clear that the fictional torture scenes were based on his medical treatment. The artificial collapse of his lung produced an emaciat-ed chest and swollen belly which, Dr. Williamson noted, were "not a pow-erful stimulus to self-esteem." Orwell's description of himself after the terrible effects of streptomycin are close to his portrayal of Winston after his torture in the novel: "The truly frightening thing was the emaciation of his body. The barrel of his ribs was as narrow as that of a skeleton: the legs had shrunk so that the knees were thicker than the thighs. . . . The curvature of the spine was astonishing. The thin shoulders were hunched forward so as to make a cavity of the chest, the scraggy neck seemed to be bending double under the weight of the skull. . . . He was aware of his ugliness, his gracelessness."[11]

It was heartbreaking, when Orwell was writing his most complex novel and wanted to use all his artistic powers to bring it to perfection, to be threat-ened by death and have to race against time to finish it. As he told Warburg in October 1948, just before he retyped the final version of the book: "I think it is a good idea but the execution would have been better if I had not writ-ten it under the influence of TB." If Orwell had had time to revise, he would have eliminated some of the inconsistencies. Though the housing shortage is extreme, Winston, an ordinary Outer Party worker, lives alone—which emphasizes his isolation and allows him to write his subversive diary. On the opening page the electricity has been cut off so he cannot take the elevator, but the telescreen continues to spy on him once he enters the flat. Winston spends his entire working life revising printed matter, but we never see anyone buying or reading books or newspapers.

Orwell said he wanted "to push the world in a certain direction, to alter people's idea of the kind of society that they should strive after." In his essay on Dickens he remarked that "in every page of his work one can see a consciousness that society is wrong somewhere at the root," but there is also an "utter lack of any constructive suggestion."[12] *Nineteen Eighty-Four* also lacks a positive vision, for everyone in the novel finally betrays everyone else: Parsons' child betrays his father; Charrington and then O'Brien betray Winston; Winston betrays Julia.

Several admirers of Orwell have commented on this defect, which derived from the fear of his own future as well as the future of mankind. Steven Runciman said that Orwell had "pity for the human condition; but not much pity for the individual human." The novelist Angus Wilson noted: "There is so little sense of pleasure and so much sense of what was wrong. That is clearly quite alarming in his work." One problem is that the totalitarian state has no ideology: "The Party seeks power entirely for its own sake. . . . Power is not a means, it is an end. . . . The object of power is power."[13] Critics noted the novel's imperfect mixture of styles, and particularly objected to the sadistic cruelty of the last part. Winston's suffering obliterates the novel's satiric wit, emphasizes his cowardice and betrayal, and suggests that the Socialist ideal of brotherhood will always be defeated.

The fundamental problem is that Orwell breaks the conventions of both literary forms that shape the novel, realism and utopian romance, and deliberately disappoints the reader's expectations. At Winston's lowest point we expect some twist that will set him free. Although a faint flicker of Orwellian humor survives in the last chapter, where we learn that Winston has to attend biweekly committee meetings on the eleventh edition of the Newspeak dictionary (a different kind of torture), the end of the novel is totally bleak. Winston, neither rescued nor rewarded, is reduced to infantilism, cowardice and self-pitying alcoholism. His enlightenment about the meaning of his life—that he is merely subject to a monstrous lust for power—coincides with the extinction of all hope. His final defeat symbolizes a victorious but weakened postwar England, dwarfed and threatened by the great powers.

Nineteen Eighty-Four succeeded brilliantly as a political fable, and continues to reverberate in our own time. It reveals Orwell's acute historical sense, his imaginative sympathy with the millions of people persecuted and murdered in the name of absolutist ideologies. The breakdown of the Soviet system and the horrors of totalitarian regimes have proved Orwell right a hundred times over. The portrayal of people trapped in a world where independent thought and the hope of escape are equally impossible links *Nineteen Eighty-Four* to Franz Kafka's grim fables and Alexander Solzhenitsyn's account of the Soviet prison camps.

V

Nineteen Eighty-Four was published during the Cold War on June 8, 1949, and created bitter political controversy. Warburg was the first to read the novel. His perceptive publisher's report noted the sado-masochism and unrelieved pessimism, and said the brief love affair between Winston and Julia merely intensified the later horrors. Julian Symons' review stated that the book was essentially about power and corruption, that Orwell was "a novelist interested in ideas, rather than in personal relationships." Orwell agreed with Symons that the novel was marred by the sensationalism of the torture scenes.

In October 1949 Aldous Huxley (who'd taught Orwell at Eton) wrote him a long, pessimistic letter. He praised the book, suggested that its horrors were destined to modulate into the brainwashing of his own *Brave New World* (1932) and expressed his fears about a devastating atomic war:

> I had to wait a long time before being able to embark on *Nineteen Eighty-Four*. Agreeing with all that the critics have written of it, I need not tell you, yet once more, how fine and how profoundly important the book is. . . .
>
> The philosophy of the ruling minority in *Nineteen Eighty-Four* is a sadism which has been carried to its logical conclusion by going beyond sex and denying it. Whether in actual fact the policy of the boot-on-the-face can go on indefinitely seems doubtful. My own belief is that the ruling oligarchy will find less arduous and wasteful ways of governing and of satisfying its lust for power, and that these ways will resemble those which I described in *Brave New World*. . . . Within the next generation I believe that the world's rulers will discover that infant conditioning and narco-hypnosis are more efficient, as instruments of government, than clubs and pris-

ons, and the lust for power can be just as completely satisfied by suggest-
ing people into loving their servitude as by flogging and kicking them into
obedience. . . . The change will be brought about as a result of a felt need
for increased efficiency. Meanwhile, of course, there may be a large-scale
biological and atomic war—in which case we shall have nightmares of
other and scarcely imaginable kinds.

Many leading critics recognized that the novel's mythic power summed
up the political experience of an entire generation. Influential reviews by
Mark Schorer in the *New York Times Book Review* and Lionel Trilling in the
New Yorker virtually guaranteed the book's success in America. Schorer
called it a "work of pure horror" that expressed Orwell's "moral and intellectual indignation before the concept of totalitarianism. . . . No other work
of this generation has made us desire freedom more earnestly or loathe tyranny with such fulness." Trilling noted Orwell's connection to the culture of
the past and Winston's severance from it, and described the novel as a "profound, terrifying and wholly fascinating book" about "the ultimate threat to
human freedom," in which "the nature of power is defined by the pain it can
inflict on others." Philip Rahv thought *Nineteen Eighty-Four* was "far and
away the best of Orwell's books," and placed it in the "melancholy mid-cen-
tury genre of lost illusions and Utopia betrayed."

Golo Mann, a liberal German, reviewed the book in the *Frankfurter
Rundschau*. Mann emphasized that the novel was not merely an attack on
Communism, and warned against the present danger of totalitarian ideology in Germany as well as Russia. As a historian, Mann particularly noted the
theme of historical truth in the book, and the way dictators strengthen their
position by controlling information and destroying records of the past.

All these reviews praised the power of Orwell's imagination and his ability to interpret complex political events in terms of human experience. More
than any other writer, Orwell had succeeded in revealing the truth to
European and American intellectuals who'd been sympathetic to the Soviet
system. Communist reviewers violently attacked the book. In *Pravda* I.
Anisimov insisted that the novel showed Orwell's "contempt for the people,
his aim of slandering man." Samuel Sillen, writing in the American *Masses
and Mainstream* called his review "Maggot-of-the-Month" and condemned
the novel as "cynical rot . . . a diatribe against the human race." James Walsh,
in the *Marxist Quarterly*, also condemned Orwell's "neurotic . . . and depressing hatred of everything approaching progress." All three claimed that since

Orwell criticized Communism he must be in favor of capitalism, and since he depicted the degradation of man he must despise the common people. These attacks made Orwell feel he must have struck home. When the Communist press called him maggot, octopus, hyena and swine, he wryly told David Astor: "they seem to be very fond of animals."[14]

Both the novelist Lawrence Durrell and the Polish poet Czeslaw Milosz (a future Nobel Prize–winner) praised Orwell's portrayal of Communist oppression. Soon after the novel appeared, Durrell, working for the British Council in Belgrade, wrote to say "how much I admire your new novel. It is intellectually the bravest and cruellest book you've done. Reading it in a Communist country is really an experience because one can see it all around one—the ever-present fact which no left-wingers of my acquaintance will dare to look in the eye." Milosz, in *The Captive Mind*, an important study of the disastrous effects of Communism on artists and intellectuals, observed that because *Nineteen Eighty-Four* "is both difficult to obtain and dangerous to possess, it is known only to certain members of the Inner Party. Orwell fascinates them through his insight into details they know well. . . . Even those who know Orwell only by hearsay are amazed that a writer who never lived in Russia should have so keen a perception into its life."[15]

In March 1949 Orwell refused the Book-of-the-Month Club's offer to publish the novel if he would take out several chapters (including Goldstein's tract and the Appendix on Newspeak) and cut it by about a quarter. He risked losing about $40,000—an enormous amount of money. But in April he told Richard Rees that the "Club have selected my novel after all, in spite of my refusing to make the changes they demanded. So that shows that virtue is its own reward or honesty is the best policy, I forget which."

The first English printing of *Nineteen Eighty-Four* was 26,500; the first American 20,000 plus 540,000 in the first two printings of the book club. The book sold, and continues to sell, phenomenally well. By the year 1984 the British Penguin edition was still selling 750,000 copies a year and the U. S. paperback 1,000 copies a day. Five years later, *Animal Farm* and *Nineteen Eighty-Four* together had sold 40 million copies in more than sixty languages, and Orwell had become the most popular English writer of our time. Orwell never owned a house or a decent car, and it was not until the last years of his life that he earned substantially more than the £1,000 a year he considered to be a comfortable income. After the spectacular success of his last novel, the enemy of capitalism had to hire an accountant and turn himself into a limited company.

The continued popularity of the novel has made it, like the novels of Dickens, part of an enduring English-speaking culture. Orwell described Kipling as "the only English writer of our time who has added phrases to the language."[16] The same is now true of Orwell. In *Nineteen Eighty-Four* alone he invented the vivid phrases, "Big Brother Is Watching You," "two minutes hate," "thought police," "thoughtcrime," "facecrime," "doublethink," "memory hole," "vaporized" and "unperson." These words uncannily expressed the ideas and feelings of people living in totalitarian societies.

Another reason for the novel's great influence was Orwell's amazingly accurate predictions. As former colonies have given way to corrupt oligarchies and dictatorships, and the Communist economies of the last half-century have failed, crumbling infrastructure and acute shortages of essential goods have become a reality for millions of people. Many repressive regimes confine dissidents to mental hospitals and "disappear" people who oppose them. Orwell was also acutely prophetic (in the novel and elsewhere) about many crucial problems of the postwar world: the breakdown of the family, the legions of homeless people, environmental pollution, deforestation, addictive drugs, fanaticism and violence in international sporting events (the new focus of nationalism), the decay of language, proliferation of atomic weapons and the permanent state of war between the superpowers, who provoke a great number of minor conflicts but never actually fight each other. Orwell's novel warned millions of people about the dangers of Communism and helped prevent the realization of the totalitarian world that he described.

16

The Art of Dying,

1949–1950

As ORWELL risked his life to finish *Nineteen Eighty-Four*, he also entertained unrealistic hopes for the future. In October 1948 he hesitantly told Julian Symons: "I could go abroad perhaps, but the journey might be the death of me, so perhaps a sanatorium might be best." Writing to Richard Rees a few months later, he finally admitted that he'd been unwise to stay on Jura: "I must from now on spend my winters within reach of a doctor—where, I don't know yet, but possibly somewhere like Brighton." He even thought that "in more reasonable times we might arrange to live every winter in Sicily." The ominous progression of his wasting disease—he suffered loss of weight, emaciation, high fever, night sweats, shortness of breath, wheezing, chest pains, severe coughing, frequent colds and spitting blood—finally forced him to leave the island in January 1949 (see Appendix IV).

Orwell decided not to return to Hairmyres, where the agonizing pneumothorax treatments had failed to cure him. After consulting Gwen O'Shaughnessy and Bruce Dick, he first chose a sanatorium near Norwich. When his admission was delayed, he entered the Cotswold Sanatorium in Cranham, 900 feet up and about five miles from Gloucester, on January 6. Dr. Dick cautiously told David Astor: "I hope the poor fellow will do well. It is now obvious that he will need to live a most sheltered life in a sanatorium environment. I fear the dream of Jura must fade out."

At Cranham Orwell lived mainly outdoors in a simple wooden cabin, an ineffectual relic of the old-fashioned tubercular treatment of rest, proper diet, sun and fresh air. In his "Last Literary Notebook," Orwell, apparently satisfied with his surroundings, precisely described the setting:

> I live in a so-called chalet, one of a row of continuous wooden huts, with glass doors, each chalet measuring about 15′ by 12′. There are hot water pipes, a washing basin, a chest of drawers & wardrobe, besides the usual bed-tables etc. Outside is a glass-roofed verandah. Everything is brought by hand—none of those abominable rattling trolleys which one is never out of the sound of in a hospital. Not much noise of radios either—all the patients have headphones.[1]

Orwell once told Connolly that he found his disease "interesting," and while at Cranham he had ample time to observe his own inexorable deterioration. In pulmonary tuberculosis, the lungs are damaged by the multiplication of bacilli in infected tissues. As bacteria attack and destroy body tissues, small rounded nodules or tubercules form, which contain bacteria and white blood cells. The bacteria cause lesions in the lung tissue, and the germs enter the sputum. The wasting disease slowly progresses from tuberculous lesions, necrosis and formation of cavities, to erosion of blood vessels and bleeding into the lungs, which, if massive, may cause drowning in one's own blood.

In *The Magic Mountain*, Thomas Mann described this pathological process, and its usually fatal resolution, as "the formation of nodules, the manifestation of soluble toxins and their narcotic effect upon the system; the breaking-down of the tissues, caseation, and the question of whether the disease would be arrested by a chalky petrifaction and heal by means of fibrosis, or [more likely] whether it would extend the area, create still larger cavities, and destroy the organ." Like Albert Camus—who suffered from the same disease and took the same course of treatment with streptomycin and P.A.S. in 1949—Orwell struggled continuously against physical pain and knew his days were numbered. And like Camus, he felt "few people have considered their case with as much horror as I did. . . . The feeling of death is familiar to me."

Though Cranham was difficult to reach, especially when few people had cars, it was much closer to London than Hairmyres, and several friends and acquaintances were able to visit. The economic historian R.H. Tawney, who lived near Cranham and was a friend of Richard Rees, came to see him.

Orwell described Tawney as "one of the few major figures in the Labour movement whom one can both respect and like personally," and gave him a rare presentation copy of *Nineteen Eighty-Four*. Charles Curran, an editor on the *Evening Standard*, reported that Orwell was still smoking his "frightful cigarettes," despite the wretched condition of his lungs, and was still eager to discuss major issues. In *Nineteen Eighty-Four* he was concerned about how to keep human values alive in a totalitarian state in which religion has been replaced by the cult of an omnipotent leader. "The problem of the world is this," he told Curran. "Can we get men to behave decently to each other if they no longer believe in God?"[2]

Other visitors recorded their alarm at the state of the sanatorium and of Orwell himself. His niece Jane Dakin "was rather horrified, really; it seemed rather stuffy and untidy and cluttered, not airy and bracing as one would suppose." To Warburg, "it looked more like a sort of Arctic concentration camp than a place where people would get well from TB." Malcolm Muggeridge, a frequent visitor during Orwell's last year, came with Anthony Powell in mid-February and "found Orwell in very good shape in the morning, and the same old trusty, lovable egotist. He looked very thin, and said that he would probably have to spend every winter henceforth in a sanatorium. . . . [He] was able to produce a bottle of rum from under his bed, which we consumed. I think he is fairly cheerful, but he said that the treatment he has to have is somewhat painful."[3] But Warburg, who arrived two months later, thought his condition was "shocking" and gave him only a 50 percent chance of recovery. Fearful that his author would die, he rushed the novel through the press and Orwell corrected proofs in the sanatorium.

Orwell's letters are not very revealing; and toward the end, when he was extremely ill and weak, they become quite repetitive. But as they record his approaching death in simple terms, they are deeply moving. Jacintha Buddicom, who'd never answered his lonely letters from Burma, belatedly realized that her childhood friend was now a famous author. She wrote to him (but didn't visit the sanatorium) and he replied with a sad history of his chronic illness: "I have been having this dreary disease (T.B.) in an acute way since the autumn of 1947, but of course it has been hanging over me all my life, and actually I think I had my first go of it in early childhood. . . . All I do is read and do crossword puzzles."

He started a second course of streptomycin, but the first dose had such a terrible effect that he had to abandon the only drug that could have saved him. Never one to complain, he said he was well looked after. But the medical examinations were as inadequate as the food and the housing. The doctors seemed less than brilliant and took only a perfunctory interest in his case. After three weeks he hadn't even seen the chief physician; and his assistant, who never even used a stethoscope, looked in every morning to ask how he felt and moved briskly on. Instead of gradually improving, by the end of March he was spitting up quantities of blood. By May, "most horribly ill," he alarmed Warburg by admitting: "I have been too feverish to go over to the X-ray room & stand up against the screen. When the picture is taken, I am afraid there is not much doubt it will show that both lungs have deteriorated badly."

Orwell maintained a keen interest in Richard, one of the strongest reasons for hanging on to life. Avril looked after him on Jura, Bill Dunn ran the farm; and she would become Richard's guardian if Orwell died. He proudly told Jacintha that though Richard, now nearly five, "can't read yet & is rather backward in talking, he's as keen on fishing as I was & loves working on the farm, where's he's really quite helpful. He has an enormous interest in machinery." Richard spent a month near Cranham; and in January 1950 was brought down from Jura for one last visit. But he had to be held at arm's length, couldn't be cuddled and kept asking Orwell: "Where have you hurt yourself?" Lettice Cooper recalled that Orwell, who was infectious, was naturally "terrified to let Richard come near him, and he would hold out his hand and push him away—and George would do it very abruptly because he was abrupt in his manner and movements. And he wouldn't let the child sit on his knee."[4] Too young to understand Orwell's behavior, Richard never knew how much his father loved him.

I I

CELIA PAGET, whom Orwell loved and trusted, made an important visit in about April 1949. They sat outside in the horribly damp little wooden hut and ate ghastly tinned peas, and Orwell seemed awfully ill. Celia was then working for the Information Research Department, which had been established by the Labour government's Foreign Office in 1948. Its purpose was "to devise means to combat Communist propaganda, then engaged in a global and damaging campaign to undermine Western power and influence."

When Celia asked about people who could write for her organization, Orwell suggested Franz Borkenau and Gleb Struve (a Russian scholar, teaching in California). He also offered to give her a list of actors, "journalists and writers who in my opinion are crypto-Communists, fellow-travellers or inclined that way and *should not be trusted as propagandists*" (my emphasis). These people, whose Communist sympathies were well known, would not lose their jobs or be harmed in any way. They would, quite simply, not be asked to write anti-Soviet propaganda for the British government.

Orwell, a great maker of lists in his notebooks, sent Celia thirty-five names, explaining that "it isn't very sensational and I don't suppose it will tell your friends anything they don't know." He felt that listing politically unreliable people would prevent them from "worming their way into important propaganda jobs where they [could] do us a lot of harm." Charlie Chaplin, Michael Redgrave and Orson Welles were mentioned without comments. But several other names were accompanied by satiric remarks: Nancy Cunard—Silly. Has money; Louis Untermeyer—Very silly; Sean O'Casey—Very stupid; Paul Robeson—Very anti-white; John Steinbeck—Spurious writer, pseudo-naif; Bernard Shaw—Reliably pro-Russian on all major issues; Kingsley Martin (his old enemy at the *New Statesman*)—Decayed liberal. Very dishonest.[5]

The recent publication of Orwell's list has provoked accusations that he betrayed his friends and his Socialist principles, and played the role of Big Brother. But when the list is seen in the political context of 1949, his behavior seems necessary, even commendable. It's important to remember that though Orwell hated Communism (and *Nineteen Eighty-Four* was in part an attack on the Russian dictatorship), he strongly supported civil rights and protested against the purge of Communists from the British Civil Service. In a forceful letter of March 1948, he wrote George Woodcock: "Is the Freedom Defence Committee taking up any position about this ban on Communists? . . . The *way* in which the government seems to be going to work is vaguely disquieting, & the whole phenomenon seems to me part of the general breakdown of the democratic outlook."

Orwell was still furious about the Russians' slaughter of 15,000 Poles at Katyn, Starobielsk and other prison camps, about the British government's attempt to cover it up and about his inability to find a British publisher for Joseph Czapski's *Souvenirs de Starobielsk* (1945), which documented these massacres. In the spring of 1949, as the Cold War intensified and opposition hardened on both sides of the Iron Curtain, Berlin was blockaded by the Russians and the West conducted a massive airlift to maintain life in their sectors of the city. In sensational espionage cases of the late 1940s, Dr. Alan Nunn May and Klaus Fuchs had been caught betraying atomic secrets to the

Soviet Union. Russia realized Orwell's great fear by exploding its first atomic bomb in 1949. In April NATO was formed and in May 1949 Chinese Communists drove the Nationalists off the mainland of China and won the long civil war. Oceania, Eurasia and Eastasia were beginning to form.

As Robert Conquest, a leading authority on the Soviet Union, recently wrote: "The charge thus amounts simply to his having made available to an agency of his own government his honest, if not infallible, opinion of the political attitudes of a number of members of the Western intelligentsia to a despotic power hostile to it and its principles."[6] By doing so, the long-standing anti-Communist Orwell did his patriotic duty. The people on his list could not have sold atomic secrets and posed no danger to Western security, but they were certainly not suited to write pro-British propaganda. As he wrote in June 1949, when clarifying the ideas of *Nineteen Eighty-Four*: "I believe that totalitarian ideas have taken root in the minds of intellectuals everywhere, and I have tried to draw these ideas out to their logical consequences. The scene of the book is laid in Britain in order to emphasize that the English speaking races are not innately better than anyone else and that totalitarianism, *if not fought against,* could triumph anywhere."

III

WHILE ORWELL was at Cranham, Sonia Brownell reentered his life. They'd first met through Cyril Connolly in the early 1940s. After rejecting his proposal in 1945, she allowed Orwell, as a consolation prize, to sleep with her. But her friend Janetta Woolley Parladé said that Sonia considered it "a disaster. She felt sorry for him and gave into his 'clumsy' efforts at lovemaking. . . . He had made love to her quickly and without any great show of passion. 'He seemed pleased,' she said, 'but I don't think he was aware that there was not any pleasure in it for me.' " But several friends thought that Sonia, who saw sex as a rebellion against her strict upbringing and as a means of coming into contact with genius, actually disliked sex and rarely got pleasure from it.

The forceful, dominant Sonia was in almost every way the opposite of the gentle, self-effacing Eileen. Born in Ranchi, Bihar, only 230 miles south of Motihari, in August 1918, she shared Orwell's Anglo-Indian origins. Her father, a freight broker with Jardine Matheson, died of a heart attack soon after her birth. In 1921 her mother married a chartered accountant, who became an alcoholic and eventually went bankrupt. The family returned to England in 1928 and Mrs. Brownell ran a boarding house in South Kensington. After 1931 she brought up her three children on her own. Strictly educated between the ages of ten and eighteen at the Convent of the Sacred Heart at Roehampton (south of London), Sonia reacted against her colonial background and unhappy family life, and strongly rejected Catholicism. Whenever she passed a nun in the street she'd spit in disgust.

In 1936 the teenage Sonia, in Switzerland to perfect her French, had a traumatic boating accident on Lake Neuchâtel. Her canoe capsized, her companion began to drown and she tried to rescue him. He seized her and pulled her down; she broke loose and, trying to stop him, held his head underwater for a few seconds. When he failed to surface, she realized he'd lost consciousness, but instead of rescuing him she panicked and swam to safety. Her guilt about the boy's death, compounded with her guilt about leaving the church, blighted her life. The French writer Michel Leiris observed that in Sonia "there could be no mistaking the presence of deep torment."

Sonia was exceptionally beautiful, with soft, rounded features, pink and white complexion, "rich golden hair, brilliant eyes, a fine oval face, and voluptuous physique"—which earned her the nickname the "Euston Road Venus" and the less complimentary "Buttocks Brownell." The art critic Adrian Stokes introduced her to the circle of painters who lived near Euston Road. She posed in the nude, and lived first with the painter Victor Pasmore, then (from 1939 to 1941) with William Coldstream, who was separated from his wife. In the summer of 1939 Coldstream painted a blurry, unflattering portrait of twenty-one-year-old Sonia, with round-necked sweater, full lips and an oversized hand on her cheek.[7]

After taking a secretarial course, Sonia worked for a few months in 1941 as John Lehmann's assistant on the magazine New Writing. Lehmann praised her energy, her "darting, gaily cynical intelligence and insatiable appetite for knowing everything that went on in the literary world: her revolt against a convent upbringing seemed to provide her life in those days with a kind of inexhaustible rocket fuel."

She spent the war as a clerk in the shipping section of the Ministry of Transport. Through Coldstream she met Connolly and Spender, co-editors of Horizon, and in 1945 became their editorial secretary. Like Lehmann, Spender believed that Sonia passionately wanted to become part of—even play a leading role in—the cultural and intellectual life of London and Paris: "She had a look of someone always struggling to go beyond herself, to escape from her social background, the convent where she was educated, into some pagan paradise of artists and 'geniuses' who would save her" — or be saved by her. Since Connolly was lazy and frequently absent, Sonia ran the Horizon office and dealt efficiently with contributors, printers and government officials who controlled paper rationing. Connolly lusted after Sonia, who rejected his advances. He disliked her domineering personality and, after she'd rejected him, accused her of lesbian tendencies and an obscure desire to take revenge on men. "I always regard Sonia as my unconscious enemy," he wrote, "unconscious because unaware of the strength of her Lesbian drives. . . . She has done me more harm than good, she is the enemy of the male principle, one has to be broken down to win her pity."[8] The last phrase seems to allude to Orwell.

A number of Sonia's close friends agreed with Connolly about her tormented attitude to sex. Diana Witherby said that "she flirted and went out with men, but underneath it all I think she did have a feeling against them, which was deep-seated." The novelist David Plante suggested that Sonia could never resolve her sexual problems: "If sex is not, or never really was, important to her privately — or if she is and always was frightened of it — she suffers the importance she imagines the world gives it, the world of either sexual fulfilment or else neurosis. She could not bear anyone thinking she is sexually neurotic." The poet Waldemar Hansen put it more bluntly by saying: "She was not promiscuous, she did not go to bed for sex — she was a 'starfucker.' "[9] For Sonia, then, flirtation and sex (if absolutely necessary), were a way, perhaps the most effective way, for a quite ordinary, undistinguished woman to play an important role in artistic life.

Sonia's character was an unusual blend of the attractive and the unpleasant. She was hardworking, warmhearted, amusing and generous — "a good sort" and very keen to promote her current favorites. She pretentiously used French expressions when English ones would do, and maddened people by arguing forcefully (even with physicists) about subjects she knew nothing about. She was also domineering, short-tempered and an appalling literary snob. Ian Angus, who edited Orwell's works with Sonia, called her "guilt-ridden and deeply anxious, which drove her at times to be reckless and self-destructive. I think all her friends at one time or another suffered from her bad behaviour."[10]

Several writers have described Sonia's appearance, mannerisms and character. The American critic Lionel Abel, who met her in Paris with her lover Maurice Merleau-Ponty, wrote that "when she wanted to make sure that those around would listen carefully to what she had to say, [she] would dramatically fling her waves of heavy blonde hair back over her shoulders and announce: 'The thing is that. . . .' The procedure was always effective." In *Anglo-Saxon Attitudes* (1956), Angus Wilson portrayed Sonia as Elvira Portway, who makes pretentious pronouncements and has a "tense mouth and strained look about her rather hysterical blue eyes." Discussing British moralizing, she exclaims: " 'It's just an English parlour-game,' twisting her hair with her fingers, 'and what's so *ghastly* is that it's got into our literature. It's all there in Morgan Forster and those people.' Gerald [Middleton] noticed that the more vague the content of her words became the more emphasis she laid on them."

In 1947 Sonia had her most intense affair with Merleau-Ponty (1908–61), "the only man she was really in love with." Thin, dark and good-looking, supremely sophisticated and married to a surgeon, Merleau-Ponty, a friend of Sartre, was a Communist fellow-traveler, prominent existentialist philosopher and professor at the Sorbonne. When they met again in 1949, he refused to leave his wife and broke off the affair. Desperately unhappy, she turned to Orwell on the rebound.

In *Animal Farm* Orwell affectionately satirized Sonia's vanity, flirtatiousness, narcissism and self-serving materialism: "Mollie, the foolish, pretty white mare who drew Mr. Jones's trap, came mincing daintily in, chewing at a lump of sugar. She took a place near the front and began flirting her white mane, hoping to draw attention to the red ribbons it was plaited with. . . . On every kind of pretext she would run away from work and go to the drinking pool, where she would stand foolishly gazing at her own reflection in the water." As winter approaches, Mollie defects to the human beings, who spoil her with lumps of sugar and scarlet ribbons.[11]

Orwell also portrayed Sonia as Julia in *Nineteen Eighty-Four*. His description of Julia's deceptively hearty demeanor—"the atmosphere of hockey-fields and cold baths and community hikes and the general clean-mindedness which she managed to carry about with her"—is a witty allusion to Sonia's lifelong rebellion against her convent school. Winston's first reaction to Julia—"He hated her because she was young and pretty and sexless, because he wanted to go to bed with her and would never do so"—expresses Orwell's frustration with Sonia, who slept with him only once.

Sonia's dislike of sexual intercourse explains the contrast in *Nineteen Eighty-Four* between Julia's leading role in the Junior Anti-Sex League (which represents Sonia's real sexual attitude) and her reckless nymphomania (which alludes to Sonia's numerous lovers and portrays Orwell's fantasies about her): "With what seemed a single movement she tore off her clothes and flung them disdainfully aside. . . . 'Have you done this before?' 'Of course. Hundreds of times—well, scores of times, anyway.' "

Orwell's comment that Julia "obviously had a practical cunning which Winston lacked" suggests that he was sceptical about Sonia's motives for marrying him. Winston's confession at their first meeting suggests that Orwell had proposed to her in his usual Kafkaesque manner: "I'm thirty-nine years old. . . . I've got varicose veins. I've got five false teeth. . . . You are ten or fifteen years younger than I am. What could you see to attract you in a man like me?" But "at the sight of the words *I love you*," as she passes him a secret note, "the desire to stay alive had welled up in him," which foreshadows Orwell's statement: "I really think I should stay alive longer if I were married." But as Winston prophetically observes: "It was impossible that this affair should end successfully; such things did not happen in real life."[12]

I V

BY SEPTEMBER 1949 it became all too clear that Cranham's facilities and treatment were inadequate and that Orwell's health was deteriorating at an alarming rate. Warburg therefore arranged for Orwell to be cared for by the amiable and charming Dr. Andrew Morland, a specialist in tuberculosis and Head of the Department of Chest Diseases at University College Hospital on Gower Street in Bloomsbury. Like Laurence O'Shaughnessy, Morland was the author of a standard textbook, *Pulmonary Tuberculosis in General Practice* (1933). Warburg called him "a doctor of the highest reputation, with a long experience of tubercular cases, who had himself suffered from it in his younger days. In addition, he had been in charge of D.H. Lawrence during the last years of his life." Dr. Morland is known today for losing both his illustrious patients.

On September 3 (three months after the publication of *Nineteen Eighty-Four*) Orwell was transferred by ambulance to University College Hospital, which gave him much better treatment and was infinitely more comfortable and convenient for visitors living in London. As at Cranham, he gave a precise catalogue of Room 65: "Room has: washbasin, cupboard, bedside locker, bed table, chest of drawers, wardrobe, 2 mirrors [which he could well do without], wireless (knobs beside bed), electric fire, radiator, armchair & 1 other chair, bedside lamp & 2 other lamps, telephone. Fees 15 guineas a week, plus extra fee for doctor, but apparently including special medicines."

By the time he reached the London hospital Orwell was clearly dying. The vitamins, fresh air and high altitudes, the injections, pneumothorax, surgical procedures and (in his case) doses of streptomycin had all been quite worthless. At this point, only sleeping pills could help him. Dr. Howard Nicholson, who assisted Dr. Morland, explained: "There was no medical treatment, really, just resting and being well looked after. He had quite extensive bilateral pulmonary tuberculosis. He was really very ill indeed. I have no doubt he suffered greatly—not pain, I don't think he had any pain, but general misery and awareness of what was happening. I'm sure it was terrible."[13]

His left lung was by now almost useless. He dreamed of death and suffered from terrifying nightmares. Friends were shocked by his morbid appearance. Fyvel said "he lay flat on his back in bed, looking terribly emaciated, his face drawn and waxen pale." With the same expression he'd used to describe the disaster at Corryvreckan, he told Fyvel's wife, after having another hemorrhage: "last night I thought I was a goner." Muggeridge's *Diaries* provide the most detailed account of his inexorable decline and hopeless despair:

> Found him, unfortunately, more poorly. He has started losing weight again, and looked altogether pretty wretched. . . . He mentioned for the first time that he found it sometimes difficult to endure his invalid life. (November 14, 1949)

> He looks quite shrunken now and somehow waxen. Said ruefully that he was having penicillin injections and they found difficulty in finding any meat into which to stick the needle." (December 20–21, 1949)

> [I found him] very deathly and wretched, alone, with Christmas decorations all round. His face looks almost dead, and reminded me, I said afterwards to Tony [Powell], of a picture I once saw of Nietzsche on his death-bed. There was also a kind of rage in his expression, as though the approach of death made him furious. . . . Poor George—he went on about the Home Guard and the Spanish Civil War, and how he would go to Switzerland soon, and all the while the stench of death was in the air. (December 25, 1949)

Seems more deathly than ever, very miserable, says he's losing 1/2-lb a week in weight and has a high temperature every day. (January 12, 1950)

Orwell had often been given up for lost, but "always lived on just to spite them." This time, however, Anthony Powell thought "it was fairly clear that he was not going to recover. Only the length of time that remained to him was in doubt."[14]

Other friends, who saw him on a good day (or good hour), were cautiously optimistic. Spender's wife, Natasha, observed him sitting up in bed and acting as if nothing were wrong. Muggeridge noted that he could still become indignant about things that troubled him: "in the hospital a day or so before he died, Orwell grew loudly vituperative about an advertisement which showed a sock suspender on the leg of a classical hero. . . . Physical beauty was a sacred thing and should be shielded from the vile devices of advertisers." Celia Paget explained how his friends tried to be optimistic though they could see quite well that he was dying: "Not knowing anything about medicine or diagnosis I think we all hoped that George might just recover somehow, but it didn't seem at all likely. He was going to be taken to Switzerland about five days after, in fact, he died, so perhaps they thought there was some hope of improvement. But I think he doubted it himself. Once when I went to visit him in hospital shortly before that he said that he had reached the lowest weight that it was possible to reach and still go on living."[15]

V

IN *Tuberculosis and Genius* Dr. Lewis Moorman observed that "it is often astonishing to behold the sinking man make plans for the future, engage in new enterprises . . . or, as I have seen, arranging for his marriage a few days before his death." Orwell fits into this textbook case. In July 1949, jilted by Merleau-Ponty, Sonia accepted his proposal, and in September their engagement was announced in the English newspapers and in *Time* magazine. As Orwell told Astor and Warburg, with morbid irony: "I intend getting married again (to Sonia) when I am once again in the land of the living, if I ever am. . . . I suppose everyone will be horrified, but it seems to me a good idea." The rationale came from Sonia, the doubts from Orwell, as he explained with unusual awkwardness in a letter to Astor: "She thinks we might as well get married while I am still an invalid, because it would give her a better status to look after me especially if, e.g., I went somewhere abroad after leaving [the hospital]. It's an idea, but I think I should have to feel a little less ghastly than at present before I could even face a registrar for 10 minutes."[16]

He admired Sonia's beauty, frankness, vigor and apparent toughness, adored seeing her and was very much in love with her. Lys Lubbock, who worked with Sonia on *Horizon*, thought "it was this radiance of health that so attracted Orwell, who perhaps saw her as a kind of life force to compensate for his own poor health"—in the same way that D.H. Lawrence was drawn to his vital wife Frieda. Grasping at straws, Orwell told Humphrey Dakin: "I've got someone who will love me now"—though love had very little to do with it.

The marriage would certainly give Sonia "better status" in more ways than one, for *Animal Farm* and *Nineteen Eighty-Four* had made Orwell one of the most famous writers in the world. But as he predicted, many friends *were* horrified. Dr. Nicholson thought it was all rather sad: "The poor old chap must have been pretty well aware of death and knew he had no future with Sonia." And David Astor remarked: "Orwell was totally unfit to marry anyone. He was scarcely alive."[17]

Everyone agrees about Sonia's striking beauty, but her friends and enemies disagree about her motives for marrying Orwell. She'd refused his invitation to visit Jura in 1947, and visited him at Cranham in the spring of 1949. She'd had affairs with a number of distinguished artists and writers (fame was essential for bedding her), but had failed to form a permanent connection with any of them. *Horizon* was about to close down. She was over thirty, had no money of her own and didn't want to go back to being a typist. So she looked carefully at her limited possibilities and focused on Orwell.

Sonia's close women-friends believed she married Orwell for altruistic reasons. Natasha Spender called her a rescuer, a carer, a worshiper of writers; an acolyte who loved the life of the mind and wanted to be a handmaiden to genius. Sonia hoped he would recover and that they'd have a life together. Janetta Parladé—who found Orwell dry, impassive, withdrawn and difficult to get on with—agreed that Sonia loved him as writer, wanted to help him and be with him. Thoughtful and considerate, Sonia *could* have nursed him if he'd recovered. Countering the charge that Sonia married Orwell for money and future royalties, Janetta insisted that Sonia was not greedy, didn't want lots of money and never lived like a rich woman. Anne Dunn, daughter of a Canadian lumber tycoon and widow of the painter Rodrigo Moynihan, offered the most positive interpretation. She thought that "Sonia married Orwell as a cause. She was tremendously idealistic and felt that she would be able to nurse him, take care of his adopted child and be the guardian of his work."[18]

Others were far more sceptical. Diana Witherby, another close friend, admitted: "it was never a case of actually being in love with him. That's the part that surprised me. I knew she wanted a real romance in her life, and I didn't think she would accept a loveless marriage." Waldemar Hansen agreed with Diana that it was not easy for Sonia to say yes to a dying man. But marrying Orwell and becoming his literary executor flattered her vanity. She could take up the offer Orwell had once made to Anne Popham to be the widow of a literary man, get his royalties and edit his unpublished works. All this, thought Robert Kee (then married to Janetta Woolley), satisfied the needs of a pretentious, ambitious woman who wanted, more than anything, to have prestige and power in the literary world.[19]

Orwell's desperate condition also eliminated the difficult problem of sex. David Astor thought there was "total unreality on both sides" about having a life together. Sonia, who would have two unconsummated marriages, was not a sexually active woman: "She admired writers, but I think she didn't contract marital relations with people easily, and I think when this man who was obviously very feeble asked her to marry, it may have suited her to marry somebody rather 'non-operational.' " Frances Partridge, a sharp-eyed survivor of the Bloomsbury Group, agreed with Astor's explanation: "Many people regard the Orwell marriage cynically and remind one that Sonia always declared her intention of marrying a Great Man. I see it principally as a neurotic one, for a marriage to a bed-ridden and perhaps dying man is as near as no marriage at all as it's possible to get."

Some people believed that Sonia, far from being idealistic and altruistic, was driven by selfish ambition. Anne Popham, who did not think she was a kind woman, was appalled by her marriage to Orwell. The novelist Francis King, an acute observer, saw Sonia's behavior in the context of her unacknowledged sexual feelings:

> He could hardly have chosen anyone worse than Sonia Orwell, who was uninterested in the boy [Richard] and totally without any maternal feelings at all. I always thought that she was basically lesbian but could not accept this. So many of her close friends, like David Plante, Joe Ackerley

and Peter Watson were gay, because she felt unthreatened by them. I don't believe for one moment that she was in love with Orwell; and the fact that he was so ill meant that a sexual relationship would be of short duration— if it took place at all. . . . My opinion of her is extremely low.[20]

Why, then, did Sonia agree to marry Orwell in 1949 after rejecting him in 1945? Was she a devoted Florence Nightingale or a mercenary Kate Croy? Sonia herself was perplexed about her motives and told Ian Angus: "The reasons why George married me are perfectly clear. What aren't clear are the reasons why I married George." Part of the answer must be that in 1949 he was a rich and famous author who made no sexual demands and would soon be dead.

Sonia, an intensely self-centered woman, naturally had trouble dealing with Orwell's grave illness. Though he was only forty-six, she told Celia: "It's rather sad to marry an old, sick man." Waldemar Hansen, visiting Orwell in the fall of 1949, saw Sonia cracking under the emotional strain and lurching around the hospital room like a frenzied Blanche DuBois. Stephen Spender recorded that she could not even come to terms with the unconsummated marriage, felt guilty about pretending to love Orwell and could be extremely callous when his wishes clashed with her own:

> I think that her own sense of her virginity has in some way been outraged, despite the fact that George was in hospital. Also she found herself incapable of really loving him, even for the short period of a few weeks before he died. . . .
> She came in about six, and found George talking to me about the death of D.H. Lawrence. . . . "Let's talk about something cheerful," said Sonia, suddenly like a bossy hospital nurse. Then she explained that she had to go to a cocktail party, and would not be back that evening. Orwell protested faintly, but she put him off, in her bustling way.

To the art critic James Lord, Sonia "admitted that it had often been a trial for her to keep [Orwell] company, so she had sometimes neglected to stay by him when she knew he wished her to, and now felt remorseful for her failure."[21] This sense of guilt later made it difficult for her to play the role of devoted widow.

Sonia has been criticized for using Orwell's money to buy an expensive engagement ring, but she never cared about jewelry. Orwell, who couldn't afford a ring for Eileen "except perhaps a Woolworth one," wanted her to have it. He was delighted to express his love, make Sonia happy and spend money on something beside hospital bills.

The civil and medical authorities, fearful of fortune-hunters fixing on their prey, required a special license for deathbed marriages. Though David Astor strongly disapproved, he helped (as always) to overcome the difficulties and arranged for the ceremony to take place in Orwell's hospital room on October 13. After consultation with Powell and Muggeridge, Orwell—sitting up in bed—wore a mauve velvet smoking jacket over his pajamas. The chaplain, Dr. Morland, Robert and Janetta Kee, and David Astor stood around the bride and groom—a blooming Renoir beauty and a gaunt El Greco saint.

Though Orwell did not seem particularly fragile or "desperate about dying," Kee was amazed by the "wildly inappropriate" marriage. Astor, who realized that his friend *was* in a desperate state, also felt it was an intensely "embarrassing occasion. We were in this tiny room, like a small cubicle, with a very sick man. . . . Orwell looked like Gandhi. He was skin and bone." After the wedding (if it can be called that) Astor gave a luncheon at the Ritz for Sonia Blair, Celia and Mamaine, the Kees, James McGibbon (Kee's publishing partner) and Roger Senhouse (of Secker & Warburg). Mamaine's husband, Arthur Koestler, was delighted when Orwell married Sonia, "wickedly praising him for rescuing her from the Connolly 'crowd.' "[22]

Orwell left his entire estate and all future royalties to Sonia, and nothing at all to Richard and Avril. He requested that Sonia make Richard her residuary legatee and had bought insurance policies to pay for Richard's education. Gwen O'Shaughnessy was the executrix and trustee of the will; Sonia and Avril the guardians of Richard; Sonia and Rees the literary executors. Orwell's assets at the time of his marriage amounted to £11,970, and his estate was probated at £9,908. Sonia later told Crick that "she had torn up three or four thousand pounds of IOUs from 'poor writers' on Orwell's death." But she greatly exaggerated her own generosity. Orwell's loans to friends amounted to £670, including £250 to Georges Kopp, £120 Paul Potts, £75 to Inez Holden, £50 to Aunt Nellie Limouzin, £50 to Jack Common, £25 to Humphrey Slater—and £100 to Sonia herself. If Sonia had to borrow from Orwell, then money was certainly an important factor in the marriage. Avril (more like Benjamin the donkey than Mollie the mare) had good reason to resent Sonia. But she told Crick that "she thought Sonia was a 'fame-hunter,' not a gold-digger. The big money came only after his death."[23] Nevertheless, everyone knew that the value of Orwell's estate would greatly increase and that very large sums of money would soon come pouring in from *Animal Farm* and *Nineteen Eighty-Four*.

VI

THOUGH ORWELL was extremely ill, he still planned a major essay on Joseph Conrad and actually began to write one on Evelyn Waugh. Fyvel wrote that Orwell admired Conrad for showing that "men were always solitary and that political life offered no moral guidance." Orwell's scattered references to Conrad give some idea of the theme of his projected essay. When reviewing a book on Stendhal he remarked, "nine times out of ten a revolutionary is merely a climber with a bomb in his pocket," a dead-on description of *Under Western Eyes*. Writing about the short stories in 1945, he made a sympathetic appraisal of Conrad's political beliefs. His European background, Orwell said, gave him "a considerable understanding of conspiratorial politics. He had an often-expressed horror of anarchists and nihilists, but he also had a species of sympathy with them, because he was a Pole—a reactionary in home politics, perhaps, but a rebel against Russia and Germany. . . . Politically he was a reactionary, and never pretended to be anything else, but he was also a member of an oppressed race, and he understood just why people throw bombs, even if he disapproved of such activities." Four years later, when the editor of a Polish émigré magazine asked his opinion of the author, Orwell replied: "I regard Conrad as one of the best writers of this century. . . . He did have a sort of grown-upness and political understanding which would have been almost impossible [for] a native English writer at that time."[24]

Waugh was the same age as Orwell and came from a similar middle-class professional background. But Waugh delighted in snobbish society and fully indulged in all the luxuries that Orwell despised: a grand country house, a London club, hedonistic cruises, elegant clothes, fine wines and expensive cigars. Prompted by Powell and Muggeridge, Waugh visited Orwell at Cranham, but left no record of this extraordinary meeting.

As with Conrad, Orwell wanted to place Waugh politically and intended to use him "as an example of the fallacy of the Marxist view that art can only be good if it is progressive." He also discussed this essay with Fyvel, who recorded his belief that "Waugh was the best English writer of his generation. . . . [But he] had moved step by step from satirizing his landed aristocracy towards identifying himself with them, as he finally did with such fatal results in *Brideshead Revisited*: here he had truly exposed his soft centre." Contrasting Waugh in his unfinished essay with the Left-wing writers of the 1930s, Orwell wrote that "In our own day, the English novelist who has most conspicuously defied his contemporaries is Evelyn Waugh. . . . His main offence in the eyes of his fellow writers has always been the reactionary political tendency which was already clearly apparent even in such light-hearted books as *Decline and Fall* and *Vile Bodies*. . . . Waugh is the latest, perhaps the last, of a long line of English writers whose real driving force is a romantic belief in aristocracy."[25]

In September 1949, the editors of the *Partisan Review* in New York gave Orwell their literary award of $1,000. He had never been honored by the British government, or any other organization, and this was the only prize he ever received.

VII

DR. MORLAND, in an innovative article "The Mind in Tubercule," emphasized the importance of the psychology of the patient and argued that it was essential "to study as fully as possible the mental states observed in persons with tuberculous disease." Always "a very optimistic chap," he believed that Orwell's marriage would bring psychological benefits. Morland was also rather keen on sending Orwell to a sanatorium in Montana-Vermala, Switzerland. In a letter to Muggeridge of January 1950 Koestler agreed that it might provide slight hope for what seemed to be a hopeless case: "I wonder what could be done about George. I know that all available specialists have already been consulted and that you and his other friends have explored all possibilities. Yet I still wonder whether the risk of getting him to Switzerland in an air ambulance should not be reconsidered. When Mamaine was ill last year I made enquiries about air-taxi ambulances and found that the service is reasonably cheap and very efficient."

Montana-Vermala, situated on a small plateau at an altitude of 5,000 feet and surrounded by lofty mountains, was a center of Swiss sanatoria. Katherine Mansfield had taken refuge there in 1921. The dying poet James Elroy Flecker, who had stayed there in the summer of 1913, found the Alpine landscape intensely depressing and wrote: "this seems to be quite the place to come to—for health, but the desolation—the black fir trees again and the horrid snowy mountains are appalling." Dr. Nicholson felt that Switzerland, with its beautiful scenery and clean air, was a much more pleasant place than London. But he didn't believe it would make the slightest difference in Orwell's case: "I think it was mainly a method of letting the patients die comfortably, in a place where they were really used to dealing with that sort of thing."[26]

The plan was for Sonia and the painter Lucian Freud (her former lover) to accompany Orwell. But the now skeletal patient was more realistic than Dr. Morland. In *Homage to Catalonia* he'd announced: "I hate mountains, even from a spectacular point of view." And he began to resist the plan to move him as early as May 1949 when, bitterly disillusioned by the failure of his medical treatments, he told Warburg: "I do hope people won't now start chasing me to go to Switzerland, which is supposed to have magical qualities. I don't believe it makes any difference where you are, & a journey would be the death of me." When Celia asked if the doctors thought he'd get better in the mountains, he caustically replied: "Either that or they don't want to have a corpse on their hands." Despite his doubts, Sonia arranged a special charter flight to Switzerland on January 25. Orwell, bucked up by Morland, laid out his new fishing rod at the bottom of his bed—all ready to pull trout from the mountain streams. But in his heart he knew, as George Bowling did in *Coming Up for Air*, that "men of forty-five can't go fishing. That kind of thing doesn't happen any longer, it's just a dream, there'll be no more fishing this side of the grave."[27]

In "How the Poor Die" Orwell said that everyone wanted to die in his own bed and with loved ones at his side, but he died in a hospital bed, alone. He did not believe in the afterlife, but was not afraid of death: he was "afraid of pain, & of the moment of dying, but not extinction." Shortly after midnight on January 21, 1950, a blood vessel in his lung ruptured and he had a massive hemorrhage. This time the bleeding did go on forever. The door to his room had glass panels and a night-light was on, but he wasn't able to ring for a nurse and no one heard his strangled cry for help. When someone came to check on him, he was already dead.[28]

The hospital could not contact Sonia, who was drinking in a nightclub with Lucian Freud and Anne Dunn. Anne has recently explained the circumstances:

Sonia lived in Percy Street [quite near the hospital] at that time. Just opposite her house was a sort of quiet nightclub where it was possible, with the strict English licencing laws, to have a drink after hours. I was there with my friend, Lucian Freud, who was due to fly to Switzerland to help Sonia transport Orwell a couple of days later. We decided to ring Sonia to see if she would like to come over and wind down with a drink. She had been at the hospital until nine that evening, when she was advised to go home and get some relaxation. There had been no sign of an imminent crisis in Orwell's health, poor as it was. In fact, the mood was upbeat—that the Swiss treatment might work a miracle. Lucian and Sonia's conversation was about travel plans. She then telephoned the hospital just to check on his evening's progress and discovered that he had hemorrhaged and had died. It came, as you can imagine, as a terrible shock.

Though Anne Dunn was present at the time, she seems to have loyally distorted the facts to put Sonia in a more favorable light. The hospital did not allow Sonia to spend all day with Orwell (it would have been far too exhausting for both of them) or to remain until 9 P.M. Shortly before his death, Orwell told Richard Rees that "Sonia comes & sees me for an hour every day & otherwise I am allowed one visitor for 20 minutes." Anthony and Violet Powell have stated that she was not there at all that day: "Sonia had a heavy cold, and from fear of infection, was unable to visit Orwell at the hospital in the few days before his death."[29] Moreover, if there was "no sign of an imminent crisis," if Orwell seemed well enough to fly to Switzerland in a few days and if the hemorrhage was completely unexpected, there was no reason for Sonia to phone the hospital in the middle of the night. Her guilt about being in a nightclub rather than with Orwell would later make her bitterly unhappy.

Though not religious, Orwell liked traditional customs. He once told Paul Potts, "quite seriously, that he liked the Church of England better than our Lord." By his own wish his funeral service (like his first wedding ceremony) took place in church Thinking of Orwell's sad last year in hospitals, his futile marriage and his early death as well as the loss of his great talent, Powell said that the funeral service at Christ Church in Albany Street, near Regent's Park, "was one of the most harrowing I have ever attended." Muggeridge, noting that Orwell's coffin was unusually long, described the funeral as "a rather melancholy, chilly affair, the congregation largely Jewish and almost entirely unbelievers; Mr. Rose, who conducted the service, excessively parsonical, the church unheated. In the front row, the Fred Warburgs. Then a row of shabby looking relatives of George's first wife, whose grief seemed to me practically the only real element in the whole affair. The bearers who carried in the coffin seemed to me remarkably like Molotov's bodyguard."[30] Powell read the lesson from the last chapter of Ecclesiastes: "man goeth to his long home, and the mourners go about the streets: Or ever the silver cord be loosed, or the golden bowl be broken. . . . Then shall the dust return to the earth as it was: and the spirit shall return unto God who gave it."

Since Orwell was not a parishioner, his wish to be buried in a country churchyard was difficult to arrange. David Astor, who owned a house in Sutton Courtenay, between the Thames and the Berkshire Downs, once again solved the problem. He persuaded the Reverend Gordon Dunstan that Orwell, a distinguished author, would be a credit to All Saints. Only Sonia and Astor were present when Orwell was buried, in the same churchyard as the former prime minister Herbert Asquith. His simple gravestone reads: "Here Lies Eric Arthur Blair. Born June 25th 1903. Died January 21st 1950." It's ironic that the burial-place of someone who feared and predicted an atomic war is now "dwarfed by the nearby cooling towers of the Didcot power station and that immediately adjacent to the churchyard is a testing laboratory for the Atomic Energy Commission."

The Orwell legend of the saintly moralist who'd sought out suffering, which he'd helped to create in his lifetime, was strengthened by two moving tributes from old friends. Koestler wrote that "his ruthlessness towards himself was the key to his personality; it determined his attitude towards the enemy within, the disease which had raged in his chest since his adolescence." Koestler called him "the most honest writer alive . . . a kind of missing link between Kafka and Swift . . . the only writer of genius among the *littérateurs* of social revolt between the two wars." V.S. Pritchett described Orwell as "a tall emaciated man with a face scored by the marks of physical suffering" and called him "the wintry conscience of a generation . . . a kind of saint."[31]

Though Orwell wanted very few material things, he didn't get any of them—even when he became wealthy at the end of his life. He wanted a handsome pram for Richard (not available in wartime), a good pair of American boots (they were sent but didn't fit), a truck for the rough roads of Jura (his wreck could not even be driven), streptomycin to cure tuberculosis (which had terrible side effects) and a second wife (who married him on his deathbed). Mabel Fierz, who knew him well, remarked that "he never found anything that was comforting, that brought him any peace and happiness. He was always on the edge, always worrying, reaching out for a solution." His old friend Cyril Connolly summed up the tragedy of his life by observing that "when at last he achieved fame and success he was a dying man and knew it. He had fame and was too ill to leave his room, money and nothing to spend it on, love in which he could not participate; he tasted the bitterness of dying."[32]

Orwell's life, in essence, was a series of irrational, sometimes life-threatening decisions. He joined the Burmese Police instead of going to university; washed dishes in Paris and tramped in England instead of pursuing a career; grew vegetables and ran a small shop in Wallington instead of encouraging Eileen to complete her degree. He fought with the hopeless Anarchists in Spain, just after his marriage, and put Eileen in danger by encouraging her to come to Barcelona during the war. He moved to London during the Blitz, when everyone else was trying to leave; and took up a suicidal residence on Jura when he was seriously ill. All these risky moves were prompted by the inner need to sabotage his chance for a happy life. But the life he chose supplied the somber material of his art.

17

Epilogue:
Orwell's Legacy

I

SONIA (as Koestler had suggested to Celia) might have bought Orwell a dinner jacket and smartened him up. But she was not interested in the kind of
life he wished to live. It's difficult to imagine her tilling the soil in rubber
boots, and she could never have put up with the remoteness and hardship of
Jura. She had no maternal instinct and was not the right woman to take care
of Richard, whom she associated with "the smell of cabbage and unwashed
nappies" in Canonbury Square.

If Orwell had lived, Richard would have gone to Westminster School in
London, but things turned out quite differently. The ailing Eileen had had
doubts about Orwell's rather cold and severe sister. She told Henry Dakin
that if she died, almost anyone could be a mother for Richard "as long as it's
not Avril." Nevertheless, the boy was brought up in Scotland (but not on Jura)
by Avril and Bill Dunn, who married, a year after Orwell died, in February
1951. Always good with machinery, Richard went to an agricultural college,
became a farmer and later sold Massey-Ferguson farm equipment. Despite
the traumas of his early life, he grew up to be a well-adjusted and happily
married man with two sons, and came into his inheritance after Sonia's death.
Avril died at the age of seventy in 1978, and her niece, Jane Dakin, much
closer to Bill Dunn's age, lived with him until his death.

Sonia took no interest in Richard, who was not an intellectual type. She gave Avril a small allowance for him of £3 a week, which caused considerable resentment in the family. As Gwen O'Shaughnessy's daughter wrote: "My mother had been appointed guardian to Rick and felt that part of the Orwell estate should go towards Rick's education and upkeep. . . . The family felt Sonia had seen a good thing and gone for it. . . . Avril told me of her reluctance to pay Rick's way and her indifference towards him."[1]

After Orwell's death Sonia tried once again to revive her affair with Merleau-Ponty, and had a number of other lovers. The publisher George Weidenfeld, for whom she worked as an editor from 1954 to 1956, described the many contradictions in her character:

Sonia was a pretty, blowsy, reddish blonde, full of *joie de vivre* and generous to a fault. She was impulsive and quick to take sides. Her literary aspirations and her penchant for high Bohemia went hand in hand with a jolly-hockeystickish streak, a relic of the colonial upbringing she tried to reject. She was very secretive about her private life. During her time with us she had a romance with John Phillips, a famous *Life* photographer. . . . Years later, during an intimate conversation about our past, Sonia burst out with the revelation that she had also had a whirlwind romance with [the Israeli general] Yigal Allon.

In 1958 the neurotic forty-year-old Sonia once again astonished her friends by marrying Michael Pitt-Rivers, a lifelong homosexual and millionaire, who'd recently served a prison sentence for his role in a notorious sexual scandal. Sonia believed that she'd be able to change his sexual tastes and rehabilitate his reputation. But he shut her out of the bedroom on their wedding night, and then took off on holiday with his boyfriend. The marriage ended a few months later and Sonia was deeply hurt.[2]

Connolly's "Happy Deaths," an unfinished novel of the late 1940s, illuminated Sonia's sexual attitudes and second marriage by describing her close friendship with Peter Watson, who'd put up the money for *Horizon*. She could truly love him "because, being homosexual, he inspired no sexual ambivalence, she could not hate him for desiring her or for desiring another woman. In the sex-war he was a kind of angel . . . who was on her side." Rayner Heppenstall bluntly remarked that Sonia "had a morbid fear of sex," but "did very well out of her two . . . *mariages blancs*."

Sonia felt responsible for looking after Orwell's reputation, and took more interest in him after he was dead than when he was alive. She donated his extensive pamphlet collection to the British Museum, and in 1960 founded the Orwell Archive at University College, London University. But admission was restricted to the happy few who'd managed to secure Sonia's permission to study Orwell's papers. Instead of preserving all the letters that Orwell had written to her, she burned them. In 1968, with her co-editor Ian Angus, she published Orwell's *Collected Essays, Journalism and Letters*, with a deliberately misleading Introduction. Trying to discourage biographers, she falsely stated that "he left no personal papers: there is nothing either concealed or spectacularly revealed in his letters. . . . There was so little that could be written about his life—except for 'psychological interpretation'—which he had not written himself." She also claimed that "with these present volumes the picture is as complete as it can be. . . . With the novels and books they make up the definitive Collected Works." In fact, her four volumes contain 2,041 pages; Peter Davison's truly definitive *Complete Works* (which includes Orwell's major books in the first nine volumes) contains more than 8,500 pages in twenty volumes.[3]

Sonia could be terribly imperious when dealing with Orwell's friends. In 1962 Steven Runciman sent Orwell's teenage letter, about sleeping rough in Cornwall, to Stephen Spender's *Encounter*. Since it showed that he didn't really like being down-and-out, and she thought it would damage his legend, she refused to allow it to be published. Heppenstall, a producer at the BBC, stated that "as controller of the Orwell copyright, she was a *veuve abusive* . . . agreeing to a radio programme on Orwell . . . only if I were excluded."

Though Orwell (like Eliot and Auden) asked that no biography be written, Sonia realized that a life would eventually be published and tried to maintain control of this project. Over the years she asked several of Orwell's friends—Koestler, Muggeridge, Symons, Michael Meyer and Dwight Macdonald—to undertake it. She would then change her mind, withdraw the offer or deny them permission to quote. Richard Ellmann and John Wain were also approached; and Wain later heard that the American academic John Aldridge "was going to do the job."

Finally, Peter Stansky and William Abrahams went ahead without approval from Sonia, who also refused them permission to quote. In 1972 and 1979 they published two volumes, covering Orwell's life up to 1938. To get even with Stansky and Abrahams for opposing her wishes, and on the basis of his brief review in the *New Statesman* of a collection of essays, *The World of George Orwell*, Sonia impulsively asked Bernard Crick to write Orwell's biography. When Crick's book was finished, she condemned it as too political, too dry and unsympathetic, and tried to prevent publication, but he had an ironclad contract and his work appeared just before her death in 1980. In 1991 Michael Shelden justly criticized Crick's biography as a large collection of facts that deliberately made no attempt to understand Orwell's inner life, and brought out a better biography, authorized by the Orwell estate.[4]

Sonia Brownell Blair Pitt-Rivers always called herself Sonia Orwell. As large sums began to roll in from Orwell's royalties, she queened it up in artistic circles. With plenty of money and the social cachet of being Orwell's widow, wrote Francis Bacon's biographer, "Sonia was free to concentrate her considerable drive on what she did best: befriending and defending writers and artists she admired and bringing them together at dinner parties which she gave tirelessly, cooking abundant food and serving unlimited wine in her comfortable house . . . in South Kensington." Just as Sonia had formed a morbid attachment to Orwell, so she also formed friendships with the aging novelists Joe Ackerley, Ivy Compton-Burnett and Jean Rhys, gave them generous help and tended them all on their deathbeds.

But Sonia, gravitating toward homosexuals and moribund old ladies, did not deliver sexually or intellectually. Once "jolly, bar-maidy and hard-drinking," she eventually lost her looks and her money, and became a blowsy drunk. Toward the end of her life, she was reduced to alcoholic pronouncements, temper tantrums and nasty outbursts. When Peter Stansky lunched with her at the White Tower on Percy Street, she boozily exclaimed: "Let's have another drink. In for a penny, in for a pound." When Janetta Parladé chided her for drinking too much, she angrily replied: "Don't you think I know all about that?"[5] She knew she was destroying herself but could not help it, and told David Plante: "I did it again. I put on my act, my widow of George Orwell act. Was I awful? I'm so drunk. Did they think I was a fool?" Embittered and miserably unhappy, she confessed to Janetta: "I wake up crying every day." Stephen Spender believed that her guilt and depression were rooted in that strange deathbed marriage, and said: "She laid herself open to the accusation that she married him for his money. . . . She blamed herself and thought she had done the wrong thing."[6]

Sonia could certainly afford to be generous. In 1982 the biographer Michael Holroyd estimated that the Orwell Estate was worth about £100,000 a year. But by the time she died, thirty years of royalties had disappeared. What was it used for and where did it go? Bernard Crick—understandably angry with Sonia, who gave him a very hard time—pointed out that she "made no charitable use of the large estate and her high living was so out of character with Orwell. . . . Her squandering of the estate on trying to create a literary salon and a coterie of clients was hardly exemplary of the name she chose to flourish." Sonia's loyal friends took a more charitable view. Anne Dunn thought the guardianship of the estate "became far more complicated than she had ever imagined and she was faced with legal problems, accounting problems that she was not qualified to deal with and that proved insuperable."

The accountant, inherited from Orwell, swindled her out of a great deal of money. He also advised her go into tax exile, where she was utterly miserable. The novelist Margaret Drabble explained that "Sonia Orwell had gone to live in Paris, thinking it would be pleasanter and cheaper to manage there on her dwindling and badly managed finances, but it had all proved a disastrous mistake: she wrote to her friends in England complaining about being in exile. She should never have gone, and now she could not afford to come back. Money and health failed, she was smoking too much, the French were unfriendly and she lived in a hole. . . . [She] ended up old and ill in a poor basement flat off the Luxembourg"—alone, without husband or children, prematurely aged, drunken and bereft. She was also completely broke, and the painter Francis Bacon paid her medical bills. She sued the accountants Harrison, Hill & Company and, after a four-year litigation, settled out of court. A week later, in December 1980, aged sixty-two, she died of a brain tumor.[7]

I I

ORWELL'S BOOKS have earned twice as much as all the stars on the Secker & Warburg list—Kafka, Gide, Mann, Svevo, Musil, Schwarz-Bart, Calvino, Kawabata, Colette and Mishima—put together, and his worldwide sales and influence are greater than any other serious writer of our time. Orwell's moral example, his political and literary impact are incalculable, but it's possible to suggest the extent of his legacy. Yasuharu Okuyama reported his powerful significance in Japan: "George Orwell was first introduced to the Japanese people at the height of the Cold War, in 1949, by the GHQ (General Headquarters) of the Allied Occupation Forces, in line with the foreign policy of the US Government. Their intention was clear: giving warning to the people against the heinous Communist influence. . . . Since Orwell was first

introduced, no less than 1,200 books and articles on Orwell have been written in Japan in Japanese."

Other scholars have emphasized his political impact in Eastern Europe.
Timothy Garton Ash, echoing the language of Orwell and Graham Greene,
called the records office of the former East German Secret Service "a min-
istry of truth occupying the former ministry of fear." When Pope John Paul
II was Archbishop of Kraków in 1977, he allowed a lecture on "Orwell's
Nineteen Eighty-Four and Contemporary Poland," banned by the authorities,
to be delivered in church. In 1984—when Orwell's works were celebrated
around the world—the Polish Solidarity Movement issued a clandestine
Orwell stamp, illegal calendars and suppressed editions of *Animal Farm* and
Nineteen Eighty-Four, and showed films based on the novels. After the
breakup of the Soviet Union in 1991, the Russian philosopher Grigori
Pomerantz echoed Czeslaw Milosz's statement in 1953 about Orwell's acute
understanding of the totalitarian state: "People read *Nineteen Eighty-Four* for
the first time and they discovered that Orwell, who got his education at Eton
and on the streets of colonial Burma, understood the soul, or soullessness, of
our society better than anyone else."[8]

Many writers on the Left never forgave Orwell for attacking both
Communists and Socialist intellectuals. After his death neo-conservatives
claimed him as one of their own and praised him for warning the world about
the totalitarian aspects of the Socialist state. A recent account of the Cold
War described *Nineteen Eighty-Four* as "the canonical text" of conservative
anti-Communism, as "the key imaginative manifesto of the Cold War" and
gave Orwell credit for having "invented . . . a complete poetics of political
invective." Another discussion noted, despite Orwell's disclaimer, that this
novel undoubtedly "benefited political conservatives." Most grotesquely, "the
John Birch Society used to sell the book, and its main office in Washington,
D.C. at one time used 1984 as the final digits of its telephone number." As
if to counter the John Birch fanatics, Left-wing city councils have honored
Orwell by giving his name to schools and squares. There is a George Orwell
School in Islington and a Plaza George Orwell at the bottom of the Ramblas,
near the old Hotel Falcón in Barcelona.

Orwell had little respect for movies, but they've carried his ideas to millions of people. Two films have been based on *Animal Farm* (1955 and 1999),
two others—the second particularly horrific—on *Nineteen Eighty-Four* (1954
and 1984). *Keep the Aspidistra Flying* inspired the witty, literate and quite
poignant *A Merry War* (1998). Ken Loach's *Land and Freedom* (1995), loose-

ly based on *Homage to Catalonia,* portrays an idealistic English Communist in the Spanish Civil War and his bitter disillusionment when his side is betrayed by the Stalinists. Orwell's cogent warning against isolationism and pacifism in the last sentence of his book on Spain (1938)—we are all "sleeping the deep, deep sleep of England, from which I sometimes fear that we shall never wake till we are jerked out of it by the roar of bombs"—was effectively distilled by Humphrey Bogart in the perennially popular *Casablanca* (1942), one of the best propaganda films ever made. In December 1941, just before the Japanese attack on Pearl Harbor, Bogart announces that America must be vigilant and prepared for war: "I bet they're asleep in New York. I'll bet they're asleep all over America."[9]

III

ORWELL'S LANGUAGE has been enormously influential and his forceful images, especially from *Nineteen Eighty-Four,* have appeared in several good poems. Robert Frost's austere, pared-down poetry uses Orwell's paradoxical phrase "freedom is slavery" to support his own scepticism, and in "How Hard It Is to Keep from Being King" he warns us (as Orwell did) to resist the enslavement of a powerful leader.

Sylvia Plath adopts O'Brien's brutal image of the future—"a boot stamping on a human face—forever"—and uses it in "Ode for Ted," "The Beekeeper's Daughter," "Berck-Plage" (in which the black boot is merciless) and "Daddy" to represent masculine oppression of a female victim. All women adore Fascists, Plath writes:

> The boot in the face, the brute
> Brute heart of a brute like you.

And in "News From Nineteen Eighty-Four," Dana Gioia presents an ironic, Audenesque version of the rapid-fire news bulletins in the novel that belie the starvation, executions and endless war under the totalitarian regime:

> The fires at the docks have been contained
> with suspects netted in a late-night sweep.
> The enemy's offensive in the East
> has been repulsed at great cost. But morale

among the senior volunteers is high.
The Worker's Festival began last night
with execution of trade dissidents.
Spring coffee rations climb to twenty grams.
Arrests continue at the Ministry.[10]

Orwell had his most lasting impact, soon after his death, on a group of young English writers known in the 1950s as The Movement. Their historian, Blake Morrison, alluding to one of Philip Larkin's key phrases, identified the character and the ideas these writers considered most significant: "George Bowling in *Coming Up for Air* (1939) is a precursor of the quietist heroes of Movement fiction. . . . Orwell's advocacy of quietism, his disillusion with the Left, his determination to be 'less deceived,' his growing fear of totalitarianism: these played a crucial role in shaping the Movement's political identity. . . . Orwellian notions of 'decency' and 'common sense' dominated post-war political aims." The poet Thom Gunn believes the expression of Orwell's ideas was as important as what he had to say: "He meant a great deal to me in the 1950s. I liked the essayist and social chronicler more than the novelist. . . . I especially admired him as a model for prose writing, and taught *Homage to Catalonia* repeatedly in my freshman writing classes at Berkeley from 1958 onward. He knew how to *qualify* his beliefs, and to show how they were qualified by his experiences—maybe the next most important thing to having beliefs at all."[11]

Robert Conquest, another Movement poet and later on (with *The Great Purge* and other books) a leading anti-Soviet historian, named Orwell, "with his principle of real, rather than ideological, honesty," as "one of the major influences on modern poetry." In his poetic tribute to Orwell, Conquest described him as fallible, but

> A *moral genius. And truth-seeking brings*
> *Sometimes a silliness we view askance,*
> *Like Darwin playing his bassoon to plants;*
> *He too had lapses, but he claimed no wings.*[12]

Philip Larkin retreated (like Orwell on Jura) from the literary world to provincial Hull. He too protested against the disappearance of the English countryside and elevated the theme of failure to high art.

Gordon Comstock's fierce protests against hypocrisy and cant in *Keep the*

Aspidistra Flying influenced both Charles Lumley, the hero of John Wain's first novel, *Hurry on Down* (1953), and Jim Dixon in Kingsley Amis' first novel, *Lucky Jim* (1954). Just as Amis' early fiction had drawn on *Coming Up for Air*, so *The Anti-Death League* (1966) portrays the grim atmosphere of *Nineteen Eighty-Four*. In *Socialism and the Intellectuals* (1957), Amis praised Orwell's honesty and clarity: "Of all the writers who appeal to the post-war intelligentsia, he is far and away the most potent. . . . No modern writer has his air of passionately believing what he has to say and of being passionately determined to say it as forcefully and simply as possible." In a review of the previous year, Amis acknowledged Orwell's pervasive influence, which transcended politics: "Orwell is one of those writers you can never quite get away from. . . . His influence seems inescapable, so that any intellectuals who may submit to having a list of their heroes wrung from them are likely to put him in the first two or three whatever their age (within reason), whatever their other preferences, and—more oddly at first sight—whatever their political affiliations."

Gordon Comstock was also the prototype for the Angry Young Men—the other dominant literary group of the 1950s. The "England Your England" section in *The Lion and the Unicorn* (1941) inspired John Osborne's hit play, *Look Back in Anger* (1957), which uses many of Orwell's characters, ideas and expressions. The cast includes an embittered Left-wing intellectual, a father who fought in the Spanish Civil War and a blimpish ex-military man. The hero, Jimmy Porter, also fulminates against the English class system, public schools and government stupidity. He, too, is nostalgic for prewar Edwardian England while realizing that his idealized memory is false. Just as Orwell had said in "Why I Write": "So long as I remain alive and well I shall continue . . . to love the surface of the earth, and to take pleasure in solid objects and scraps of useless information," so Osborne writes of the tubercular hero, named after Orwell, in *Epitaph for George Dillon* (1958): "He never allowed himself one day of peace. He worshipped the physical things of this world, and was betrayed by his own body."[13]

Many contemporary writers have paid tribute to Orwell and defined the importance of his work. Alan Sillitoe, another of the Angry Young Men, particularly admired Orwell's moral traits: "I think really the word integrity would stand high on my list of his qualities, for it shines through in all his writings." Apart from *A Clergyman's Daughter* and *Coming Up for Air*, "it's top marks from me. He showed that integrity, honesty if you like, and delightfully clear English go together and produce something hard to beat." The novelist and critic David Lodge recalled that "as a young university teacher I read Orwell's prewar novels and realised that he was a seminal influence on the 50s generation of British Angry Young Men who in turn directly influenced my own early attempts to write fiction. But I think I still admire him most as an essayist and documentary writer, for his 'truth-telling' quality (which is of course partly a rhetorical feat)."[14]

Orwell's dark vision of the future powerfully influenced the novels of Ray Bradbury and Anthony Burgess, as well as the plays of Tom Stoppard. Bradbury's *Fahrenheit 451* (1953) takes up Orwell's theme of political repression through the destruction of culture, and his hero, Montag, is employed to destroy books as Winston Smith is to destroy the factual record. The novel portrays a dissident community whose people memorize great literary works in order to pass on "the human heritage."

In Anthony Burgess' *The Malayan Trilogy* (1956–59) the Abang, a corrupt Malay potentate whose title literally means "elder brother," "had read George Orwell and was struck by the exquisite appropriateness of the title of the Ruler of Oceania. It had amused him for a time to consider sticking posters throughout Dahaga, posters bearing below the image of his own powerful head, the legend," in Malay, Big Brother Is Watching You. Burgess' *A Clockwork Orange* (1962) considers the Orwellian theme of the lust for power and discusses the problem of evil itself. This satiric fable is set, like *Nineteen Eighty-Four*, in the near future in England, a work-state where teenage criminals roam free at night, and where political expediency has replaced the rule of law and the ethical code. The narrator, a sociopathic delinquent, takes pleasure, like Orwell's O'Brien, in the idea of grinding his boot into a human face. Burgess' *1985* (1978) jolts us into Future Britain, where organized labor dominates the will of the individual, Workers' English is the new official language, street toughs spout Latin, the Arab-owned Al-Dorchester welcomes converts to Islam and Bill the Symbolic Worker looks on from the myriad wall posters.

The Czech-born Tom Stoppard wrote two plays with Orwellian themes. *Professional Foul* (1978), like *Nineteen Eighty-Four*, attacks intellectuals for their hypocrisy and collusion with repression. *Every Good Boy Deserves Favour* (1978) is set in a Soviet psychiatric hospital, where a dissident is being punished. An orchestra accompanies the action, and the play's central metaphor expresses the conflict between the "orchestration" of society and the discordant note represented by the dissident. Stoppard's hero, like Winston Smith, clings obstinately to the distinction between right and wrong, truth and lies, despite the doctors' abuse of language and attempt to disorient him with drugs. Stoppard was also moved by Orwell's winning mixture of documentary truth and personal integrity: "I was fascinated to be told what it was like to be hit by a bullet (*Homage to Catalonia*)—more 'technical' than *A Farewell to Arms* (which I know was not a bullet). The novel about 'going back' (*Coming Up for Air*) hit a nerve with me. Much later, I went back similarly to my first English memories, with similar results. But, in a nutshell, Orwell suggested a standard of honesty—of intellectual honesty."[15]

Down and Out in Paris and London, in which (Tom Wolfe said) "Orwell went through the experience in order to write about it . . . as a reporter," and *Homage to Catalonia*, which showed that good reporting not only describes the larger political and military issues but also captures the spirit of the place, influenced both the concepts and methods of participatory journalism from Mary McCarthy, Norman Mailer and Truman Capote to Joan Didion, George Plimpton and Tom Wolfe. Mailer also admired the humane aspect of *Keep the Aspidistra Flying*: "it's a book that in a funny way I think has had a salutary effect upon me; it's given me more charity and compassion than I might have had naturally by myself. Orwell's always good for that." He also liked the stylistic principles described in "Politics and the English Language": "I've admired him enormously for years. He's one of my favorite writers. . . . I don't think there's a man writing English today who can't learn how to write a little better by reading his essays. Even his maxims and instructions on how to write well are superb."[16]

Paul Theroux wrote that in Africa in the 1960s, when he was starting out as a novelist, "Orwell was my model. I think Vidia [Naipaul] belittled him so as to loom larger in my life." Later on, however, Naipaul praised Orwell's courage in breaking away from conventional forms and subjects, in stripping "himself of all his earliest assumptions" about social class, elite education and colonialism. Naipaul called him "the most imaginative man in English history [because] he travelled in a new direction."

Angus Wilson admired Orwell's revelations in *The Road to Wigan Pier* about poverty in the industrial towns of northern England: "Orwell's absolute concern with the iniquities of unemployment at that time, and of the lies that were being told, both on the Right and the Left, about what was happening, were, for people like me, *the* kind of guiding light. So I think Orwell was one of my great heroes."[17] Doris Lessing praised his political perception, which intensified her disillusionment with Communism: "The reaction to *Homage to Catalonia* was the first expression we on the left had of the poisonous vendettas the comrades were capable of. I would say the nastiness of the campaign against Orwell hastened our reaction against the Communist Party. And then there was *Animal Farm*. More nastiness, unfairness, slanders. . . . *Animal Farm* and *Nineteen Eighty-Four* are wonderful." John le Carré observed that Orwell's life and works fused into a noble ideal: "Orwell meant and means a great deal to me. . . . *Burmese Days* still stands as a splendid cameo of colonial corruption. Orwell's commitment to the hard life is a lesson to all of us. I taught at Eton. It always amused me that Blair-Orwell, who had been to Eton, took great pains to disown the place, while Evelyn Waugh, who hadn't been to Eton, took similar pains to pretend he had. Orwell's hatred of greed, cant, and the 'me' society is as much needed today as it was in his own time—probably more so. He remains an ideal for me—of clarity, anger and perfectly aimed irony." All these authors found something different to admire in Orwell, but also discovered a unity between the experience, the style and the man.

Despite his vast influence Orwell was never part of a movement and never founded a school. He remained a solitary, individualistic writer whose reputation and stature derived from his personal example as much as from his work. Carlyle's description of Samuel Johnson's poverty, illness, courage and commitment applies with equal force to Orwell himself:

> This great mournful [man] guided his difficult confused existence wisely; led it *well*, like a right-valiant man. That waste chaos of Authorship by trade; that waste chaos of Scepticism in religion and politics, in life-theory and life-practice; in his poverty, in his dust and dimness, with the sick body and the rusty coat: he made it do for him, like a brave man. . . . He had a lodestar, as the brave all need to have: with his eye set on that, he would change his course for nothing.[18]

Writing in an anxious, atheistic age, Orwell fought for social justice and believed that it was essential to have both personal and political integrity. He has taken his place with Johnson, Blake and Lawrence in the English tradition of prophetic moralists.

Appendix I

The Geography of
Kipling's "Mandalay"

THE MEANING of "Mandalay" (1892), one of Kipling's most famous and memorable ballads, depends on its evocation of the exotic East. So haunting are the place-names, so insistent the rhythm, that readers have not noticed that its geography is wildly inaccurate. The speaker, in cold, faraway London, recalls the attraction of the Orient, contrasting the harsh, gritty, drizzly Bank, Chelsea and the Strand to the sunny, lazy, carefree life—represented by the playful flying fishes—in Moulmein, Rangoon and Mandalay. The "old Moulmein Pagoda" is Kyaikthanlan, whose hilltop site offers breathtaking views of the city and harbor. The "sludgy, squdgy creek" is the Salween River, in the dry season, at Moulmein. And the paddle steamers of the Irrawaddy Flotilla Company sail the river to Mandalay. Supiyawlat was the queen of King Thibaw, who was deposed and exiled after victory in the Third Anglo-Burmese War of 1885 gave the British control of the entire country. The "*hathis* pilin' teak" wood are the elephants.

The British soldier-narrator believes that the wind-blown palm trees and the tinkly temple-bells express the longing of his colorfully dressed, cheroot-smoking, banjo-playing, pretty and affectionate Burmese girl. She worships a "heathen" image of Buddha and, luckily for him, is unaware of the moral laws and sexual prohibitions of the Ten Commandments. Here, too, she is contrasted to the grubby, beefy-faced London housemaids who behave with propriety and know nothing of sex or love. Though the exotic setting, warm climate and complaisant women draw the soldier to the East, the malarial fever, which continues to plague him, is a grim reminder of the tropics. Indeed, he remembers the boat setting sail "With our sick beneath the awnings when we went to Mandalay."

In other respects, however, the poem makes no sense at all. Why, if a girl is in Moulmein—about 175 miles east of Rangoon and (via Rangoon) near- ly 500 miles south of Mandalay—would she want her beloved soldier to take the distant "road to Mandalay" instead of coming back to her and to Moulmein? In any case, there was no actual "road" to Mandalay. In Kipling's time passengers, including soldiers, took a thirty-day voyage from Liverpool, through the Suez Canal, to Aden, Bombay, Colombo, Madras and Rangoon (but not to Moulmein). Then, avoiding the rough cart-track, they traveled north to Mandalay by riverboat.

Moulmein is on the Gulf of Martaban, on the northern end of the Andaman Sea. To the west of Moulmein, across the Bay, is the coast of cen- tral Burma; to the east, across the land, is Siam. So the dawn does *not* come up "like thunder outer China 'crost the Bay!" For China, even Indochina, is nowhere near Moulmein or its Bay.

Kipling, though known for his technical expertise, must have either nod- ded or, relying on faulty memory, failed to consult a map when he wrote this famous poem. It made Orwell—and thousands of others—hear "the East a- callin' "; and Orwell ironically echoed its evocative opening line in his grim account of a depressed industrial town—which has no pier—*The Road to Wigan Pier.*

Appendix II

Allusions in *Burmese Days*

Works, v. 2:

80	"What shall it profit"	Bible, Mark 8:36
48	*Civis Romanus sum*	Cicero, *In Verrem*, 4.57
27	*eheu fugaces!*: "Alas, the fleeting years slip by"	Horace, *Odes*, 2.14.1
41	"They build a prison"	Tacitus, *Agricola*, 30
152	"In India, do as the English do"	St. Ambrose, *Advice to St. Augustine*
150	"Abandon your noses, all who enter here"	Dante, *Inferno*, 3.9
239	"when wilt thou blow"	ballad, "O Western wind"
title page	"This desert inaccessible"	Shakespeare, *As You Like It*, 2.7.111
17, 33, & 241	"Lead on, Macduff"	*Macbeth*, 5.8.33
36	"take them for all in all"	*Hamlet*, 1.2.187
153	"that obscene trunk of humours"	*I Henry IV*, 2.4.494–496
156 & 162	"Where is the life that late I led?"	*The Taming of the Shrew*, 4.1.143
203	"The gods are just"	*King Lear*, 5.3.170–171
42	"counsel ignoble ease"	Milton, *Paradise Lost*, 2.227
270	"the conquering hero comes!"	Handel, *Joshua*
152	"the usual village Hampdens"	Gray, "Elegy in a Country Churchyard"
83	"a green, unpleasant land"	Blake, Preface to *Milton*
222	"'cept of course Jorrocks and all that"	Surtees, *Jorrocks's Jaunts and Jollities*

Works, v. 2:

69	"whisky to the right of you"	Tennyson, "The Charge of the Light Brigade"
73	"a spiritual Mrs. Wititterly"	Dickens, *Nicholas Nickleby*
124	"Mr. Chollop"	*Martin Chuzzlewit*
183	"leaving her sentences unfinished, like Rosa Dartle"	*David Copperfield*
250	"Much better hang the wrong fellow"	*Bleak House*
223	"Alone, alone in the sea of life enisled"	Arnold, "To Marguerite"
40	"the trees avenge themselves"	Ibsen, *The Wild Duck*
30 & 243	"Sacrificed to the Paget MPs"	Kipling, "The Enlightenment of Pagett, M.P."
36 & 37	"the white man's burden"	"The White Man's Burden"

Appendix III

Getting at the Truth

I

As a biographer, I'm often more puzzled than enlightened by personal interviews. Establishing the facts is tricky enough, and the truth can be elusive. The people I talk to may be old, have frail health or failing memories. They sometimes "remember" what's been written or said instead of what actually happened, or say what they think I want to hear. They may even lie to make themselves look better. At work on the life of Orwell, I came across a new difficulty in literary biography: ideological blindness.

When I went to England to do research I had the names of two men, Frank Frankford and Sam Lesser, who'd fought against Franco in the Spanish Civil War. Frankford, who'd been in the Anarchist POUM (United Marxist Workers Party) militia with Orwell, and was now aged eighty-five, had agreed to see me; but I didn't know anything about Lesser, or if he was still alive. After talking to them I realized that the two men, fighting on different fronts, Barcelona and Madrid, had in fact been intimately connected. Lesser had changed the life of Frankford, and Frankford had been searching for him for the last sixty years.

I knew that Frankford had played a notorious role in Orwell's life. In 1937 Frankford was arrested in Barcelona for trying to sell paintings stolen from museums or looted from churches. After his release from jail with the help of an English intermediary, the British *Daily Worker* of September 14, 1937, published a story about him. In the article Frankford accused the POUM, and especially its commander, Georges Kopp, of secretly helping the Fascists on the Aragón front and deliberately rebelling against their Communist allies in Barcelona.

To validate the story the *Daily Worker* claimed that it had first appeared in the Spanish press, and then quoted Frankford's detailed accusations: "Every night at 11 p.m. the sentries heard the rattle of a cart, and we could tell from its light that it was crossing the space between the positions on our left and the Fascist lines. We were ordered never to shoot at this light. . . . Near Huesca . . . one night we saw Commandant Kopp returning from the Fascist lines." Two days later, to lend authenticity to the story, the *Daily Worker* printed Frankford's corrections. He now said he wasn't so sure: "he was not *certain* that the carts actually crossed the line, nor had he *himself* actually seen Kopp returning from the Fascist lines."

Frankford's false statement that the POUM had collaborated with the Fascist forces in Aragón was repeated in a vicious book by Georges Soria, *Trotskyism in the Service of Franco: Facts and Documents on the Activities of the P.O.U.M.*, which was brought out in London in 1938 by the Communist publishers Lawrence & Wishart. This book was used to justify the Communist extermination of their former POUM allies in Barcelona. Frankford's condemnation did great harm to former comrades, like Kopp, who were arrested, imprisoned and tortured, and like Orwell, who were hunted down and threatened with execution.

Frankford's accusations were forcefully refuted by Orwell's article in the British *New Leader* of September 24, which was signed by fourteen members of the British contingent. He concluded: "it is quite obvious that all these wild statements . . . were put into Frankford's mouth by the Barcelona journalists, and that he chose to save his skin by assenting to them, because at that time it was extremely dangerous to be known to have any connection with the P.O.U.M." The Left-wing politician Fenner Brockway later verified this statement. In his autobiography, *Inside the Left* (1942), Brockway wrote that when "the boy" (Frankford was actually twenty-four) returned to London he came to the office of the Independent Labour Party, which was affiliated with the POUM, and spoke to John McNair, who had escaped from Barcelona with Orwell: "He broke down crying and begged forgiveness. He had been imprisoned in Barcelona, and had been presented with the document to sign as a condition of freedom."

But forty-two years later, in December 1979, Frankford repeated his accusations to Orwell's biographer. Bernard Crick wrote:

Frankford denies that he ever broke down or asked forgiveness; says that he never signed anything, but simply gave an interview to Sam Lessor [*sic*] of *The Daily Worker* which he embellished, and he sticks to his story that there was fraternisation and crossing of the lines on occasion (which seems plausible), but he is "not sure" whether he ever thought that guns rather than fruit and vegetables ever figured in such movements, though "there are things still to be explained." (When I asked him if he was not angry at *The Daily Worker* for putting words into his mouth, Mr. Frankford replied: "Quite legitimate in politics, I am a realist.")

Four years later, when closely questioned in an Arena television program of December 1983, Frankford squirmed uneasily and forced out a fake smile. He now denied that he'd ever made the accusations and insisted: "I don't remember that. . . . I don't think I ever said that . . . that wasn't true and I wouldn't have said that." When asked about the propriety of publishing such stories, he replied with surprising cynicism: "Certain tactics are legitimate when you are fighting a battle like this." Not at all horrified that such statements could be attributed to him, he said, "it rather amuses me."

II

ON A long shot, before seeing Frankford, I called Lesser's old phone number. Now eighty-three, he answered in a gruff, aggressive voice. When I mentioned my book on Orwell, he became extremely hostile and asked: "What the hell are you ringing me for?" I said I understood that he'd been in the Spanish Civil War. He exclaimed that he was a Communist who'd fought and was wounded with the International Brigades, and was violently antagonistic to both Orwell and the POUM.

As I questioned him about his background, he first vented his anger, then calmed down and became more friendly. He'd spent his whole professional life as a journalist on the *Daily Worker*. Since his brother was also on the paper, he'd reversed the letters of his last name and used the byline "Sam Russell." When I said his brother must have been the greater Lesser and he the lesser Lesser, he laughed and we broke the ice.

Still repeating the old lies—which he may have believed after a lifetime of professional lying—Lesser claimed that the POUM had started the revolution in Barcelona behind the front and stabbed the Communists in the back. He also maintained that members of the POUM had driven around Barcelona in the ambulances so desperately needed at the front. The POUM, he said, had plenty of medical supplies when the International Brigades had nothing at all. When he was wounded he had to be evacuated by ox-cart. I listened patiently to these angry assertions, hearing the bitterness of past years, and didn't try to refute them.

III

DESPITE ALL his contradictory interviews, ranging over sixty years, Frankford was still eager to talk again when I turned up in 1998. I realized that I was dealing with a deaf and probably muddled old man. I had made the appointment over the phone with his wife, but he then called back to get my address so he could send me directions to his house in Wells, Somerset. The directions never reached me (and his house *was* hard to find) because he really couldn't hear me on the phone. I arrived late and hungry at noon. Mrs. Frankford gave me a sandwich and poured me a glass of Spanish wine. So I struggled to eat, drink, ask questions, take notes, look at the documents he offered me and copy whatever I could—all at the same time.

Though apparently robust, the stocky, white-haired Frankford had trouble hearing my questions and his memories were clearly embellished. After discussing his background and explaining why he went to Spain, he claimed (like most other British volunteers on the Aragón front) that *he* was the one standing next to Orwell when he was shot through the throat and caught him when he fell. Frankford maintained that just before he was shot Orwell "was telling us of his experiences working in a Paris brothel"—unlikely, since he had worked in a restaurant.

Frankford readily admitted that he disliked Orwell because of "his attack on the English working class" in *The Road to Wigan Pier* (1937), which he had read in Spain. Frankford resented the way Orwell had assumed leadership of the British contingent and disliked Orwell's belief that "everything he did was right." He was also annoyed that Stafford Cottman (another British member of the POUM), rather than himself, had been invited to Spain for the Arena television program. He didn't seem to realize that his role in events in Barcelona precluded such an invitation.

Frankford then described his arrest, along with his mate "Tankie," who'd served in the Tank Corps in World War I. The Spanish Police saw Frankford reading an English book, suspected him of being a spy and stopped him for questioning. They found the looted art, arrested him and put him in prison. An Englishman, Sam Lesser, got him out of jail and advised him to leave Spain as soon as possible. But he didn't know if Lesser had published the *Daily Worker* story and didn't know where Lesser was—though he'd been try-ing to find him for a very long time. When I said I had just spoken to Lesser and had his address and phone number, Frankford was astonished.

We then got down to the sticky question. Though Frankford was still a Communist, he now conceded that the "POUM was all right" and had been "badly treated during the political maneuvering and struggle for power." Apparently contrite and eager to clear his name, though stumbling for words, he showed me a xeroxed page from Brockway's book, and admitted that he had indeed broken down and begged forgiveness in London. The *Daily Worker* "twisted and changed the meaning of what I said," he exclaimed. Pathetically, and rather touchingly, he pleaded: "Don't blame me for any-thing. I never meant those things to be put down that way!" I asked, for the record, if the accusations he'd made in 1937 were true or false. "Just say 'yes' or 'no'," I said. Vague, evasive, yet eager to please, he thought for a long time. Finally, he said he wasn't sure.

I V

I WENT back to London and called Lesser again. Friendlier this time, but more wary, he said that after being invalided out of the International Brigades he became Communist Party representative, head of English-language broadcasting (i.e., propaganda) and *Daily Worker* correspondent in Barcelona. When I mentioned Frankford's name, Lesser said he might have known him in Hackney (a working-class district in London's East End) before they went to Spain. But he could not recall getting Frankford out of prison and said he would surely have remembered that good deed if he had done so. When I mentioned the *Daily Worker* story, he asked: "Was it signed?" When I said it wasn't, he claimed he had no recollection of writing it. Then he added: "Maybe it was true."

What, then, *is* the truth? Frankford said Lesser got him out of prison and he was certainly in a position to do so. Frankford's arrest gave the Communists an opportunity to smear the POUM and helped justify their extermination. Lesser, Barcelona correspondent of the *Daily Worker*, must have written that lying story. He was, it seems, both Frankford's benefactor and betrayer.

Frankford's accusations, refuted by Orwell, were certainly false. Brockway's account of Frankford's remorse (witnessed by McNair) is convincing. Why then did Frankford "stick to his story" and repeat his lies to Crick, yet retract essential parts of his statement—as he did long ago in Spain—and claim to be a cynical realist when he was really a disillusioned fantasist? Was it stubbornness, pride, bravado or bitterness?

His uneasy recantation on television, reinforced by his guilt-ridden pleas when I interviewed him, seemed inspired by bad conscience. Was he a victim, manipulated and humiliated by the Communists he still believed in, or a Communist agent, planted in the POUM to discredit the militia? My interviews with Frankford and Lesser reveal that the political battle-lines of the 1930s have endured into the 1990s. Hard-liners still believe it's ethical to lie in the service of Communism—even when the system has withered and supporters like Frankford have begun to crack. They continue to repeat what Orwell in 1940 called "the smelly little orthodoxies which are now contending for our souls."

Appendix IV

A History of Illness

Henley, Feb. 1905: Bronchitis.

Childhood: "Defective bronchial tubes and a tubercular lesion in one lung which was not discovered till many years later." "Wheezes like a concertina."

Eton, 1918: Chronic cough. Pneumonia.

Eton, 1921: Second case of pneumonia.

Katha, Burma, 1927: Dengue fever. "The climate ruined my health."

Southwold, late 1927: Ill in bed, perhaps with dengue fever.

Paris, Mar. 7–22, 1929: Influenza. Two weeks in Hôpital Cochin.

Uxbridge, Dec. 1933: Third case of pneumonia. Two weeks in Uxbridge Cottage Hospital.

Zaragoza, Mar. 1937: Blood poisoning in hand. Ten days in Monflorite Hospital.

Huesca, May 20, 1937: Shot through throat by sniper's bullet. Three weeks in hospital at Barbastro and Sanatorium Maurín, Barcelona.

Wallington, Mar. 8, 1938: Lung hemorrhage. "The bleeding seemed prepared to go on forever."

Aylesford, Kent, Mar. 15–Sept. 1, 1938: Preston Hall Sanatorium.

Marrakech, Dec. 1938: "He has been worse here than I've ever seen him."

Southwold, Apr. 1939: In bed with temperature of 102°.

Greenwich, Jan. 30–Mar. 13, 1940: Influenza.

Mortimer Crescent, London, Jan. 20–Feb. 11, 1943: Bronchitis.

Cologne, late Mar. 1945: Lung disease. In military hospital for a few days. "I thought at one time it was all up with me."

Canonbury Square, mid-Feb. 1946: Lung hemorrhage, refuses to call a doctor. Two weeks in bed.

Canonbury Square, winter 1946–47: In bed for several weeks with severe bronchitis.

Jura, Sept.–Dec. 1947: Loses twenty pounds, seems to be wasting away, feels deathly sick.

Jura, Dec. 1947: Tuberculosis diagnosed.

East Kilbride, Dec. 20, 1947–July 28, 1948: Hairmyres Hospital. Streptomycin treatment fails.

Jura, Sept. 1948: Suffers relapse and returns to bed.

Cranham, Glos., Jan. 6–Sept. 2, 1949: Seriously ill with tuberculosis in Cotswold Sanatorium.

London, Sept. 3, 1949: Transferred to University College Hospital.

London, Jan. 21, 1950: Dies of tubercular hemorrhage.

Notes

1. An Edwardian Childhood

1. *Imperial Gazetteer of India* (Oxford, 1908), 18.5; George Orwell, *The Complete Works*, ed. Peter Davison, assisted by Ian Angus and Sheila Davison (London: Secker & Warburg, 1998), 10.524 ("A happy vicar," Dec. 1936); David Edward Owen, *British Opium Policy in China and India* (New Haven, 1934), pp. 305, 282–283; Frederic Wakeman, Jr., *Policing Shanghai, 1927–1937* (Berkeley, 1995), pp. 34–35.

2. The photographs of Frank Limouzin and of Ida holding Eric appear in Miriam Gross, ed., *The World of George Orwell* (London, 1971), after p. 6, and of the *ayah* with Eric in Bernard Crick, *George Orwell : A Life* (Boston, 1980), opposite p. 222.

3. *Works*, 7. 37–38; Jane Dakin Morgan, in Crick, *Orwell*, p. 13; *Works*, 7.138.

4. Interview with Orwell's housekeeper, Susan Watson, London, November 12, 1998; Stephen Wadhams, *Remembering Orwell* (Markham, Ontario, Canada: Penguin Books, 1984), p. 3; Michael Shelden, *Orwell: The Authorized Biography* (New York, 1991), p. 21.

5. Wadhams, *Remembering Orwell*, p.3; *Works*, 18.242 (Letter to Andrew Gow, April 13, 1946); *Works*, 19.332 (Letter, May 4, 1948); Ian Hamilton, *The Trouble with Money* (London, 1998), pp. 88–89.

6. Wadhams, *Remembering Orwell*, pp. 29–30; 30; Interview with Orwell's nephew, Henry Dakin, Rosthwaite, Keswick, Cumbria, November 26, 1998; *Works*, 4.40.

7. Jacintha Buddicom, *Eric and Us: A Remembrance of George Orwell* (London,

1974), p. 19; *Works*, 19.384, 379 ("Such, Such"); *Works*, 20.206 ("Literary Notebook," 1949); *Works*, 19.377.

8. *Works*, 19.373 ("Such, Such"); *Works*, 19.501("Literary Notebook," 1948); Humphrey Dakin, in Crick, *Orwell*, p. 127; Jacintha Buddicom, in Shelden, *Orwell*, p. 67; Buddicom, *Eric and Us*, p. 110.

9. *Works*, 17.410–411 ("Bare Christmas for the Children," Dec. 1, 1945); Wadhams, *Remembering Orwell*, p. 14; Buddicom, *Eric and Us*, pp. 97; 32.

10. Buddicom, *Eric and Us*, p. 58; *Works*, 16.472 ("As I Please," Nov. 2, 1944); Audrey Coppard and Bernard Crick, *Orwell Remembered* (London: BBC, 1984), p. 86.

2. Misery at St. Cyprian's

1. W.H.J. Christie, "St. Cyprian's Days," *Blackwood's Magazine*, 309 (May 1971), 387; Henry Longhurst, *My Life and Soft Times* (London, 1971), p. 26; Hugo Vickers, *Cecil Beaton: A Biography* (New York, 1985), p. 16.

2. Gavin Maxwell, *The House of Elrig* (New York, 1965), p. 81; *Works*, 19.358; 362; James Joyce, *A Portrait of the Artist as a Young Man* (1916; New York: Compass, 1956), p. 50 and *Works*, 19.362.

3. *Works*, 19.357; 364; Maxwell, *House of Elrig*, p. 81; David Ogilvy, *Blood, Brains & Beer: An Autobiography* (New York, 1978), p. 15; Cyril Connolly, *Enemies of Promise* (1938; New York, 1960), pp. 166, 169.

4. Buddicom, *Eric and Us*, p. 46; *Works*, 2.38 (the last eight words of this sentence were silently deleted from the Popular Library edition [New York, 1958], p. 36, of the novel); *Works*, 4.39.

5. Ogilvy, *Blood, Brains & Beer*, pp. 15-16; *Works*, 12.164 (Review, May 24, 1940); Robert Pearce, "The Prep School and Imperialism: The Example of Orwell's St. Cyprian's," *Journal of Educational Administration and History*, 22 (January 1991), 44.

6. *Works*, 4.43–44; *Works*, 19.356; 359; Jeremy Lewis, *Cyril Connolly: A Life* (London, 1997), p. 35.

7. Mrs. Vaughan Wilkes, in Peter Stansky and William Abrahams, *The Unknown Orwell* (New York, 1972), 38; Sir John Grotrian, in Crick, *Orwell*, p. 29; *Works*, 19.379.

8. *Works*, 19.383; *Works*, 10.10–12; Christie, "St. Cyprian's Days," pp. 396–397; Lewis, *Cyril Connolly*, p. 37.

9. Samuel Hynes, *The Auden Generation* (London, 1976), pp. 18–19; Gross, *World of Orwell*, illustration nos. 7 and 8 (in his otherwise excellent book on Connolly, Jeremy Lewis mistakenly writes that Connolly commented on Blair's poem instead of the other way round); Connolly, Arena Television, "Orwell in 1984," Orwell Archive, University College, London University; Connolly, *Enemies of Promise*, pp. 170–171. Connolly thought, later on, that Orwell's prediction might have been made at Eton, not at St. Cyprian's.

10. *Works*, 11.253–254 (Letter, Dec. 14, 1938); Lewis, *Connolly*, p. 39; Maxwell, *House of Elrig*, p. 91; Longhurst, *My Life and Soft Times*, p. 37.

11. Vickers, *Cecil Beaton*, pp. 16–17; *Works*, 19.379.

3. Slacking Off at Eton

1. Harold Acton, *More Memoirs of an Aesthete* (1970; London, 1986), p. 152; Sir Steven Runciman, "Eton Days with Eric Blair," in Yasuharu Okuyama, *George Orwell* (Tokyo: Waseda University Press, 1983), p. 10 (Professor Okuyama kindly sent me a copy of his book); Malcolm Muggeridge, in Gross, *World of Orwell*, p. 173.

2. Harold Nicolson, in *The Old School*, ed. Graham Greene (1934; Oxford, 1984), pp. 85, 91; Denys King-Farlow, in Stansky, *Unknown Orwell*, p. 85; *Works*, 7.122; Buddicom, *Eric and Us*, pp. 68, 78, 90.

3. Lewis, *Cyril Connolly*, p. 49; *Works*, 5.118; Connolly, *Enemies of Promise*, p. 185; John Lehmann, *The Whispering Gallery: Autobiography* (London, 1965), p. 96; Interview with Sir Steven Runciman, Lockerbie, Scotland, November 29, 1998.

4. Christopher Hollis, *Eton* (London, 1960), p. 15; Shelden, *Orwell*, p. 77; Robert Louis Stevenson, "The Suicide Club," *New Arabian Nights* (New York, 1909), p. 25; Christopher Hollis, *A Study of George Orwell* (Chicago, 1956), p. 13.

5. Connolly, *Enemies of Promise*, p. 194; Hollis, *Study of Orwell*, p. 15; Tom Hopkinson, "George Orwell: Dark Side Out," *Cornhill*, 166 (1953), 453–454; Christopher Hollis, "George Orwell and His Schooldays," *Listener*, 51 (March 4, 1954), 382; Denys King-Farlow, in Crick, *Orwell*, p. 49.

6. Runciman, in Okuyama, *George Orwell*, pp. 7–8; Hollis, *Listener*, p. 383; James Owen, "A Meeting with Sir Steven Runciman," *Spectator*, 280 (August 15, 1998), 38; Runciman, in Okuyama, *George Orwell*, pp. 13; 10; Interview with Sir Steven Runciman.

7. *Works*, 10.56; Hollis, *Eton*, p. 23; *Works*, 12.270 ("My Country Right or Left," Autumn 1940).

8. *Works*, 12.270; 5.130; 10.77.

9. Shelden, *Orwell*, p. 70; Sir Anthony Wagner, in Crick, *Orwell*, p. 74; *Works*, 19.380 ("Such, Such"); *Works*, 5.107; Connolly, *Enemies of Promise*, pp. 210–211.

10. *Works*, 19.381; Crick, *Orwell*, p. 55; *Works*, 16.275 ("As I Please," July 7, 1944).

11. Lehmann, *Whispering Gallery*, p. 105; Sybille Bedford, *Aldous Huxley: A Biography*, (New York, 1974), pp. 92; 89; Aldous Huxley, *Antic Hay* (1923; London: Penguin, 1948), p. 15; Interview with Sir Steven Runciman.

12. Sir Steven Runciman, in *Aldous Huxley, 1894–1963: A Memorial Volume*, ed. Julian Huxley (London, 1965), pp. 27–28; Wadhams, *Remembering Orwell*, p. 21, and Coppard, *Orwell Remembered*, p. 53.

13. *Works*, 10.52; *Works*, 7.167; Gow, in Crick, *Orwell*, pp. 51 and 59; Runciman, in Okuyama, *George Orwell*, p. 12.

14. Tim Card, *Eton Renewed: A History from 1860 to the Present Day* (London, 1994), p. 161; Letter from A.S.F. Gow to Jeffrey Meyers, January 1, 1969, first published in Jeffrey Meyers, *A Reader's Guide to George Orwell* (London, 1975), pp. 32–33.

15. Connolly, *Enemies of Promise*, p. 238; Interview with Michael Meredith, Eton, December 2, 1998; Interview with Sir Steven Runciman; Hollis, *George Orwell*, p. 26 and Hollis, *Listener*, p. 383.

16. *Works*, 4.7; Buddicom, *Eric and Us*, pp. 116–117; Runciman, in Okuyama, *George Orwell*, p. 14.

17. The Eton Library has Eric's copy of G.K. Chesterton's book of comic verse, *Greybeards at Play*, 1900 (whose title may have alluded to the masters), with his pen-and-ink bookplate, "Eric Blair—His Book," and his drawing of a rocky Middle Eastern seascape, including palm trees, domed mosque and fortified castle. The library also owns Orwell's presentation copy of *Nineteen Eighty-Four* to the historian R.H. Tawney, who visited him in a sanatorium in 1949, the year the book was published. See [Michael Meredith], *100 Books, Manuscripts and Pictures, 1800–1996, in the Eton College Library* (Eton, 1996). Mr. Meredith kindly gave me a copy of this catalogue.

18. *Works*, 12.104 ("Inside the Whale," March 11, 1940); *Works*, 16.102 ("As I Please," Feb. 18, 1944); Mabel Fierz, in Coppard, *Orwell Remembered*, p. 96; *Works*, 12.147.

19. Interview with David Astor, London, November 15, 1998; *Works*, 19.412; Richard Rees, *George Orwell: Fugitive from the Camp of Victory* (1962; Carbondale, Illinois, 1965), p. 134; Christie, "St. Cyprian's Days," p. 391.

4. Policing Burma

1. Judicial and Public File 6079 for the year 1922, India Office Library, see Jeffrey Meyers, "Orwell in Burma," *American Notes & Queries*, 11 (December 1972), 52–54; *Works*, 19.6 ("As I Please," Jan. 3, 1947); *Works*, 12.121 ("Notes on the Way," March 30, 1940); *Works*, 10.143.

2. Sir Herbert White, *A Civil Servant in Burma* (London, 1913), p. 153; Sir J.G. Scott, *Burma: A Handbook of Practical Information*, 3rd revised edition (London, 1921), p. 77; Richard Curle, *Into the East*, Preface by Joseph Conrad (London, 1923), pp. 28; 45; 46; Somerset Maugham, *The Gentleman in the Parlour* (London, 1930), pp. 6–7.

3. Muggeridge, in Gross, *World of Orwell*, p. 171; *Works*, 16.143 (Review, April 6, 1944); White, *Civil Servant in Burma*, p. 253; V.C. Scott O'Connor, *Mandalay and Other Cities of the Past in Burma* (London, 1907), pp. 72–73.

4. Maurice Collis, *Into Hidden Burma* (London, 1953), p. 58; Curle, *Into the East*, pp. 75; 76; *Works*, 2.296; Bill Tydd, *Peacock Dreams* (London: British Association of Cemeteries in South Asia, 1986), p. 14.

5. *Works*, 12.270 ("My Country Right or Left," Autumn 1940); Roger Beadon, "With Orwell in Burma," *Listener*, 81 (May 29, 1969), 755; Maung Htin Aung, "Orwell of the Burma Police," *Asian Affairs*, 60 (June 1973), 185; Beadon, "With Orwell in Burma," p. 755.

6. Maung Htin Aung, "George Orwell and Burma," *Asian Affairs*, 57 (February 1970), 19; 22; *Works*, 10.502 ("Shooting an Elephant,"); Aung San Suu Kyi, *Freedom from Fear*, revised edition (New York, 1995), p. 126.

7. John Cady, *A History of Modern Burma* (Ithaca, New York, 1958), p. 242; *Works*, 12.405 ("England Your England," Feb. 1941); *Works*, 15.48 ("Comment," April 2, 1943).

8. Dennis Collings, in Coppard, *Orwell Remembered*, p. 82; Cady, *History of Modern Burma*, pp. 275; 247–248.

9. Philip Woodruff, *The Men Who Ruled India: The Guardians* (1954; London, 1965), p. 52; Shelden, *Orwell*, p. 97; *Works*, 5.136.

10. *Imperial Gazetteer of India: Provincial Series. Burma* (Calcutta: Superintendent of Government Printing, 1908), 1.333; *Works*, 12.268 ("War Diary," Sept. 24, 1940); Stansky, *Unknown Orwell*, pp. 181–182.

11. *Works*, 18.128 (Letter, March 14, 1946); Curle, *Into the East*, p. 54; *Murray's Handbook for Travellers in India, Burma and Ceylon*, 12th edition (London, 1926), p. 644; *Imperial Gazetteer: Burma*, 1.432–433; Collis, *Into Hidden Burma*, p. 77; May Hearsey, *Land of Chindits and Rubies* (London: privately printed, 1982), p. 94 (Peter Davison kindly sent a Xerox copy).
    Besides evoking "the old Moulmein pagoda," Kipling (in "In the Neolithic Age," 1895) also wrote:

> And the wildest dreams of Kew are the facts of Khatmandhu,
> And the crimes of Clapham chaste in Martaban.

12. Anthony Powell, "George Orwell: A Memoir," *Atlantic Monthly*, 220 (October 1967), 63; Wadhams, *Remembering Orwell*, p. 28; George Stuart, in *Works*, 10.88n; Roger Beadon, in Bernard Crick, "Appendix," *George Orwell: A Life*, 3rd edition (Harmondsworth: Penguin, 1992), p. 589.

13. Wadhams, *Remembering Orwell*, p. 24; Crick, "Appendix," p. 587; *Works*, 16.117 (March 10, 1944); *Works*, 5.138.

14. Jack Common, "Orwell at Wallington," *Stand*, 22:3 (1980–81), 35; Kay Welton Ekevall, in Coppard, *Orwell Remembered*, p. 100; Jack Common, in Wadhams, *Remembering Orwell*, p. 50.

15. Acton, *More Memoirs of an Aesthete*, p. 153; Anthony Powell, *Journals, 1987–1989* (London, 1996), p. 221; Maung, "Orwell and Burma," p. 28; *Works*, 17.442 ("The Sporting Spirit," Dec. 14, 1945); *Works*, 10.501.

16. Maung, "Orwell and Burma," p. 23; Hollis, "Orwell and His Schooldays," p. 383 and Hollis, *George Orwell*, p. 27; *Works*, 5.135.

17. Martin Wynne, ed., *On Honourable Terms: The Memoirs of Some Indian Police Officers, 1915–1948* (London: British Association of Cemeteries in South Asia, 1985), p. 12; Maung, "Orwell of the Burma Police," p. 181; Shelden, *Orwell*, p. 95; Peter Davison, *George Orwell: A Literary Life* (New York, 1996), p. 46.

18. A.J. Langguth, *Saki: A Life of Hector Hugh Munro* (New York, 1981), p. 40; *Works*, 14.34; 12.147 (Letter, April 17, 1940).

19. *Works*, 10.245 (Review, May 1932); *Works*, 2.250; 10.508 (Review, Oct. 17, 1936).

20. Maung, "Orwell of the Burma Police," p. 183; *Works*, 16.451; 20.213 ("Literary Notebook," 1949); *Works*, 10.207–210.

21. *Works*, 10.506n; 10.501–508. In *Animal Crackers* (1930), Groucho Marx says: "One morning I shot an elephant in my pajamas. How he got into my pajamas I'll never know."

On March 22, 1926, under the headline "Rogue Elephant Shot," the *Rangoon Gazette* reported that Major E.C. Kenny, subdivisional officer, Yamethin, when on tour "came across a rogue elephant . . . and brought it down to the delight of the villagers. The elephant had killed a villager and caused great havoc to the plantation. It is not known whether or not this is the elephant claimed by the Bombay Burma Trading Corporation" (quoted in letter from Peter Davison to Jeffrey Meyers, April 6, 1999).

For a detailed description of the heavyweight workers in the jungle, see U Toke Gale, *Burmese Timber Elephant* (Rangoon: Trade Corporation, 1974). For an unusual account of legal issues in Burma in the 1920s, using Eric Blair as a fictional protagonist, see Norval Morris, *The Brothel Boy and Other Parables of the Law* (New York, 1992).

5. The Joy of Destitution

1. Ruth Pitter, in Coppard, *Orwell Remembered*, p. 71; *Works*, 4.50; Mabel Fierz, in Coppard, *Orwell Remembered*, p. 95 and BBC Television, "The Road to the Left," January 10, 1971, Orwell Archive.

2. Crick, *Orwell*, pp. 144–145; Avril Dunn, "My Brother, George Orwell," *Twentieth Century*, 169 (March 1961), 257; *Works*, 18.384 ("The Cost of Letters," 1940).

3. *Works*, 10.485 (Letter, June 9, 1936); *Works*, 18.243 (Letter, April 12, 1946). Eton College Library now owns Orwell's presentation copy of this book.

4. *Works*, 4.47–48; Ruth Pitter, in Crick, *Orwell*, p. 106; Ruth Pitter, in Coppard, *Orwell Remembered*, pp. 71, 74; *Works*, 16.231 ("As I Please," May 26, 1944).

5. Interview with Henry Dakin; Humphrey Dakin, in Stansky, *Unknown Orwell*, p. 264 and Arena Television, "Orwell in 1984," Orwell Archive; Jane Dakin Morgan, in Coppard, *Orwell Remembered*, p. 86.

6. *Works*, 5.138–140; 5.142; Dennis Collings, in Coppard, *Orwell Remembered*, p. 78.

7. *Works*, 11.99 (Review, Nov. 27, 1937); Jack London, *The People of the Abyss* (1903; Oakland, Calif., 1982), p. vii; *Works*, 10.227 (Letter, Sept. 4, 1931).

8. *Works*, 18.388 (Letter, Sept. 5, 1946); *Works*, 12.86; Ernest Hemingway, *A Moveable Feast* (New York, 1964), p. 11; *Works*, 1.16–17.

9. Louis Bannier, in Wadhams, *Remembering Orwell*, p. 42; Ruth Pitter, in Stansky, *Unknown Orwell*, p. 274; *Works*, 18.460.

10. Mabel Fierz, in Coppard, *Orwell Remembered*, p. 95; *Works*, 1.104 (*Down and Out*); Loelia, Duchess of Westminster, *Grace and Favour* (London, 1961), p. 225.

11. Geoffrey Gorer, in BBC Television, "The Road to the Left," Orwell Archive; *Works*, 12.129 ("New Words," Feb. 1940); *Works*, 10.268.

12. Wadhams, *Remembering Orwell*, p. 39; Brenda Salkeld, in Stansky, *Unknown Orwell*, p. 280 and Arena Television, "Orwell in 1984," Orwell Archive.

13. *Works*, 4.155–156; 10.269 (Letter, Sept. 19, 1932); *Works*, 2.53; 4.155–156; 7.108–109; 9.126.

14. *Works*, 10.250 (Letter, June 14, 1932); *Works*, 10.253 (Letter, July 8, 1932); *Works*, 10.271 (Letter, Oct. 19, 1932); *Works*, 10.275–276 (Letter, Nov. 30, 1932).

15. Interview with Adrian and Stephanie Fierz, London, November 14, 1998; Rayner Heppenstall, *Four Absentees* (London, 1960), p. 51; Letter from Fay Fierz Evans to Jeffrey Meyers, December 28, 1998; Letter from Adrian Fierz to Jeffrey Meyers, January 2, 1999.

16. Mabel Fierz, BBC Television, "The Road to the Left," Orwell Archive; Adrian Fierz, "Reminiscences of Eric Blair," in Okuyama, *George Orwell*, pp. 23, 21; Letter from Adrian Fierz to Jeffrey Meyers, January 26, 1999; Interview with Adrian and Stephanie Fierz; Mabel Fierz, BBC Television, "The Road to the Left," Orwell Archive. Orwell equates scoutmasters with homosexuals in *Burmese Days* (2.78).

17. Mabel Fierz, BBC Television, "The Road to the Left," Orwell Archive; Peter Stansky and William Abrahams, *Orwell: The Transformation*, (London, 1979), p. 30; Letter from Mabel Fierz to Eric Blair, [Summer 1932], Orwell Archive; Letter from Adrian Fierz to Jeffrey Meyers, January 2, 1999; Interview with Adrian and Stephanie Fierz.

18. *Works*, 20.88 (Letter, April 17, 1949); Rayner Heppenstall, *The Intellectual Part* (London, 1963), p. 151.

19. *Works*, 18.301; 16.492 (Review, Dec. 7, 1944); *The Master Eccentric: The Journals of Rayner Heppenstall, 1969–1981*, ed. Jonathan Goodman (London, 1986), p. 51n; Katherine Middleton Murry, *Beloved Quixote: The Unknown Life of John Middleton Murry* (London, 1986), p. 177.

20. Mark Benny, *Almost a Gentleman* (London, 1966), p. 106; *Works*, 4.175, 90; Richard Rees, *For Love or Money* (London, 1960), p. 152.

21. *Works*, 10.198; Edouard Roditi, "When Orwell Was Still Eric Blair," p. 7, unpublished typescript, Orwell Archive.

6. Among School Children

1. *Works*, 12.209; Dennis Collings, in Coppard, *Orwell Remembered*, p. 79.

2. R.S. Peters, "A Boy's View of George Orwell," *Psychology and Ethical Development* (London, 1974), pp. 461–463; R.S. Peters, in Stansky, *Unknown Orwell*, p. 266; *Works*, 7.70.

3. *Works*, 10.320 (Letter, July 20, 1933); Cyril Connolly, *The Evening Colonnade* (1963; New York, 1975), p. 342; John Friend, "Gold Leaf and Caterpillars in Godforsaken Hayes," *Middlesex Advertiser Gazette* (Uxbridge), January 22, 1981, p.

14; Interview with Geoffrey Stevens, Hayes, Middlesex, November 14, 1998.
Mr. Stevens made a point of correcting a statement in Crick's *Orwell*, p. 138:
"The previous head master had just begun a six-year sentence in prison for inde-
cent assault." In fact, the master left under a cloud *after* Blair's time at the school.
He had embezzled a small amount of money, but had never assaulted a boy or
gone to prison.

4. *Works*, 10.276 (Letter, Nov. 30, 1932) and 10.249 (Letter, June 14, 1932); *Works*,
   3.197, 215, 214; *Works*, 12.163.

5. *Works*, 10.338 (Poem, April 1934); Avril Dunn, "My Brother, George Orwell," p.
   257.

6. *Works*, 12.148 (Letter, April 17, 1940); Letter from Anthony Curtis to Jeffrey
   Meyers, December 16, 1998; Wyndham Lewis, *One-Way Song* (London, 1933), p.
   132.

7. T.S. Eliot, in Gillian Fenwick, *George Orwell: A Bibliography* (New Castle,
   Delaware, 1998), p. 2.

8. Cecil Woolf and Rabbi Bertram Korn, Introduction to Frederick Rolfe, Baron
   Corvo, *Letters to Leonard Moore* (London: Nicholas Vane, 1960), p. 10; *Works*,
   19.221 (Letter to George Woodcock, Oct. 25, 1947).

9. *Works*, 10.252 (Letter, July 1, 1932); Sheila Hodges, *Gollancz: The Story of a
   Publishing House, 1928–1978* (London, 1978), p. 107; Shelden, *Orwell*, p. 158;
   Fredric Warburg, *An Occupation for Gentlemen* (London, 1960), p. 222.

10. Powell, "George Orwell," p. 62. A brief survey of pseudonyms from Mark
    Rutherford and Lewis Carroll to Blaise Cendrars and Ignazio Silone does not
    reveal the reasons for their adoption. Women (George Sand, George Eliot and
    Isak Dinesen) wished to disguise their gender; the French went in for "Madonna"-
    like single names (Voltaire, Stendhal, Colette, Céline and Vercors). Twain suggest-
    ed his profession, Conrad replaced an unpronounceable Polish surname,
    O. Henry, Saki and Man Ray were catchy and cute.

11. *Works*, 10.190; *Works*, 1.1–2; 20.210 ("Literary Notebook," 1949); *Works*, 1.54;
    1.67–68; 1.79.

12. *Works*, 1.74; 1.136; 1.206-207; 1.215–216.

13. Jeffrey Meyers, ed., *George Orwell: The Critical Heritage* (London, 1975), p. 42;
    Herbert Gorman, "On Paris and London Pavements," *New York Times Book
    Review*, August 6, 1933, p. 4; Humbert Possenti, Letter to the *Times* (London),
    January 31, 1933, p. 6; *Works*, 10.303 (Letter, Feb. 11, 1933).

14. Meyers, *Orwell: Critical Heritage*, p. 40; Henry Miller, Letter to Orwell, August
    1936, Orwell Archive; Henry Miller, in *Writers at Work: The "Paris Review"
    Interviews: Second Series*, (1963; New York, 1965), p. 181; Interview with Orwell's
    nieces, Jane Dakin Morgan and Lucy Dakin Bestley, Keswick, Cumbria,
    November 26, 1998; Buddicom, *Eric and Us*, p. 131.

15. *Works*, 10.347; 10. 348–349 (Letter to Salkeld, Sept. 1943); *Works*, 10.375 (Letter,
    Feb. 16, 1935).

16. *Works*, 10.482 (Letter, May 23, 1936); 10.511; 10.513.

17. Heppenstall, *Four Absentees*, pp. 51; 63; *Works*, 16.402 ("As I Please," Sept. 5, 1944); Heppenstall, *Four Absentees*, pp. 85–86; Interview with Margaret Heppenstall, Deal, Kent, November 16, 1998; Heppenstall, *Journals*, p. 22n.

18. *Works*, 10.374 (Letter to Salkeld, Feb. 16, 1935); Interview with Sally Jerome, Huddersfield, December 1, 1998; Interview with Adrian and Stephanie Fierz; Interview with Kay Welton Ekevall, London, November 14, 1998; Kay Ekevall, in Stansky, *Orwell: The Transformation*, p. 82. Photographs of Kay and Sally appear in this book opposite p. 115. In a private joke, Orwell lists "Lady Pamela Westrope" in an imaginary social column in *Burmese Days* (2. 96).

19. In her privately printed pamphlet *Kindling Memories for the Future* (London Voices Poetry Workshop, n.d.), p. 40, Kay Ekevall wrote: "his full-length polemic in *The Road to Wigan Pier* reveals how shallow was his knowledge of Socialism, Socialists and the working-class." Kay Ekevall kindly gave me a copy of this book.

20. *Works*, 5.101; 18.317–318; Aung San Suu Kyi, *Freedom from Fear*, p. 72 and *Murray's Handbook*, p. 617; *Works*, 2.121.

21. Orwell's sketch-map appears as the frontispiece to *Burmese Days* in *Works*, volume 2.

    In Burmese, the titles *U*, *Ko* and *Ma* (as well as *Daw* and *Maung*) are prefixes, like "Mr." and "Mrs." *U* literally means "uncle" and indicates an important position. *Ko*, as in Flory's servant Ko S'la, literally means "older brother" and indicates, for a man of his age, low status. *Ma*, as in his mistress Ma Hla May, means "sister."

22. Cady, *History of Burma*, p. 276. According to Orwell's contemporary Maurice Collis, *Into Hidden Burma*, p. 133, even an exceptionally Westernized and Oxbridge-educated Burmese, let alone U Po Kyin, "would not have got into the Rangoon clubs, where no polish, no charm, no culture could recommend an Asiatic."

    Maung Htin Aung wrote in "Orwell of the Burma Police," p. 185, that in Katha "the District Medical Officer and ex-officio superintendent of the jail was South Indian ('Dravidian')," whose real name was Krishnaswami. Nothing more is known about him.

23. Meyers, *Orwell: Critical Heritage*, p. 51; *Works*, 2.216; 2.70; 2.37–40; Friedrich Nietzsche, "Notes" (1874), *The Portable Nietzsche*, trans. and ed. Walter Kaufmann (New York, 1954), p. 48.

24. Beadon, "With Orwell in Burma," p. 755; Letter from Geoffrey Gorer to Orwell, July 16, 1935, Orwell Archive; Letter from Compton Mackenzie to Orwell, November 20, 1936, Orwell Archive; Cyril Connolly, "New Novels," *New Statesman and Nation*, 10 (July 6, 1935), 18.

7. Eileen and Wigan Pier

1. *Works*, 19.336 (Letter, May 10, 1948); *Works*, 10.348 (Letter, early Sept. 1934); *Works*, 3.300, 3.299 and 3.41.

2. Hodges, *Gollancz*, p. 106; *Works*, 10.243 (Letter, April 26, 1932); *Works*, 10.496 (Letter, Aug. 26–27, 1936).

3. *Works*, 10.351 (Letter, Oct. 3, 1934); *Works*, 18.411 (Letter, Sept. 28, 1946); *Works*, 3.259.

4. Rosalind Obermeyer, in Crick, *Orwell*, p. 172; Letter from David Whitaker, St. Hugh's College, to Jeffrey Meyers, March 29, 1999; Letter from Catherine O'Shaughnessy Moncure to Jeffrey Meyers, March 17, 1999; Elisaveta Fen, *A Russian's England: Reminiscences of Years 1926–1940* (Warwick, England: Paul Gordon, 1976), pp. 343, 345.

   According to Fen, Eileen was tall, to Lettice Cooper she was of medium height and to Crick she was small. Eileen's Moroccan identity card lists her height as 17 cm less than Orwell's, which would make her about 5'8"—rather tall, as Fen says, for a woman in the 1930s.

5. Lettice Cooper, in Shelden, *Orwell*, p. 358; Interview with Jane Morgan and Lucy Bestley; Lettice Cooper, *Black Bethlehem* (London, 1947), pp. 153–154; Cyril Connolly, in Crick, *Orwell*, p. 173.

6. Elisaveta Fen, "George Orwell's First Wife," *Twentieth Century*, 168 (August 1960), 116 (spaced dots in the original); *Works*, 10.394 (Letter, Sept. 24 1935); Interview with Kay Welton Ekevall; *Works*, 10.485 (Letter, June 9, 1936); Elisaveta Fen, in Crick, *Orwell*, p. 200; Humphrey Dakin, in T.R. Fyvel File, Orwell Archive.

7. Lettice Cooper, in Wadhams, *Remembering Orwell*, pp. 116–117; *Works*, 11.171 (Letter, July 5, 1938).

8. Elisaveta Fen, in Crick, *Orwell*, p. 200; Stansky, *Orwell: The Transformation*, p. 158; *Works*, 7.99; 11.222 (Letter, Oct. 12, 1938).

9. Denys King-Farlow, in Stansky, *Orwell: The Transformation*, p. 167 (spaced dots in the original); Benny, *Almost a Gentleman*, p. 107; Common, "Orwell at Wallington," pp. 33–34; *Works*, 11.261–262 (Letter, Dec. 26, 1938).

10. *Works*, 12.148 (Letter, April 17, 1940); Heppenstall, *Four Absentees*, p. 146; Geoffrey Gorer, in Crick, *Orwell*, p. 171.

11. Richard Rees in BBC Television, "The Road to the Left," Orwell Archive; Steven Runciman, in Okuyama, *George Orwell*, p. 10; Fen, *Russian's England*, p. 349; Lettice Cooper, "Eileen Blair," p. 5, unpublished typescript, Orwell Archive.

12. Interview with Adrian and Stephanie Fierz; *Works*, 20.204–205.

13. *Works*, 4.154; 16.232 (Letter, May 27, 1944); *Works*, 18.320; 10.490 (Review, July 23, 1936); Meyers, *Critical Heritage*, pp. 65–69.

14. Letter from Connolly to Orwell, April–May 1936, Orwell Archive; *Works*, 10.484n (Powell to Orwell); Letter from Geoffrey Gorer to Orwell, April 21, 1936, Orwell Archive; *Works*, 10.401 (newspaper report).

15. Crick, *Orwell*, p. 184; A.J.P. Taylor, *English History, 1914–1945* (New York, 1965), p. 238.

16. May Deiner, in Crick, *Orwell*, pp. 185–186; W.H. Auden, *Letters from Iceland* (London, 1937), p. 49; *Works*, 5.17; 5.98; 5.15; 5.58.

17. Thomas Carlyle, "Chartism," *Critical and Miscellaneous Essays* (London, 1888), 3.259; *Works*, 5.20–21.

   In July 1988, wearing a battery lamp and carrying a gas mask, I also went 964 meters down a mine. After riding a conveyor belt and tramcar, I walked, while bent over, a final 300 meters underground to the coal face in Haworth, north Nottinghamshire. There was winding gear at the pithead, the miners still used a modern form of the Davy lamp and it was still extremely hot, dusty and dangerous. Showers have been built so the miners can go home clean, but a stern reminder warned the men not to piss in the baths.

18. *Works*, 5.108; 5.171, 5.167; 5.169, 5. 207.

19. *Works*, 5.138, 5.140; Charles Dickens, *Little Dorrit* (1857; Oxford, 1953), p. 63; T.E. Lawrence, *Seven Pillars of Wisdom* (New York, 1935), p. 564; Quoted in Anthony Kenny, *A Path from Rome* (Oxford, 1985), p. 68.

20. Meyers, *Critical Heritage*, pp. 91–99; 104–107; Edith Sitwell, *Selected Letters, 1919–1964*, ed. John Lehmann and Derek Parker (New York, 1970), p. 62; Arthur Bryant, Preface to G.A.W. Tomlinson, *Coal Miner* (London, 1937), pp. 10–11.

21. Meyers, *Critical Heritage*, pp. 115–118; Dwight Macdonald, "Varieties of Political Experience," *New Yorker*, 35 (March 29, 1959), pp. 137–146; Richard Rees, BBC Television, "The Road to the Left," Orwell Archive; *Works*, 12.56 ("Charles Dickens," 1940).

8. Fighting for Spain

1. *Works*, 16.289 ("Spanish Memories," July 16, 1944); Alan Judd, Review of Shelden's *Orwell*, *Washington Post Book Review*, November 17, 1991; Fen, *Russian's England*, p. 417.

2. Philip Mairet, in Crick, *Orwell*, p. 206; *Works*, 10.241; Letter from Dr. Kenneth Sinclair-Loutit to Jeffrey Meyers, January 9, 1999.

3. Crick, *Orwell*, p. 162; Robert Dowse, *Left in the Centre: The Independent Labour Party, 1893–1940* (London, 1966), pp. 194, 197; *Works*, 12.106; Henry Miller, in *Writers at Work*, p. 181; *Works*, 16. 403 ("As I Please," Sept. 5, 1944).

4. Paul Preston, *The Spanish Civil War, 1936–1939* (London, 1986), p. 177; Ronald Fraser, *Blood of Spain: An Oral History of the Spanish Civil War* (1979; New York, 1986), p. 341; Pierre Broué and Émile Témine, *The Revolution and the Civil War*, trans. Tony White (London, 1972), pp. 71–72; Carr, in Gross, *World of Orwell*, p. 69; Letter from Dr. Kenneth Sinclair-Loutit to Jeffrey Meyers.

5. *Works*, 13.398 (Pacifism Controversy, July 12, 1942); Letter from Victor Alba to Jeffrey Meyers, January 29, 1999.

6. Cyril Connolly, "Barcelona," *The Condemned Playground: Essays, 1927–1944* (London, 1945), p. 186; Willy Brandt, *My Life in Politics* (New York, 1992), p. 102; Jason Gurney, *Crusade in Spain* (London, 1974), p. 49; *Works*, 11.28 (Letter, June 8, 1937).

7. *Works*, 13.497 ("Looking Back on the Spanish Civil War," 1942); John McNair, *Spanish Diary*, ed. Don Bateman (Stockport, Lancs., 197-), p. 14; Frank Frankford, in Wadhams, *Remembering Orwell*, p. 77; José Rovira, in Shelden, *Orwell*, p. 251.

8. Ilya Ehrenburg, *Eve of War, 1933–1941*, trans. Tatiana Shebunia and Yvonne Kapp (London, 1963), p. 138; Raymond Carr, *Spain, 1808–1939* (Oxford, 1966),

pp. 660, 679; Hugh Thomas, *The Spanish Civil War* (New York, 1961), pp. 364–365.

9. *Works*, 13.498 ("Looking Back," 1942); *Works*, 12.246 ("War Diary," Aug. 1940); Bob Edwards, Introduction to *Homage to Catalonia* (London: Folio Society, 1970), p. 7; Harry Milton, in Wadhams, *Remembering Orwell*, p. 82.

10. *Works*, 12.271 ("My Country Right or Left," Autumn 1940); Edwards, Introduction to *Homage to Catalonia*, p. 7; *Works*, 16.460; Stafford Cottman, in James Hopkins, *Into the Heart of the Fire: The British in the Spanish Civil War* (Stanford, 1998), p. 205; Stafford Cottman and Bob Edwards, in Wadhams, *Remembering Orwell*, pp. 81, 79.

11. Benjamin Lewinski, in Shelden, *Orwell*, p. 260; *Works*, 11.52 (Review, July 31, 1937); Hopkins, *Into the Heart of the Fire*, p. 206.

12. Letter from Michel Kopp to Jeffrey Meyers, December 9, 1998; Letter from Pierre Kopp to Jeffrey Meyers, December 22, 1998; and Interview with Quentin Kopp, Chesterfield, November 28, 1998; Bert Govaerts, "Georges Kopp," *Vrij Nederland*, August 24, 1985, translated and paraphrased in Hopkins, *Into the Heart of the Fire*, pp. 400 n120; 406 n23; *Works*, 9.182–183.

13. Stafford Cottman in T.R. Fyvel, *George Orwell: A Personal Memoir* (New York, 1982), p. 134; Jack Branthwaite, in Wadhams, *Remembering Orwell*, p. 84; *Works*, 11.17 (Letter, April 12, 1937).

14. Isaac Deutscher, *Stalin: A Political Biography* (1949; New York, 1960), p. 425; Eileen Blair, in Crick, *Orwell*, p. 220; Brandt, *My Life in Politics*, p. 105; Burnett Bolloten, *The Spanish Civil War: Revolution and Counterrevolution* (Chapel Hill, North Carolina, 1991), p. 498; Townsend Ludington, *John Dos Passos: A Twentieth Century Odyssey* (New York, 1980), p. 373; Gurney, *Crusade in Spain*, p. 185.

15. Georges Kopp, in Meyers, *Reader's Guide to George Orwell*, p. 173 n13 (May 31, 1937) and *Works*, 11.25; Harry Milton, in Wadhams, *Remembering Orwell*, p. 90.

16. *Works*, 11.27; *Works*, 11.25 (Kopp to O'Shaughnessy, June 10, 1937); *Works*, 11.29 (Eileen to O'Shaughnessy); Heppenstall, *Four Absentees*, p. 204.

17. Rees, *Love or Money*, p. 153; *Works*, 11.31 (in the Archivo Histórico Nacional de España, Madrid); Hopkins, *Into the Heart of the Fire*, pp. 205–208.

18. John McNair, in Warburg, *An Occupation for Gentlemen*, p. 237; *Works*, 12.103.

19. Letter from Georges Kopp to Eileen Blair, January 10, 1939, Orwell Archive; *Works*, 11.339n; Telegram from Kopp to Eric and Eileen Blair, December 18, 1938, Orwell Archive; Letter from Kopp to Blair, August 12, 1939, Orwell Archive; *Works*, 11.53 (Letter, July 31, 1937).

20. Connolly, *Evening Colonnade*, p. 341; Peter Quennell, *Customs and Characters* (Boston, 1982), p. 2.

21. Malcolm Muggeridge, "Langham Diary," *Listener*, October 6, 1983, p. 18; John Morris, "Some Are More Equal Than Others: A Note on George Orwell," *Penguin New Writing*, 40 (1950), 90; Julian Symons, "Orwell—A Reminiscence," *London Magazine*, 3 (September 1963), 38.

22. Noel Annan, *Our Age: English Intellectuals Between the World Wars—A Group*

Portrait (New York, 1990), pp. 210–211; Malcolm Muggeridge, in Gross, *World of Orwell*, p. 172; Cyril Connolly, in "George Orwell: Some Letters," *Encounter*, 18 (January 1962), 56; Connolly, BBC Television, "The Road to the Left," Orwell Archive.

23. *Works*, 10.491 (Review, July 23, 1936); *Works*, 17.413 (Review, Dec. 2, 1945); *Works*, 17.21 (Review, Jan. 14, 1945).

24. *Works*, 18.319; 11.88 (Letter, Oct. 12, 1937); Albert Camus, in Frederick Benson, *Writers in Arms: The Literary Impact of the Spanish Civil War* (New York, 1967), p. 302.

25. Juan Negrín, in Herbert Matthews' review of *Homage to Catalonia*, Meyers, *Critical Heritage*, p. 149; Cecil Day-Lewis, *A Time to Dance* (London, 1935), p. 58; Ralph Bates, in Hopkins, *Into the Heart of the Fire*, p.236; *Works*, 16.394 ("Arthur Koestler," Sept. 11, 1944).

26. Adrian Smith, *The "New Statesman": Portrait of a Political Weekly* (London, 1996), p. 246; *Works*, 11.51 (Review of Borkenau, July 31, 1937); *Works*, 11.71 (Letter, Aug. 19, 1937).

    The shadowy Yvonne Davet, who began corresponding with Orwell in August 1937, translated *Homage to Catalonia* before the war, though it was not published in France until 1955. Gide's biographer writes that "as a young woman in Avignon [in 1937], she wrote Gide passionately admiring letters," and eventually became his intelligent, efficient and hardworking secretary. Gide said that "she works like an angel, because everything she does is an act of love. . . . She's very pretty and emotional, but too obviously interested in only one subject in the world"—Gide. By 1947 "her passion, always ready to explode, was beginning to wear Gide down" (Alan Sheridan, *André Gide: A Life in the Present* [London, 1998], p. 591).

27. Malcolm Muggeridge, *Chronicles of Wasted Time* (London, 1972), 1.175; *Works*, 11.67 (Letter, Aug. 3–6, 1937); Fredric Warburg, BBC interview, February 19, 1963, Orwell Archive; Warburg, BBC Television, "The Road to the Left," Orwell Archive.

28. *Works*, 17.208 (Letter, July 1, 1945); *Works*, 18.320.

29. *Works*, 1.130; 5.141; George Orwell, *Homage to Catalonia*, Introduction by Lionel Trilling (New York: Beacon, 1952), pp. 1–2. In a rare error of judgment, the editor of *The Complete Works* moved Chapter 5 (and Chapter 11) to the end of the book, but failed to see that without Chapter 5 the political discussion that follows in Chapter 8 now makes no sense, and the force of Orwell's conclusion is lost. I have therefore used the American edition of *Homage to Catalonia*.

30. Michael Seidman, "The Unorwellian Barcelona," *European History Quarterly*, 20 (April 1990), 164, 175; *Works*, 11.416 (Review, Dec. 1939); Orwell, *Homage to Catalonia*, pp. 32; 99; 129; 209.

31. *Works*, 13.501 ("Looking Back on the Spanish War," 1942); *Works*, 16.42 ("Can Socialists Be Happy?" Dec. 24, 1943); André Malraux, *The Walnut Trees of Altenburg*, trans. A.W. Fielding (London 1952), p.119; Orwell, *Homage to Catalonia*, p. 185.

32. Meyers, *Critical Heritage*, pp. 121–151; V.S. Pritchett, "The Spanish Tragedy," *New Statesman and Nation*, 15 (April 30, 1938), 734, 736.

9. Morocco and *Coming Up for Air*

1. Letter from Desmond Young to Orwell, December 28, 1937, Orwell Archive; "The Man Who Would Be King," *Best Short Stories of Rudyard Kipling*, ed. Jeffrey Meyers (New York: Signet, 1987), p. 88; *Works*, 11.121; 11.122n; 11.123 (Letter, Feb. 12, 1938).

2. *Works*, 11.128 (Eileen to Jack Common, March 14, 1939); *Works*, 11.127; 11.128–129 (Eileen to Jack Common); Medical report, in Shelden, *Orwell*, p. 289; *Works*, 11.165 (Eileen to King-Farlow) and 11.190 n2 (Medical report, Nov. 7, 1938); *Works*, 11.130 (Letter, late March 1938).

3. George Kayne, Walter Pagel and Laurence O'Shaughnessy, *Pulmonary Tuberculosis: Pathology, Diagnosis, Management and Prevention* (1939), 4th edition (London, 1964), p. 428; F.B. Smith, *The Retreat of Tuberculosis, 1850–1950* (New York, 1988), p. 166.

4. *Works*, 11.129 (Eileen to Jack Common, March 14, 1938); *Works*, 11.228n (John Sceats); Ian Hyle, "Man of Vision," obituary of Reynolds, *The Friend*, December 26, 1958, p. 1664; Letter from Reginald Reynolds to Orwell, August 22, 1945, Orwell Archive.

5. Hyle, "Man of Vision," p. 1664; *Works*, 7.228; Reginald Reynolds, *My Life and Crimes* (London: Jarrolds, 1956), pp. 212–213; James Boswell, *Life of Johnson*, ed. G.B. Hill and L.F. Powell (Oxford, 1971), 4.427. For a photograph of Orwell in his shabby, almost shredded jacket, see the back cover of Vernon Richards, *George Orwell At Home: Essays and Photographs* (London: Freedom Press, 1998).

6. *Works*, 13.247 (Letter, March 26, 1942); Reynolds, *My Life and Crimes*, p. 214.

7. Arnold Bennett, *Journal* (New York, 1933), p. 755; *Works*, 19.417 (Review, Aug. 7, 1948); *Works*, 17.456 (Letter, late 1945).

8. *Works*, 11.199 (Eileen to her mother, Sept. 15, 1938); *Works*, 11.206 (Eileen to Marjorie Dakin, Sept. 27, 1938); *Works*, 11.249 (Eileen to Mary Common, Dec. 5, 1938); Fen, "Orwell's First Wife," p. 121; *Works*, 11.321 (Letter, Jan. 20, 1939).

9. Lettice Cooper, "Eileen Blair," p. 5, unpublished typescript, Orwell Archive; *Works*, 11.325 (Jan. 27, 1939); Acton, *More Memoirs of an Aesthete*, p. 153; Fyvel, *George Orwell*, p. 109; *Works*, 11.253 (Letter, Dec. 14, 1938); *Works*, 11.417, 420.

10. Fen, *Russian's England*, p. 419; *Works*, 11.336 (Letter, March 1, 1939); *Works*, 11.348–349 (Letter, March 31, 1939); Fen, *Russian's England*, pp. 431–432; *Works*, 19.341 (Letter, May 24, 1948).

11. *Works*, 11.344–345 (Letter, March. 19, 1939); *Works*, 11.350 (Eileen to Mary Common, April 9, 1939); Mabel Fierz, in Wadhams, *Remembering Orwell*, p. 44; *Works*, 11.365 (Letter, July 14, 1939); Rees, *George Orwell*, p. 137.

12. Orwell, *Homage to Catalonia*, pp. 231–232; *Works*, 12.394 (*Lion and Unicorn*, Feb. 1941); *Works*, 7.238; 7.25; 7.20.

   In *Coming Up for Air* (7.20) Bowling says: "I'm fat but I'm thin inside. Has it ever struck you that there's a thin man inside every fat man?" Five years later, in *The Unquiet Grave* (1944; London, 1961), p. 58, the obese Connolly (who may have inspired Bowling's physical appearance) lifted this idea and wrote:

"Imprisoned in every fat man is a thin one wildly signalling to be let out."

13. *Works*, 12.191 (Review, June 21, 1940); *Works*, 19.336 (Letter, May 10, 1948); *Works*, 7.143; 19.336 (Letter, May 10, 1948).

14. *Works*, 7.169, 7.160; D.H. Lawrence, *Letters. Volume II, 1913–1916*, ed. George Zytaruk and James Boulton (Cambridge, England, 1981), pp. 431–432; *Works*, 7.168–169.

15. Bertrand Russell, *Autobiography, 1944–1969* (New York, 1969), p. 115; *Works*, 7.106–107; Meyers, *Critical Heritage*, pp. 152–174; Letter from Ethel Mannin to Orwell, October 30, 1939, Orwell Archive.

10. London in the Blitz

1. *Works*, 12.137 (Letter, April 3, 1940); Common, "Orwell at Wallington," p. 33; Fen, "Orwell's First Wife," p. 122; Lydia Jackson, in Wadhams, *Remembering Orwell*, p. 68; Fyvel, *George Orwell*, p. 105.

2. Lettice Cooper, *Black Bethlehem*, pp. 153–154, 177, 181–182; *Works*, 12.6 (Letter, Jan. 10, 1940); Symons, "Orwell—A Reminiscence," p. 39; *Works*, 12.277 ("War Diary," Oct. 1940).

3. George Woodcock, *The Crystal Spirit: A Study of George Orwell* (Boston, 1966), p. 13; Stephen Spender, in Shelden, *Orwell*, p. 325; Interview with Celia Paget Goodman, Cambridge, England, November 24, 1998.

4. V.S. Pritchett, *"A Cab at the Door" and "Midnight Oil"* (London: Penguin, 1974), p. 407; Connolly, *Evening Colonnade*, p. 341; *Works*, 12.262 and 12.468 ("War Diary," Sept. 1940 and April 1941).

5. Fyvel, *George Orwell*, p. 109; Lettice Cooper, "Eileen Blair," p. 3, unpublished typescript, Orwell Archive; *Works*, 12.452 ("War Diary," March 20, 1941); *Works*, 12.197 ("War Diary," June 24, 1940).

6. Powell, "George Orwell," p. 65; For Karl Schnetzler, see *Works*, 18.98n.

7. Letter from Georges Kopp to Eileen, September 8, 1940, Orwell Archive; *Works*, 15.175n (Letter from Kopp to Orwell, July 26, 1943); Interview with Quentin Kopp; Letter from Michel Kopp to Jeffrey Meyers, December 9, 1998.

8. William Empson, in Gross, *World of Orwell*, p. 94; Powell, "George Orwell," p. 65; *Works*, 12.186 ("War Diary," June 1940); Philip Zeigler, *London at War: 1939–1945* (London, 1995), pp. 107, 103–104, 106.

9. *Works*, 12.202 ("War Diary," June 30, 1940); *Works*, 13.249 ("War Diary," March 1942); Patricia Donahue, in Wadhams, *Remembering Orwell*, p. 119; Fredric Warburg, *All Authors Are Equal* (London, 1973), p. 38. A photo of the dangerous spigot-mortar appears in S.P. Mackenzie, *The Home Guard: A Military and Political History* (Oxford, 1995).

10. *Works*, 4.78; 18.302; 12.545 (Review, Aug. 16, 1941); *Works*, 12.512 (Review, June 14, 1941); *Works*, 12.304 (Review, Dec. 7. 1940).

11. *Works*, 12.543–544 (Review, Aug. 9, 1941); *Works*, 12.314–315 (Review, Dec. 21, 1940).

12. *Works*, 12.21; 12.31; 12.51; 12.53; 12.56; *Works*, 12.74; 12.72; Letter from David Lodge to Jeffrey Meyers, October 11, 1998.

13. *Works*, 12.88–89; 12.97; 12.104; 12.103–104; Humphrey Carpenter, *W.H. Auden: A Biography* (Boston, 1981), p. 219; *Works*, 12.110.

14. Meyers, *Critical Heritage*, pp. 177–190; V.S. Pritchett, "Back to Jonah," *New Statesman and Nation*, 19 (March 16, 1940), 370; *Works*, 12.392; 12.404; 12.406; Andrew Motion, *Philip Larkin: A Writer's Life* (New York, 1993), p. 45.

15. T.R. Fyvel, "A Writer's Life," *World Review*, 16 (June 1950), 18; Richard Cockett, *David Astor and "The Observer"* (London, 1991), pp. 2; 126 (David Astor kindly gave me a copy of this book); Interview with David Astor.

16. *Works*, 11.113 (Review, Feb. 5, 1938); *Works*, 12.359 (Review, Jan. 4, 1941); John Banville, review of David Cesarani's *Arthur Koestler: The Homeless Mind*, *London Review of Books*, February 18, 1999, p. 19.

17. *Works*, 17.409 (Review, Nov. 30, 1945); *Works*, 16.399; Fredric Warburg, BBC Television, "The Road to the Left," Orwell Archive.

18. Iain Hamilton, *Koestler* (New York, 1982), pp. 81; 166; Iain Hamilton, Interview with Koestler, p. 23, Edinburgh University Library; Arthur Koestler, in Coppard, *Orwell Remembered*, p. 169.

19. Arthur and Cynthia Koestler, *Stranger on the Square*, ed. Harold Harris (London, 1984), p. 187; Frances Spalding, *Stevie Smith: A Biography* (New York, 1989), p. 151; Interview with David Astor, London.

   Down and Out, written before Orwell had known any Jews, has many anti-Semitic remarks. An extraordinarily disagreeable red-haired Jew owned a second-hand clothes shop in Paris, paid incredibly low prices and tried to swindle his customers, and "it would have been a pleasure to flatten the Jew's nose." His Russian friend Boris, hating to live with a Jew who didn't have "the decency to be ashamed of it," told the story of a horrible old Jew with a Judas Iscariot beard who pimped for his own daughter. He concluded that "a Russian officer's spittle was too precious to be wasted on Jews." A third Jew, with a first-rate plan for smuggling cocaine into England, took 6,000 francs from his victims and double-crossed them by giving them face-powder instead of cocaine (*Works*, 1.16; 34; 124–126).

   But as soon as he began to meet Jewish friends—Jon Kimche, Rosalind Obermeyer and Michael Sayers in Hampstead; Benjamin Lewinski and Harry Milton in Spain; Fyvel and Koestler (with whom he disagreed about Zionism and Palestine); Victor Gollancz and Fredric Warburg in publishing and, later on, A.J. Ayer, Julian Symons and Michael Meyer—his attitude changed and hostility to Jews disappeared from his work. In an essay on "Anti-Semitism in Britain," published in the *Contemporary Jewish Record* in April 1945, Orwell warned that "anti-Semitism is on the increase, that it has been greatly exacerbated by the war, and that humane and enlightened people are not immune to it" (*Works*, 17.64).

11. Wartime Propagandist

1. *Works*, 13.5 (Editorial note); Interview with Martin Esslin, London, November 29, 1998; *Works*, 13.354 ("War Diary," June 10, 1942) and *Works*, 9.148.

2. Martin Esslin, "Television and Telescreen," *On "Nineteen Eighty-Four,"* ed. Peter Stansky (Stanford, California, 1983), p. 127 and Interview with Martin Esslin; *Works,* 9.62.

3. Elisabeth Knight, in Shelden, *Orwell,* p. 344; Orwell, in Fyvel, *George Orwell,* p. 122; *Works,* 14.103 ("War Diary," Oct. 15, 1942); William Empson, in Gross, *World of Orwell,* p. 96.
   Empson's short essay, though extremely intelligent and perceptive, contains at least four major errors and is a minefield for the biographer. Orwell was *not* writing *Animal Farm* while employed by the BBC; he was *not* a "Burmese Editor"; he did *not* say "the working classes smell"; he did *not* resign from the BBC to care for his son after the death of his wife. He left the BBC in November 1943, adopted the child in June 1944, and Eileen died in March 1945.

4. Bahadur Singh, in Crick, *Orwell,* p. 284; Malcolm Muggeridge, *Chronicles of Wasted Time,* 2.78; Sunday Wilshin, in Wadhams, *Remembering Orwell,* p. 126; Herbert Read, in Woodcock, *Crystal Spirit,* p. 26.

5. *Works,* 15.12 (Letter, March 4, 1943); *Works,* 14.157 ("Imaginary Interview with Swift," Nov. 2, 1942); *Works,* 13.466 ("Voice," Aug. 11, 1942); *Works,* 14.20 ("Voice," Sept. 8, 1942).

6. Woodcock, *Crystal Spirit,* p. 7; Morris, "Some Are More Equal Than Others," p. 90; *Works,* 15.248n (Brander's survey); Laurence Brander, *George Orwell* (London, 1954), p. 8. Though Orwell made hundreds of broadcasts, there is, oddly enough, no recording of his voice in the BBC Sound Archives.

7. *Works,* 13.229 ("War Diary," March 14, 1942); *Works,* 13.470–471; (Letter, Aug. 11, 1942); Orwell, *Homage to Catalonia,* p. 65; *Works,* 13.288–289.

8. *Works,* 13.381–382 ("War Diary," July 1, 1942); *Works,* 15.206; *Works,* 14.214 (Letter, Dec. 2, 1942).

9. I've also found this strange mixture in several other people. The poet-critic Geoffrey Grigson, the literary scholars Donald Greene and Marvin Mudrick had ferocious reputations, but were humane and sympathetic in person. Wyndham Lewis, however, could be pretty rough both in writing and in person.

10. *Works,* 11.67 (Letter, Aug. 3–6, 1937); Stephen Spender, in Crick, *Orwell,* p. 243; *Works,* 13.110–111; *Works,* 13.395 and 399; 15.165 (Letter, July 11, 1943). Philip Larkin thought Orwell's poem "As One Non-Combatant to Another" good enough to include in his *Oxford Book of Twentieth Century English Verse* (Oxford, 1973), pp. 517–521.

11. *Works,* 13.395 and 399 (Pacifism Controversy, Sept. 1942); *Works,* 14.214; Woodcock, *Crystal Spirit,* p. 3.

12. Interview with Henry Dakin (photographs of Langford Court and Mortimer Crescent appear in John Thompson's *Orwell's London* [London, 1984], p. 60); Anthony Powell, *To Keep the Ball Rolling* (1976–1982; London: Penguin, 1983), pp. 131–132; Celia Goodman, "Inez Holden: A Memoir," *London Magazine,* 9–10 (December 1993–January 1994), 33; *Works,* 17.307–308.

13. Jack Barbera and William McBrien, *Stevie: A Biography of Stevie Smith* (1985; New York, 1988), pp. 116–117; 139; Anthony Powell, *Journals, 1990–1992*

(London, 1997), p. 135; Interview with Celia Paget Goodman.

14. *Works*, 4.18 (*Aspidistra*); Celia Paget, in Shelden, *Orwell*, p. 383; Crick, *Orwell*, p. 320.

15. *Works*, 12.540; Inez Holden, in Crick, *Orwell*, pp. 293–294; Michael Meyer, *Words Through a Windowpane* (New York, 1989), p. 66.

16. *Works*, 13.213; Wells, in Peter Lewis, *George Orwell: The Road to 1984* (New York, 1981), p. 5; Norman and Jeanne Mackenzie, *H.G. Wells: A Biography* (New York, 1973), p. 431; Interview with Michael Meyer, London, November 18, 1998; *Works*, 19.406.

17. *Works*, 17.311–312 (Profile of Bevan, Oct. 14, 1945); Interview with Michael Foot, London, November 17, 1998; Letter from Antonia White to Orwell, April 27, 1944, Orwell Archive; Letter from Gerald Brenan to Orwell, June 26, 1944, Orwell Archive.

18. *Works*, 19.37 ("As I Please," Jan. 31, 1947); *Works*, 4.84; *Works*, 16.46 ("As I Please," Dec. 31, 1943); *Works*, 16.231 ("As I Please," May 26, 1944).

19. *Works*, 16.55 (Jan. 7, 1944); *Works*, 16.272 (June 30, 1944); *Works*, 16.363 (Sept. 1, 1944); *Works*, 18.238 (April 12, 1946).

12. Fatherhood and Eileen's Death

1. *Works*, 12.146; Kay Welton Ekevall, in Wadhams, *Remembering Orwell*, p. 57; *Works*, 16.283 (Inez Holden's Journal); Fyvel, *George Orwell*, p. 148; *Works*, 19.462 (Letter, Oct. 29, 1948).

2. Fyvel, *George Orwell*, p. 147 ; *Works*, 17.43 ("As I Please," Feb. 9, 1945); *Works*, 9.22; 9.3.

3. *Works*, 18.396 (*Vogue* profile, Sept. 15, 1946); *Works*, 18.18 ("Just Junk," Jan. 5, 1946); Woodcock, *Crystal Spirit*, pp. 22–23.

4. *Works*, 18.99 ("The Moon Under Water," Feb. 9, 1946); Paul Potts, "Don Quixote on a Bicycle: In Memoriam George Orwell," *London Magazine*, 4 (March 1957), 40; Arthur Koestler, Susan Watson and Jane Dakin Morgan, in Coppard, *Orwell Remembered*, pp. 168, 218, 89.

5. *Works*, 17.122, 106; 17.130; Acton, *More Memoirs of an Aesthete*, p. 152; A.J. Ayer, *A Part of My Life* (New York, 1977), p. 287; A.J. Ayer, in Martine de Courcel, ed., *Malraux: Life and Work* (London, 1976), p. 56.

6. Letter from Hemingway to Harvey Breit, April 16, 1952, in Jeffrey Meyers, *Hemingway: A Biography* (New York, 1985), p. 416; Ernest Hemingway, *True at First Light* (New York, 1999), pp. 139–140.
   In his 1957 essay Paul Potts does not mention the Orwell-Hemingway meeting. But when he reprinted it and wanted to flesh out his thin book *Dante Called You Beatrice* (1960), he made up an entirely predictable encounter at the Hôtel Scribe between the shy Englishman and the blustering American. Hemingway is hostile and obscene until Orwell reveals his identity, then offers him a bottle of Scotch. Potts' account ends just where it should begin, as Orwell enters Hemingway's room and they begin to talk, but he did not have the ability to invent their conver-

sation. In any case, Hemingway was holding court at the Ritz, not the Scribe. Both Crick (324–325) and Shelden (375–376) quote Potts' imaginary account as if it were true.

7. *Works*, 17.53 and 61; *Works*, 17.63 (Letters from Wodehouse to Orwell, Aug. 1, 1945 and from Wodehouse to Denis Mackail, Aug. 11, 1951).

8. *Works*, 17.105 (Eileen to Lettice Cooper); *Works*, 17.96–99 (Eileen to Orwell, March 21, 1945).

9. *Works*, 17.112 (Eileen to Orwell, March 29, 1945); Letter from Catherine Moncure to Jeffrey Meyers, March 17, 1999; Coroner's Inquest, in Crick, *Orwell*, p. 328.

10. Fyvel, *George Orwell*, p. 128; (See *Works*, 17.119 for Orwell hearing the fatal news in Paris, not Cologne); Julian Symons, in Wadhams, *Remembering Orwell*, p. 145; *Works*, 17.118; 17.124.

11. *Works*, 18.249 (Letter, April 18, 1946); Orwell, in a letter from Koestler to David Astor, Jan. 21–25, 1950, Orwell Archive; *Works*, 17. 236 (Letter, Aug. 1, 1945).

12. Celia Paget Goodman, in Wadhams, *Remembering Orwell*, p. 163; Storm Jameson, *Journey from the North: Autobiography* (London, 1970), 2.131; Celia Paget Goodman in Wadhams, *Remembering Orwell*, p. 164; Interview with Celia Paget Goodman; Celia Paget Goodman, in Crick, *George Orwell*, p. 334.

13. T.R. Fyvel, "Arthur Koestler and George Orwell," *Astride the Two Cultures: Arthur Koestler at 70*, ed. Harold Harris (London, 1975), p. 155; Arthur Koestler, "A Rebel's Progress to George Orwell's Death," *The Trail of the Dinosaur* (London, 1955), p. 102.

14. Letter from Celia Paget Goodman to Jeffrey Meyers, February 7, 1999; Conversation with Michael Shelden, September 15, 1998.

15. Anne Popham Bell, in Wadhams, *Remembering Orwell*, p. 166; Interview with Anne Popham Bell, Firle, East Sussex, November 23, 1998; *Works*, 18.248–249 and 153–154 (Letters, April 16 and March 15, 1946); Franz Kafka, *Letters to Felice*, ed. Erich Heller and Jürgen Born, trans. James Stern and Elisabeth Duckworth (London, 1974), pp. 216, 293, 315.

13. *Animal Farm* and Fame

1. Susan Watson, in Coppard, *Orwell Remembered*, p. 217; Susan Watson, in Wadhams, *Remembering Orwell*, p. 157; Susan Watson, in Crick, *Orwell*, pp. 347, 349; *Works*, 12.246 ("War Diary," 1940); Interview with Dr. Howard Nicholson, Laughton, East Sussex, November 23, 1998; Most of the material in this section comes from my interview with Susan Watson.

2. *Works*, 19.88; Letter from Victor Gollancz to Orwell, March 23, 1944, Orwell Archive; Hodges, *Victor Gollancz*, p. 109; *Works*, 17.207.

3. Michael Howard, *Jonathan Cape, Publisher* (London, 1971), p. 179; Letter from Jonathan Cape to Leonard Moore, June 16, 1944, Orwell Archive; *Works*, 16.276 ("As I Please," July 7, 1944); *Works*, 16.266 n1.

4. Interview with Michael Meyer; Eliot, in Meyers, *Critical Heritage*, pp. 19–20; *Works*, 8.17–18; 18.123 (Letter, Feb. 1946).

5. Warburg, *Occupation for Gentlemen*, p. 14; *Works*, 19.88; 19.451 (Letter, Oct. 9, 1948); *Works*, 8.86; 8.80.

6. T.S. Eliot, "Tradition and the Individual Talent," *Selected Essays, 1917–1932* (New York, 1932), p. 7; *Works*, 18.320; *Works*, 8.90.

   Orwell's inscription in his Everyman's edition of Milton reveals that he'd seriously, if reluctantly, studied *Paradise Lost* at Eton in 1920–21: "E.A. Blair K[ing's] S[cholar]. Bought this book Much against his will For the study of Milton a poet for whom he had no love" (Buddicom, *Eric and Us*, p. 122).

7. *Works*, 11.317 (Review, Jan. 12, 1939); *Works*, 8.22; 8.95; Karl Marx, *Economic and Philosophic Manuscripts of 1844*, trans. Martin Milligan, ed. and intro. Dirk Struik (New York, 1964), p. 111; Joseph Conrad, *Under Western Eyes* (1911; New York: Anchor, 1963), p. 113.

8. Letter from Empson to Orwell, August 24, 1945, Orwell Archive; Peter Viereck, "Bloody-Minded Professors," *Confluence*, 1 (September 1952), pp. 36–37; Meyers, *Critical Heritage*, pp. 195–205; Arthur Schlesinger, Jr., "Mr. Orwell and the Communists," *New York Times Book Review*, August 25, 1946, pp. 1, 28.

9. William Empson, in Gross, *The World of Orwell*, p. 99. The talking animals spawned a great many children's books, from Jane Doe's derivative and amateurish *Anarchist Farm* (Gualala, California, 1996) to Martin Waddell's prize-winning *Farmer Duck* (1991), in which the lazy farmer is driven out by the oppressed animals who take over the farm and work happily together—an ending that deliberately missed the point of Orwell's book.

10. Letter from Frank Morley to Orwell, April 16, 1946, Orwell Archive; *Works*, 18.115 (Letter, Feb. 19, 1946).

    According to Fenwick, *George Orwell: A Bibliography*, pp. 103, 107, "by 1973 more than 2 million Penguin copies had been sold, and it continues to sell about 140,000 copies a year." By 1973 the U.S. Signet edition "had sold over 5,000,000 copies, and continues to sell more than 350,000 a year."

11. *Works*, 16.411–412 ("London Letter," Winter 1944); Anthony Powell, in "Orwell," BBC World Service, December 30, 1983 (Celia Paget Goodman kindly gave me this tape); Symons, "Orwell: A Reminiscence," p. 41. In his novel *The Military Philosophers* (London, 1968), p. 215, Powell uses the Orwellian phrase "Big Brother."

12. Letter from Lady Violet Powell to Jeffrey Meyers, December 13, 1998; *Works*, 12.151 (Review, Apr. 25, 1940); Malcolm Muggeridge, *The Thirties* (1940; London, 1971), p. 11; Malcolm Muggeridge, Introduction to *Animal Farm* (New York: Time, 1965), p. xx.

13. *Works*, 16.221 (*The English People*, 1947); *Works*, 13.314–316 (Review, May 10, 1942); Meyers, *Critical Heritage*, pp. 224–226; 309–311; *Works*, 18.244 (Letter, April 13, 1946).

14. Escape to Jura

1. *Works*, 12.188; Interview with David Astor; *Works*, 18.205 ("British Cookery," March 29, 1946); *Works*, 12.153 (Review, April 26, 1940).

2. W.H. Murray, *The Hebrides* (London, 1966), p. 56; Margaret Fletcher Nelson, in Wadhams, *Remembering Orwell*, p. 171; Lewis, *George Orwell*, p. 111.

3. Rees, *George Orwell*, p. 140; Lewis, *George Orwell*, p. 108; Bill Dunn and David Astor, in Wadhams, *Remembering Orwell*, pp. 184–185; 170; Sonia Orwell, BBC interview, May 20, 1963, Orwell Archive; Crick, *Orwell*, p. 354, states that "the climate was mild" and the island salubrious.

4. Margaret Fletcher, in Roger Ratcliffe, "The Dream Island Where Orwell Had His Nightmare Vision," *Sunday Times* (London), May 22, 1983, p. 5; *Works*, 19.461 (Letter, Oct. 29, 1948); Bill Dunn, in Crick, *Orwell*, p. 364.

5. Interview with Richard Blair, near Rugby, Warwickshire, November 25, 1998; Letter from Georges Kopp to Orwell, March 20, 1946, Orwell Archive; *Works*, 18.250 (Letter, April 18, 1946).

6. Interview with Richard Blair; Interview with Jane Morgan and Lucy Bestley; Rees' painting is reproduced in Lewis, *George Orwell*, p. 75.

7. *Works*, 20.107 (Letter, May 7, 1949); Letter from Michel Kopp to Jeffrey Meyers, December 9, 1998; Interview with Jane Morgan and Lucy Bestley.

8. Letter from Catherine Moncure to Jeffrey Meyers, March 17, 1999; David Holbrook, *The Inevitable Price*, pp. 72; 73 (David Holbrook kindly gave me a copy of his unpublished novel); Interview with David Holbrook, Cambridge, England, November 24, 1998.
   Orwell gave a similar account of the deer. See *Works*, 18.411 ("Domestic Diary," Sept. 28, 1946): "Two stags standing close together near the old stable, about 100 yards from the road, & roaring in a very bellicose manner, apparently at me."

9. Holbrook, *The Inevitable Price*, pp. 81; 78; 80; Interview with David Holbrook.

10. Susan Watson, in Michael Simmons, "Beauty of the Bleak," *Guardian*, October 16, 1993, p. 62; Interview with Susan Watson; Katie Darroch, in Crick, *Orwell*, p. 358; Interview with Jane Morgan.

11. *Works*, 10.501 ("Shooting an Elephant," 1936); *Works*, 12.392 ("England Your England," 1941); *Works*, 20.5 ("Reflections on Gandhi," 1949); *Works*, 16. 233 ("Salvador Dali," 1944).
    The opening of the Dali essay may have come from Heine through Dostoyevsky. In *Notes from Underground*, trans. Andrew MacAndrew (1864; New York: Signet, 1961), p. 122, Dostoevsky mentions "Heine's remark to the effect that sincere autobiographies are almost impossible and that a man is bound to lie about himself."

12. *Works*, 12.282 (Review, Nov. 9, 1940); *Works*, 13.210 ("Re-discovery of Europe," March 10, 1942); *Works*, 13.151–152, 156, 160 ("Rudyard Kipling"); *Works*, 14.279, 283 ("W.B. Yeats").

13. *Works*, 13.30 ("The Art of Donald McGill"); *Works*, 16.347, 349, 350, 354 ("Raffles and Miss Blandish"); *Works*, 16.234, 238, 239, 240 ("Salvador Dali").

14. Julian Symons, "Meeting Wyndham Lewis," *Critical Occasions* (London, 1966), p. 189; *Works*, 17.349 ("Good Bad Books," Nov. 2, 1945); *Works*, 18.287 ("London Letter," Summer 1946).

15. Wyndham Lewis, *Letters*, ed. W.K. Rose (Norfolk, Conn., 1963), p. 403; Wyndham Lewis, *Rude Assignment* (London, 1950), pp. 79–80; Interview with Hugh Gordon Porteous, Cheltenham, Sept. 21, 1978.

    Macdonald, who'd left *Partisan* in 1944 to found *Politics* and was keen to have Orwell's contributions, responded to his cautious request "for a pair of American shoes, in separate parcels, since 'then it's not worth anyone's while to pinch them, unless there happened to be a one-legged man at the dock.' " In December 1946, after buying a splendid pair of size 12 walking shoes for $8.95, Macdonald scuffed them up a bit, packed them with some garb and sent them in a package marked "old clothes" (Letter from Michael Macdonald to Jeffrey Meyers, October 3, 1998 and Letter from Dwight Macdonald to Orwell, December 21, 1946, Orwell Archive).

16. Martin Martin, *A Description of the Western Isles of Scotland, Circa 1695*, ed. Donald Mcleod (1703: Stirling: Eneas Mackay, 1934), p. 270; Clyde Cruising Club, *Sailing Directions and Anchorages. Part 2: Kintyre to Ardnamurchan* (Glasgow, 1981), p. 36. For a photo of the formidable whirlpool of Corryvrecken, see Donald Budge, *Jura, An Island of Argyll: Its History, People and Story* (Glasgow: John Smith, 1960), opposite p. 16.

17. Lucy Bestley, in Wadhams, *Remembering Orwell*, p. 190; Interview with Richard Blair; Interview with Henry Dakin; Interview with Lucy Bestley.

18. *Works*, 19.190 ("Domestic Diary," Aug. 19, 1947); *Works*, 20.202–203; Warburg, *Occupation for Gentlemen*, p. 234.

15. The Dark Vision of *Nineteen Eighty-Four*

1. *Works*, 20.204 ("Literary Notebook," 1949); J.B. Pick, "A Bed at Hairmyres," *Scots Magazine*, 121 (April 1984), 44; Alan Campbell, *Hairmyres: The History of the Hospital, 1904–1993* (Hamilton, Scotland: Lanarkshire Health Board, 1994), p. 22.

2. Interview with Dr. James Williamson, Edinburgh, November 17, 1998; Williamson, in Wadhams, *Remembering Orwell*, pp. 197–198; *Works*, 19.247 (Letter, Jan. 1, 1948); Letter from Dr. James Williamson to Bernard Crick, September 12, 1983, Orwell Archive.

3. *Works*, 19.394; *Works*, 19.340 ("Diary," May 21, 1948).

4. Warburg, *All Authors Are Equal*, p. 99; Campbell, *Hairmyres*, pp. 22–23; Interview with Dr. James Williamson; Fyvel, *George Orwell*, p. 156; *Works*, 19.450 (Letter, Oct. 9, 1948).

5. Sonia Brownell, in Fyvel, *George Orwell*, p. 160; T.R. Fyvel, "Remembering Fred Warburg," *Encounter*, 59 (August 1982), 35; Interview with Richard Blair; *Works*, 20.23 (Letter, Jan. 18, 1949).

6. *Works*, 16.208 (*The English People*, May 1944); *Works*, 19.438 ("The Labour Government After Three Years," Oct. 1948); *Works*, 9.63.

7. *Works*, 16.138 ("As I Please," March 11, 1944); For the sinking of the *City of Benares*, see the *Times* (London), September 28, 1940, p. 4.

8. *Works*, 9.32; 9.30; 9.71; *Works*, 19.381.

9. *Works*, 9.138; 9.132; 9.172–173.

10. *Works*, 9.264; *Works*, 19.359 ("Such, Such"); *Works*, 9.280.

11. David Astor, in Wadhams, *Remembering Orwell*, p. 199; Interview with Dr. James Williamson; *Works*, 9.284-285.

12. *Works*, 19.457 (Letter, Oct. 22, 1948); *Works*, 18.318 ("Why I Write"); *Works*, 12.22 ("Charles Dickens," March 1940).

13. Steven Runciman, in Okuyama, *George Orwell*, p. 15; Angus Wilson, Arena Television, "Orwell in 1984," Orwell Archive; *Works*, 9.275-276.

14. Meyers, *Critical Heritage*, 247–293; Aldous Huxley, *Letters*, ed. Grover Smith (New York, 1969), pp. 604–605; Mark Schorer, "An Indignant and Prophetic Novel," *New York Times Book Review*, June 12, 1949, p. 1; Lionel Trilling, "Orwell on the Future," *New Yorker*, 25 (June 18, 1949), pp. 78–83; Interview with David Astor.

15. Letter from Lawrence Durrell to Orwell, June–July 1949, Orwell Archive; Czeslaw Milosz, *The Captive Mind*, trans. Jane Zielenko (New York, 1953), p. 42.

16. *Works*, 20.82 (Letter, April 8, 1949); John Rodden, *Politics of Literary Reputation: The Making and Claiming of "St. George" Orwell* (New York, 1989), p. 16; *Works*, 13.157 ("Rudyard Kipling," Feb. 1942).

16. The Art of Dying

1. *Works*, 19.460; *Works*, 20.23 (Letter, Jan. 18, 1949); Pick, "A Bed at Hairmyres," p. 48; *Works*, 20.70 ("Literary Notebook," March 21, 1949).

2. Thomas Mann, *The Magic Mountain*, trans. H.T. Lowe-Porter (1924; London, 1957), p. 432; Olivier Todd, *Albert Camus: A Life*, trans. Benjamin Ivry (New York, 1997), pp. 259, 162; *Works*, 20.28 (Letter, Jan. 27, 1949); *Works*, 20.119n (Orwell to Charles Curran, May 28–29, 1949).

3. Jane Morgan, in Wadhams, *Remembering Orwell*, p. 203; Fredric Warburg, in Coppard, *Orwell Remembered*, p. 197; Malcolm Muggeridge, *Like It Was: Diaries*, ed. John Bright-Holmes (London, 1976), pp. 323–324.

4. Buddicom, *Eric and Us*, p. 150; *Works*, 20.116 (Letter, May 16, 1949); Buddicom, *Eric and Us*, p. 151; Interview with Richard Blair; Lettice Cooper, in Wadhams, *Remembering Orwell*, p. 196.

5. Interview with Celia Paget Goodman; *Works*, 20.318–319 (Editorial note); *Works*, 20.322 (Letter, April 6, 1949); *Works*, 20.103 (Letter, May 2, 1949); *Works*, 20.244-256 (Orwell's List, April 1949).

6. *Works*, 19.301 (Letter, March 23, 1948); Robert Conquest, "In Celia's Office,"

Times Literary Supplement, August 21, 1998, p. 4; *Works*, 20.136 (Letter, June 15, 1949).

7. Janetta Woolley Parladé in Shelden, *Orwell*, p. 409; *Works*, 20.308n (Leiris on Sonia, 1987); James Lord, *A Gift for Admiration: Further Memoirs* (New York, 1998), p. 114; Interview with Anne Popham Bell (on Sonia and the Euston Road painters). See *The Paintings of William Coldstream, 1908–1987* (London: Tate Gallery, 1990), p. 82. This portrait, once owned by J.B. Priestley, has disappeared.

8. John Lehmann, *I Am My Brother* (London, 1960), pp. 143-144; Stephen Spender, *Journals, 1939–1983*, ed. John Goldsmith (New York, 1986), p. 433; Letter from Cyril Connolly to Anne Dunn, in Michael Shelden, *Friends of Promise: Cyril Connolly and the World of "Horizon"* (New York, 1989), p. 75.

9. Diana Witherby, in Wadhams, *Remembering Orwell*, p. 213; David Plante, *Difficult Women* (1983; New York, 1984), p. 172; Interview with Waldemar Hansen, New York, Sept. 20, 1998.

10. Interviews with Anne Popham Bell; Robert Kee, London, November 17, 1998; Michael Meyer; Celia Paget Goodman; Joanna Kilmartin, London, November 16, 1998; Janetta Woolley Parladé, London, November 16, 1998; Anthony and Sarah Curtis, London, November 15, 1998 (Mabel Fierz liked to contradict experts in the same way); Letter from Ian Angus to Jeffrey Meyers, June 27, 1999.

11. Lionel Abel, *The Intellectual Follies* (New York, 1984), p. 209; Angus Wilson, *Anglo-Saxon Attitudes* (1956; London: Penguin, 1958), pp. 172–173; Interview with Celia Paget Goodman (on Merleau-Ponty); *Works*, 8.2–3, 30. Sonia was also the model for Ada Leitwardine in Anthony Powell's *Books Do Furnish a Room* (1971).

12. *Works*, 9.126, 128; 12; 17; 33, 131; 133; 115; *Works*, 20.159 (Letter to Fredric Warburg, Aug. 22, 1949); *Works*, 9.118.

13. Warburg, *All Authors Are Equal*, p. 108; *Works*, 20.166 ("Literary Notebook," Sept. 1949); Interview with Dr. Howard Nicholson; Dr. Howard Nicholson, in Wadhams, *Remembering Orwell*, p. 214. For Morland's obituary, see the *Times* (London), July 15, 1957, p. 14.

14. Fyvel, *George Orwell*, pp. 162; 1; Muggeridge, *Like It Was: Diaries*, pp. 361–362, 366, 368, 371; Ian Hunter, *Malcolm Muggeridge: A Life* (London, 1980), pp. 177–178; Powell, "George Orwell," p. 67.

15. Interview with Natasha Spender, London, November 20, 1998; Malcolm Muggeridge, Introduction to *Burmese Days* (New York: Time, 1962), p. xiii; Letter from Celia Paget Goodman to Jeffrey Meyers, January 7, 1999.

16. Lewis Moorman, *Tuberculosis and Genius* (Chicago, 1940), p. xxix; *Works*, 20.159 (Letter to Warburg, Aug. 22, 1949); *Works*, 20.147 (Letter to Astor, July 18, 1949); *Works*, 20.165 (Letter to Astor, Sept. 5, 1949).

17. Lys Lubbock and Humphrey Dakin, in Shelden, *Orwell*, pp. 410, 441; Interview with Dr. Howard Nicholson; Interview with David Astor.

18. Interview with Natasha Spender; Interview with Janetta Parladé; Letter from Anne Dunn to Jeffrey Meyers, Dec. 28, 1998.

19. Diana Witherby, in Shelden, *Orwell*, pp. 438; Interview with Waldemar Hansen; Interview with Robert Kee.

20. Interview with David Astor; David Astor, in Wadhams, *Remembering Orwell*, p. 211; Frances Partridge, *Everything to Lose: Diaries, 1945–1960* (London, 1985), p. 98 (Oct. 18, 1949—five days after Orwell's marriage); Interview with Anne Popham Bell; Letter from Francis King to Jeffrey Meyers, Oct. 15, 1998; Letter from Ian Angus to Jeffrey Meyers, June 27, 1999.

21. Interviews with Celia Goodman and Janetta Parladé (on the engagement ring); Interview with Waldemar Hansen; Stephen Spender, *Journals*, pp. 108–109; Lord, *Gift for Admiration*, p. 122.

22. Interview with Robert Kee; David Astor, in Wadhams, *Remembering Orwell*, p. 210; Cesarani, *Arthur Koestler*, p. 347.

23. Bernard Crick, "On the Orwell Trail," *Essays on Politics and Literature* (Edinburgh, 1989), p. 217; For Orwell's assets and debtors, see *Works*, 20.218 ("Literary Notebook," late 1949); Bernard Crick, Letter, *Times Literary Supplement*, November 1, 1991, p. 15.

24. Fyvel, *George Orwell*, p. 167; *Works*, 11.379 (Review, July 27, 1939); *Works*, 17.191, 196 (Reviews, June 24 and 28, 1945); *Works*, 20.47 (Letter, Feb. 25, 1949). Orwell admired Koestler for similar reasons.

25. Evelyn Waugh, *Letters*, ed. Mark Amory (New Haven, 1980), p. 211n; Fyvel, *George Orwell*, p. 168; *Works*, 20.75 ("Evelyn Waugh," April 1949).

26. Andrew Morland, "The Mind in Tubercule," *Lancet*, January 23, 1932, p. 176; Koestler, *Stranger on the Square*, p. 90; John Sherwood, *No Golden Journey: A Biography of James Elroy Flecker* (London, 1973), p. 189; Interview with Dr. Howard Nicholson; Dr. Howard Nicholson in Wadhams, *Remembering Orwell*, p. 215.

27. Orwell, *Homage to Catalonia*, p. 40; *Works*, 20.116 (Letter, May 16, 1949); Interview with Celia Paget Goodman; *Works*, 7.237.

28 *Works*, 20.203 ("Literary Notebook," 1949); Interview with Dr. Howard Nicholson.

29. Letter from Anne Dunn to Jeffrey Meyers, December 28, 1998; *Works*, 20.169 (Letter, Sept. 17, 1949); Letter from Violet Powell to Jeffrey Meyers, December 13, 1998.
    Shelden, *Orwell*, p. 442, says the hospital managed to find and call Sonia—not the other way round.

30. Potts, "Don Quixote on a Bicycle," p. 44; Powell, *To Keep the Ball Rolling*, p. 321; Muggeridge, *Like It Was: Diaries*, p. 376.

31. Interview with David Astor; Cockett, *David Astor and the "Observer"*, p. 130; Koestler, "A Rebel's Progress," pp. 102–104; Meyers, *Critical Heritage*, p. 294.

32. Mabel Fierz, in Wadhams, *Remembering Orwell*, p. 44; Cyril Connolly, "George Orwell," *Previous Convictions* (New York, 1963), p. 317.

7. Epilogue: Orwell's Legacy

1. Sonia Orwell, in Michael Shelden, *Friends of Promise*, p. 160; Interview with Henry Dakin; Letter from Catherine Moncure to Jeffrey Meyers, March 17, 1999.

2. George Weidenfeld, *Remembering My Good Friends* (New York, 1994), p. 240; Interviews with Richard Blair, Celia Paget Goodman, Natasha Spender and Janetta Parladé (on Sonia and Pitt-Rivers).

3. Shelden, *Friends of Promise*, p. 77; Heppenstall, *Journals*, p. 263; Sonia Orwell, Introduction to George Orwell, *Collected Essays, Journalism and Letters*, 4 volumes (New York, 1968), 1: xvi, xix, xvi–xvii.

   For my reviews of Sonia's and Davison's editions, see Meyers, *Critical Heritage*, pp. 373–381; and Jeffrey Meyers, "A Voice That Naked Goes," *London Magazine*, (February–March 2001).

4. Interview with Sir Steven Runciman; Heppenstall, *Journals*, p. 263; Letter from John Wain to Jeffrey Meyers, October 21, 1970.

   Orwell's publisher Tom Rosenthal found it extremely difficult to deal with Sonia, who "once went beserk over a single word on the jacket blurb for an Orwell reprint and demanded the pulping of 20,000 large books" ("Putting on her Orwell's Widow Act," *Daily Telegraph*, June 27, 1998).

   In the spring of 1968 I won a grant from my university to do research at the Orwell Archive. I wrote in advance to the director of the library asking if I could read the unpublished letters and manuscripts, and duly received his permission. But when I arrived that summer and certified in writing that I was not working on a biography, I was icily informed that the unpublished material was closed and that I could read only what was already in print (which I had already done). I appealed to the English sense of fairness but was told that only Sonia Orwell could grant me access to the papers, and that she would never do so.

   For my reviews of the Orwell biographies, see *Modern Fiction Studies*, 19 (Summer 1973), 250–256; *Virginia Quarterly Review*, 58 (Spring 1982), 353–359; and *Boston Globe*, October 27, 1991, p. A-16.

5. Michael Peppiatt, *Francis Bacon: The Anatomy of an Enigma* (New York, 1996), p. 203; Interview with Michael Meyer; Interview with Peter Stansky, Hillsborough, California, September 19, 1998; Interview with Janetta Parladé.

6. Plante, *Difficult Women*, p. 97; Stephen Spender, in Wadhams, *Remembering Orwell*, p. 211.

7. Bernard Crick, Letter, *Times Literary Supplement*, November 1, 1991, p. 15; Letter from Anne Dunn to Jeffrey Meyers, December 28, 1998; Margaret Drabble, *Angus Wilson: A Biography* (1993; London, 1996), pp. 533, 605; Interviews with Richard Blair, Celia Paget Goodman, Natasha Spender and Janetta Parladé.

8. Yasuharu Okuyama, *Orwell: The Man for All Times* (Tokyo: Waseda University Press, 1999), pp. 10, 9; Timothy Garton Ash, *The File* (New York, 1997), p. 20; See William Blair, "Orwell and Poland's Solidarity Movement," *Polish-American Journal*, January 1996, p. 13 and Peter Stansky, "The Orwell Year," *Dictionary of Literary Biography Yearbook, 1984*, ed. Jean Ross (Detroit: Gale, 1985), pp. 52–62; David Remnick, *Lenin's Tomb* (New York, 1993), p. 122.

9. Fred Inglis, *The Cruel Peace* (London, 1991), pp. 103–104; Abbot Gleason,

Totalitarianism: The Inner History of the Cold War (New York, 1995), p. 84, both quoted in John Newsinger, *Orwell's Politics* (London, 1999), p. 122; Julius Epstein, Philip Epstein and Howard Koch, *Casablanca*, ed. Richard Anobile (New York, 1974), p. 77.

Orwell—who had the same high bristling hair, long cadaverous face, prominent nose, sad eyes and mournful expression as Cézanne's portrait of his patron and friend Victor Choquet (1877)—inspired sculpture and paintings as well as satires and plays. A crude relief of his head appears on a plaque at the corner of Pond Street and South End Road in Hampstead, where he worked in the bookstore in 1934–35. Richard Rees painted his bedroom in Barnhill, and Warburg's wife Pamela de Bayou did a vivid charcoal portrait in the summer of 1940. The plaque is reproduced in *The World of George Orwell*, opposite p. 159; de Bayou's drawing appears in Warburg's *All Authors Are Equal*, opposite p. 36.

Orwell's sickening account in *Down and Out* of how food is prepared in luxurious French restaurants was mentioned in a kitchen scene in the BBC television comedy series "Fawlty Towers." The "Pseuds' Corner" column in *Private Eye* evolved directly from Orwell's examples of pretentious jargon in "Politics and the English Language" (1946). At least three plays have been written about him: Robert Holman's *Outside the Whale* (1976) portrays his years as a schoolmaster, Steven Lowe's *Divine Gossip* (1988) his impoverished period in Paris, Michael MacEwoy's *The Last Man in Europe* (1998)—the original title of *Nineteen Eighty-Four*—about his time in the Cranham sanatorium.

10. Robert Frost, *Poetry*, ed. Edward Connery Lathem (New York, 1975), p. 460; Sylvia Plath, *Collected Poems*, ed. Ted Hughes (New York, 1981), p. 223 (See also pp. 29, 118, 197); Dana Gioia, *The Gods of Winter* (St. Paul: Graywolf, 1991), p. 29.

    Stevie Smith and Anthony Powell modeled characters on Orwell; and his works have also inspired titles, allusions, postcolonial and futuristic novels, fictionalized versions of biography and history. The title of Nancy Mitford's *Love in a Cold Climate* (1949) comes from *Keep the Aspidistra Flying* (4.135) just as Iris Murdoch's *The Book and the Brotherhood* (1987) alludes to Goldstein's book and Big Brother in *Nineteen Eighty-Four*. In *Mr. Sammler's Planet* (1970; New York: Fawcett, 1971), p. 42, Saul Bellow mentions Orwell's remark that British radicals were free to speak because they were "all protected by the British Navy." In William Boyd's *A Good Man in Africa* (1981), the Orwellian hero, Morgan Leafy, is a comic version of John Flory. Overweight, alcoholic and depressive, he pursues a girl in a steamy, inhospitable and snobbish postcolonial society.

    György Dalos' *1985: A Historical Report* (1982) also continues the genre of *Nineteen Eighty-Four*. Margaret Atwood, who greatly admired Orwell's literary essays, acknowledged that "*Animal Farm* and *1984* were obviously important for *The Handmaid's Tale*" (1985) (Letter from Margaret Atwood to Jeffrey Meyers, October 27, 1998). Her novel depicts a corrupt and claustrophobic totalitarian society, based on a global stalemate and formalized spheres of influence. David Caute, who's written important books on Communism, has in *Dr. Orwell and Mr. Blair* (1994) given a fictionalized account of how Orwell came to write *Animal Farm*.

    Orwell's work could also be misused. Claude Simon's *The Georgics* (1981), which alludes to Orwell's first name, attempts to incorporate the action of *Homage to Catalonia* into his own fiction. Rewriting Orwell's text without quoting it directly and paraphrasing great chunks of material without analysis or insight, Simon, while criticizing Orwell's attempt to represent reality, makes the subject both pretentious and boring.

11. Blake Morrison, *The Movement: English Poetry and Fiction of the 1950s* (1980; London, 1986), pp. 94–95; Letter from Thom Gunn to Jeffrey Meyers, October 19, 1998.

12. Robert Conquest, Introduction to *New Lines* (London, 1956), p. xv; Robert Conquest, "George Orwell," *Arias From a Love Opera* (London, 1968), p. 32.

13. Kingsley Amis, *Socialism and the Intellectuals* (London, 1957), p. 8; Kingsley Amis, "The Road to Airstrip One," *Spectator*, 197 (August 31, 1956), 292; *Works*, 18.319–320; John Osborne and Anthony Creighton, *Epitaph for George Dillon* (New York, 1958), p. 87.

14. Letter from Alan Sillitoe to Jeffrey Meyers, October 1, 1998; Letter from David Lodge to Jeffrey Meyers, October 11, 1998.

15. Anthony Burgess, *The Malayan Trilogy* (1956–59; London: Pan, 1964), p. 247; Letter from Tom Stoppard to Jeffrey Meyers, December 14, 1998. My discussion of Bradbury, Burgess and Stoppard is based on Valerie Meyers, *George Orwell* (London, 1991), pp. 143–145.

16. Tom Wolfe, *The New Journalism* (New York, 1973), p. 45; Norman Mailer, BBC Television, "The Road to the Left," Orwell Archive; Norman Mailer, Arena Television, "Orwell in 1984," Orwell Archive.

17. Letter from Paul Theroux to Jeffrey Meyers, October 2, 1998; Bharati Mukherjee and Robert Boyers, "A Conversation with V.S. Naipaul," *Salmagundi*, 54 (Fall 1981), 11; Angus Wilson, BBC Television, "The Road to the Left," Orwell Archive.

18. Letter from Doris Lessing to Jeffrey Meyers, October 1, 1998; Letter from John le Carré to Jeffrey Meyers, September 27, 1998; Thomas Carlyle, *On Heroes and Hero Worship* (1841; London: Everyman, 1959), p. 411.

Bibliography

I

Orwell, George. *Down and Out in Paris and London* (1933)
    Burmese Days (1934)
    A Clergyman's Daughter (1935)
    Keep the Aspidistra Flying (1936)
    The Road to Wigan Pier (1937)
    Homage to Catalonia (1938)
    Coming Up for Air (1939)
    Animal Farm (1945)
    Nineteen Eighty-Four (1949)
    Complete Works. Ed. Peter Davison, assisted by Ian Angus and Sheila
        Davison. 20 volumes. London: Secker & Warburg, 1998.

II

Atkins, John. *George Orwell: A Literary and Biographical Study*. New York: Ungar,
    1954.
Beadon, Roger, "With Orwell in Burma," *Listener*, 81 (May 29, 1969), 755.
Brander, Laurence. *George Orwell*. London: Longmans, 1954.
Buddicom, Jacintha. *Eric and Us: A Remembrance of George Orwell*. London: Leslie
    Frewen, 1974.
Christie, W.H.J., "St. Cyprian's Days," *Blackwood's Magazine*, 309 (May 1971),
    385–397.
Common, Jack, "Orwell at Wallington," *Stand*, 22:3 (1980–81), 32–36.
Connolly, Cyril. *Enemies of Promise*. 1938; New York: Anchor, 1960.
Coppard, Audrey, and Bernard Crick. *Orwell Remembered*. London: BBC, 1984.
Crick, Bernard. *George Orwell: A Life*. Boston: Atlantic–Little, Brown, 1980.
Dunn, Avril, "My Brother, George Orwell," *Twentieth Century*, 169 (March 1960),
    255–261.
Edwards, Bob. Introduction to *Homage to Catalonia*. London: Folio Society, 1970. Pp.
    5–11.

n, Elisaveta, "George Orwell's First Wife," *Twentieth Century*, 168 (August 1960), 115–126.

Fen, Elisaveta. *A Russian's England: Reminiscences of Years 1926–1940*. Warwick: Paul Gordon, 1976. Pp. 341–349, 377–378, 417–419, 430–432, 448–449.

Fenwick, Gillian. *George Orwell: A Bibliography*. Newcastle, Delaware: Oak Knoll Press, 1998.

Fyvel, T.R. *George Orwell: A Personal Memoir*. New York: Macmillan, 1982.

Gross, Miriam, ed. *The World of George Orwell*. London: Weidenfeld & Nicolson, 1971.

Heppenstall, Rayner. *Four Absentees*. London: Barrie & Rockcliff, 1960.

Heppenstall, Rayner. *The Master Eccentric: The Journals of Rayner Heppenstall, 1969–1981*. Ed. Jonathan Goodman. London: Allison & Busby, 1986. Pp. viii, 11, 22, 51n, 52n, 76, 112n, 118, 119n, 141n, 175, 257–258, 262–263. On Sonia: 32, 117, 119, 258, 262–263.

Hollis, Christopher, "George Orwell and His Schooldays," *Listener*, 51 (March 4, 1954), 382–383.

Hollis, Christopher. *A Study of George Orwell*. Chicago: Henry Regnery, 1956.

Hopkinson, Tom, "George Orwell: Dark Side Out," *Cornhill*, 166 (1953), 450–470.

Koestler, Arthur. "A Rebel's Progress to George Orwell's Death." *The Trail of the Dinosaur*. London: Collins, 1955. Pp. 102–105.

Lewis, Jeremy. *Cyril Connolly: A Life*. London: Cape, 1997.

Maung Htin Aung, "George Orwell and Burma," *Asian Affairs*, 57 (February 1970), 19–28.

Maung Htin Aung, "Orwell of the Burma Police," *Asian Affairs*, 60 (June 1973), 181–186.

McNair, John, "George Orwell: The Man I Knew," *Controversy*, 1 (1962), 3–5.

Meyers, Jeffrey. *A Reader's Guide to George Orwell*. London: Thames and Hudson, 1975.

Meyers, Jeffrey. *George Orwell: The Critical Heritage*. London: Routledge & Kegan Paul, 1975.

Meyers, Jeffrey, and Valerie. *George Orwell: An Annotated Bibliography of Criticism*. New York: Garland, 1977.

Meyers, Valerie. *George Orwell*. London: Macmillan, 1991.

Morris, John, " 'Some Are More Equal Than Others': A Note on George Orwell," *Penguin New Writing*, 40 (1950), 90–97.

Okuyama, Yasuharu. *George Orwell*. Tokyo: Waseda University Press, 1983. In Japanese, with interviews in English with Sir Steven Runciman, "Eton Days with Eric Blair," pp. 6–17, and "Mr. F.A.S. Fierz's Reminiscences of Eric Blair," pp. 18–25.

Peters, R.S. "A Boy's View of George Orwell." *Psychology and Ethical Development*. London: Allen & Unwin, 1974. Pp. 460–463.

Potts, Paul, "Don Quixote on a Bicycle: In Memoriam, George Orwell," *London Magazine*, 4 (March 1957), 39–47.

Powell, Anthony, "George Orwell: A Memoir," *Atlantic Monthly*, 220 (October 1967), 62–68.

Pritchett, V.S., "George Orwell," *New Statesman*, 39 (January 28, 1950), 96.

Rees, Richard. *George Orwell: Fugitive from the Camp of Victory.*1962; Carbondale: Southern Illinois University Press, 1965.

Reynolds, Reginald. *My Life and Crimes*. London: Jarrolds, 1956. Pp. 211–215.

Rodden, John. *The Politics of Literary Reputation: The Making and Claiming of "St.*

George" Orwell. New York: Oxford, 1989.

Shelden, Michael. *Orwell: The Authorized Biography*. New York: HarperCollins, 1991.

Stansky, Peter, and William Abrahams. *The Unknown Orwell*. New York: Knopf, 1972.

Stansky, Peter, and William Abrahams. *Orwell: The Transformation*. London: Constable, 1979.

Symons, Julian, "Orwell, A Reminiscence," *London Magazine*, 3 (September 1963), 35–49.

Wadhams, Stephen. *Remembering Orwell*. Introduction by George Woodcock. Markham, Ontario, Canada: Penguin, 1984.

Warburg, Fredric. "From Wigan to Barcelona." *An Occupation for Gentlemen*. Boston: Houghton Mifflin, 1960. Pp. 220–238.

Warburg, Fredric. "*Animal Farm* and *Nineteen Eighty-Four*." *All Authors Are Equal*. New York: St. Martin's, 1973. Pp. 7–15, 35–58, 92–120, 205–206.

Woodcock, George. *The Crystal Spirit: A Study of George Orwell*. Boston: Little, Brown, 1966.

Index

Compiled by Valerie Meyers